Elementary Hindi
प्राथमिक हिन्दी

Elementary
Hindi

प्राथमिक हिन्दी

An Introduction to the Language

RICHARD DELACY AND SUDHA JOSHI

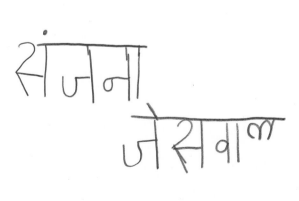

TUTTLE Publishing

Tokyo | Rutland, Vermont | Singapore

इजा को समर्पित — *For Ija*

The Tuttle Story: "Books to Span the East and West"

Many people are surprised to learn that the world's largest publisher of books on Asia had its humble beginnings in the tiny American state of Vermont. The company's founder, Charles E. Tuttle, belonged to a New England family steeped in publishing.

Immediately after WW II, Tuttle served in Tokyo under General Douglas MacArthur and was tasked with reviving the Japanese publishing industry. He later founded the Charles E. Tuttle Publishing Company, which thrives today as one of the world's leading independent publishers.

Though a westerner, Tuttle was hugely instrumental in bringing a knowledge of Japan and Asia to a world hungry for information about the East. By the time of his death in 1993, Tuttle had published over 6,000 books on Asian culture, history and art—a legacy honored by the Japanese emperor with the "Order of the Sacred Treasure," the highest tribute Japan can bestow upon a non-Japanese.

With a backlist of 1,500 titles, Tuttle Publishing is more active today than at any time in its past—inspired by Charles Tuttle's core mission to publish fine books to span the East and West and provide a greater understanding of each.

Published by Tuttle Publishing, an imprint of Periplus Editions (HK) Ltd.

Copyright © 2009 by Richard Delacy and Sudha Joshi
This paperback edition Copyright © 2014 Richard Delacy and Sudha Joshi
Cover image © R. Gino Santa Maria | Dreamstime.com

Library of Congress Cataloging-in-Publication Data

Delacy, Richard.
    Elementary Hindi : an introduction to the language / Richard Delacy and Sudha Joshi. -- 1st ed.
        xiii, 337 p. : ill. ; 26 cm. + 1 MP3 audio CD (223 min., 36 sec. : digital ; 4¾ in.)
    ISBN 978-0-8048-3962-4 (hbk.)
1. Hindi language--Textbooks for foreign speakers--English. 2. Hindi language--Grammar. I. Joshi, Sudha. II. Title.
    PK1933.D45 2009
    491.4'382421--dc22
                    2009013677

Distributed by:

North America, Latin America & Europe
Tuttle Publishing, 364 Innovation Drive,
North Clarendon, VT 05759-9436 U.S.A
Tel: 1 (802) 773 8930; Fax: 1 (802) 773 6993
info@tuttlepublishing.com
www.tuttlepublishing.com

Asia-Pacific
Berkeley Books Pte Ltd, 61 Tai Seng Avenue #02-12,
Singapore 534167
Tel: (65) 6280-1330; Fax: (65) 6280-6290
inquiries@periplus.com.sg
www.periplus.com

First Paperback Edition
18 17 16 15 14   5 4 3 2 1   1402HP

ISBN 978-0-8048-4499-4

Printed in Singapore

TUTTLE PUBLISHING® is a registered trademark of Tuttle Publishing, a division of Periplus Editions (HK) Ltd.

Contents

Acknowledgments

Elementary Hindi was initially developed as course materials by Sudha Joshi to teach introductory Hindi at the tertiary level in Australia. It was revised and further developed by Sudha Joshi and Richard Delacy with the addition of newer materials, conversations and recordings with the help of a grant from the Federal Australian Government and then published by La Trobe University (Bundoora) for use in college level courses. We would like to thank La Trobe University and particularly John Fitzgerald for releasing to us the copyright for the earlier edition. Many people have made valuable suggestions and criticisms from which we have benefited enormously, including Ali Asani, Richard Barz, Tino Batbro, Craig Bird, David Bradley, Tanya Caulfield, Philip Claxton, Eli Franco, Francesca Gaiba, Linda Hemphill, Naseem Hines, Dharini Kakkad, Mridula Kakkad, Guy Leavitt, Kama Maclean, Ronald Stuart McGregor, Parimal Patil, Sarah Pinto, Nicolas Roth, Ralph Saubern, Sunil Sharma, Rashid Sultan, Reena Tandan-Verma, Kate Tempany, and the many students who used these materials at universities in Australia and the United States, including Monash University, La Trobe University, The University of Chicago, The University of Illinois at Chicago and Harvard University. We would also like to acknowledge the debt that we owe to all those who have previously produced materials for the study of Hindi at the introductory level as well as reference grammars. We have learnt much from their labors on this subject. In addition we are grateful to Jaclyn Michael, Sukhdev Purewal, Benjamin Siegel, and Devin Dirk Smith for permission to use photographs, and to Amit Basole, Vivek Sharma, and Shilpi Suneja for their audio work. Finally, we would also like to thank our editor at Tuttle Publishing, Sandra Korinchak, for her expert advice, suggestions and patience, as well as the design team at Tuttle for the attractive presentation of these materials. Any errors and inaccuracies remain those of the authors. We would appreciate comments and suggestions that will help us to improve these materials further. These can be e-mailed to: richarddelacy@gmail.com.

Introduction

Hindi is the official language of the Republic of India and the first language of approximately half of the population, from Bihar in the east to Rajasthan in the west and from the border of Nepal to Maharasthra in the center of the country. It is also the official language of several north Indian states and is taught in schools as a second or third language outside the Hindi-speaking region, making it an important lingua franca throughout the rest of India since independence in 1947. With its pan-Indian reach Hindi is employed as the language of most films in the largest film industry in Asia, "Bollywood," situated in Mumbai (Bombay), as well as of a significant proportion of television programming. Both films and television in Hindi are consumed across South Asia and wherever South Asians have settled abroad. No less important is the rich literary heritage of Hindi that includes poetic traditions extending back several centuries as well as modern prose literature from the late nineteenth century.

Spoken Hindi possesses a tremendous variety of registers across the length and breadth of the north of India. All of these spoken forms vary to differing degrees and, depending on the individuals, are more or less mutually intelligible to speakers of other registers. Hindi's many spoken forms are generally included under the rubric of "Modern Standard Hindi," the codified written form of the language based on the spoken language that evolved in and around Delhi (khaṛī bolī) over two hundred years ago. This form of Hindi is employed as the medium of instruction in many schools at the primary and high school levels and used more or less in official discourse as well as in the various media across north India. It is also this form of Hindi that possesses, at a basic spoken level, a close relationship lexically and grammatically with Urdu, another major language of India and the national language of Pakistan, written in a modified form of the Arabic script.

Given its prominence, Modern Standard Hindi is presented in introductory textbooks such as this one, with the view that knowledge of a basic standard form enables the student to go on to read literary texts, watch Hindi films and engage with various other forms of media. Learning this form of Hindi also allows the student to communicate effectively with the widest possible range of speakers across the Hindi-speaking region in the north, putting the student in a good position to begin to develop an appreciation for the nuances of Hindi's many different regional spoken registers.

Who Should Use This Book

Elementary Hindi is aimed at those with no background in Hindi. For this reason it focuses on literacy as well as developing basic listening and speaking skills. The script in which Hindi is written, called Devanagari or Nagari, is the most efficient system of representation for the sounds of the language, and is also easy to master. In addition to Hindi, it is also employed to write several other north Indian languages as well as Nepali. It contains 46 characters in their basic form. The Devanagari script is written from left to right and there is almost a one-to-one correspondence between the characters and the sounds that they represent. As a result, it is very easy to learn.

In *Elementary Hindi* the Devanagari writing system is introduced gradually over the course of the first six lessons. The characters are not introduced in their dictionary order but in an order that is easiest for English speakers. They are explained in manageable groups with plenty of systematic reading practice that does not rely on a messy transliteration scheme. A Roman letter value is only provided once, when the characters are introduced. It is recommended that students complete all of the reading practice. We have found over many years that by building quickly from characters to meaningful words and colloquial utterances, students' trepidation at learning a new script quickly vanishes. For this reason, the first six chapters focus most intensely on the script, together with some basic structures and verbal paradigms.

After the script is introduced most of the basic structures of the language are presented in the remaining lessons, enabling the beginner to reach a point at the end of this book at which he or she can understand simple written prose with the help of a dictionary and can begin to engage in simple conversations on a range of topics. Because of the unique manner in which the script is introduced over the first six lessons, there is some repetition of concepts and vocabulary that would not ordinarily occur in a conventional grammar of Hindi. However, it was necessary to structure the textbook this way in order to help the learner build up to complete sentences before the complete syllabary has been introduced.

The available lexicon in Hindi is vast, given that it has drawn from several sources as it evolved into its current form. Particularly important are words that have come into Hindi from Sanskrit, Persian, Arabic, Turkish, Portuguese and English. The pronunciation of many of the words that have come into Hindi from English, Persian and Arabic in particular has been modified with their adoption into Hindi. There are conventions that are employed (such as a dot under a character) to indicate that words contain sounds that came originally from these languages and that their "correct" pronunciation should approximate sounds in those languages. However, many Hindi speakers do not differentiate between the original sounds and their modified forms and for the most part people do not write the dots under characters to represent these sounds either. We have used these conventions in *Elementary Hindi* to reflect the alternate pronunciation of these sounds.

How to Use This Book

Elementary Hindi is divided into a Textbook that contains 24 lessons, an Audio CD, and a Workbook containing activities and conversations that closely follow the structure of the Textbook. Whether you are learning Hindi in a classroom setting or on your own, *Elementary Hindi* will help you learn the basics of the language.

The lessons in the **Textbook** are designed so that learners may complete a lesson a week over approximately 24 weeks. Individual learners are encouraged to take as long as they require to absorb the material in each lesson. Each Textbook lesson contains explanations, examples of the grammatical concepts in practice, various exercises and cultural information that will reinforce the material and make the learning process enjoyable. The Textbook's *Practice* exercises are in a format conducive to group work, so independent learners will want to approach these with an eye toward experiencing each facet of the exercises—creating the questions, then creating the answers, for example. The Practice exercises can be utilized in the classroom in numerous ways by a teacher. Students can translate individual Practices and/or listen to them on the CD, create and answer the questions or try to ask them of a partner. The teacher also can ask questions of students to ensure that they have understood the content of the passages. Students can also be asked to prepare the passages and conversations prior to the class to maximize their effectiveness. A key to all of the exercises is also provided.

The **Audio CD** allows learners to hear all of the Textbook's Hindi passages and conversations, along with their questions and answers. It also includes the sounds and reading activities that are in the Workbook, and the Workbook's conversations, questions and answers. Throughout, the symbol 💿 indicates the items that have corresponding audio.

The **Workbook** offers *Activities* that are designed for thorough practice of the concepts and vocabulary in each chapter, and its material should be completed as concepts are covered in the Textbook. The Workbook also contains a key to every activity so that learners can monitor their own progress. Activities are designed so that learners can understand with relative ease what is expected of them and may further consolidate their knowledge while taking control of their learning experience through self-correction. It is recommended that teachers assign the Workbook Activities to be completed outside of the class.

The primary aim of this course is to bring learners to a point where they possess the tools to go on to become fluent in Hindi. Hence, we have tried to cover as many of the basic structures of the language that will assist a person in reaching this point. Because Hindi possesses a large vocabulary we believe that beginners can best spend their time focusing on assimilating these basic structures, but we also recommend that they attempt to learn as many new words as they can while doing this. The most effective way to learn new vocabulary, however, is to encounter it again and again in different contexts, and also to use it repeatedly, rather than memorizing single words in isolation. For this reason, an attempt has been made to restrict the vocabulary in this book largely to what may be considered "everyday words" and to use them repeatedly, rather than insisting that students rote learn individual words from the lessons.

Note to Teachers: To use *Elementary Hindi* in class, instructors will find it most effective to develop their lesson plans around each Textbook chapter's grammatical concepts. The Workbook exercises may then be assigned to the students to complete (and correct) as homework.

The book is designed to focus rigorously on the basic structures of Modern Standard Hindi, introducing them in a way that is most comfortable for the student. The vocabulary that has been introduced in *Elementary Hindi* reflects the fact that in order to have even a basic "natural" conversation, students must be exposed to a significant lexicon. Students should be encouraged to integrate words of their choosing as they go along, but we do not recommend that teachers drill students in vocabulary learning.

A teacher's guide is available from the publisher; to request it, please e-mail academicsales@tuttlepub lishing.com

List of Abbreviations

The following abbreviations are used throughout the book.

adj	adjective
adv	adverb
conj	conjunction
f	feminine
inter	interrogative
invar	invariable
m	masculine
part	participle
pl	plural
pp	postposition
pro	pronoun
rel	relative
sing	singular
v.i.	verb, intransitive
voc	vocative
v.t.	verb, transitive

The Basic Sentence; Asking Questions

THE DEVANAGARI SYLLABARY

The Devanagari script contains 46 characters (35 consonants and 11 vowels) in their basic form. Each of these represents a single syllable. Hence, the Devanagari script is said to be a syllabary rather than an alphabet. In this lesson, eight consonants and four vowels are introduced.

Consonants

In its basic form each consonant is pronounced together with an inherent *a* (अ) vowel (a lower-mid or mid-central vowel, similar to the vowel sound in the English word *but*).

The eight consonants introduced in this lesson are:

क/क़	न	प	म	य	ल	व	ह
ka/qa	na	pa	ma	ya	la	va/wa	ha

क/क़ ka/qa

This is first consonant in the syllabary. It is pronounced like the **k** in the word *speaker*. It is an *unaspirated voiceless velar plosive*. When written with a dot underneath (क़ **qa**) it is produced further back in the throat. However, many speakers of Hindi do not differentiate between the two sounds.

न na

This character is pronounced as **n** in the English word *none*. It is an *unaspirated voiced dental nasal plosive*.

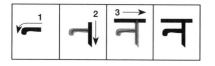

प pa

This character is pronounced as **p** in the word *spun*. It is an *unaspirated voiceless bilabial plosive*.

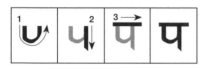

म ma

This sound is equivalent to **m** in the word *money*. It is a *bilabial nasal*.

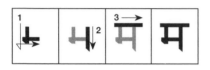

य ya

This is equivalent to the sound **y** in the word *young*. It is a *voiced palatal semi-vowel*.

ल la

This character is pronounced as **l** in the word *lug*. It is a *voiced alveolar lateral*.

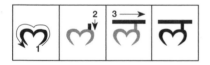

व va/wa

In some words this character is pronounced like the **v** in *vowel* and in some words like the **w** in *wow*. It is often pronounced somewhere between these two sounds. व is quite often pronounced as **v** at the beginning of words (*word initial*) and **w** in the middle (*word medial*) and at the end (*word final*). It is a *voiced labio-dental semi-vowel* or *fricative*.

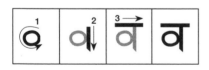

ह ha

This character is a *fricative* consonant similar to **h** in *hunt*. It is *voiceless* when it occurs at the beginning of a word and *voiced* otherwise.

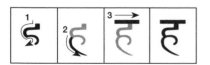

Vowels

There are four vowels introduced in this lesson.

अ	आ	ई	ऐ
a	**ā**	**ī**	**ai**

Apart from the first vowel अ **a**, each vowel can be represented by two forms:

1. the full form
2. the mātrā form

1. The full form of a vowel is written when the vowel occurs at the beginning of a word. It is also written in a word when it follows another syllable (either consonant + vowel, or vowel).
2. The mātrā form is an abbreviated symbol that represents a vowel when it is pronounced with a consonant *in place of* the inherent अ **a** vowel. The mātrā forms are written above, below, to the left and to the right of consonants.

अ/ऋ a

This is pronounced as **a** in the word *but*. It is a *lower-mid* or *mid-central unrounded* vowel. It is the only vowel in Devanagari that does not possess a mātrā (abbreviated) form because each consonant in its primary form is pronounced with the inherent अ vowel. There are two alternative forms of the vowel. While the first is now the standard form, the second is still encountered in printed and hand-written texts.

आ/ऋा (T) ā

This is pronounced similar to the **a** in the word *father*. It is *low central unrounded* vowel. There are also two full forms of this vowel. As with अ above, the first form is now the standard form.

The mātrā form of आ is T. Writing this mātrā form with each of the consonants thus far learned replaces the inherent अ vowel with a long आ vowel.

का/क़ा	ना	पा	मा	या	ला	वा	हा
kā/qā	nā	pā	mā	yā	lā	vā	hā

ई (ी) ī

This is a *long high front* vowel. It is pronounced like the **ee** in the English word *need*.

Its mātrā form when it is pronounced with a consonant is ी. This is written *after* the consonant. When pronounced with an ī vowel the consonants thus far introduced are written in the following manner:

की/क़ी	नी	पी	मी	यी	ली	वी	ही
kī/qī	nī	pī	mī	yī	lī	vī	hī

ऐ (ै) ai

This vowel may be pronounced two ways. The first pronunciation is similar to the vowel sound in the word *bad*. It is a *long low front* vowel. The second pronunciation is a diphthong[1] similar to the diphthong **a + i** in the word *height*. This pronunciation occurs where ऐ is followed by the semi-vowel य and also often occurs in the learned pronunciation of Sanskrit words borrowed into Hindi.

The mātrā form of ऐ is ै. It is written *above* the consonant. The eight consonants combined with ऐ are written in the following manner:

कै/क़ै	नै	पै	मै	यै	लै	वै	है
kai/qai	nai	pai	mai	yai	lai	vai	hai

---

1. A *diphthong*—from the Greek, meaning literally "two sounds"—is a vowel sound that changes noticeably while being pronounced; the tongue moves upwards during pronunciation.

PRACTICE

Now see if you can pronounce the words below using the characters that have been introduced in this lesson.

In Hindi all nouns are assigned a gender, either masculine (*m*) or feminine (*f*). This has to be learned along with the word.

अली Ali (name)　　नाई barber (*m*)　　या or (*conj*)
आना to come (*v.i.*)　नानी (maternal) grandmother (*f*)　लाई brought (*v.i.*)
ऐ O!　　　　पीना to drink (*v.t.*)　व and (*conj*)
कला art (*f*)　　पैना sharp, acute　वाला wallah
का 's　　　मामा (maternal) uncle (*m*)　ही only, just
कै vomiting (*f*)　माली gardener (*m*)　है is (*v.i.*)
ना no　　　मैना Indian black bird (*f*)

📖 *Before continuing, complete Activity 1.1 in the Workbook.*

RULES FOR PRONUNCIATION

In the Devanagari script each character represents a single syllable. When these are combined to form words their pronunciation is governed by the following rules.

The Inherent अ

In Hindi each consonant character in its basic form (i.e., without a vowel mātrā) represents the consonant sound along *with* an inherent अ **a** vowel. In the pronunciation of words, however, there occur several circumstances where the inherent अ is not pronounced with the consonant, or its pronunciation is slightly modified:

1. When another vowel (in mātrā form) is written and pronounced with the consonant.
2. When no vowel is pronounced with the consonant.
3. When the inherent अ sound is modified by surrounding consonants and vowels in the word.
4. Before a suffix.

1. The inherent अ is not pronounced when a vowel mātrā occurs with a consonant.

क ka,　　क् k + आ ā　=　का kā
क ka,　　क् k + ई ī　=　की kī
क ka,　　क् k + ऐ ai　=　कै kai

2. In certain positions in a word the inherent अ is not pronounced.

a) Generally the inherent अ is not pronounced with a consonant at the end of a word.
कम **kam** less
कल **kal** tomorrow, yesterday (*m*)

However, when the final consonant is a semi-vowel (य or व) it is difficult to stop the pronunciation of अ completely.

आय **āya** income (*f*)
नाव **nāva** (or **nāu**) boat (*f*)

b) The inherent अ is also silent within a word, but not in the first syllable of the word and not when preceded or followed by another silent inherent अ.

कलकल **kalkal** a sweet, soft sound (*m*)
नमकीन **namkīn** salty, salted (*adj.*), a salty dish of snacks (*m*)
नमक **namak** salt (*m*)

c) When two or more consonants are pronounced without the inherent अ vowel, this is often represented in Devanagari by modifying the forms of the consonants and joining them together. Such conjoined forms are called *conjunct consonants*.

क्या **kyā** what? (*interrogative pronoun*)
(क् + य + आ)

3. The presence of the consonant ह in a word may affect the pronunciation of a *preceding* inherent अ vowel. If the consonant ह is not followed by a full vocalic sound (if there is very little or no vowel produced with the ह), then a *preceding* inherent अ vowel is often pronounced by many speakers like **e** in the word *get*.

यह **yeh** third person pronoun (he, she, it, this—close to speaker)
पहला **pehlā** first, foremost, primary
कहना **kehnā** to say[2]
महल **mehal** palace (*m*)
However:
महीना **mahīnā** month (*m*)

4. Before a suffix.

An inherent अ occurring before a suffix is considered to be in a word final position and, hence, is generally not pronounced. For example, in Hindi the infinitive form of verbs is formed by attaching the suffix ना to the verb stem. If the verb stem ends in a consonant, the अ is omitted.

पहनना **pehnnā** to wear
कहना **kehnā** to say
मानना **mānnā** to accept, agree

Finally, the third person pronoun वह (he, she, it, that—far from the speaker) is pronounced by some speakers entirely irregularly as **vo**, the **o** being similar to that in the word *low*.

---

2. The word कहना is the infinitive form of the verb (i.e., *to say*). The stem is कह and the infinitive marker (*to*) is represented by ना. Therefore, the end of the stem is effectively the end of the word and hence, its pronunciation adheres to rule number 2 above. The infinitive form of all verbs ends in ना.

Read out loud the following words according to the rules for pronunciation above.

अपना one's own	क़लम pen (*f*)	मकान house (*m*)
आम mango (*m*); ordinary, general	कहना to say (*v.t.*)	महल palace (*m*)
ईमान faith, belief, integrity (*m*)	नमक salt (*m*)	महीना month (*m*)
ऐनक spectacles (*f*)	पहनना to wear (*v.t.*)	यह this, he, she, it (near)
कमल lotus (*m*)	पानी water (*m*)	वह that, he, she, it (far)

📖 *Before continuing, complete Activity 1.2 in the Workbook.*

Word Order

The regular word order in a Hindi sentence is: Subject – (Object) – Verb

Every sentence must have at least a subject and only one finite verb. The verb is contained in the *predicate*. Word order in Hindi is relatively flexible and changing the regular word order changes the emphasis in the sentence.

Punctuation

Punctuation marks in Hindi are the same as those used in English, with the exception of the mark for a period. This is generally indicated by the use of a vertical line (|) called a virām (pause, rest). Individual words are distinguished by a horizontal line drawn at the top of the word.

यह	मकान है।	This/it is a house.
(subject)	(predicate)	

यह मकान	नया है।	This house is new.
(subject)	(predicate)	

Asking Questions

When asking questions, ordinarily the interrogative comes directly *before* the verb. The first interrogative introduced in this lesson is:

क्या **kyā** what? (*interrogative pronoun*)

When क्या is placed directly *before* the verb in the sentence, it may be translated as *what*.

यह क्या है?　　What is this?
वह क्या है?　　What is that?

क्या may also be placed at the beginning of the sentence. When this is the case, it is not translated as *what* but simply transforms the sentence into a question. This is similar to placing the verb at the beginning of the sentence in English.

यह मकान है।　　This is a house.
क्या यह मकान है?　*Is* this a house?

Occasionally speakers omit क्या when it is employed to mark a question at the beginning of the utterance. In such cases, a raised intonation at the end of the sentence indicates the presence of a question.

PRACTICE

This exercise is best done with a partner. Pointing to the various words listed below, ask a partner the following questions.

यह क्या है?	What is this?	वह क्या है?	What is that?
(क्या) यह... है?	Is this ... ?	(क्या) वह... है?	Is that ... ?

When asking questions, use यह while pointing to objects that are closer to you and वह for objects that are closer to the listener and farther away from you. When responding to questions, use the opposite pronoun. Ask at least five questions each. You may omit क्या at the start of a sentence when it marks a question and simply raise your intonation at the end of the question.

आम mango (*m*)　　पान betel leaf (*m*)　　महल palace (*m*)
क़लम pen (*f*)　　ऐनक spectacles (*f*)　　मैना Indian black bird (*f*)
मकान house (*m*)　　पानी water (*m*)
नमक salt (*m*)　　कमल lotus (*m*)

Before proceeding to Lesson 2, complete Activities 1.3 and 1.4 in the Workbook.

LESSON **2** दूसरा पाठ

Greetings; Introductions

In this lesson, six consonants and three vowels are introduced. In addition to this, the symbol that represents the nasalization of a syllable is also explained.

Consonants

The six consonants explained in this lesson are:

ज/ज़	त	द	ब	र	स
ja/za	ta	da	ba	ra	sa

ज/ज़ ja/za

This character is pronounced like the **j** in the word *judge*. It is described as a *voiced unaspirated palatoalveolar affricate*. When written with a dot underneath (ज़), the pronunciation is changed to **z**. This sound is described as a *voiced alveolar fricative* (friction of the breath) and occurs only in words of English, Arabic and Persian origin. Some Hindi speakers do not distinguish between the pronunciation of ज and ज़.

त ta

This is similar to the **t** produced in the word *ton*. The tongue should touch the back of the upper teeth. It is described as an *unaspirated voiceless dental plosive*.

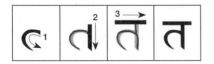

द da

This is similar to the **d** in the word *does* except that the tongue should touch the back of the upper teeth. It is described as an *unaspirated voiced dental plosive*.

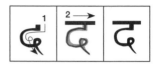

ब ba

The pronunciation of this character is similar to the **b** in the word *bun*. It is described as an *unaspirated voiced bilabial plosive*.

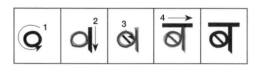

र ra

The pronunciation of this character is similar to the **r** in *run* but it is pronounced with a trill. When making this sound, ideally the tip of the tongue *taps* several times in quick succession against the ridge of the upper teeth. It is described as a *voiced alveolar trill*.

स sa

The pronunciation of this character is similar to the **s** in the word *sun*. It is described as a *voiceless alveolar sibilant fricative*.

Vowels

There are three vowels introduced in this lesson.

इ (ि) i

The pronunciation of this vowel is similar to the **i** in the word *sit*. It is described as a *high front unrounded* vowel.

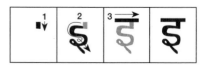

The mātrā form of the vowel इ is ि . This mātrā form is written to the left of the consonant but it is pronounced after the consonant. When pronounced with the vowel इ the six consonants introduced in this lesson appear in the following manner.

जि/ज़ि	ति	दि	बि	रि	सि
ji/zi	ti	di	bi	ri	si

उ (‸) u

This vowel is pronounced as **oo** in the word *book*. It is described as a *short high back rounded* vowel.

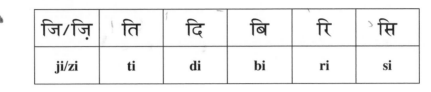

The mātrā form of उ is ‸. This is written underneath the consonant, except in the case of र, where it is written to the side.

जु/ज़ु	तु	दु	बु	रु	सु
ju/zu	tu	du	bu	ru	su

ए (ˋ) e

The pronunciation of this vowel is similar to the sound in the word *bay*. It is described as a *high-mid front unrounded* vowel.

The mātrā form of ए is ˋ. It is written above the consonant.

जे/ज़े	ते	दे	बे	रे	से
je/ze	te	de	be	re	se

Conjunct Consonants (स्त and स्क)

In Lesson 1 the concept of a conjunct consonant was introduced (see p. 6). Here the conjunct form of the character स is presented. When स occurs as the first member of a conjunct consonant, it loses its vertical line:

स् + त = स्त sta नमस्ते **namaste** greeting and goodbye (lit: "I bow to you")

स् + क = स्क ska नमस्कार **namaskār** greeting and goodbye (lit: "I bow to you")

Nasalization

Nasalization is the pronunciation of a syllable through the nose. In Hindi it is called *anunāsik* and is represented by a symbol called *candrabindu* (*candra* = moon, *bindu* = dot) because it looks similar to a dot resting above a crescent moon.

ँ
candrabindu

This is written *above* the line at the top of the word, directly over the syllable that is nasalized. When there is the occurrence of a vowel mātrā, all or part of which appears above the line, the candrabindu is reduced to a dot.

जी हाँ **jī hã** yes   जी नहीं **jī nahī̃** no[1]

बाज़ार market (*m*)

---

1. The first word जी is honorific and is generally used as a polite suffix to denote respect (although in this example it may be expressed either before or after the words for "yes" and "no.") It is advisable to use these more respectful forms for "yes" and "no" rather than merely हाँ and नहीं.

PRACTICE

See if you can pronounce the words below using the characters that have been introduced in this lesson.

आज today	किताब book (*f*)	नमस्ते greeting and goodbye
आदमी man (*m*)	क़ीमत price (*f*)	पता address (*m*)
आसान easy	जी नहीं no	बाज़ार market (*m*)
इमारत building (*f*)	जी हाँ yes	मिलना to meet, find (*v.i.*)
उदास sad	तारा star (*m*)	रुपया rupee (*m*)
कमरा room (*m*)	दुआ prayer (*f*)	सस्ता cheap
क़मीज़ shirt (*f*)	देना to give	

📖 *Before continuing, complete Activity 2.1 in the Workbook.*

GRAMMAR

The Postposition का

In Hindi, English prepositions such as *in*, *on*, *in front of*, *by*, etc. *follow* rather than precede the noun, pronoun or adverb to which they relate. For this reason they are called *post*positions. For example, the phrase *in the room* is expressed in Hindi as *room in*. Postpositions indicate the relationship between particular words in the sentence.

The first postposition introduced in this course is the postposition का , which equates to *'s* that is used in English.

1. का is described as the possessive postposition because it indicates a relationship of possession between particular words in a sentence, such as nouns, pronouns and adverbs. It functions exactly the same way as *'s* in English.

   दीपक का मकान   Deepak's house (*m*)

2. का changes to के when the object or person *possessed* is masculine plural and to की when the object or person possessed is feminine (either singular or plural).

दीपक का मकान	Deepak's house (*m sing*)
दीपक के मकान	Deepak's houses (*m pl*)
दीपक की कहानी	Deepak's story (*f sing*)
दीपक की कहानियाँ*	Deepak's stories (*f pl*)

   * This is the plural form of the noun कहानी.

It is important to remember that the transformation of का to के or की takes place for the number and gender of the object or person *possessed*, not for the number and gender of the *possessor*. The order of the phrase is always the same:

   possessor का/के/की possessed.

Pronouns

A pronoun is a word that is used in place of a noun (i.e., *I, we, you*, etc.). In Hindi there are nine personal pronouns. The personal pronouns relate to the person speaking (1st person), the person being spoken to (2nd person) and the person being spoken about (3rd person). In the case of the 2nd and 3rd person pronouns, often the plural forms are used to refer to an individual to be polite.

In this lesson seven of the nine personal pronouns are presented, using the letters that have been introduced thus far.

1st person
मैं I (*sing*)
हम we (*pl*) Some people employ this in place of मैं.

2nd person
आप you (*pl*) This is the most respectful 2nd person pronoun. It may refer to a single person (being polite) or to more than one person.

3rd person
यह he/she/it/this (*sing*) This is employed when the person or thing is close to the speaker (either physically or contextually). It is also a demonstrative pronoun (*this*).

ये they/these/he/she (*pl*) This is employed to talk about a person, people or things *close* to the speaker. It is best to employ this plural form when talking about a single person who is present. It is also a demonstrative pronoun (*these*).

वह he/she/it/that (*sing*) This form of the pronoun is employed to talk about a person or thing that is *far* from the speaker (physically or contextually). It is also a demonstrative pronoun (*that*). Many speakers pronounce this pronoun as **vo**.

वे they/those/he/she (*pl*) This is employed to talk about a person, people or things *far* from the speaker. As with ये, this plural form may be employed to talk respectfully about a single person. It is also a demonstrative pronoun (*those*). Many speakers pronounce this pronoun as **vo**.

There are two more 2nd person pronouns (the intimate and the informal) which are introduced in Lesson 4.

Pronouns + का
The form of most of these pronouns changes when they are governed by का *'s*.

Pronoun + का

मैं I + का	=	मेरा my
हम we + का	=	हमारा our
आप you + का	=	आपका your
यह he/she/it/this + का	=	इसका his/her/its/of this
ये they/these/he/she + का	=	इनका their/of these/his/her
वह he/she/it/that + का	=	उसका his/her/its/of that
वे they/those/he/she + का	=	उनका their/of those/his/her

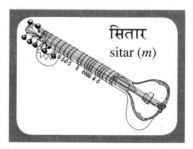

सितार
sitar (*m*)

In those cases where का *'s* is not incorporated into the pronoun it is ordinarily attached but may also be written separately; that is, इनका or इन का.

मेरी माँ my mother (*f*)
हमारे नाम our names (*m pl*)
इनका दाम the price of these (*m sing*)
उनके मकान their houses (*m pl*)
आपकी क़मीज़ your shirt (*f*)

Greetings

There are several ways to greet a person and to say goodbye in Hindi. The two most common greetings and expressions of farewell are:

नमस्ते "I bow to you." ("hello" and "goodbye")
नमस्कार "I bow to you." ("hello" and "goodbye")

The polite suffix जी, which can be affixed to both first names and family names (सुनीता जी **Sunita ji**, वाजपेयी जी **Vajpayee ji**), may also be used with these greetings.

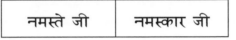

नमस्ते जी	नमस्कार जी

In more formal contexts the expression of one of these greetings may be accompanied by the action of folding the hands in front of the chest and slightly bowing the head. Shaking hands is also common. The English greeting "hello" is also popular among some speakers.

When asking the name of a third person present, it is best to use the plural forms of the pronouns with का — इनका his, her, their (close to the speaker), उनका his, her, their (far from the speaker):

नमस्ते जी, आपका नाम क्या है? नमस्ते, मेरा नाम ... है।
Hello. What is your name? Hello. My name is ....

इनका नाम क्या है? इनका नाम ... है।
What is his/her/their name? His/her/their name is ....

उनका नाम क्या है? उनका नाम ... है।
What is his/her/their name? His/her/their name is ....

There are some other greetings that you will encounter in later lessons.

📖 *Before going on to Lesson 3, complete Activities 2.2, 2.3, 2.4 and 2.5 in the Workbook.*

बड़ा गुम्बद मसजिद

मसजिद की दक्षिणी दीवार पर अंकित एक लेख के अनुसार यह तीन गुम्बद की इमारत सिकन्दर लोदी के राज्यकाल,(हिजरी 900 सन् 1494) में बनायी गयी।

मसजिद के प्रार्थनागृह के सामने पांच खुली मिहराबें हैं, और उनके ऊपर टोड़ेदार छज्जे। इमारत के पिछले कोनों में बने ढालू मीनार तुगलक शैली में हैं, किन्तु उनके स्थान से यह ज्ञात होता है जैसे की वे प्रारम्भिक मुगल एवं सूर काल के अठभुजी बुर्जों के पूर्वज हों। इसी प्रकार मसजिद के दक्षिण तथा उत्तर की ओर बनी गोरवनुमा खिड़कियां भी परवर्ती मसजिदों

Explanatory tablet in Lodi Gardens

Introducing Kavita

THE DEVANAGARI SYLLABARY

In this lesson, five consonants and three vowels are introduced. This brings the total number of consonants introduced to 19 (out of 35) and the vowels to 10 (out of 11).

Consonants

The five consonants explained in this lesson are:

ख/ख़	घ	च	ड़	ध
kha/<u>kha</u>	gha	ca	ṛa	dha

ख/ख़ kha/<u>kha</u>

This is the *aspirated* form of क. Its pronunciation is similar to **kh** in the word *blockhead*. When pronouncing this consonant, a breath of air (aspiration) should be released with the sound. It is described as a *voiceless aspirated velar plosive*. When written with a dot underneath, ख़, this consonant corresponds to a *velar fricative* consonant produced with only a partial closure of the air-passage. ख़ is only found in words that have come into Hindi from Persian and Arabic and is often not distinguished from ख by many Hindi speakers.

घ gha

This is an aspirated consonant pronounced much as **gh** in the word *loghouse*. It is described as a *voiced aspirated velar plosive*.

च **ca**

The pronunciation of this consonant is similar to **ch** in the word *church*. It is described as a *voiceless unaspirated palatoalveolar affricate*.

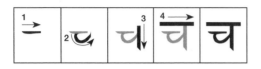

ड़ **ṛa**

This is a difficult consonant for English speakers to pronounce. It is similar in pronunciation to the **r** in the word *party*. The tongue touches the roof of the mouth before quickly flapping down during the production of this consonant. It is described as a *voiced unaspirated retroflex flap*.

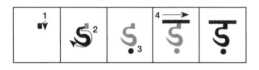

ध **dha**

This is the *aspirated* form of द. It is pronounced like the **dh** in the word *roadhouse*. It is described as a *voiced aspirated dental plosive*. That is, the tongue touches the back of the top teeth during the production of this consonant.

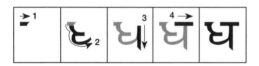

Vowels

There are three new vowels introduced in this lesson. They are:

ऊ (ू) **ū**

This is the long form of the vowel उ (p. 11) and is pronounced like the **oo** in the word *soon*. It is a *long high back rounded* vowel. Its mātrā form is ू . This is written under the consonant except when it combines with the consonant र, where it is written alongside the consonant रू (cf. रू p. 11).

The consonants introduced in this lesson with the vowel ऊ appear in the following manner:

खू/ख़ू	घू	चू	डू	धू	रू
khū/k͟hū	ghū	cū	ḍū	dhū	rū

ओ/ओ (ो) o

This is a *long rounded back mid* vowel similar to the **o** in the word *both*. Just as with the vowels अ and आ, there are two alternative full forms of this vowel and its partner (औ) below.

The **mātrā** form of this vowel, written after the consonant, is ो.

The consonants introduced in this lesson with the vowel ओ appear in this manner:

खो/ख़ो	घो	चो	ड़ो	धो
kho/kho	gho	co	ḍo	dho

औ/औ (ौ) au ≈ ɔ

The pronunciation of this sound is somewhat similar to the vowel sound in the English word *saw*. It is described as a *low-mid to mid-back rounded* vowel. It may also be pronounced as a diphthong, similar to the diphthong **a + u** in the word *ouch*. This pronunciation occurs where औ is followed by the semi-vowel व and also often occurs in the learned pronunciation of Sanskrit words in Hindi.

The mātrā form of औ when it is pronounced with a consonant is ौ. This is written after the consonant.

The consonants introduced in this lesson with the vowel औ appear like this:

खौ/ख़ौ	घौ	चौ	ड़ौ	धौ
khau/khau	ghau	cau	ṛau	dhau

Conjunct Consonants (न्द and ल्ल)

In this lesson the conjunct forms of two more characters, न and ल, are introduced. Both of these lose their vertical line when attached to the following character:

न् + द = न्द **nda**   हिन्दुस्तान **hindustān** India

ल् + ल = ल्ल **lla**   दिल्ली **dillī** Delhi

PRACTICE

See if you can pronounce the words below using the characters that have been introduced in this lesson.

अख़बार newspaper (*m*)   घर home (*m*)   बोलना to speak (*v.t.+v.i.*)
अमरूद guava (*m*)   घूमना to wander (*v.i.*)   लड़का boy (*m*)
आँख eye (*f*)   चलना to move (*v.i.*)   लड़की girl (*f*)
ऊँचा high   चाँदनी moonlight (*f*)   रोज़ day (*m*); daily
ओर direction (*f*)   ज़रूर certainly   समोसा samosa (*m*)
और and, more   जूता shoe (*m*)   सुबह morning (*f*)
कोई someone, anyone   तारीख़ date, history (*f*)   सोचना to think (*v.t.*)
ख़रीदना to buy (*v.t.*)   दूध milk (*m*)   हूँ am (*v.i.*)
खाना food (*m*); to eat (*v.t.*)   नौकरी work, employment (*f*)   होना to be (*v.i.*)

📖 *Before continuing, complete Activity 3.1 in the Workbook.*

GRAMMAR

Adjectives

An adjective is a word that qualifies a noun, pronoun or another adjective. In Hindi adjectives that end in a long आ vowel change to indicate agreement with the *number*, *gender* and *case*[1] of the noun etc. that they qualify. All other adjectives are invariable. There are also some आ ending adjectives that do not change.

1. **आ ending adjectives.**

    Most adjectives that end in आ change in the following manner:

    a) If the noun they qualify is masculine singular there is *no change*.

    b) If the noun they qualify is masculine plural, (or in the oblique case), आ *changes* to ए.

    c) If the noun that they qualify is feminine singular *or* plural, आ *changes* to ई.

    ऊँचा high, tall (*adj*)
    ऊँचा मकान a tall house (*m sing*)
    ऊँचे मकान tall houses (*m pl*)
    ऊँची दीवार a high wall (*f sing*)*

        *The adjective will take the same ending (ई) for feminine plural nouns.

---

1. For a full explanation of case, see p. 52.

The postposition का may be understood as transforming the noun, pronoun or adverb it follows into an –आ ending adjective.

मेरा नाम my name (*m sing*)
मेरे मकान my houses (*m pl*)
मेरी क़मीज़ my shirt (*f sing*)

2. **Exceptional आ ending invariable adjectives.**

There are a few आ ending adjectives that *do not change* for the gender, number and case of the noun. Here are some of the more common ones.[2]

सवा one-and-a-quarter
बढ़िया **baṛhiyā** excellent
घटिया **ghaṭiyā** inferior
दुखिया unfortunate, unhappy, sad
पैदा born
ज़रा a little
ज़िंदा **zindā** alive
ताज़ा fresh (This is both variable and invariable.)

ज़रा नमक a little salt (*m sing*)
ताज़ा अमरूद fresh guavas (*m pl*)
दुखिया औरत unhappy woman (*f sing*)

3. **All other adjectives.**

Adjectives ending in any other vowel or consonant remain *unchanged* irrespective of the gender, number, or case of the noun they qualify.

लाल मकान a red house (*m sing*)
लाल मकान red houses (*m pl*)
लाल दीवार a red wall (*f sing*)

---

2. The words here with roman transliteration include characters that have not yet been introduced.

PRACTICE

 Meeting Kavita

Kavita is a college student in India. She lives in Delhi and studies with her friend Deepak. Here Kavita tells you a little about herself.

नमस्ते। मेरा नाम कविता है।
आपका नाम क्या है?
मैं हिन्दुस्तानी लड़की हूँ।
क्या आप हिन्दुस्तानी हैं? क्या आप अमरीकी हैं?
यह कौन है? यह मेरा दोस्त है। इसका नाम दीपक है।
यह मेरा घर है। मेरा घर दिल्ली में है। मेरा घर बड़ा है।
यह मेरी किताब है। मेरी किताब नीली है।

Glossary

हिन्दुस्तानी Indian	कौन who (*inter*)	दोस्त friend (*m/f*)	घर home (*m*)
अमरीकी American	किताब book (*f*)	नीला blue	लड़का boy (*m*)
बड़ा big	लाल red	हूँ am (*v.i.*)	लड़की girl (*f*)

 Translate the following questions and ask a partner.

1. What is the name of the girl? _Kavita_

2. What is your name? _____

3. Is Kavita an Indian girl? _____

4. Are you an Indian? _____

5. Are you an American? _____

6. Who is the boy? _____

7. Is Kavita's book red? ....

8. Is Kavita's home big? ....

9. Is your home big? ....
   (If your home is not big, you can answer in the negative.)

📖 *Before proceeding to Lesson 4, complete Activities 3.2, 3.3 and 3.4 in the Workbook.*

More about Deepak

THE DEVANAGARI SYLLABARY

In this lesson, four consonants and one vowel are introduced. This brings the total number of consonants learned to 23 and completes the 11 vowels.

Consonants

The four consonants introduced in this lesson are:

ग/ग़	ड	ढ़	फ/फ़
ga/ga	ḍa	ṛha	pha/fa

ग/ग़ ga/ga

The pronunciation of this consonant is similar to the **g** in the word *gun*. It is described as a *unaspirated voiced velar plosive*. When written with a dot underneath it is pronounced as a *voiced velar* or *post velar fricative*, that is, farther back in the throat. This sound occurs in Perso-Arabic words. Many speakers of Hindi do not differentiate between the two sounds.

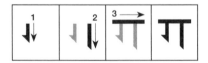

ड ḍa

The pronunciation of this character is similar to the **d** in the word *hard* but the tongue touches the top of the mouth. It is described as an *unaspirated voiced retroflex plosive*.

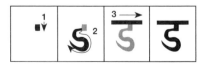

ढ़ ṛha

This is the *aspirated* partner of ड़ (introduced in Lesson 3). It is an *aspirated voiced retroflex flap*. The tongue touches the roof of the mouth before quickly flapping down during the production of this consonant.

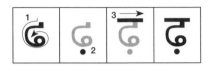

फ/फ़ pha/fa

There are two possible pronunciations of this consonant. The first (without the dot underneath) is the *aspirated* form of प introduced in Lesson 1. This is similar to the pronunciation of **p** in the word *putt*, but with more of a breath. It is a *bilabial aspirated voiceless plosive*. The second pronunciation (with the dot underneath) is similar to the **f** in the word *fly*. It is a *labio-dental fricative* and occurs in words from Persian, Arabic and English.

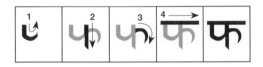

Vowels

The final vowel in the Devanagari syllabary is introduced in this lesson.

ऋ (ृ) ṛ

This vowel occurs in words of Sanskrit origin that have come into Hindi. It is pronounced like the consonant र trilled + the vowel इ as in the English word *rip*. The mātrā form of this vowel is ृ . This is joined to the bottom of the consonant (except ह). Some speakers pronounce this vowel as **r + u**.

All of the vowels in the order that they appear in the syllabary are:

अ	आ	इ	ई	उ	ऊ	ऋ	ए	ऐ	ओ	औ
a	ā	i	ī	u	ū	ṛ	e	ai	o	au

Here is how they appear in their mātrā forms with a consonant:

क	का	कि	की	कु	कू	कृ	के	कै	को	कौ
ka	kā	ki	kī	ku	kū	kṛ	ke	kai	ko	kau

Conjunct Consonants (म्ह)

In this lesson one new conjunct consonant is introduced. This is the modified form of the consonant म. There are two alternatives for representing म in a conjunct form:

1. A dot above the line and directly over the previous syllable: ˙
2. A modified form without the vertical stroke: ᒧ

1. म may be written as a dot only when it occurs in a conjunct cluster with the following consonants— प, फ, ब, भ (the *labial* consonants).

2. With all other consonants, it is written in the modified form.

     म् + ह = म्ह **mha**
     तुम्हारा **tumhārā** your (second person pronoun तुम + का)

PRACTICE

See if you can pronounce the words below using the characters that have been introduced in this lesson.

अगर if	ग़रीब poor	फ़ुरसत spare time (*f*)
अफ़सर officer (*m*)	चिढ़ाना to tease (*v.t.*)	फूल flower (*m*)
ऋतु season (*f*)	डाक mail (*f*)	माँगना to demand (*v.t.*)
काग़ज़ paper (*m*)	तुम्हारा your	लिफ़ाफ़ा envelope (*m*)
काफ़ी enough	पढ़ना to read, study (*v.t.*)	लोग people (*m*)
कृपा mercy (*f*)	पढ़ाई studies (*f*)	हृदय heart (*m*)
गला throat (*m*)	फल fruit (*m*)	

📖 *Now complete Activity 4.1 in the Workbook.*

साधु sadhu (*m*)

GRAMMAR

Pronouns

In Lesson 2 seven of the nine personal pronouns were introduced. Here the remaining two personal pronouns are added to complete the list of personal pronouns. The interrogative pronouns are also introduced. It is important to remember that plural pronouns are ordinarily employed for an individual to denote respect towards the person addressed or the person about whom one is speaking.

मैं I (*1st person sing*).

हम we (*1st person pl*). Regionally this pronoun is sometimes used for the 1st person singular as well as plural.

तू you (*2nd person sing intimate*). This pronoun is employed to address children, God, animals, younger siblings and intimate friends. It can also be employed to indicate disrespect.

तुम you (*2nd person pl familiar*). This pronoun is employed for those of equal social status and when addressing members of the family.

आप you (*2nd person pl polite*). This polite plural pronoun may be employed both for an individual and for more than one person. It should be used when addressing elders as well as those whom one does not know.

यह he/she/it/this (*3rd person sing* — close).
This pronoun is used to indicate a person or thing close to the speaker. This form should not be employed to talk about people present unless they can be addressed as तू.

वह he/she/it/that (*3rd person sing* — far). This is used to indicate a person or thing far from the speaker. It is pronounced as वो by many speakers.

ये these/they/he/she (*3rd person pl* — close). This is used to indicate people or things close to the speaker. It is also employed for individuals to indicate respect.

वे those/they/he/she (*3rd person pl* — far). This is employed for people or things *far* from the speaker. It is also employed to show respect for an individual. It is pronounced as वो by many speakers.

कोई someone/somebody/anybody (*sing*). This refers to an unspecified person when used as a pronoun.

कौन who (*inter*). This is both the singular and plural form of the interrogative pronoun. Its regular place in the sentence is directly before the verb.

क्या what (*inter*). When this interrogative occurs directly before the verb, it corresponds to *what* in English. When it occurs at the beginning of a sentence, it transforms the sentence into a question. (See p. 8.)

There is also a relative pronoun जो *who*, *which*, *that*. For a full description of जो, see p. 223.

Pronouns + का

In Lesson 2 the forms of the pronouns thus far discussed were introduced when followed by the postposition का. These are considered to be आ ending adjectives. Thus, the ending will change depending on the number, gender and case[1] of the noun or pronoun that follows.

This is a list of the forms of all of the pronouns you know thus far, when they are followed by का 's.

मैं I + का	=	मेरा my
हम we + का	=	हमारा our
तू you + का	=	तेरा your
तुम you + का	=	तुम्हारा your
आप you + का	=	आपका your
यह he/she/it/this + का	=	इसका his/her/its/of this
ये they/these/he/she + का	=	इनका their/of these/his/her
वह he/she/it/that + का	=	उसका his/her/its/of that
वे they/those/he/she + का	=	उनका their/of those/his/her
कोई anybody/somebody/anyone + का	=	किसी का anybody's/somebody's/anyone's
कौन who (*sing*) + का	=	किसका whose*
कौन who (*pl*) + का	=	किनका whose (*pl*)*

*The interrogative कौन has both a singular and a plural form when followed by a postposition.

The Verb होना *to be* (Simple Present Tense)

The verb *to be* in the simple present form is conjugated for the number and the person of the subject in the sentence.

	Singular	Plural
1st person	मैं हूँ I am	हम हैं we are
2nd person	तू है you are	तुम हो you are
		आप हैं you are
3rd person	यह है he/she/it/this is	ये हैं these/they are
	वह है he/she/it/that is	वे हैं those/they are

Where Are You From?

There are two ways to ask where a person is from in Hindi. In the first of these the postposition का is employed. In this question one is literally asking, "Where are you of?" का changes to की or के depending on the number and gender of the person addressed.

दीपक - कविता, तुम कहाँ की हो?
कविता - मैं दिल्ली की हूँ।
(कहाँ where?; दिल्ली Delhi)

Deepak — "Where are you from, Kavita?"
Kavita — "I am from Delhi."

1. For a full description of case, see p. 52.

LESSON **5** पाँचवाँ पाठ

Kavita's Family

In this lesson, five new consonants are introduced. This brings the total number of consonants learned to 28. In addition to these consonants, the symbol *visarg* is introduced. This symbol represents an aspiration akin to a repetition of the vowel sound that it follows.

Consonants

The five consonants introduced in this lesson are:

छ	ठ	थ	भ	श
cha	ṭha	tha	bha	śa

छ cha

This is the *aspirated* form of च. It is pronounced as the **ch** in *church-hill* and is described as a *voiceless aspirated palatal plosive*.

ठ ṭha

This character is pronounced with the tongue tip touching the ridge of the mouth. Its pronunciation is similar to that of **t** in the word *train* but with the tongue farther back and with a breath. This is a *voiceless aspirated retroflex plosive*.

थ tha

This is the *aspirated* partner of त, that is, an *aspirated voiceless dental plosive*. It is very similar in pronunciation to the **t-h** in *meet here*. The tip of the tongue touches the back of the upper teeth and there should be an expulsion of breath with the production of the consonant.

भ bha

This consonant is the *aspirated* form of ब. This means that a breath of air is expelled with its pronunciation. It is similar to the pronunciation of **b-h** in the word *clubhouse*. It is described as an *aspirated voiced bilabial plosive*.

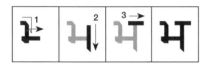

श śa

This is very similar to the pronunciation of **sh** in the word *shoe*. It is described as a *voiceless prepalatal fricative*.

Conjunct Consonants (श्त, ध, च्छ)

There are two new conjunct consonants introduced in this lesson. They are the conjunct forms of the consonants श and च.

There are two alternative forms of the consonant श when it appears as the first member of a conjunct cluster. In the first (modern standard) form, the vertical line is omitted.

> श् + त = श्त śta
> नाश्ता breakfast, light refreshment (*m*)

With the consonants च, र, ल and व (as well as the vowel ऋ) an alternative modified form of श is often employed:

> श् + व = श्व (also श्व) śva
> ईश्वर God (*m*)

When च appears as the first member of a conjunct cluster, it loses its vertical line:

> च् + छ = च्छ ccha
> अच्छा good, okay, fine

Visarg

In Devanagari the symbol : (*visarg*) represents an echo of the vowel that it follows together with a breath similar to an "**h**" sound. The visarg occurs in some Sanskrit words that have come into Hindi and is often not pronounced when it occurs in the middle of a word.

अतः (**at*aha***) therefore

दुःख (**du*hu*kh**) sorrow (*m*)   This word may also be written as दुख (and pronounced as **dukh**).

थाली thali (metal plate)

PRACTICE

See if you can pronounce the words below using the characters that have been introduced in this lesson.

अच्छा good, okay	खुशी happiness (*f*)	भारत India (*m*)
अस्पताल hospital (*m*)	गोश्त meat (*m*)	भूलना to forget (*v.i.*)
अतः thus, therefore	ठीक okay	मच्छर mosquito (*m*)
आवश्यक necessary	देश country (*m*)	शनिवार Saturday (*m*)
आशा hope (*f*)	नाश्ता breakfast, snack (*m*)	शराब alcohol (*f*)
कठिन difficult	बीमार ill, sick	शुरू beginning (*m*)
कभी sometime	भाई brother (*m*)	

📖 *Now complete Activity 5.1 in the Workbook.*

शौचालय toilet

GRAMMAR

The Verb होना *to be* (Simple Past Tense)

The verb होना *to be* when conjugated in the simple past tense (was, were) is modified for the gender and number of the subject. The paradigm for होना in the simple past tense is:

	Singular (m/f)	**Plural (m/f)**
1st person	मैं था/थी I was	हम थे/थीं we were
2nd person	तू था/थी you were	तुम थे/थीं you were
		आप थे/थीं you were
3rd person	यह था/थी he/she/it/this was	ये थे/थीं these/they were (he/she was)
	वह था/थी he/she/it/that was	वे थे/थीं those/they were (he/she was)

Terms for Some Close Relations

There are several words for "parents" in Hindi. The two most important combine common words for "mother" and "father":

माता-पिता "mother-father" and माँ-बाप "mother-father."

The first of these is more formal and should be used when talking to someone about their parents. The second term is more informal and is more commonly used to talk about one's own parents.

The term वालिदैन "parents" is also common, although it is more likely to be used in Urdu than in Hindi.

The most common term for one's maternal grandparents in Hindi is नाना "grandfather" and नानी "grandmother." For one's paternal grandparents the terms दादा "grandfather" and दादी "grandmother" are used.

PRACTICE

Meeting Kavita's Family

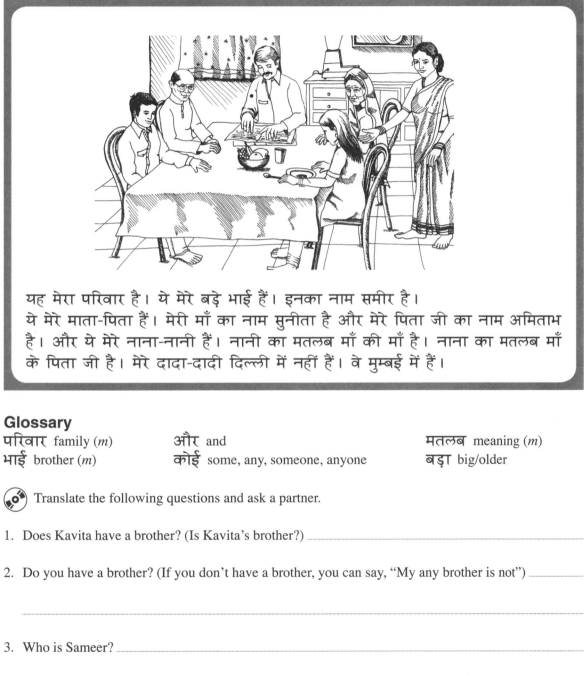

यह मेरा परिवार है। ये मेरे बड़े भाई हैं। इनका नाम समीर है।
ये मेरे माता-पिता हैं। मेरी माँ का नाम सुनीता है और मेरे पिता जी का नाम अमिताभ
है। और ये मेरे नाना-नानी हैं। नानी का मतलब माँ की माँ है। नाना का मतलब माँ
के पिता जी है। मेरे दादा-दादी दिल्ली में नहीं हैं। वे मुम्बई में हैं।

Glossary

परिवार family (*m*)   और and   मतलब meaning (*m*)
भाई brother (*m*)   कोई some, any, someone, anyone   बड़ा big/older

Translate the following questions and ask a partner.

1. Does Kavita have a brother? (Is Kavita's brother?) _____

2. Do you have a brother? (If you don't have a brother, you can say, "My any brother is not") _____

_____

3. Who is Sameer? _____

4. Are Kavita's (maternal) grandparents in Delhi? _____

5. Are Kavita's (paternal) grandparents in Delhi? _____

6. Are your (maternal/paternal) grandparents in … ? (the name of your city) ....

....

7. What is the meaning of नाना-नानी? ....

📖 *Before continuing, complete Activity 5.2 in the Workbook.*

GRAMMAR

The Use of कितना and कैसा
कैसा How, what sort of, what kind of? (quality)
कैसा is an adjective and as such it belongs to the category of आ ending adjectives that change for the *gender*, *number* and *case*[1] of the noun that is being qualified. It is employed to inquire about the *quality* of the noun that it qualifies.

When कैसा occurs in the predicate, it is often translated as *how?*

आप कैसे हैं? How are you (*m*)?
तुम कैसी हो? How are you (*f*)?

When कैसा occurs *before* the noun it qualifies, it may be translated as *what kind/sort of?*

वह कैसा अख़बार है? *What sort of* newspaper is that?

वे कैसे लोग हैं? *What sort of* people are they?

यह कैसी किताब है? *What kind of* book is this?

कितना how much, many? (quantity)
कितना is an आ ending adjective that is employed to inquire about the *quantity* of the noun that it qualifies. It may also be used rhetorically to express how good or bad something may appear to the speaker.

यह दीवार कितनी ऊँची है? *How (much)* high is this wall?

अरे, ये फूल कितने ख़ूबसूरत हैं! *How (much)* beautiful are these flowers!

वहाँ कितने आदमी खड़े हैं? *How many* men are standing there?

यह कितनी अच्छी बात है! *What* a great thing/matter this is!

---

1. For a full explanation of case, see p. 52.

PRACTICE

How Are You? How's the Weather?

The most common way of asking *How are you?* utilizes the word कैसा *how?* If you are good friends, you are more likely to use the second person familiar pronoun तुम.

आप कैसे/कैसी हैं? How are you? (*m/f polite*)
तुम कैसे/कैसी हो? How are you? (*m/f informal*)

There are several words that can be used in response.

मैं ... हूँ। I am ....   अच्छा/अच्छी good
ठीक okay
मज़े में at perfect ease

or you can say

बस, आप सुनाइये। Fine, you tell me. (*polite*)
बस, तुम सुनाओ। Fine, you tell me. (*informal*)
  (बस = that's all, that will do, enough)

When talking about the weather (मौसम), the following words can be employed:
(बहुत) अच्छा (very) good
ठीक okay
(बहुत) ख़राब (very) bad
सुहावना charming
बढ़िया excellent

आज का मौसम कैसा है? How is today's weather?
आज मौसम कैसा है? How is the weather today?
आज का मौसम अच्छा है। Today's weather is good.
आज मौसम अच्छा है। The weather today is good.

कविता - नमस्ते दीपक तुम कैसे हो?
दीपक - मज़े में हूँ। तुम सुनाओ।
कविता - बस। मैं ठीक हूँ। कल तुम कैसे थे?
दीपक - कल मैं बीमार था। कल तुम कैसी थीं?
कविता - कल मैं अच्छी थी। कल का मौसम कैसा था?
दीपक - कल का मौसम सुहावना था। आज का मौसम ख़राब है।
कविता - आज मौसम ख़राब नहीं है, दीपक।

Glossary
मज़े में at ease   बीमार sick, ill   सुहावना pleasing, charming
ठीक okay   मौसम weather (*m*)   ख़राब bad

(🔘) Answer the following questions and ask them of a partner:

1. आप कैसे/कैसी हैं? ....

2. कल आप कैसे थे (कैसी थीं)? ....

3. आज का मौसम कैसा है? ....

4. क्या आज का मौसम बहुत ख़राब है? ....

5. कल का मौसम कैसा था? ....

6. क्या कल का मौसम बहुत अच्छा था? ....

📖 *Before continuing, complete Activity 5.3 in the Workbook.*

GRAMMAR

Word Order

In Lesson 1 the basic word order of a Hindi sentence (*subject – object – verb*) was introduced. In addition to these parts of speech, there are several other parts of speech that can be said to have a *regular word order* in the sentence. Ordinarily in Hindi the emphasis in a sentence falls on the part of speech that occurs in a penultimate position.

1. Interrogative Adverbs and Pronouns.
   Interrogative adverbs and pronouns (e.g., *what*, *where*, *who*) are generally placed directly before the verb.

   यह क्या है? What is this?
   क़लम कहाँ है? Where is a/the pen?
   आप कौन हैं? Who are you?

2. Adjectives.
   These are generally placed *before* the noun or pronoun that they qualify. They may also form part of the predicate.

   यह पक्का मकान है। This is a strong house.
   यह मकान पक्का है। This house is strong.
   यह मकान कितना पक्का है? How strong is this house?

3. The negative adverb नहीं *not* is ordinarily placed directly before the verb. If there also is an interrogative, it generally comes before the negative adverb.

   क़लम वहाँ क्यों नहीं है? Why isn't the pen there?

4. Adverbial phrases that tell *when*, *where* or *how* an action takes place (such as *here*, *in the room*, *tomorrow*, *in the morning*, *slowly*, etc.) generally are placed either before the verb or at the beginning of the sentence.

> यहाँ वह लड़का था। Over here there was that boy.
> वह लड़का यहाँ था। That boy was (over) here.
> कल वह लड़का यहाँ नहीं था। Yesterday that boy was not (over) here.

If there is an interrogative adverb it will occur between these adverbs and the verb.

> कल वह लड़का यहाँ क्यों नहीं था? Why wasn't that boy here yesterday?

PRACTICE

📖 *Turn to the Workbook and complete Activity 5.4 before moving on to Lesson 6.*

LESSON **6** छठा पाठ

Meeting Deepak's Family

In Lesson 6 the remaining seven consonants are introduced. This completes the Devanagari syllabary.

Consonants

The final seven consonants are:

ङ	झ/ऴ	ञ	ट	ढ	ण/ग	ष
ṅa	jha	ña	ṭa	ḍha	ṇa	ṣa

ङ ṅa

This is similar to **n** in the word *king*. It is difficult to pronounce alone, and cannot occur in a *word initial position* or *final position*. In other words, it occurs only when followed by the velar consonants, namely, क, ख, ग and घ. It is described as a *velar nasal plosive*.

झ/ऴ jha

This character is the *aspirated* partner of ज. It is an *aspirated voiced palatal plosive* and is pronounced like the **-dgeh-** in the word *hedgehog*. There are two possible written forms of this consonant. The first of these is now considered the standard form.

ञ ña

This character is another of the five nasal consonants. It is pronounced with the back of the tongue touching the roof of the mouth like the **n** in the word *inch* and is described as a *palatal nasal*. It does not occur in a *word initial position* or *word final position* and is found only in combination with other consonants of the same series (च, छ, ज and झ).

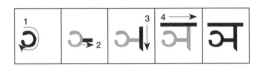

ट ṭa

This character represents a retroflex **t**. This means that the tip of the tongue should touch the ridge of the mouth at the time of pronunciation. It is an *unaspirated voiceless retroflex plosive*. Its aspirated partner is ठ.

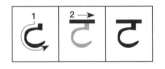

ढ ḍha

This character is a *retroflex* consonant and the *aspirated* partner of ड. During the production of this consonant the tip of the tongue should be placed on the ridge of the mouth and flapped down. At the same time a breath of air should be expelled.

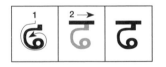

ण/ण ṇa

This is also a nasal consonant. It cannot occur in a *word initial position*. It has two forms, both of which are commonly encountered, and is described as a *retroflex nasal plosive*.

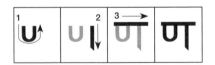

ष ṣa

This character represents another **sh** sound. It is pronounced as the **sh** in the word *flush*. ष is described as a *voiceless retroflex sibilant fricative*.

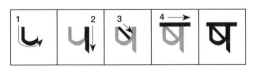

The Complete Syllabary

These final seven characters complete the Devanagari syllabary. Now we can display the entire syllabary in the order that the characters appear in the dictionary. Conventionally the vowels appear first, followed by all of the consonants.

अ	आ	इ	ई	उ	ऊ	ऋ	ए	ऐ	ओ	औ	अं	अः

After the vowels, the consonants appear in their series. These are arranged according to the point of articulation in the mouth, beginning with the *velar* consonants (those pronounced in the throat).

velar consonants (produced in the throat)	क/क़	ख/ख़	ग/ग़	घ	ङ
palatal consonants (produced using the tongue and hard palate)	च	छ	ज	झ/ॼ	ञ
retroflex consonants (produced with the tip of the tongue on the ridge of the mouth)	ट	ठ	ड (ड़)	ढ (ढ़)	ण/ण़
dental consonants (produced with the tongue against the back of the top teeth)	त	थ	द	ध	न
labial consonants (formed with the lips)	प	फ/फ़	ब	भ	म
liquids and semi-vowels	य	र	ल	व	
sibilants and fricatives	श	ष	स		
aspirate	ह				

Conjunct Consonants

A few modified forms of particular characters have been introduced in earlier lessons when they occur in conjunct clusters. In this lesson, you will learn the forms of most of the more common variations. These can be divided into six groups, depending on the particular modification to the consonant that takes place. In all cases, conjunct clusters are read from left to right and then top to bottom.

1. The first group of conjunct forms includes only the consonants क and फ. Both of these end in a short, horizontal half-stroke.

    क्या **kyā** what? (*also question marker*)
    शक्कर **śakkar** sugar (*f*)
    रफ़्तार **raftār** speed (*f*)
    मुफ़्त **muft** free

गंगा नदी The Ganges River

2. The second group consists of consonants that lose the vertical line when they are joined to the following consonant. This includes the majority of the consonants in the syllabary.

ख ग घ च ज त थ ध प
ब भ य ल व श ष स

विख्यात **vikhyāt** famous	ख्याल **khyāl** idea, thought (*m*)
ग्यारह **gyārah** eleven	बग्घी **bagghī** buggy (*f*)
अच्छा **acchā** good	बच्चा **baccā** child (*m*)
छज्जा **chajjā** balcony (*m*)	राज्य **rājya** state, province (*m*)
त्याग **tyāg** renunciation (*m*)	कुत्ता/कुत्ता **kuttā** dog (*m*)
पृथ्वी **pṛthvī** earth (*f*)	तथ्य **tathya** fact (*m*)
ध्यान **dhyān** attention (*m*)	अध्यापक **adhyāpak** teacher (*m*)
प्यास **pyās** thirst (*f*)	चप्पल **cappal** sandal (*f*)
शब्द **shabd** word (*m*)	ब्याह **byāh** marriage (*m*)
अभ्यास **abhyās** practice (*m*)	सभ्य **sabhya** civilized (*adj*)
अय्यर **ayyar** a name	
जल्दी **jaldī** haste (*f*)	दिल्ली **dillī** Delhi (*f*)
व्यवहार **vyavahār** behavior (*m*)	व्यापार **vyāpār** business (*m*)
नाश्ता **nāśtā** snack, breakfast (*m*)	चश्मा **caśmā** spectacles, eye glasses (*m*)
शिष्य **śiṣya** disciple (*m*)	कष्ट **kaṣṭ** difficulty, pain (*m*)
नमस्कार **namaskār** greeting (*m*)	पुस्तक **pustak** book (*f*)

3. The third group of conjunct characters contains all of the nasal consonants: ङ, ञ, ण/ग, न, म. When they appear as the first member of a consonant cluster, they may either be written in a modified form and joined to the following consonant or as a dot above the horizontal line. Nasal conjuncts will only occur with a consonant of the series to which they belong in the syllabary.

ङ (combines with क, ख, ग, घ)
शङ्कर/शंकर **śaṅkar** Shiva (*m*)
कङ्घी/कंघी **kaṅghī** comb (*f*)
पङ्खा/पंखा **paṅkhā** fan (*m*)

ञ (combines with च, छ, ज, झ)
सञ्जय/सञ्जय/संजय **sañjay** Sanjay
चञ्चल/चञ्चल/चंचल **cañcal** restless, fickle (*adj*)

ण/ण (combines with ट, ठ, ड, ढ)
अण्डा/अरडा/अंडा **aṇḍā** egg (*m*)
ठण्डा/ठरडा/ठंडा **ṭhaṇḍā** cold
घण्टा/घरटा/घंटा **ghaṇṭā** hour, bell (*m*)

न ¹ (combines with त, थ, द, ध)
सुन्दर/सुंदर **sundar** beautiful
सन्त/संत **sant** saint (*m*)

  a) When न combines with त, थ, द or ध, it may be written as a dot or in the modified form.

  b) When न combines with र, श and स, it should be written as a dot. When it combines with म etc. it should be written in the modified form ` ॆ `.
मुन्नी/मुन्नी **munnī** child (*f*)
नन्हाँ **nanhā̃** tiny, wee, small (as in child)

म ² (combines with प, फ, ब, भ)
चम्मच **cammac** spoon (*m*)
कम्बल/कंबल **kambal** blanket (*m*)
तुम्हारा **tumhārā** your (from तुम)

4. The fourth group consists of the consonants that have a rounded shape: ट, ठ, ड, ढ, द and ह. As the first member of a consonant cluster, these characters may be represented in two ways. The consonants can be joined one on top of the other, or the symbol ੍ (हलंत **halant**) may be written under the first consonant to represent the omission of the अ vowel.

चिट्ठी/चिट्ठी **ciṭṭhī** letter (*f*)
छुट्टी/छुट्टी **chuṭṭī** holiday (*f*)
पाठ्य-पुस्तक/पाठ्यपुस्तक **pāṭhya-pustak** textbook (*f*)
लड्डू/लड्डू **laḍḍū** (an Indian sweet) (*m*)
धनाढ्य/धनाढ्य **dhanāḍhya** wealthy
कद्दू/कद्दू **kaddū** pumpkin (*m*)
चिह्न/चिह्न **cihn** sign (*m*)
ब्राह्मण/ब्राह्मण **brāhmaṇ** Brahman (*m*)

5. The fifth group consists only of the consonant र, which takes three forms depending on whether it occurs as the first member or the final member of the conjunct cluster and the character with which it is combined.
  a) When र occurs as the first member of the cluster it is written above the line *after* the consonant to which it is joined.
    धर्म **dharm** justice, duty, religion (*m*)   सर्दी **sardī** cold, winter (*f*)

---

1. न may also combine with म, य, र, व, श, स, and ह.
2. When म combines with प, फ, ब, or भ, it may be written as a dot but when it combines with म, न, य, ल, and ह the conjunct form ॆ is employed.

b) When र occurs as the second member of the consonant cluster it is written as a diagonal stroke at the bottom of the consonant it follows.

चक्र **cakra** circle (*m*)
ग्राहक **grāhak** customer (*m*)

c) When र is the second member after any of the rounded consonants, ट, ठ, ड, ढ, द, ह, छ, it is written under the consonant thus ॒ or ॕ (or in the case of ह, in the consonant).

ट्रेन **ṭren** train (*f*)
राष्ट्र **rāṣṭra** nation (*m*)
द्रव्य **dravya** substance, money (*m*)
ह्रास **hras** decay (*m*)

ट्रेन **ṭren** train (*f*)

6. The final group consists of the exceptional conjunct consonants.

क् + ष = क्ष/क्ष	परीक्षा **parīkṣā** examination (*f*)	
क् + र = क्र	क्रिया **kriyā** action, verb (*f*)	
क् + त = क्त	भक्त **bhakt** devotee (*m*)	
ज् + अ = ज्ञ	ज्ञान **jñān** knowledge (pronounced **gyān**) (*m*)	
त् + त = त्त	पत्ता **patta** leaf (*m*)	
त् + र = त्र	मित्र **mitra** friend (*m*)	
द् + ध = द्ध	शुद्ध **śuddh** pure	
द् + भ = द्भ	अद्भुत **adbhut** wonderful, astonishing	
द् + य = द्य	विद्या **vidya** knowledge (*f*)	
द् + व = द्व	द्वार **dvār** door (*m*)	
न् + न = न्न	मुन्ना **munnā** baby (*m*)	
श् + ऋ = शृ	शृंगार **śṛṅgār** beautification, adornment* (*m*)	
श् + च = श्च/श्च	निश्चय **niścay** decision (*m*)	

श्‍ + र = श्र श्री śrī Mr. (*adj* + *m*)
श्‍ + व = श्व/श्व ईश्वर īśvar God (*m*)
ह्‍ + ऋ = हृ हृदय hṛday heart* (*m*)
ह्‍ + व = ह्व ह्वाइट hvāiṭ white
ह्‍ + य = ह्य असह्य asahya unbearable

> * These are not actually conjunct consonants but the consonant together with the mātrā form of the vowel ऋ.

PRACTICE

See if you can pronounce the words below using the characters that have been introduced in this lesson.

अंगूठी a ring (*f*)	ठंड cold (*f*)	प्रेम love (*m*)
अंग्रेज़ी English language (*f*)	ढूँढना to search (*v.t.*)	ब्राह्मण Brahmin (*m*)
आज्ञा order (*f*)	ढेर heap, pile (*m*)	महाराष्ट्र Mahrashtra (*m*)
आश्रम hermitage (*m*)	निर्बल weak	मिट्टी soil, earth (*f*)
कक्षा class (*f*)	पत्र letter (*m*)	वर्षा rain (*f*)
कुत्ता dog (*m*)	पृथ्वी the earth (*f*)	संस्कृत Sanskrit (*f*)
झूठ a lie (*m*)	प्रश्न question (*m*)	समझना to understand
टमाटर tomato (*m*)	प्रसन्नता happiness (*f*)	(*v.t.* + *v.i.*)
टिकट ticket (*m/f*)	प्रार्थना prayer (*f*)	

RULES FOR PRONUNCIATION

Nasalization and Nasal Consonants

Distinguishing between the nasalization of a vowel and a nasal consonant when it appears as the first member of a consonant cluster and is written as a dot can be a difficult task. Confusion may occur when nasalization (represented by the candrabindu symbol, ँ) is reduced to a dot ं due to the presence of a vowel mātrā above the horizontal line at the top of the word or at the discretion of the writer or printer. The following guidelines help to clarify when a dot represents nasalization and when it represents a nasal consonant.

1. A dot ं (*anusvār*) often represents a nasal consonant as the first member of a consonant cluster, *particularly when the preceding vowel is short.* (See 3 above.) In such cases, the dot will represent the nasal consonant of the class of the consonant that follows.

velar (क, ख, ग, घ)	ङ	अङ्क or	अंक number, numeral (*m*)
palatal (च, छ, ज, झ)	ञ	अञ्चल or	अंचल outer portion of a sari (*m*)
retroflex (ट, ठ, ड, ढ)	ण/ण	ठण्ड / ठण्ड or	ठंड cold (*f*)
dental (त, थ, द, ध)	न	हिन्दी or	हिंदी Hindi language (*f*)
labial (प, फ, ब, भ)	म	लम्बा or	लंबा tall

2. The candrabindu symbol ˘ represents the nasalization of a syllable. Ordinarily (but not always) this will contain a *long vowel*.

आँख **ãkh** eye (*f*)   हाँ **hã** yes
ऊँट **ũṭ** camel (*m*)   आँधी **ãndhī** storm (*f*)

When a vowel mātrā occurs above the horizontal line, candrabindu ˘ is reduced to a dot.

नहीं **nahī̃** no   हैं **haĩ** is/are

3. In some printed texts, sometimes a dot is used uniformly to represent all nasalization.

आंख **ãkh** eye (*f*)   हां **hã** yes
ऊंट **ũṭ** camel (*m*)   आंधी **ãndhī** storm (*f*)

4. As was previously mentioned, a nasal consonant only occurs with a following consonant of the same class, with another nasal or with य र ल व श ष स and ह. The euphonic change that takes place is quite natural. These five nasal consonants can also be written in a modified conjunct form.

PRACTICE

📖 *Now turn to the Workbook and complete Activity 6.1 before continuing.*

THE DEVANAGARI SYLLABARY

Looking Up Words in a Dictionary
The order of words in a conventional monolingual or Hindi-English dictionary follows systematically the order of the syllabary, with each syllable in a word arranged according to this order.

First appear all of the vowels headed by anusvār and visarg.
अं अः (These are not actually vowels and cannot appear alone in *word initial position*.)
अ आ इ ई उ ऊ ऋ ए ऐ ओ औ

After the vowels appear the consonants in their series.

velar consonants	क/क़	ख/ख़	ग/ग़	घ	ङ*
palatal consonants	च	छ	ज/ज़	झ	ञ*
retroflex consonants	ट	ठ	ड(ड़)*	ढ(ढ़)*	ण/ण*
dental consonants	त	थ	द	ध	न
labial consonants	प	फ/फ़	ब	भ	म
liquids and *semi-vowels*	य	र	ल	व	
sibilants and *fricatives*	श	ष	स		
aspirate	ह				

* These never appear in a *word initial position*.

For example, the order of the words in the dictionary that begin with क would follow the same sequence as the vowels above.

क का कि की कु कू कृ के कै को कौ

1. If a syllable has a nasalization (ँ), an anusvār (ं) or a visarg (ः), these will occur at the beginning of the syllable.

कं/कँ कः क का कि की कु कू कृ के कै को कौ

For example,

चं *precedes* च

    चंचल fickle *precedes* चकमा trick (*m*)

गाँ *precedes* गा

    गाँव village (*m*) *precedes* गाड़ी car (*f*)

दुः *precedes* दु

    दुःख sorrow (*m*) *precedes* दुआ prayer (*f*)

2. Conjunct consonants occur at the *end* of a syllable after all of the vowels that occur with the particular consonant.

    कौशेय silky (*adj*) *precedes* क्या what (*pro*)

3. The consonants ङ, ञ, ण, ड़, and ढ़ never occur in word initial position. The consonants ड़ and ढ़ follow the consonants ड and ढ respectively.

PRACTICE

📖 *Now complete Activity 6.2 in the Workbook.*

GRAMMAR

Asking One's Age
There are two ways to ask the age of a person in Hindi.

1. आपकी उम्र क्या है?   What is your age?

2. आप कितने साल के/की हैं?   How old are you? (of how many years are you?)

There are two ways to respond to this question.

1. मेरी उम्र ... साल की है।   My age is (of) ... years.

2. मैं ... साल का/की हूँ।   I am of ... years.
(For a list of all numbers from 1–50, see Lesson 16, p. 151.)

PRACTICE

 **Meeting Deepak's Family**

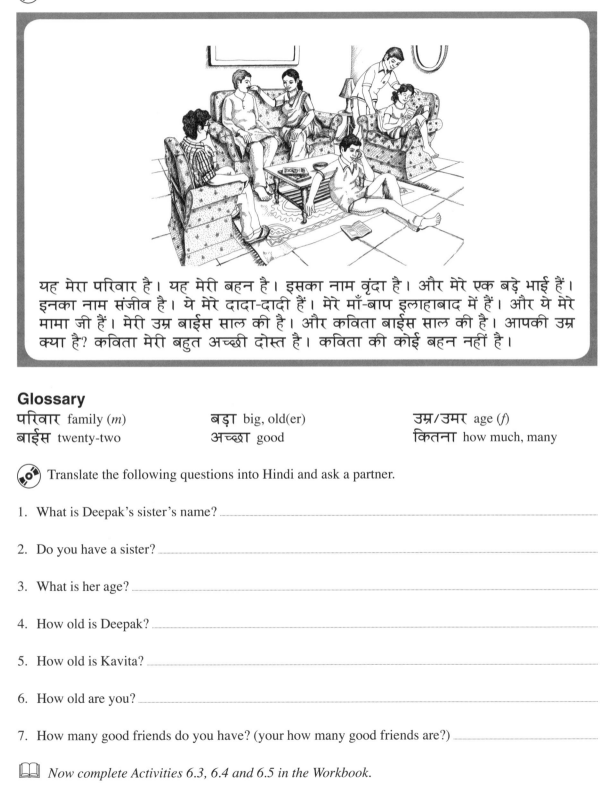

यह मेरा परिवार है। यह मेरी बहन है। इसका नाम वृंदा है। और मेरे एक बड़े भाई हैं। इनका नाम संजीव है। ये मेरे दादा-दादी हैं। मेरे माँ-बाप इलाहाबाद में हैं। और ये मेरे मामा जी हैं। मेरी उम्र बाईस साल की है। और कविता बाईस साल की है। आपकी उम्र क्या है? कविता मेरी बहुत अच्छी दोस्त है। कविता की कोई बहन नहीं है।

Glossary

परिवार family (*m*)   बड़ा big, old(er)   उम्र/उमर age (*f*)

बाईस twenty-two   अच्छा good   कितना how much, many

Translate the following questions into Hindi and ask a partner.

1. What is Deepak's sister's name? ....

2. Do you have a sister? ....

3. What is her age? ....

4. How old is Deepak? ....

5. How old is Kavita? ....

6. How old are you? ....

7. How many good friends do you have? (your how many good friends are?) ....

Now complete Activities 6.3, 6.4 and 6.5 in the Workbook.

Some More Greetings; To Want/Need

PRACTICE

Outside the Library पुस्तकालय के बाहर

Kavita and Deepak meet a friend, Imran, in front of the library at the university.

दीपक	– नमस्ते कविता, आज तुम कैसी हो?
कविता	– आज मैं बिल्कुल ठीक हूँ। तुम सुनाओ।
दीपक	– बस, सब ठीक है। आजकल तुम्हारे भाई कैसे हैं?
कविता	– वे ठीक हैं। आजकल तुम्हारी बहन का क्या हाल है?
दीपक	– वह अच्छी है। अच्छा, इमरान आदाब। कैसे हो तुम?
इमरान	– मज़े में हूँ। तुम दोनों कैसे हो?
दीपक	– बस! इमरान, आज तुम्हारी माँ का जन्मदिन है, न?
इमरान	– जी हाँ, आज अम्मी जान बहुत ख़ुश हैं।
कविता	– अच्छा, उनकी क्या उम्र है?
इमरान	– उनकी उम्र पचास साल की है।
दीपक	– अरे वाह! अच्छी बात है।

Glossary

परिवार family (*m*)	सुनाओ tell, relate (imperative) (*v.t.*)	आजकल these days
बिल्कुल absolutely	आदाब "greetings" (*voc*)	मज़े में in fine health
हाल state, condition (*m*)	बहुत very, much	ख़ुश happy
दोनों both	जन्मदिन birthday (*m*)	पचास fifty
अम्मी जान mother dear (*f*)	न isn't it?	क्योंकि because
अरे वाह! Oh wow!	क्यों why (*inter*)	
बड़ा big, old(er)	उम्र/उमर age (*f*)	

See if you can answer the following questions. Then, ask these questions of a partner.

1. आज कविता कैसी है? _____

2. आज क्या दीपक ठीक है? _____

3. आज कौन मज़े में है? _____

4. आज तुम्हारा क्या हाल है? _____

5. क्या इमरान दीपक और कविता का दोस्त है? _____

6. आज इमरान की माँ क्यों ख़ुश हैं? _____

7. क्या आज तुम्हारी माँ का जन्मदिन है? _____

8. क्या आज तुम्हारे पिता जी का जन्मदिन है? _____

GRAMMAR

Some More Greetings

In Lesson 2, two common greetings in Hindi were introduced, नमस्ते and नमस्कार. They are employed as a form of greeting, similar to "hello," as well as to say goodbye. There are several other expressions of greeting and farewell employed in Hindi. Some of these are considered more formal expressions in Hindi and some are primarily used to address respectfully speakers of Urdu.

प्रणाम "Reverential salutation" (a formal term often used to greet elders).

राम राम An orthodox Hindu greeting.

आदाब (अर्ज़) "Greetings" (either आदाब or आदाब अर्ज़ may be used with little difference in meaning); predominantly used when greeting a speaker of Urdu.

अस्सलाम अलैकुम "Peace be upon you" (वालैकुम अस्सलाम "And peace be upon you," said in response); predominantly used when greeting a speaker of Urdu.

ख़ुदा हाफ़िज़ "May God protect you" (used in Urdu when parting).

The Polite Suffixes

In addition to the polite suffix जी (lit. "heart, mind," Lesson 2, p. 15), the word साहब *sahib* may also be employed as a polite suffix for males after both first names and family names. When employed with family names it approximates "Mr." It is commonly used with English names, Muslim names and with the term भाई "brother" as a polite way to address a stranger. The word साहिबा *sahiba,* "madam," is generally employed with (mainly married) Muslim women's names and with the term बेगम "lady."

जॉन साहब John *sahib*
मुज़फ़्फ़र साहब Muzaffar *sahib*
सुलतान साहब Mr. Sultan (or Sultan *sahib*)
डॉक्टर साहब Doctor *sahib*
भाई साहब! Sir!
ज़ेबा साहिबा Zeba *sahiba*

Case

There are two cases in Hindi: the *direct* case and the *oblique case.* A noun, pronoun or adjective that is governed by a postposition is said to be in the *oblique case.* Often the particular word governed by the postposition is declined to reflect this. Nouns, pronouns and adjectives that are not followed by postpositions are said to be in the *direct* case. The form a noun (or adjective) takes when governed by a postposition is determined by its gender, its number and what occurs in a *word final position.* Pronouns take various forms depending on the particular postposition that follows. Finally (and most importantly), any word that is governed by a postposition cannot influence the conjugation of the verb.

Consider the following phrase:

ख़ालिद का यह बड़ा मकान
this big house of Khalid
(lit: *Khalid's this big house*)

1. Here ख़ालिद is in the *oblique case* (followed by the postposition का *'s*)
2. The postposition का, the pronoun यह, the adjective बड़ा and the noun मकान are said to be in the *direct case* (not followed by a postposition).

Consider the same phrase with the addition of the postposition में *in.*

ख़ालिद के इस बड़े मकान में
in this big house of Khalid
(lit: *Khalid's this big house in*)

1. The noun ख़ालिद is in the *oblique case* due to the postposition का.
2. Here the postposition का, the pronoun यह *this*, the adjective बड़ा *big* and the noun मकान *house* are all in the *oblique case* (followed by a postposition में).

In this lesson, the forms of pronouns followed by various postpositions are introduced, as well as the declension of masculine nouns.

Pronouns with Postpositions

The following table shows the forms that the pronouns take when governed by various postpositions. The majority of postpositions comprise two or three words beginning either with के or की (such as के लिये *for, in order to*). Single word postpositions (except for को and ने) govern the forms of the pronouns in the manner of में *in* shown in the table. This list is for your reference; you aren't expected to memorize these forms immediately. For a list of some of the more common postpositions, see p. 242.

Direct Case	Oblique Case				
	+ का *'s*	+ के लिये *for, in order to*	+ में *in*	+ को *(object marker)* [1]	ने *(ergative part.)* [2]
मैं *I*	मेरा	मेरे लिये	मुझमें	मुझको/मुझे	मैंने
हम *we*	हमारा	हमारे लिये	हममें	हमको/हमें	हमने
तू *you*	तेरा	तेरे लिये	तुझमें	तुझको/तुझे	तूने
तुम *you*	तुम्हारा	तुम्हारे लिये	तुममें	तुमको/तुम्हें	तुमने
आप *you*	आपका	आपके लिये	आपमें	आपको	आपने
यह *he/she/it/this*	इसका	इसके लिये	इसमें	इसको/इसे	इसने
वह *he/she/it/that*	उसका	उसके लिये	उसमें	उसको/उसे	उसने
ये *he/she/they/these*	इनका	इनके लिये	इनमें	इनको/इन्हें	इन्होंने
वे *he/she/they/those*	उनका	उनके लिये	उनमें	उनको/उन्हें	उन्होंने
कौन *who*	किसका	किसके लिये	किसमें	किसको/किसे	किसने
कौन* *who (pl)*	किनका	किनके लिये	किनमें	किनको/किन्हें	किन्होंने
क्या *what*	किसका	किसके लिये	किसमें	किसको/किसे	किसने
कोई *someone/anyone some/any*	किसी का	किसी के लिये	किसी में	किसीको	किसी ने
कोई* *some (pl)*	किन्हीं का	किन्हीं के लिये	किन्हीं में	किन्हीं को	किन्हीं ने
जो* *who/that/which*	जिसका	जिसके लिये	जिसमें	जिसको/जिसे	जिसने
जो* *who/that/which (pl)*	जिनका	जिनके लिये	जिनमें	जिनको/जिन्हें	जिन्होंने

1. For an explanation of को, see pp. 56, 65, 71.
2. For an explanation of ने, see p. 100
* Both कौन and कोई have plural oblique forms that are included in this list. जो is the relative pronoun. See p. 223 for an explanation of जो.

(Many speakers of Hindi have replaced the forms मुझे/मुझको and तुझे/तुझको with मेरे को and तेरे को respectively.)

Masculine Nouns

Masculine nouns in Hindi are declined for number and case (direct/oblique) according to what occurs in a word final position. There are three classes of masculine nouns:

1. Masculine nouns that end in आ
2. All other masculine nouns
3. Exceptional आ ending masculine nouns

Let's look at each more closely.

1. Masculine nouns that end in आ

Masculine nouns that end in आ decline in the following manner.

Singular Direct	Singular Oblique	Plural Direct	Plural Oblique
कमरा room	कमरे में in a/the room	कमरे rooms	कमरों में in (the) rooms

2. All other masculine nouns

All other masculine nouns decline in the following manner.

Singular Direct	Singular Oblique	Plural Direct	Plural Oblique
घर home	घर में in a/the home	घर homes	घरों में in (the) homes

Masculine nouns that end in the long vowels ई and ऊ shorten these vowels in the plural oblique form and in the case of ई, add the semi-vowel य before the oblique ending.

Singular Direct	Singular Oblique	Plural Direct	Plural Oblique
आदमी a/the man	आदमी में in a/the man	आदमी men	आदमियों में in (the) men
आलू potato	आलू में in a/the potato	आलू potatoes	आलुओं में in (the) potatoes

3. Exceptional आ ending masculine nouns

There are some आ ending masculine nouns that follow the pattern of (2). These are mainly nouns that signify a relationship and have a reduplicative form (मामा maternal uncle, चाचा paternal uncle, नाना maternal grandfather, दादा paternal grandfather) as well as some words that have come into Hindi from Sanskrit (राजा king, पिता father).

Singular Direct	Singular Oblique	Plural Direct	Plural Oblique
राजा king	राजा में in a/the king	राजा kings	राजाओं में in (the) kings
मामा maternal uncle	मामा में in a/the uncle	मामा uncles	मामाओं में in (the) uncles

The Vocative Case

The vocative form of the noun is used when calling out to or addressing someone. The vocative forms of masculine nouns are the same as the singular oblique form and the plural oblique form without the nasalization. Often the vocative particles ओ, हे, अरे (अरी for feminine nouns) are employed when calling out to someone.

Singular	Plural
ओ लड़के! Hey/Oh boy!	ओ लड़को! Hey/Oh boys!
ओ धोबी! Hey/Oh washerman!	ओ धोबियो! Hey/Oh washermen!
हे राजा! Hey/Oh king!	हे राजाओ! Hey/Oh kings!

PRACTICE

📖 *Now turn to the Workbook and decline the masculine nouns given in Activity 7.1.*

GRAMMAR

Declension of Adjectives

When qualifying masculine nouns in the oblique case, आ ending adjectives must also be inflected. The oblique form of आ ending adjectives is the same as the plural form.

Singular Direct	Singular Oblique	Plural Direct	Plural Oblique
अच्छा लड़का a/the good boy	अच्छे लड़के को (to) a/the good boy	अच्छे लड़के (the) good boys	अच्छे लड़कों को (to the) good boys

वहाँ एक बड़ा मंदिर है।
There is a big temple over there.

उस बड़े मंदिर में कृष्ण की मूर्ति है।
In that big temple there is a statue of Krishna.

वहाँ दो बड़े मंदिर हैं।
There are two big temples over there.

उन बड़े मंदिरों में कोई नहीं है।
There is no one in those big temples.

Because the postposition का *'s* transforms the noun or pronoun it governs into an आ ending adjective, it acts in the same way as other आ ending adjectives in the oblique case.

उसके बड़े मकान में कोई नहीं है।
There is no one in his/her big house.

There is no additional change to adjectives qualifying feminine nouns in the oblique case (see p. 20).

PRACTICE

📖 *Complete Activities 7.2 and 7.3 in the Workbook before continuing.*

GRAMMAR

The Use of चाहिए (wanted/needed)

1. The invariable verbal form चाहिए *wanted/needed* is employed in useful expressions where the object needed/wanted is a *noun or pronoun*. The person who needs/wants is governed by the postposition को.[1]

X को y चाहिए।   X wants/needs y.

Singular	Plural
मुझको/मुझे चाहिए I want/need	हमको/हमें चाहिए we want/need
तुझको/तुझे चाहिए you want/need	तुमको/तुम्हें चाहिए you want/need
	आपको चाहिए you want/need
इसको/इसे चाहिए she/he/it/this/wants/needs	इनको/इन्हें चाहिए he/she/they/these want(s)/need(s)
उसको/उसे चाहिए she/he/it/that/wants/needs	उनको/उन्हें चाहिए he/she/they/those want(s)/need(s)
किसको/किसे चाहिए who wants/needs	किनको/किन्हें चाहिए who want/need
किसी को चाहिए someone/anyone/wants/needs	किन्हीं को चाहिए some want/need

---

1. को is an important postposition that performs several functions in a Hindi sentence. For a more comprehensive explanation of को, see pp. 65, 71.

चाहिए may also be written as चाहिये with no change in pronunciation or meaning.

मुझे संतरा चाहिये।
I want/need an orange.

लड़की को छुट्टी नहीं चाहिये।
The girl doesn't want/need a vacation.

2. Expressions employing चाहिये may be placed in the past with the addition of the simple past form of the verb होना *to be* (था, थे, थी, थीं). This is conjugated for the gender and number of the object or person that is wanted/needed.

मुझे एक संतरा चाहिए था।
I wanted/needed an orange (*m sing*).

मेरी माँ को दो संतरे चाहिये थे।
My mother wanted/needed two oranges (*m pl*).

दीपक को एक किताब चाहिये थी।
Deepak wanted/needed a book (*f sing*).

आफ़ताब को दो किताबें चाहिये थीं।
Aftab wanted/needed two books (*f pl*).*

  * For an explanation of feminine nouns, see p. 59.

PRACTICE

 What Does Kavita Want? कविता को क्या चाहिये?

नमस्ते दोस्तो। वैसे मेरी ज़िंदगी बहुत अच्छी है। मुझे बहुत कुछ नहीं चाहिये। परीक्षा में मुझको अच्छे नंबर चाहिये। और हाँ, अभी मुझे चाय चाहिये। मेरे भाई को बहुत पैसे चाहिये। और उन्हें एक नयी गाड़ी चाहिये। तुम्हें क्या चाहिये? पैसे? शांति? ज़िंदगी में किसे शांति नहीं चाहिये? दुनिया में सब लोगों को शांति चाहिये, न? बस, मुझे बहुत कुछ नहीं चाहिए।

Glossary

वैसे actually, in that way	परीक्षा exam (*f*)	शांति peace (*f*)
ज़िंदगी life (*f*)	अभी right now	दुनिया में in the world
बहुत कुछ very much	पैसे money (*m pl*)	सब लोग all people (*m*)
बहुत very, much	नया new	न isn't it?
कुछ नहीं nothing	गाड़ी car (*f*)	बस enough, that's all

Translate the following questions in Hindi and ask a partner.

1. Does Kavita want/need a lot of (much) money? _____

2. Do you want/need a lot of money? _____

3. Does Kavita's brother want/need a new car? _____

4. Do all the people in the world want/need peace? _____

5. Does Kavita want/need coffee or tea right now? _____

6. Who wants/needs good grades (अच्छे नंबर) on the exam? _____

📖 *Now turn to the Workbook and complete Activities 7.4 and 7.5.*

How Many Siblings Do You Have?

GRAMMAR

Feminine Nouns

As with masculine nouns, feminine nouns also decline for number, gender and case, according to what appears in a *word final position*. Feminine nouns, regardless of their ending, only change in the *plural direct* and the *plural oblique case*. There are two classes of feminine nouns:

1. Feminine nouns that end in इ, ई or इया.
2. All other feminine nouns.

1. **Feminine nouns that end in इ, ई or इया**

इ — add याँ in plural direct, यों in plural oblique.
ई — shorten to इ and add याँ in plural direct, यों in plural oblique.
इया — add ँ in plural direct, changing या to यों in plural oblique.

Singular Direct	Singular Oblique	Plural Direct	Plural Oblique
रात्रि night	रात्रि में in a/the night	रात्रियाँ nights	रात्रियों में in (the) nights
साड़ी sari	साड़ी में in a/the sari	साड़ियाँ saris	साड़ियों में in (the) saris
चिड़िया bird	चिड़िया में in a/the bird	चिड़ियाँ birds	चिड़ियों में in (the) birds

2. **All other feminine nouns.**

Feminine nouns that end in any other character are declined simply by adding एँ in the plural direct and ओं in the plural oblique.

Singular Direct	Singular Oblique	Plural Direct	Plural Oblique
चीज़ thing	चीज़ में in a/the thing	चीज़ें things	चीज़ों में in (the) things
भाषा language	भाषा में in a/the language	भाषाएँ languages	भाषाओं में in (the) languages
जोरू wife	जोरू में in a/the wife	जोरुएँ* wives	जोरुओं* में in (the) wives

* Feminine words ending in a ऊ vowel shorten this vowel before the addition of एँ and ओं in the plural direct and oblique.

The Vocative Case

As is the case with masculine nouns, the vocative forms of feminine nouns are the same as the singular oblique form and plural oblique form without the nasalization.

Singular	Plural
ओ लड़की! Hey/Oh girl!	ओ लड़कियो! Hey/Oh girls!
हे औरत! Hey/Oh woman!	हे औरतो! Hey/Oh women!

PRACTICE

📖 *Now turn to the Workbook and decline the feminine nouns in Activity 8.1.*

💿 **How Many Brothers and Sisters Do You Have? आप के कितने भाई-बहन हैं?**

Just as the most common terms for "parents" are a combination of the words for "mother and father" in Hindi (see p. 34), भाई "brother" and बहन "sister" are also combined—भाई-बहन—for "brothers and sisters" or "siblings."

In this passage Kavita talks about herself and her brother.

हम दो भाई-बहन हैं। मेरे एक भाई हैं, समीर। आजकल वे ऑस्ट्रेलिया में हैं। पहले मेरे परिवार के सब लोग बंबई में थे। मेरे पिता जी के दो भाई हैं। मेरे पिता जी के एक भाई के दो लड़के हैं और दूसरे भाई की दो लड़कियाँ हैं। दीपक के दो भाई-बहन हैं। आप के कितने भाई-बहन हैं? आप के भाइयों के नाम क्या हैं? आप की बहनों के नाम क्या हैं?

Glossary

आजकल these days	पहले previously	परिवार family (*m*)
सब all	लोग people (*m*)	पिता father (*m*)
लड़का boy (*m*)	दूसरा other, second	लड़की girl (*f*)

Answer the following questions in Hindi.

1. कविता के कितने भाई-बहन हैं? ....

2. आजकल कविता के भाई कहाँ हैं? ....

3. क्या पहले कविता के परिवार के सब लोग बंबई में थे? ....

....

4. आप के कितने भाई-बहन हैं? ....

5. आपके भाइयों और बहनों के नाम क्या हैं? ....

6. कविता के पिता जी के भाइयों के कितने लड़के-लड़कियाँ हैं? ....

....

Now turn to the Workbook and complete Activity 8.2.

GRAMMAR

The Imperative Mood

The imperative mood is used to give commands and to make requests. There are five forms of the imperative. Often the pronoun is left unexpressed in the imperative mood. Beginners are advised initially to use polite forms of the imperative.

1. The intimate imperative—used mostly with तू.
2. The familiar imperative—used mostly with तुम, and occasionally with आप.

3. The polite/formal imperative—used with आप.
4. The polite future imperative—used with आप.
5. The infinitive as imperative—used with तू, तुम.

Let's look at each of these forms more closely.

1. The intimate imperative

The stem of the verb is used to express the intimate form of the imperative. The stem of the verb is obtained by removing the suffix ना from the infinitive.

बोलना	बोल
to speak	speak

This form of the imperative is employed in circumstances where the pronoun तू is commonly used, that is, to address God, young children, in situations of intimacy, or of anger and contempt.

बैठना	बेटे, (तू) यहीं बैठ।
to sit	Son, sit right here.

2. The familiar imperative

The familiar imperative is formed by the addition of ओ to the verb stem. It is used in circumstances where the pronoun तुम is employed. Verb stems ending in ई and ऊ shorten these vowels before the addition of ओ. In the case of ई, the semi-vowel य may also be inserted.

खाना	(तुम) यह जलेबी खाओ।
to eat	Eat this jalebi.

खोलना	(तुम) खिड़की खोलो।
to open	Open the window.

पीना	मेरे दोस्त, (तुम) चाय पियो।
to drink	Drink [some] tea, my friend.

छूना	(तुम) यह गर्म चीज़ मत* छुओ।
to touch	Don't touch this hot thing.
	* See below (p. 64) for an explanation of मत.

Exceptional Form

The verbs देना *to give* and लेना *to take* have exceptional forms in the familiar imperative.

देना	(तुम) अभी किताब दो!
to give	Give the book now!

लेना	(तुम) यह चाय लो।
to take	Take this tea.

The familiar form of the imperative is occasionally used in particular expressions with the polite/plural form of the second person pronoun (आप). This usage is considered non-standard.

सुनाना	आप कैसे हैं?
to relate	How are you?
	बस। आप सुनाओ।
	I'm fine. You relate (to me how you are).

3. **The polite/formal imperative**
    The formal imperative is employed with the pronoun आप. It is formed by attaching इए (also written इये) to the stem of the verb.

बैठना	(आप) यहाँ बैठिये/बैठिए।
to sit	Please sit here.

रखना	(आप) तशरीफ़ रखिये/रखिए।
to place	Please sit down.
	(Please place your nobleness.)

Exceptional Forms
The four verbs करना *to do*, पीना *to drink*, देना *to give* and लेना *to take* are exceptional in the formal imperative.

करना	कीजिये/कीजिए	(आप) यह काम अभी कीजिये।
to do	please do	Please do this work right now.
पीना	पीजिये/पीजिए	(आप) चाय पीजिए।
to drink	please drink	Please drink tea.
देना	दीजिये/दीजिए	(आप) एक किताब दीजिये।
to give	please give	Please give a book.
लेना	लीजिये/लीजिए	(आप) यह क़लम लीजिए।
to take	please take	Please take this/the pen.

4. **The polite future imperative**
    To form the polite future imperative गा is added to the formal imperative. The polite future imperative is used almost like the future tense. That is, it is often employed to indicate some time further in the future than at the time of the command.

भेजना	(आप) चिट्ठी जल्दी भेजियेगा।
to send	Please be kind enough to send a letter soon.

आना	आप कल आइयेगा।
to come	Will you kindly come tomorrow? (Please come tomorrow.)

5. **The infinitive as imperative**

The infinitive of the verb may also be employed as an imperative. When used as an imperative it too indicates that the action is to be undertaken at some point in time further than the immediate future. This form is also used to give more generalized commands or directions. It is used with persons you would address with the pronouns तू or तुम.

आना   (तू/तुम) कल फिर आना।
to come   Come again tomorrow.

रखना   (तू/तुम) चाय मेज़ पर रखना।
to place   Place the tea on the table.

The Prohibitive

The prohibitive (negative imperative) is formed by placing मत or न directly before the verb. न is considered a more polite, softer form of negation than मत, which is considered more emphatic. Occasionally the use of नहीं (generally placed after the verb) is also encountered.

जाना   वहाँ मत जाना।
to go   Don't go there.

पीना   गंदा पानी मत पियो।
to drink   Don't drink dirty water.

लेना   इतने पैसे न लीजिये।
to take   Please don't take so much money.

ज़रा, कृपया and मेहरबानी से/करके

An imperative may be softened by introducing it with one of the following adverbial phrases.

ज़रा a little, a bit (*adj*); slightly, please, kindly (*adv*)
कृपया kindly, please (*adv*)
मेहरबानी से/करके with kindness, compassion (*adv*)

ठहरना   ज़रा यहाँ एक मिनट ठहरो।
to wait, stay Kindly wait here for a minute.

GRAMMAR

The Use of को (a)

को is an important postposition that performs several different functions in a sentence. The first of these was encountered in Lesson 7 (p. 56). There it was explained that को governs the subject when using the invariable verb form चाहिए (*wanted/needed*). In this lesson some more functions of को are introduced.

1. **को with the Direct Object**

   को governs the direct object (that word or phrase that receives the action of the verb) of a sentence, if that object is *animate and denotes a particular being*. It is possible to see this at work in the imperative mood introduced in this lesson.

   | बिठाना | (आप) उस लड़के को यहाँ बिठाइए। |
   | to seat (someone) | Please seat that boy (down) here. |

   | देखना | उस आदमी को देखो। |
   | to look | Look at (see) that man. |

   Occasionally को is used with an inanimate object for emphasis.

   | पढ़ना | (तुम) रोज़ इसे पढ़ो। |
   | to read | Read this daily. |

2. **को with the Indirect Object**

   Some verbs take two objects: a *direct object* and an *indirect object*. The verb देना *to give* is one such verb. In such cases, the indirect object, which is generally animate, will be followed by the postposition को.

   | देना | मुझे किताब दो। |
   | to give | Give a/the book to me. |

   In this sentence, the direct object (that receives the action of the verb) is "the book" (किताब) and the indirect object is "me" (मुझे). The subject of the command (left unexpressed) is "you" (तुम).

   | लिखना | (तुम) मुझको ख़त लिखो। |
   | to write | Write me a letter. |

   | बेचना | (तुम) इस लड़के को सेब मत बेचना। |
   | to sell | Don't sell apples to this boy. |

PRACTICE

Now turn to the Workbook and complete Activity 8.3.

PRACTICE

 **What Does Deepak Want? दीपक को क्या चाहिये?**

> नमस्ते मेरे दोस्तो। तुम लोग कैसे हो? मेरी दोस्त कविता को क्या चाहिये था? क्या तुम लोगों को याद है? हाँ, उसे परीक्षा में अच्छे नंबर चाहिये थे। मुझे क्या चाहिये? मुझको सिर्फ़ एक चीज़ नहीं चाहिये। मुझे बहुत चीज़ें चाहिये। पढ़ाई के बाद मुझको अच्छी नौकरी चाहिये। कल लाइब्रेरी से मुझे दो किताबें चाहिये थीं। मेरी बहन को एक नया सेल फ़ोन चाहिए और मेरे भाई को बहुत पैसे चाहिये थे लेकिन अब उसे कुछ नहीं चाहिये। बस, हमें इतना ही चाहिये।

Glossary

दोस्त friend (*m/f*)	क्या तुम लोगों को याद है?	चीज़ thing (*f*)
परीक्षा exam (*f*)	Do you (people) remember?	नया new
पढ़ाई के बाद after studies	सिर्फ़ only, just	अब now
इतना ही just this much	नौकरी job, employment (*f*)	

Translate the following questions into Hindi and then ask a partner.

1. What had Kavita wanted/needed? ....

2. What does Deepak want/need? ....

3. Does Deepak want many things? ....

4. What had Deepak wanted/needed yesterday? ....

5. Does Deepak's sister want much money? ....

📖 *Now turn to the Workbook and complete Activities 8.4 and 8.5.*

LESSON **9** नवाँ पाठ

What Do You Do?

The Imperfect Present Tense

The imperfect present tense is employed to express actions of a habitual nature that occur in the present. As the name suggests, the action is ongoing and, hence, is considered *imperfect*. This tense is used specifically to express everyday statements such as *I live in Delhi*, or *I learn Hindi*.

There are two parts to the verbal unit in the imperfect present tense: the *imperfect participle* and the *tense marker*.

बोलना	बोलता	हूँ
to speak	*imperfect participle*	*tense marker*

1. Take the stem of the verb.

बोलना	बोल
to speak	speak

2. Add:
   ता for a masculine singular subject.
   ते for a masculine plural subject.
   ती for feminine singular *and* plural subjects.

बोलता	बोलते	बोलती

3. Add the appropriate form of होना (हूँ, है, हो, हैं) for the person and number of the subject.

बोलता   speak (imperfect participle—*m sing*)
(मैं) बोलता हूँ   I speak (*m sing*)

It is important to remember that both parts of the verbal unit together form the imperfect present tense. Here, the form of होना should *not* be translated as *am, is, are*.

रहना   वह लड़का दिल्ली में रहता है।
to live   That boy lives in Delhi.

सीखना   मैं हिन्दी सीखता हूँ।
to learn   I (*m*) learn Hindi.

It can also be used to express an action that is to take place in the immediate future.

चलना   अच्छा, मैं चलता हूँ।
to move   Okay, I'm (*m*) off (*I move*).

With masculine subjects:

Singular	Plural
मैं बोलता हूँ I speak	हम बोलते हैं we speak
तू बोलता है you speak	तुम बोलते हो you speak
	आप बोलते हैं you speak
यह बोलता है he/it/this speaks	ये बोलते हैं he/they/these speak
वह बोलता है he/it/that speaks	वे बोलते हैं he/they/those speak

With feminine subjects:

Singular	Plural
मैं बोलती हूँ I speak	हम बोलती हैं we speak
तू बोलती है you speak	तुम बोलती हो you speak
	आप बोलती हैं you speak
यह बोलती है she/it/this speaks	ये बोलती हैं she/they/these speak
वह बोलती है she/it/that speaks	वे बोलती हैं she/they/those speak

Word Order

1. When the imperfect present tense is negated, the regular position of the negative adverb, नहीं, is directly before the participle. The tense marker (हूँ, है, हो, हैं) is generally omitted but may be expressed for particular emphasis.

मैं हिन्दी बोलता हूँ।
I (*m*) speak Hindi.

मैं हिन्दी नहीं बोलता।
I (*m*) don't speak Hindi.

If the subject is feminine plural, the imperfect participle is nasalized in the negative.

वे लड़कियाँ हिन्दी बोलती हैं।
Those girls speak Hindi.

वे लड़कियाँ अंग्रेज़ी नहीं बोलतीं।
Those girls don't speak English.

2. The regular word order of interrogative adverbs is directly before the imperfect participle. If there is also a negative adverb, it is placed between the interrogative and the participle.

तुम अंग्रेज़ी क्यों बोलते हो?
Why do you (*m*) speak English?

तुम हिन्दी क्यों नहीं बोलतीं?
Why don't you (*f*) speak Hindi?

PRACTICE

📖 *Now turn to the Workbook and complete Activity 9.1 before continuing.*

💿 ### What Do You Do? आप क्या करते हैं?
Read the passage below, which explains some background about the lives of Deepak and Kavita.

कविता और दीपक दोनों छात्र हैं। वे दिल्ली के एक कॉलेज में पढ़ते हैं। कविता के पिता जी सेना में हैं और उस की माँ डॉक्टर है। आजकल वे दिल्ली में रहते हैं। दीपक के माता-पिता इलाहाबाद में रहते हैं। दीपक के पिता भारतीय रेल में काम करते हैं और उसकी माँ स्कूल में टीचर है। दीपक दिल्ली में एक मामा के साथ रहता है। दीपक की बहन इलाहाबाद में रहती है। वह कभी-कभी दिल्ली आती है। दीपक का भाई दिल्ली में आई॰ टी॰ में काम करता है। आजकल कविता का भाई ऑस्ट्रेलिया में रहता है। वहाँ वह पढ़ाई करता है। अब आप बताइए, आप कहाँ रहते हैं और क्या करते हैं?

Glossary

दोनों both	छात्र student (*m*)	पढ़ना to study, read (*v.t.*)
सेना army (*f*)	आजकल these days	रहना to live (*v.i.*)
भारतीय Indian	रेल railways, rail (*f*)	काम करना to do work,
x के साथ with x	कभी-कभी sometimes	to work (*v.t.*)
वहाँ there	पढ़ाई करना to do study, to study (*v.t.*)	आना to come (*v.i.*)
बताना to tell (*v.t.*)	करना to do (*v.t.*)	अब now

💿 Answer the following questions.

1. दिल्ली में कौन रहता है? ....

2. दिल्ली के कॉलेज में कौन पढ़ता है? ....

3. क्या आप कॉलेज में पढ़ते हैं? (पढ़ती हैं) ....

4. आप क्या करते हैं? (करती हैं) ....

5. क्या दीपक के पिता सेना में हैं? ....

6. क्या कविता की माँ डॉक्टर है? ....

7. क्या कविता का भाई दिल्ली में आई॰ टी॰ में काम करता है? ....

....

8. क्या आप छात्र हैं? ....

9. क्या आप नौकरी करते हैं? ....

GRAMMAR

The Use of को (b)

The postposition को is one of the most important postpositions in Hindi and is used in a number of distinct senses. The first of these was briefly introduced in Lesson 8. It was explained that को generally governs the *direct object* of a sentence when it is animate and denotes a particular being. Sometimes it is used with inanimate direct objects for emphasis. It is also used with the *indirect object*. In this lesson, we will learn more about these usages, as well as about two other functions of को.

1. को **with the direct object of the verb**
   a) If the direct object of the verb is animate and denotes a particular being it is ordinarily marked by को.

जानना	मैं उस दुकानदार को जानती हूँ।
to know	I (*f*) know that shopkeeper.

   In this example the subject of the verb is the pronoun मैं *I*. The direct object (marked by को) is *that shopkeeper* (उस दुकानदार को).

   b) If the direct object does not refer to a particular being, को may not necessarily be employed.

ढूँढना	वह नौकर ढूँढती है।
to search	She searches for servants.

In this example the direct object is a category (servant) rather than a particular being.

c) को may follow a direct object that is not animate. Ordinarily this indicates a particular emphasis or occurs when the object is represented by a pronoun.

पढ़ना	वह इस अख़बार को पढ़ता है।	मैं इसे नहीं पढ़ती।
to read	He reads *this* newspaper.	I (*f*) don't read it/this.

For a list of the pronouns followed by को, see p. 53.

2. को with the indirect object

Some verbs take two objects, a direct object and an indirect object. Some common verbs of this nature are *to give*, *to sell*, *to tell*, *to explain*, *to teach*, and *to show*. In such cases, the indirect object, which will most often be animate, takes को.

देना	ओ लड़के! लड़कियों को वे किताबें देना।
to give	Hey boy! (You) give those books to (the) girls.

In this example, the direct object of the verb is *the books* (किताबें) and the indirect object is *the girls* (लड़कियों को).

दिखाना	मैं आपको एक फ़िल्म दिखाता हूँ।
to show	I (*m*) show you a film.

3. को with the destination of a verb of motion

को is employed to mark the destination of a verb of motion, although it is frequently left unexpressed and *never* used when the destination is a person.

वह आदमी हर साल भारत (को) जाता है।
That man goes to India every year.

In this example को may or may not be expressed with very little change in the sense.

कल मेरे घर (   ) आइएगा।
Please come to my home tomorrow.

In this example को is ordinarily not expressed after a noun such as घर *home*. It is clear from the declension of the possessive pronoun that both the noun and the pronoun are in the oblique case.

Some common verbs of motion are: आना *to come*, जाना *to go*, चलना *to move*, पहुँचना *to arrive*.

If the destination of a verb of motion is a person, then that person is marked by the postposition के पास *near*, rather than by को.

अभी डॉक्टर के पास जाओ।
(You) go to the doctor right now.

वह मेरे पास कुछ पूछने के लिये आती है।
She comes to me in order to ask something.

4. **को with days of the week and dates**
Some adverbial expressions that indicate the time an action takes place are governed by को.[1] The first of these that we will learn are days of the week and dates.

सोमवार को वे लड़कियाँ विश्वविद्यालय जाती हैं।
Those girls go to university on Monday.

दो तारीख़ को मेरे घर आना।
Come to my home on the second.

PRACTICE

📖 *Now turn to the Workbook and complete Activities 9.2 and 9.3 before continuing.*

💿 What Do You Do on Monday? सोमवार को आप क्या करते हैं?
Deepak and Kavita are sitting in an upmarket café in New Delhi having coffee.

कविता - कल सोमवार है। सोमवार को तुम क्या करते हो?
दीपक - सोमवार को मैं जल्दी कॉलेज जाता हूँ, क्यों?
कविता - फिर क्या करते हो?

---

1. Some of these expressions may be governed by other postpositions as well. In some such expressions को may be left unexpressed. For a full description of adverbial expressions, see p. 91.

दीपक — कॉलेज के बाद मैं मामा जी के घर वापस जाता हूँ। सोमवार को मैं मामी के साथ रात का खाना बनाता हूँ। तुम क्या करती हो?

कविता — मैं माँ के पास जाती हूँ। माँ सोमवार को देर तक सर्जरी में काम करती है। सोमवार को मैं उस की मदद करती हूँ। उस के बाद हम ख़ान मार्केट जाते हैं। कल तुम हमारे साथ बाज़ार आना।

दीपक — बहुत अच्छा।

Glossary

कल tomorrow/yesterday (*m*)
जाना to go (*v.i.*)
वापस जाना to return (*v.i.*)
मामी aunty (*f*)
देर तक until late
बुधवार Wednesday (*m*)
ख़ान मार्केट Khan Market
    (a market in Delhi)

सोमवार Monday (*m*)
फिर then
खाना food (*m*)
बनाना to make, prepare (*v.t.*)
x की मदद करना to help x (*v.t.*)
शनिवार Saturday (*m*)
जल्दी quickly, early; haste (*f*)
x के बाद after x

रात का खाना dinner (*m*)
x के पास near x
सर्जरी surgery (*f*)
मंगलवार Tuesday (*m*)

Translate the following questions into Hindi and ask a partner.

1. Does Deepak go to college early on Monday? _____

2. Does Kavita help her mother on Monday? _____

3. Do you go to college on Monday? _____

4. Do you go home early on Tuesday? _____

5. Do you go to the supermarket* on Saturday? ....
   * Use the word सुपर मार्केट "*supermarket.*"

6. Do you cook dinner on Wednesday? ....

📖 *Now turn to the Workbook and complete Activities 9.4 and 9.5 before continuing.*

LESSON **10** दसवाँ पाठ

Where Did You Use to Live?

What Time Do You …? आप कितने बजे …?

The expression कितने बजे ("how many have struck") in Hindi equates to "At what time…?"

The simplest way to answer to this is to replace कितने *how many/much* with a number, which translates to "x o'clock." For example, चार बजे *four o'clock*. (For divisions of time other than hourly, see p. 176.)

आप सुबह कितने बजे उठते हैं? What time do you (*m*) get up in the morning?
मैं आठ बजे उठता हूँ। I (*m*) get up at eight o'clock.

कविता रोज़ सुबह सात बजे उठती है। वह नहाती है और फिर आठ बजे नाश्ता करती है। सोमवार को वह सुबह नौ बजे कॉलेज जाती है। चार बजे वह सर्जरी में माँ के पास जाती है। वहाँ वह माँ की मदद करती है। छै बजे वह और उसकी माँ बाज़ार जाती हैं। सोमवार को कविता के पिता रात का खाना बनवाते हैं। बुधवार को वह बारह बजे कॉलेज जाती है। गुरुवार को वह कॉलेज में सारे दिन रहती है। दीपक रोज़ सुबह आठ बजे उठता है। वह रात का खाना आठ बजे खाता है। दीपक सोमवार, मंगलवार और गुरुवार को क्लास में जाता है। बुधवार को और शुक्रवार को वह पुस्तकालय में दिन-भर पढ़ता है। कविता कभी-कभी शुक्रवार को पुस्तकालय में पढ़ती है, दीपक के साथ।

Glossary

रोज़ daily	उठना to get up, rise (*v.i.*)	नहाना to bathe (*v.t. + v.i.*)
नाश्ता करना to eat breakfast (*v.t.*)	सुबह morning (*f*)	जाना to go (*v.i.*)
x की मदद करना to help x (*v.t.*)	खाना बनवाना to have food made (*v.t.*)	सारे दिन the entire day
रात का खाना dinner (*m*)	खाना to eat (*v.t.*)	पुस्तकालय library (*m*)
दिन-भर the entire day	पढ़ना to study, read (*v.t.*)	कभी-कभी sometimes

Answer the following questions.

1. रोज़ सुबह आठ बजे कौन उठता है? _____

2. कविता रोज़ नाश्ता कितने बजे करती है? _____

3. सोमवार को कविता कितने बजे माँ के पास जाती है? _____

4. दीपक और कविता कॉलेज कितने दिन जाते हैं _____

5. आप रोज़ कितने बजे उठते हैं (उठती हैं)? _____

6. क्या कविता कभी दीपक के साथ पुस्तकालय में पढ़ती है? _____

7. दीपक रात का खाना कितने बजे खाता है? _____

8. आप रात का खाना कितने बजे खाते हैं (खाती हैं)? _____

GRAMMAR

The Verb होना *to become, occur, happen, take place*

The verb होना is also employed in the imperfect present tense, where it may be translated as *to become*, *happen*, *occur*, *take place*. Just as with other verbs, the formation of होना in the imperfect present requires the imperfect participle (होता, होते, होती) together with the appropriate simple present form of होना *to be* (हूँ, है, हो, हैं).

होना
to happen, occur, take place, become

यहाँ क्या काम होता है?
What work takes place here?

Remember that in the imperfect present the auxiliary verb (हूँ, है, हो, हैं) does *not* mean *am, is, are*, but indicates that the action takes place in the present.

In the imperfect present tense, होना *to become, occur, happen, take place* is often employed to express:

1. A general or eternal truth.
2. Growth or occurrence.
3. Causation.

1. **A general or eternal truth.**
   Such statements as *the earth is round* or *there are seven days in the week* are often expressed using the imperfect present form of the verb होना.

यह गुलाब लाल है।
This rose is red. (a single rose)

गुलाब लाल होते हैं।
Roses are red. (roses are generally red)

ऑस्ट्रेलियन लोग आराम-प्रिय हैं।
Australian people are easygoing.

ऑस्ट्रेलियन लोग आराम-प्रिय होते हैं।
(Generally) Australian people are easygoing.

साल में बारह महीने होते हैं।
There are twelve months in a year. (*in the year twelve months happen*)

2. **Growth or occurrence**

In some cases the use of होना in the imperfect present can be rendered as *to grow*, *take place*, *occur*.

क्या उस चिड़ियाघर में शेर है? क्या चिड़ियाघरों में शेर होते हैं?

Is there a lion in that zoo? Do lions generally occur in zoos?

ऑस्ट्रेलिया में गेहूँ होता है।

Wheat grows (occurs) in Australia.

स्वर्ग में सब कुछ होता है। (सब कुछ everything)

There is everything in heaven.

होली का त्यौहार वसंत ऋतु में होता है। (वसंत ऋतु spring, *f*)

The festival of Holi takes place in the spring.

हर सोमवार को उस समय टीचर कक्षा में होता है। (कक्षा class, *f*)

Every Monday at that time, the teacher is in class.

3. **Causation**

Occasionally, होना expresses causation.

धूप से मेरे सिर में दर्द होता है।

I get a headache from sunlight. (*from sunlight in my head pain occurs*)

सिगरेट पीने से कैंसर होता है।

Cancer is caused by cigarette smoking. (*from drinking cigarettes cancer occurs*)

PRACTICE

📖 *Now turn to the Workbook and complete Activity 10.1 before continuing.*

GRAMMAR

The Habitual Past Tense

The habitual past tense is used to express actions that took place in the past as a habit. In other words, the action took place more than once as in the statements *I used to work in this building*, and *I used to live in Bombay*.

The formation of the habitual past is similar to the formation of the imperfect present tense. The imperfect participle is still employed, but the simple present form of होना (हूँ, है, हो, हैं) is substituted with the past form of होना (था, थे, थी, थीं).

जाना	मैं जाता हूँ।
to go	I (*m*) go.

जाना	मैं जाता था।
to go	I (*m*) used to go.

With masculine subjects:

	Singular	**Plural**
1st person	मैं जाता था I used to go	हम जाते थे we used to go
2nd person	तू जाता था you used to go	तुम जाते थे you used to go
		आप जाते थे you used to go
3rd person	यह जाता था he/it/this used to go	ये जाते थे he/they/these used to go
	वह जाता था he/it/that used to go	वे जाते थे he/they/those used to go

With feminine subjects:

	Singular	**Plural**
1st person	मैं जाती थी I used to go	हम जाती थीं we used to go
2nd person	तू जाती थी you used to go	तुम जाती थीं you used to go
		आप जाती थीं you used to go
3rd person	यह जाती थी she/it/this used to go	ये जाती थीं she/they/these used to go
	वह जाती थी she/it/that used to go	वे जाती थीं she/they/those used to go

If the sentence is negated, the regular place of the negative adverb (नहीं) is directly before the verb. Unlike the imperfect present tense (see p. 69), the auxiliary verb is not omitted in the negative in the habitual past tense.

सोना	मैं उस कमरे में नहीं सोता था। मैं इस कमरे में सोता था।
to sleep	I (*m*) didn't use to sleep in that room. I (*m*) used to sleep in this room.

PRACTICE

 Where Did Kavita and Deepak Use to Live? कविता और दीपक कहाँ रहते थे?
Kavita and Deepak are studying at the table in Kavita's living room.

दीपक - कविता, तुम दो साल पहले कहाँ रहती थीं?

कविता - हम बंबई में रहते थे। हम दादा-दादी के साथ रहते थे। अब हम नाना-नानी के
साथ रहते हैं। मैं और मेरे भाई बंबई में स्कूल में पढ़ते थे। अब मेरे भाई ऑस्ट्रेलिया
में कॉलेज में पढ़ते हैं और हम दिल्ली में रहते हैं। तुम पहले इलाहाबाद में रहते थे,
न?

दीपक - हाँ, माँ-बाप और बहन अभी भी इलाहाबाद में रहते हैं लेकिन अब मैं और मेरा भाई
दिल्ली में मामा जी के साथ रहते हैं। मेरी बहन कभी-कभी दिल्ली आती है। तुम
जानती हो न, कि मेरा भाई आई० टी० में काम करता है।

कविता - हाँ। और तुम्हारे दादा-दादी कहाँ रहते हैं?

दीपक - वे इलाहाबाद में रहते हैं माँ और पिता जी के साथ। और नाना-नानी बनारस में
रहते हैं। पहले वे इलाहाबाद में रहते थे।

Glossary

साल year (*m*)	काम करना to (do) work (*v.t.*)	कि that (*conj*)
दादा-दादी (paternal) grandparents (*m*)	पहले previously, ago	रहना to live (*v.i.*)
x के साथ with x	नाना-नानी (maternal) grandparents (*m*)	न isn't it; no
अभी भी even now	पढ़ना to read, study (*v.t.*)	आना to come (*v.i.*)
जानना to know (*v.t.*)	कभी-कभी sometimes	

Construct a narrative about yourself based on the conversation above. Where do you live now (अब)?
Where did you (use to) live two years ago? Or five years ago? Did you (use to) live in India five years ago?

Or in America? Do you live with (your)* parents? Did you (use to) live with (your) parents three/four/five years ago (तीन/चार/पाँच साल पहले)? Did you (use to) study in school in …? Did you (use to) live with friends (दोस्तों के साथ)? Or with (your) wife (पत्नी के साथ), husband (पति के साथ), brother/s (भाई/भाइयों के साथ) and/or sister/s (बहन/बहनों के साथ) five years ago? Do you work now?

    * Do not include "your" in Hindi.

📖 *Now turn to the Workbook and complete Activity 10.2.*

GRAMMAR

Plural Polite Agreement

You will have noticed that the pronoun आप *you* is considered a plural pronoun, even when it is used to address one person. This means that when the verb is conjugated for this pronoun, it must be conjugated in the plural. When आप is employed to address more than one person, often the word लोग *people* (*m*) is added to clarify this.

> आप बहुत शरीफ़ आदमी हैं, वर्मा जी।
> You are a true gentleman, Mr. Varma. (*You are a very noble man, Varma ji.*[1])

> काम करना   आप लोग बहुत काम करते हैं।
> to (do) work   You people (*m*) do much work.

From this we can see that respect or deference towards a person is indicated in Hindi by employing plural forms. In the third person the plural forms ये/वे are also employed for this purpose particularly when the person who is being spoken about is present. All other parts of speech that show agreement for number, including adjectives (see p. 20) and masculine nouns (see p. 54), will also ordinarily be placed in the plural.

It should be remembered that the second person pronoun तुम is also a plural pronoun, even though it does not denote the same degree of respect as आप. As with आप, when employing तुम to refer to more than one person, the word लोग *people* is often used to clarify this.

> मेरे पिता जी वहाँ खड़े हैं।
> My father is standing over there.

In this example, there is only one पिता *father*. The adjectives (मेरे *my* and खड़े *standing*) are declined in the plural to denote respect and the verb is also conjugated in the plural. The degree of respect is further reinforced by the use of the polite suffix जी.

> तुम किसके बेटे हो?
> Whose son are you?

---

1. Here the word जी is translated as *Mr.* but it is really a polite suffix and may be attached to either first names or family names of both males and females. For more on this, see p. 15.

In this example there is only one बेटा *son*. However, because the second person plural pronoun तुम has been employed, the adjective किसका *whose* and the noun are declined in the plural.

Feminine nouns are not pluralized for respect.

तुम किसकी बेटी हो?
Whose daughter are you?

The Use of अपना *one's own*

In Lesson 4 the pronouns were introduced together with the possessive postposition का *'s*. When a second reference is made to the subject of a sentence, as the possessor of something or someone, the form अपना *one's own* is used in place of the possessive forms of the pronouns. It is declined like regular आ ending adjectives, that is, for the number, gender and case of the person or thing possessed. Depending on the subject, अपना may be translated as *my (own), our (own), his/her (own), their (own)*, etc.

1. अपना declines as an आ ending adjective.
2. It refers back to the logical subject of the sentence.
3. It is used in place of the possessive pronouns (मेरा, हमारा, तेरा, तुम्हारा, आपका, इसका, उसका, इनका, उनका, etc.) when a second reference is made to the subject of the sentence.

जानना	वह अपना नाम नहीं जानता।
to know	He doesn't know his (own) name.
	वह उसका नाम नहीं जानता।
	He doesn't know his/her/its name.

In the first example, अपना refers to the subject of the sentence वह *he*. In the second example, it is clearly someone else's name and not that of the subject. Hence, अपना has not been employed.

जाना	मैं अपनी माँ के साथ शहर जाती हूँ।
to go	I (*f*) go to the city with my (own) mother.
	मैं और मेरी माँ शहर जाते हैं।
	My mother and I go to the city.

In the first example, अपना is employed because it refers back to the subject of the sentence मैं *I*. In the second example the subject is मैं *I* and मेरी माँ *my mother*, thus, अपना is not employed.

देना	(आप) मुझे अपनी किताब दीजिये।
to give	Please give me your (own) book.
	(आप) मुझे मेरी किताब दीजिए।
	Please give me my book.

In the first example, the book is possessed by the subject आप *you*. In the second example, the book is possessed by the direct object मुझे *me*. Therefore, अपना cannot be employed here.

While such references in English can sometimes be ambiguous, the use of अपना in Hindi makes it quite clear whether the thing possessed belongs to the subject or not.

पढ़ना	वह अपनी किताब पढ़ती है।
to read	She reads her (own) book.
	वह उसकी किताब पढ़ती है।
	She reads her/his book. (someone else's book)

If there are two clauses in the sentence, then **अपना** refers only to the subject of the clause in which it appears.

कहना	मैं मेधा से कहती थी कि* मुझे अपनी किताब दीजिए।
to say	I (f) used to say to Medha, "Please give me your (own) book."
	(*I used to say with Medha that* please give me your [own] book)

When the subject is plural, often **अपना** is repeated to show that the possession refers to everybody individually.

लिखना	सब लोग अपना-अपना नाम लिखो।
to write	All of you people write your (own) names.
जाना	छुट्टी में सब लोग अपने-अपने घर जाते हैं।
to go	Everyone goes (to their own) home during (in) the holiday.

PRACTICE

Whose Cell Phone? Whose Friends? किस का सेल है? किस के दोस्त हैं?
Kavita and Deepak are sitting on the steps of the library.

कविता - चलो, क्लास से पहले हम कैंटीन में चलते हैं। चाय पीते हैं।

दीपक - मुझे चाय नहीं चाहिये। मैं आजकल कॉफ़ी ज़्यादा पीता हूँ।

कविता – ठीक है, बाबा। अगर कॉफ़ी चाहिये तो कॉफ़ी पियो, मेरा क्या! मेरा सेल कहाँ है? मैं कुछ दोस्तों को बुलाती हूँ।

दीपक – अपने दोस्तों को या मेरे दोस्तों को?

कविता – अपने दोस्तों को, और क्या! अपने दोस्तों के साथ हर बुध को क्लास से पहले कैंटीन में चाय पीती हूँ।

दीपक – ठीक है। एक मिनट मुझे अपना सेल दो। मैं एक फ़ोन करता हूँ।

कविता – तुम्हारा अपना सेल नहीं है?

दीपक – है,* लेकिन आज वह घर पर है। हर बुध को मैं अपने भाई के साथ शहर में खाना खाता हूँ।

कविता – जल्दी फ़ोन करो। मुझे अपनी किताब दो। तब तक मैं उसे देखती हूँ।

दीपक – ठीक है। किताब लो और अपना फ़ोन दो।

*Deepak's response "है" is short for **मेरा अपना सेल है।**

Glossary

x से पहले before x   चलना to move, go (*v.i.*)   पीना to drink (*v.t.*)
ज़्यादा more, much, many   अगर if   कुछ some
मेरा क्या! what's it to me?   बुलाना to call, invite (*v.t.*)   बुध(वार) Wednesday (*m*)
या or (*conj*)   और क्या what else   सेल cell phone (*m*)
देना to give (*v.t.*)   फ़ोन करना to phone (*v.t.*)   शहर city (*m*)
खाना खाना to eat food (*v.t.*)   जल्दी quickly   तब तक until then
देखना to see, look (*v.t.*)   लेना to take (*v.t.*)

Answer the following questions, or ask them of a partner.

1. क्या कविता अपने दोस्तों को बुलाती है? _____

2. क्या दीपक कविता के भाई को फ़ोन करता है? _____

3. हर बुध को दीपक किस के साथ शहर में खाना खाता है? _____

4. क्या दीपक कविता को कविता की किताब देता है? _____

5. क्या कविता दीपक से अपनी किताब लेती है? _____

6. आज दीपक का सेल कहाँ है? _____

7. कविता को चाय चाहिये या कॉफ़ी? _____

Now complete Activities 10.3 and 10.4 in the Workbook.

What Do You Study?

GRAMMAR

अपने-आप, आप (ही), स्वयं, खुद *(by) oneself*

In Lesson 10 the reflexive adjective अपना *one's own* was introduced. It was explained that this form is employed where a reference is made back to the subject of the sentence as the possessor of something or someone. In addition to अपना *one's own* there are four other similar words[1] that are reflexive in nature and can function as pronouns or adverbs:

अपने-आप (by) oneself
आप (ही) (by) oneself
स्वयं (by) oneself (pronounced **svayam**)
खुद (by) oneself

पढ़ना	वह अपने-आप हिन्दी पढ़ती है।
to study/read	She studies Hindi (by) herself.
काम करना	(तुम) अपने-आप काम करो।
to do work	Do the work (by) yourself.
टाइप करना	मैं हिंदी में स्वयं टाइप करती थी।
to type	I (*f*) used to type in Hindi (by) myself.
जानना	वह खुद को नहीं जानता।
to know	He doesn't know himself.

Occasionally simply आप ही or आप is used in place of अपने-आप.

जाना	वह अमीर आदमी आप ही बैंक में जाता है।
to go	That wealthy man goes to the bank himself.

---

1. The existence of several alternatives is due to the fact that Hindi draws its vocabulary from several sources. स्वयं comes directly from Sanskrit, खुद is from Persian and अपने-आप and आप derive from Sanskrit words.

PRACTICE

📖 *Turn to the Workbook and complete Activity 11.1.*

💿 **What Do You Study? आप क्या पढ़ते हैं?**

In Hindi there are two common ways of talking about studying something.
1. x की पढ़ाई करना to study x (*to do x's study*)
2. x पढ़ना to study/read x

Here, Kavita and Deepak talk about their studies over tea in a café.

दीपक - कविता, क्या तुम अपने-आप अपनी पढ़ाई करती हो?

कविता - हाँ, मैं हमेशा अपने-आप पढ़ाई करती हूँ। तुम क्या करते हो?

दीपक - इतिहास की पढ़ाई खुद करता हूँ। लेकिन ईकनॉमिक्स में एक दोस्त मेरी मदद करता
है।

कविता - मैं अंग्रेज़ी की पढ़ाई स्वयं करती हूँ लेकिन एक दोस्त के साथ अंग्रेज़ी का अभ्यास
करती हूँ। हिन्दी में ईकनॉमिक्स का मतलब "अर्थशास्त्र" है, न?

दीपक - हाँ। क्या तुम जीव-विज्ञान अपने-आप पढ़ती हो?

कविता - मतलब है कि बाइऔलौजी? नहीं, मैं अपनी दो सहेलियों के साथ उसकी पढ़ाई करती
हूँ। दीपक, क्या तुम खुद गाड़ी चलाते हो?

दीपक - हाँ, आजकल अपने-आप चलाता हूँ। पहले मामा के साथ चलाता था।

Glossary

अपने-आप (by) oneself
इतिहास history (*m*)
अंग्रेज़ी English (language) (*f*)
x का अभ्यास करना
  to practice x (*v.t.*)
जीव-विज्ञान biology (*m*)
गाड़ी चलाना to drive a car (*v.t.*)
असल में in reality

पढ़ाई करना to study
  (to do study) (*v.t.*)
x की पढ़ाई करना to study x (*v.t.*)
लेकिन but (*conj*)
स्वयं (by) oneself
मतलब meaning (*m*)
सहेली female friend of a female (*f*)
पहले previously

हमेशा always
x की मदद करना
  to help x (*v.t.*)
अभ्यास practice (*m*)
अर्थशास्त्र economics (*m*)
खुद (by) oneself
कहना to say (*v.t.*)
कि that (*conj*)

Translate the following questions into Hindi and ask a partner.

1. Does Deepak study history (by) himself?

2. Do you always do your study (by) yourself?

3. Does Deepak drive a car (by) himself?

4. Did Deepak previously (use to) drive a car by himself?

5. Does Kavita really always study (by) herself?

6. Does Kavita study biology with her (own) friends?

7. Do you study Hindi yourself?

GRAMMAR

The Narrative Past Tense

The habitual past tense is also sometimes employed to narrate events that happened sometime in the past. It is mainly found in the written language and is often called the "narrative past." The only difference in the form of this from the habitual past tense is that the auxiliary verb is omitted. It is used chiefly when the writer is reminiscing or recalling past memories, as in the sentence *When I was a girl I would often visit my relatives in Delhi during the holidays.*

The formation of this tense simply requires that the auxiliary form of होना *to be* is omitted.
  If the subject is feminine plural, the imperfect participle is nasalized.

जाना to go

Imperfect Present
हर रविवार को हम अपनी नानी के पास जाते हैं।
Every Sunday we to go to (near) our (own) grandmother.

Habitual Past

बचपन में हर रविवार को हम अपनी नानी के पास जाते थे।

In childhood, every Sunday we used to go to our (own) grandmother. (lit: In childhood, every Sunday we used to go near our (own) grandmother.)

Narrative Past Tense

बचपन में हर रविवार को हम अपनी नानी के पास जाते।

In childhood, every Sunday we would go to our (own) grandmother. (lit: In childhood, every Sunday we would go near our (own) grandmother.)

बचपन में हर रविवार को वे लड़कियाँ अपनी नानी के पास जातीं।

In childhood, every Sunday those girls used to go to their (own) grandmother.
(In childhood, every Sunday those girls *would go* near their (own) grandmother.)

दौड़ना to run	रोज़ स्कूल के बाद अप्पू बरगद के पेड़ तक दौड़ता और अपनी दीदी के साथ खेलता।
	Every day after school Appu would run to the banyan tree and would play with his older sister.
खेलना to play	

Contrary to Fact Statements

The imperfect present tense without the auxiliary verb होना may also be used to express statements that are contrary to fact. This is one way of expressing such things as *If you spoke Hindi, then I could understand you*. The connotation is that you do not speak Hindi and, hence, I *cannot* understand you. These are also sometimes called "counterfactual statements."

These types of expressions involve two clauses. The first clause contains a condition that is unfulfilled and which makes the condition impossible.

1. The first clause is introduced by अगर/यदि *if*. This *may* be omitted.
2. The second clause is introduced by तो *then*. This *cannot* be omitted.
3. The verbs are conjugated without the auxiliary verb होना *to be* (हूँ, है, हो, हैं).

बोलना to speak	अगर आप हिन्दी बोलते तो मैं आपकी बात समझती। *If you (m) spoke Hindi then I (f) would understand you.*
समझना to understand	*(I would have understood your talk/matter)*
अच्छा होना to be/become good	यदि मैं भारत जाता तो मेरी हिन्दी अच्छी होती। *If I (m) had gone to India then my Hindi would be good.*

While the form of the verb looks similar to the *narrative past*, the context and the presence of तो and यदि/अगर will clarify that this is a statement that is contrary to fact.

The यदि/अगर may be left unexpressed with no change in the meaning.

नहाना	तुम रोज़ नहातीं तो साफ़ रहतीं।*
to bathe	*If* you (*f*) bathed daily *then* you would stay clean.
साफ़ रहना	
to remain clean	

* When the verb is conjugated for a plural feminine subject, the imperfect participle is nasalized. This is similar to the nasalization of the feminine plural in the negative in the imperfect present tense and in the narrative past.

In a negative statement that is contrary to fact, either नहीं or न may be employed.

कहना	अगर तुम ऐसा न कहतीं तो वह कमरे से न जाता।
to say	*If* you (*f*) hadn't said this *then* he wouldn't have left the room.
	(*if you hadn't said such then he wouldn't have gone from the room*)

PRACTICE

 Now complete Activities 11.2 and 11.3 in the Workbook.

If I Were a Rich Man... अगर मैं अमीर होता तो ...
Here Kavita and Deepak discuss what they would do if they were wealthy.

दीपक	- कविता, अगर तुम बहुत अमीर होतीं तो कहाँ रहतीं?
कविता	- अगर मैं बहुत अमीर होती तो मैं न्यू यॉर्क में रहती।
दीपक	- न्यू यॉर्क में तुम क्यों रहतीं?
कविता	- पता नहीं। न्यू यॉर्क इतना बड़ा शहर है और वहाँ अलग-अलग तरह के लोग रहते हैं। वहाँ ज़रूर बहुत मज़ा आता। तुम कहाँ रहते?
दीपक	- अगर मैं अमीर होता तो मैं तब भी दिल्ली में रहता।
कविता	- दिल्ली में क्यों रहते? दिल्ली की क्या ख़ासियत है?

दीपक – दिल्ली बहुत अच्छा शहर है। यहाँ सब कुछ मिलता है।

कविता – अगर तुम बहुत अमीर होते तो क्या तुम कॉलेज में पढ़ते?

दीपक – यह बहुत अच्छा सवाल है। अगर मैं बहुत अमीर होता तो शायद मैं कॉलेज में नहीं पढ़ता। मैं नहीं जानता। क्या तुम पढ़ाई करतीं? क्या तुम डॉक्टर बनतीं?

कविता – हाँ, अगर मैं बहुत अमीर होती तो तब भी मैं पढ़ाई करती।

दीपक – अगर अमीर होतीं तो क्या एक नयी गाड़ी ख़रीदतीं?

कविता – अपने लिये नहीं ख़रीदती, लेकिन माँ-बाप के लिये ख़रीदती।

Glossary

अमीर wealthy
इतना this much, such
लोग people (*m*)
मज़ा आना to be enjoyable (enjoyment to come) (*v.i.*)
ख़ासियत quality, special feature (*f*)
सवाल question (*m*)
बनना to become, to be made (*v.i.*)
अपने लिये for oneself

नौकरी करना to work (*v.t.*)
क्यों why (*inter*)
अलग-अलग different
ज़रूर certainly
तब भी even then
मिलना to be available (*v.i.*)
शायद perhaps (*conj*)
गाड़ी car (*f*)
x के लिये for x

किसको to whom
पता नहीं (I) don't know
तरह type (*f*)
पढ़ना to read/study (*v.t.*)
जानना to know (*v.t.*)
ख़रीदना to buy (*v.t.*)
कभी ever, sometimes

Answer the following questions. The form in parentheses is the feminine form of the verb.

1. अगर आप बहुत अमीर होते (होतीं) तो आप कहाँ रहते (रहतीं)?

2. अगर आप बहुत अमीर होते (होतीं) तो क्या आप दिल्ली में रहते (रहतीं)?

3. अगर आप बहुत अमीर होते (होतीं) तो आप क्या ख़रीदते (ख़रीदतीं)?

4. अगर आप बहुत अमीर होते (होतीं) तो क्या आप नयी गाड़ी ख़रीदते (ख़रीदतीं)?

5. अगर आप बहुत अमीर होते (होतीं) तो क्या आप कभी नौकरी करते (करतीं)?

6. अगर आप बहुत अमीर होते (होतीं) तो आप किसको पैसे देते (देतीं)?

GRAMMAR

Adverbs of Time

In Lesson 9 the use of को was introduced with the days of the week and dates when they are employed adverbially (see p. 73). The postpositions को and में *in* may be used with other time words as well to create adverbs that tell us when an action takes place. Unlike with days of the week and dates, the postposition is not always expressed with other time words. Learning when the postposition is expressed or may or may not be expressed can take some time. The use of postpositions to express the time of an action may be divided into three categories.

1. No postposition is employed.
2. A postposition is left unexpressed with an oblique form of the time word.
3. A postposition may or may not be expressed.

1. **No postposition is employed**

   Some words that express time are not governed by a postposition when used adverbially. Either they were never governed by one or it disappeared over time. Below is a list of some common words in this category.

अब now	तब then	कब when?
आज today (*m*)	कल yesterday/tomorrow (*m*)*	आजकल these days
हमेशा/सदा always	फिर then, again	अक्सर/प्रायः often
रोज़ daily†	प्रतिदिन daily	निरंतर continuously
लगातार continuously	बार-बार again and again	एकदम immediately
फ़ौरन/तुरंत immediately	झट/झटपट quickly	एक दिन one day (*m*)
सुबह morning (*f*)	परसों the day before yesterday/the day after tomorrow	

* कल is not ordinarily followed by a postposition when it is used for *yesterday* but may be followed by को when it means *tomorrow*.

† रोज़ is also a noun meaning *day* (*m*).

आज	आज उस का जन्मदिन है।
today	Today is her/his birthday.

कल	कल क्या आप विश्वविद्यालय में नहीं थे?
yesterday/tomorrow	Weren't you at university yesterday?

आजकल	आजकल तुम विश्वविद्यालय में क्यों नहीं होते?
these days	Why aren't you at university these days?

हमेशा	वह लड़का हमेशा अपना काम जल्दी करता था।
always	That boy used to always do his work quickly.

2. **A postposition is left unexpressed with an oblique form of the time word**

a) The group includes time words that are declined because they are in the oblique but the postposition is ordinarily left unexpressed. One such word that functions in this manner is the word सवेरा *morning* (*m*).

उठना	मैं सवेरे आठ बजे उठता हूँ।
to rise	I rise at eight o'clock *in the morning*.

In the expression *in the morning*, it is clear from the declension of सवेरा (to सवेरे) that it is in the oblique case (see m. nouns, p. 53) and so the postposition is left unexpressed.

b) Occasionally a time word is qualified by an adjective or pronoun (such as *on that day*) which appears in the oblique. In such circumstances ordinarily no postposition is expressed.

वह *that*	उस दिन ( ) आप क्या करते हैं?
दिन *day* (*m*)	What do you do *on that day*?

Here, the declension of the pronoun वह to उस indicates that the expression उस दिन *on that day* is in the oblique and therefore being used adverbially.

पिछला *behind, previous*	पिछले हफ़्ते तुम कहाँ थे?
हफ़्ता *week* (*m*)	Last week where were you?

In this example, the phrase पिछले हफ़्ते is in the oblique case but the postposition has been left unexpressed.

Here is a list of the more common adverbial expressions that fall into this group.

पिछले हफ़्ते last week	पिछले महीने last month
अगले हफ़्ते next week	अगले महीने next month
इस हफ़्ते this week	इस महीने this month
उस हफ़्ते that week	उस महीने that month
किस हफ़्ते which week?	किस महीने which month?
किसी हफ़्ते some week	किसी महीने some month
पिछले साल/वर्ष/बरस last year	इस समय/वक़्त at this time
अगले साल/वर्ष/बरस next year	उस समय/वक़्त at that time

इस साल/वर्ष/बरस this year
उस साल/वर्ष/बरस that year
किस साल/वर्ष/बरस which year?
किसी साल/वर्ष/बरस some year
उस दिन/रोज़ on that day
इन दिनों these days
उन दिनों those days
किस दिन which day?
किन दिनों which days?
किसी दिन some day
इस क्षण/पल at this moment
उस क्षण/पल at that moment
किस क्षण/पल at which moment?
किसी क्षण/पल at any/some moment
सवेरे in the morning
पहले previously, ago*
एक बजे at one o'clock (बजना to strike)
दो बजे at two o'clock (and so on)
कितने बजे at what time?

किस समय/वक़्त at which time?
किसी समय/वक़्त at some time

पिछली बार last time/turn
अगली बार next time/turn
इस बार this time/turn
उस बार that time/turn
किस बार which time/turn?

    * As in कुछ दिन पहले *a few days ago.*

For some adverbial expressions of time there are several synonymous words that are commonly employed. For example, there are three common words for *year* in Hindi, and two common words for *day*, *time*, and *moment*.

With some of these adverbial expressions the postposition में *in* is occasionally employed to give a sense of *during*. For example, उस महीने में *during that month.*

3. **A postposition may or may not be expressed**

In the final category fall all of those time words where the postposition must be expressed (such as days of the week and dates), as well as those words with which in some adverbial expressions the postposition may or may not appear. Such expressions should be noted when you encounter them. As a guideline, when a noun is preceded by an adjective (as in 2 above) the postposition is often (but not always) omitted. The most important words to note in adverbial expressions in this category are:

दोपहर midday, afternoon (*f*)
रात night (*f*)
शाम evening (*f*)

In adverbial expressions such as *this morning, this afternoon, this evening, tonight,* the word आज *today* is ordinarily used to express the current day. When referring to a time on another day, as in the expressions *that morning, that afternoon,* etc., in Hindi the expression उस दिन is generally employed with the time of day.

आज सवेरे this morning
आज दिन में today, during the day

उस दिन सवेरे on that morning
उस दिन, दिन में during that day

आज दोपहर को midday in the afternoon today   उस दिन दोपहर को that afternoon
आज शाम (को) this evening   उस दिन शाम को that evening
आज रात (को) tonight   उस दिन रात को that night

क्या कल रात आप घर में थीं?
Were you (*f*) home last night?

आज शाम को मेरे घर आइये।
Come to my house this evening.

उस दिन शाम को मैं घर में नहीं था।
I (*m*) wasn't home that evening.

आज रात को बाहर मत जाइये।
Don't go out(side) tonight.

रात में यहाँ कोई नहीं आता।
No one comes here during the night.

दो तारीख़ को मेरे घर आइये।
Come to my house on the second (date).

सोमवार को हमारी हिन्दी की क्लास होती है।
Our Hindi class takes place on Monday.

काम करना to do work	दिन में अपना सब काम करो। रात को मत करो। Do all your work during the day. Don't do (it) at night.

Finally, when a day of the week is specified as well as a particular time of the day, often the day of the week is governed by का, not by को.

करना to do	बुधवार की शाम को सात बजे तुम क्या करते हो? What do you do on Wednesday at 7 P.M.?
पढ़ाई करना to (do) study	हर हफ़्ते इतवार की सुबह मेरा भाई पढ़ाई करता था। Every week on Sunday mornings my brother used to study.

PRACTICE

📖 *Now turn to the Workbook and complete Activities 11.4 and 11.5 before continuing on to Lesson 12.*

LESSON 12 बारहवाँ पाठ

Where Were You Born?
Where Did You Grow Up?

What's Your Daily Routine? आपकी दिनचर्या क्या है?

Kavita explains her routine.

मेरी दिनचर्या क्या है? क्या आप लोगों को याद है? मैं रोज़ सवेरे सात बजे उठती हूँ। मैं नहाती हूँ और फिर नाश्ता करती हूँ। सोमवार को मेरी एक क्लास सुबह होती है। मैं सुबह नौ बजे कॉलेज पहुँचती हूँ। सोमवार की शाम को चार बजे मैं माँ के पास जाती हूँ। हफ़्ते में तीन दिन माँ अपनी सर्जरी में काम करती है। वहाँ मैं दो घंटे उस की मदद करती हूँ। उस दिन पिता जी रात का खाना बनवाते हैं। मंगलवार को मेरी कोई क्लास नहीं होती। मैं दोपहर को लाइब्रेरी में जाती हूँ। वहाँ अक्सर दीपक होता है। हम अक्सर मंगलवार की शाम को सिनेमाहाल में हिन्दी फ़िल्म देखते हैं। बुधवार को क्लास से पहले मैं अपने दोस्तों के साथ कैंटीन में जाती हूँ और वहाँ चाय पीती हूँ। गुरुवार को मैं सारे दिन कॉलेज में रहती हूँ। रोज़ रात को हम खाना नौ बजे खाते हैं। कभी-कभी माँ खाना बनाती है और कभी-कभी पिता जी बनवाते हैं। रात को मैं दो घंटे पढ़ाई करती हूँ। फिर मैं सोती हूँ। अब आप बताइये, आप रोज़ कितने बजे उठते हैं? कितने बजे नाश्ता करते हैं? कॉलेज कितने बजे जाते हैं? रात को कितने बजे सोते हैं?

Glossary

दिनचर्या daily routine (*f*)
सवेरा morning (*m*)
नाश्ता करना to eat breakfast (*v.t.*)
शाम evening (*f*)
x की मदद करना to help x (*v.t.*)
दोपहर midday, afternoon (*f*)
देखना to see, look (*v.t.*)
खाना food (*m*); to eat (*v.t.*)
बताना to tell (*v.t.*)

क्या आप लोगों को याद है?
Do you (people) remember?
उठना to get up (*v.i.*)
सुबह morning (*f*)
x के पास near x
दिन day (*m*)
अक्सर often
सारा entire
बनवाना to have made (*v.t.*)

दफ़्तर office (*m*)
नहाना to bathe (*v.t.* + *v.i.*)
पहुँचना to arrive (*v.i.*)
घंटा hour (*m*)
कोई any, some
सिनेमाहाल movie theater (*m*)
रोज़ daily; day (*m*)
सोना to sleep (*v.i.*)
टेलीविज़न television (*m*)

Translate the following questions into Hindi and ask a partner.

1. What time (कितने बजे) do you get up daily? _____

2. What time do you eat breakfast daily in the morning? _____

3. What time do you bathe daily in the morning? _____

4. What time do you go to college/the office on Tuesday morning? _____

5. What time do you eat lunch in the afternoon on Wednesday? _____

6. What time do you go home on Thursday('s) evening? _____

7. What time do you eat dinner on Friday('s) night? _____

8. What time do you sleep on Saturday('s) night? _____

9. How many hours (कितने घंटे) a day (daily) do you watch television? _____

GRAMMAR

The Indicative Past Tense

The indicative or simple past tense is used to express a single action that is complete. It does not indicate when the action was completed. In this way, it should not be confused with the habitual past (see p. 78), which refers to an action that is ongoing, but at some point in the past. The past tense is used to express such statements as *I went to India* and *I did my work*. These statements do not indicate *when* these actions took place, only that they are complete. This tense can also be used to describe an action that will be complete in the immediate future, such as *I will be right back*.

To form the indicative past tense:

1. Take the stem of the verb.

2. Add the appropriate perfective ending:
   आ (masculine singular)
   ए (masculine plural)
   ई (feminine singular)
   ईं (feminine plural)

Let's look at an example, using the verb चलना *to move*.
   चलना to move
   चल move (stem)

With masculine subjects:

Singular	Plural
मैं चला I moved	हम चले we moved
तू चला you moved	तुम चले you moved
	आप चले you moved
यह चला he/it/this moved	ये चले he/they/these moved
वह चला he/it/that moved	वे चले he/they/those moved

With feminine subjects:

Singular	Plural
मैं चली I moved	हम चलीं we moved
तू चली you moved	तुम चलीं you moved
	आप चलीं you moved
यह चली she/it/this/that moved	ये चलीं she/they/these moved
वह चली she/it/that moved	वे चलीं she/they/those moved

If the stem of the verb ends in आ, ए or ओ then the semi-vowel य is inserted before the masculine singular ending is added. All other forms may be written either way.

आना **to come**	सोना **to sleep**
आया came (*m sing*)	सोया slept (*m sing*)
आये/आए came (*m pl*)	सोये/सोए slept (*m pl*)
आयी/आई came (*f sing*)	सोयी/सोई slept (*f sing*)
आयीं/आईं came (*f pl*)	सोयीं/सोईं slept (*f pl*)

Verb stems that end in ई or ऊ shorten these vowels before the suffix is attached. Those that end in ई also insert a semi-vowel य in masculine singular and may insert the semi-vowel य in the masculine plural.

पीना **to drink**	छूना **to touch**
पिया drank (*m sing*)	छुआ touched (*m sing*)
पिये/पिए drank (*m pl*)	छुए touched (*m pl*)
पी drank (*f sing*)	छुई touched (*f sing*)
पीं drank (*f pl*)	छुईं touched (*f pl*)

The following forms are exceptional and should be noted.

	m sing	**m pl**	**f sing**	**f pl**
करना to do	किया done	किये/किए	की	कीं
लेना to take	लिया taken	लिये/लिए	ली	लीं
देना to give	दिया given	दिये/दिए	दी	दीं
जाना to go	गया gone	गये/गए	गयी/गई	गयीं/गईं
होना to happen, etc.	हुआ happened	हुए	हुई	हुईं

Note the difference between the simple past of होना (था/थे/थी/थीं—*was/were*) and the past tense of होना (हुआ, हुए, हुई, हुईं—*became, occurred, took place*, etc.).

PRACTICE

📖 *Now turn to the Workbook and complete Activity 12.1.*

💿 Where Were You Born? Where Did You Grow Up?
आप कहाँ पैदा हुए? आप कहाँ बड़े हुए?

The most common way of asking where (or when) a person was born utilizes the adjective पैदा *born, created, produced* with the verb होना *to become, occur.* पैदा does not change regardless of the gender of the subject. The verb *to grow up* is expressed by बड़ा होना *to become big.* बड़ा declines like all आ ending adjectives.

पैदा होना to be born, created, produced, begotten
बड़ा होना to grow up (to become big)

कविता – दीपक, तुम कहाँ पैदा हुए?

दीपक – मैं इलाहाबाद में पैदा हुआ। तुम कहाँ पैदा हुई?

कविता – मैं दिल्ली में पैदा हुई। तुम्हारी बहन कहाँ पैदा हुई?

दीपक – वह और मेरे भाई दोनों इलाहाबाद में पैदा हुए। हम तीनों इलाहाबाद में बड़े हुए। लेकिन तुम लोग पहले बंबई में रहते थे, न?

कविता – हाँ, मैं बंबई में बड़ी हुई। बहुत साल तक हम बंबई में रहे, दादा-दादी के साथ। उस से पहले मेरे माँ-बाप दिल्ली में रहते थे। मेरे पिता जी दिल्ली के रहनेवाले हैं और मेरी माँ उत्तराखंड के पहाड़ों में पैदा हुई। अगर मेरी माँ दिल्ली पढ़ाई के लिये नहीं आती तो शायद वे नहीं मिलते।

Glossary

पैदा होना to be born (*v.i.*)
बड़ा होना to grow up (*v.i.*)
x का रहनेवाला होना to be
  a resident of x (*v.i.*)

उत्तराखंड Uttarakhand (a state
  to the northwest of Uttar Pradesh)
पहाड़ mountain (*m*)
मिलना to meet (*v.i.*)

कहाँ where (*inter*)
तक up till, for
x के लिये for x
दोनों both
शायद perhaps

Translate the following questions into Hindi, then ask them of a partner.

1. Where was Deepak born? _____

2. Where was Kavita born? _____

3. Where did Kavita grow up? _____

4. Where did Deepak, his brother and his sister grow up? _____

5. Where were you born? _____

6. Where did you grow up? _____

7. Did you grow up in India? _____

GRAMMAR

The Use of ने

Now that the past tense has been introduced, in which an action occurred and was completed once at some point in the past, we must discuss the use of the postposition ने.

Consider the following sentences.

| बैठना | कविता कुर्सी पर बैठी। |
| to sit | Kavita sat on a/the chair. |

| करना | कविता ने कुछ काम किया। |
| to do | Kavita did some work (*m*). |

Both of these actions were completed in the past. In both cases, the agent of the action was female. However, in the second example, the agent कविता is governed by the postposition ने and the verb is not conjugated for a feminine subject. Earlier (see Lesson 7, p. 52) we learned that any word that is governed by a postposition cannot influence the conjugation of the verb. In this second example, the verb is conjugated in the masculine singular for काम *work*.

The difference between these two sentences is that in the second example, the verb is *transitive* (takes an object).[1] Thus, we can say that in the indicative past tense, when the verb is transitive, the subject of the action must be governed by the postposition ने. The verb will then agree with the object, if it is expressed and not governed by a postposition.

At this point it is useful to review the pronouns and how their forms change when they are governed by the postposition ने.

मैं - मैंने = I	हम - हमने = we
तू - तूने = you	तुम - तुमने = you
	आप - आपने = you
यह - इसने = he/she / it / this	ये - इन्होंने = these/they
वह - उसने = he/she / it / that	वे - उन्होंने = those/they
कौन - किसने = who (*sing*)	कौन - किन्होंने = who (*pl*)
कोई - किसी ने = someone (*sing*)	कोई - किन्हीं ने = some people (*pl*)
जो - जिसने = who (*sing*)*	जो - जिन्होंने = who (*pl*)*

* For an explanation of relative and correlative pronouns, see p. 223.

देखना	मैंने लड़के को देखा।
to see	I saw the boy.

In this example, the subject (agent) of the action is governed by ने and the object is governed by को (see p. 65). In such cases, the verb will be conjugated in the masculine singular.

देना	उसने मुझे एक किताब दी।
to give	He/she gave me a book.
पूछना	उसने पूछा कि तुम इतने उदास क्यों हो?
to ask	He/she asked, "Why are you so sad?"

Both of these examples contain transitive verbs in the perfective form. In the first sentence, however, there is an object that is not marked by a postposition, किताब *book* (*f*). Therefore, the verb is conjugated for this feminine singular noun. This is called objectival construction (where the verb is conjugated for the object). In the second sentence, there is nothing to conjugate the verb पूछना *to ask*. It is a transitive verb in the perfective form, but the object is not expressed (i.e., *words, sentences,* etc.). Therefore, the verb is conjugated in neutral construction (*m sing*).

---

1. Verbs that do not take an object are considered *intransitive*.

Exceptional Verbs

There are some verbs that are considered transitive in English but in Hindi in the past tense are not considered transitive. In addition to this, there are some verbs that can function as both transitive and intransitive in the past tense.

Verbs that are considered intransitive in the past:
लाना to bring
डरना to fear (x से = from x).
मिलना to meet (x से = with x)
भूलना to forget

Verbs that may function as either transitive or intransitive:
समझना to understand, consider
बोलना to speak
लड़ना to fight (x से = with x).
बदलना to change

लाना to bring	मैं लड़के को यहाँ नहीं लायी। I (*f*) didn't bring the boy here.
मिलना to meet	दीपक कविता से मिला। Deepak met Kavita.
डरना to be afraid	वह लड़की कुत्ते से डरी। That girl feared (from) the dog.
बोलना to speak	लड़की मुझसे बोली। The girl spoke to (with) me. लड़की ने झूठ बोला। The girl told (spoke) a lie (*m*).
समझना to understand	माफ़ कीजिये, मैं नहीं समझा। Please excuse (me), I didn't understand. मैंने उसकी बात समझी। I understood what he/she said. (his/her talk)

Special Use of the Past Tense

The past tense is occasionally employed idiomatically to give a sense of the immediate future.

आना to come	मैं अभी आयी। I (*f*) am coming right now.
लाना to bring	मैं अभी चाय लाया। I'll (*m*) bring the tea right now.

PRACTICE

📖 *Complete Activity 12.2 in the Workbook before continuing.*

💿 **Did You Watch the Film Last Night? क्या तुमने कल रात वह फ़िल्म देखी?**
Kavita and Deepak discuss what they did last night.

कविता - हे दीपक, क्या हाल है?

दीपक - ठीक हूँ। तुम सुनाओ। कल रात तुमने क्या किया?

कविता - मैंने टी० वी० में एक फ़िल्म देखी और फिर एक किताब पढ़ी। तुमने क्या किया?

दीपक - मैंने कुछ नहीं किया। तुमने कौन-सी फ़िल्म देखी?

कविता - मैंने शाह रुख़ ख़ान की एक पुरानी हिन्दी फ़िल्म देखी, डी० डी० एल० जे०। ज़ी टी० वी० में फ़िल्म आयी। तुमने नहीं देखी?

दीपक - नहीं। कल रात मैं जल्दी सोया। मेरी तबीयत ठीक नहीं थी।

कविता - क्या हुआ?

दीपक - मेरे सिर में दर्द था। मैं लगभग आठ बजे सोया। तुमने कौन-सी किताब पढ़ी?

कविता - मैंने एक उपन्यास पढ़ा। वह अमिताव घोष की नयी किताब है।

दीपक - अच्छा। किताब कैसी है?

कविता - बहुत अच्छी है। अच्छा, कल रात क्या तुमने खाना खाया?

दीपक - नहीं। सरदर्द की वजह से मैंने खाना नहीं खाया।

Glossary

कुछ some, something (with negative, "nothing")

कौन-सा which

शाह रुख़ ख़ान Shah Rukh Khan (a famous actor)

डी० डी० एल० जे० *DDLJ* (दिलवाले दुल्हनिया ले जाएँगे, the title of a popular Hindi film, *The One with the Heart Gets the Bride*)

ज़ी टी० वी० Zee TV (a popular television channel in India)

आना to come (*v.i.*)

जल्दी early, quickly

सोना to sleep (*v.i.*)

तबीयत health, disposition (*f*)

सिर head (*m*)

दर्द pain (*m*)

लगभग approximately

उपन्यास novel (*m*)

अमिताव घोष Amitav Ghosh (the name of a famous Indian author)

खाना to eat (*v.t.*)

सरदर्द headache (*m*)

x की वजह से on account of, because of x

💿 Write the questions (using the characters' names) for the answers below. Then ask the questions of a partner.

1. _____ जी हाँ, कल रात उसने एक फ़िल्म देखी।
   (Use क्या [*question marker*])

2. _____ उसने फ़िल्म टी० वी० में देखी। (Use कहाँ *where*)

3. _____ कल रात दीपक की तबीयत ठीक नहीं थी।
   (Use कैसा *how*)

4. _____ क्योंकि उसके सिर में दर्द था। (Use क्यों *why*)

5. _____ कल रात उसने एक उपन्यास पढ़ा।
   (Use क्या *what*)

6. _____ जी नहीं, उसने खाना नहीं खाया।
   (Use क्या [*question marker*])

7. _____ कल रात वह लगभग आठ बजे सोया।
   (Use कितने बजे *at what time*)

GRAMMAR

Use of कि *that*

कि *that* is a conjunction that joins two sentences or clauses where one contains direct speech, a para-phrase of someone's speech, thought(s) or something that is known.

कहना	उसने कहा कि वह लड़की उन्नीस साल की है।
to say	He/she said (that), "That girl is nineteen years of age." (*is of nineteen years*)
पूछना	मैं रोज़ आपसे पूछती/पूछता हूँ कि आप कैसी हैं?
to ask	I ask you everyday (that) "How are you?"
सोचना	वह सोचती है कि हिन्दी बहुत अच्छा विषय है।
to think	She thinks that Hindi is a very good subject.
रहना	मुझे मालूम है कि तुम कहाँ रहती हो।
to live	I know (that) where you (*f*) live.
	(*to me it is known that you where live*)
	With the verb मालूम होना the logical subject is governed by को।

PRACTICE

📖 *Now turn to the Workbook and complete Activity 12.3.*

LESSON **13** तेरहवाँ पाठ

Do You Have Money?

GRAMMAR

How Do You Go to College? आप कॉलेज कैसे जाते हैं?

The word कैसे is an adverb that may be translated as *how, in what manner*. When discussing how you go to work, to school, to India, etc., all forms of transportation are followed by the postposition से *from, with, by, than, since*. The only exception to this occurs when talking about walking somewhere, for which the adverb पैदल *on foot* is used without a postposition.

गाड़ी (कार) से by car, vehicle
रेलगाड़ी (ट्रेन) से by train
जहाज़ से by ship
हवाई जहाज़ से by plane
(मोटर)साइकिल से by (motor)cycle
रिक्शे से by rickshaw
ऑटो(रिक्शे) से by auto(rickshaw)
बस से by bus
but:
पैदल on foot

आप दफ़्तर कैसे जाते हैं? How do you (*m*) go to the office?
मैं बस से जाता हूँ। I (*m*) go by bus.

आप स्कूल कैसे जाती हैं? How do you (*f*) go to school?
मैं पैदल जाती हूँ। I (*f*) go on foot.

PRACTICE

 Sitting in the university canteen, Kavita and Deepak discuss how they get around.

कविता - दीपक, तुम कॉलेज कैसे आते हो?

दीपक - मैं कभी गाड़ी से आता हूँ और कभी मेट्रो से आता हूँ। तुम कैसे आती हो?

कविता - ज़्यादातर मेट्रो से आती हूँ। बुध की सुबह पिता जी के साथ गाड़ी से आती हूँ।

दीपक - और सोमवार की शाम को तुम अपनी माँ की सर्जरी में कैसे जाती हो?

कविता - माँ की सर्जरी ख़ान मार्केट के पास है। वहाँ मैं ऑटो से जाती हूँ। और फिर माँ और मैं ख़ान मार्केट तक पैदल जाते हैं। वहाँ से सर्जरी पैदल वापस जाते हैं और फिर गाड़ी से घर जाते हैं।

Glossary

कैसे how, by what manner/means	सुबह morning (*f*)	फिर then (*conj*)
कभी sometime(s)	शाम evening (*f*)	चलना to move, go (*v.i.*)
गाड़ी car, vehicle (*f*)	ख़ान मार्केट Khan Market	वापस जाना to return (*v.i.*)
से by, with, from, since	(a market in Delhi)	आना to come (*v.i.*)
मेट्रो metro (*f*)	के पास near	दफ़्तर office (*m*)
ज़्यादातर mostly	ऑटो autorickshaw (*m*)	स्कूल school (*m*)

 Translate the following questions into Hindi. Then ask them of a partner.

1. How does Deepak go to college? _____

2. How does Kavita go to college? _____

3. How do you come to school/college/the office*? ....

4. How do Kavita and her mother go to Khan Market on Monday? ....

5. Do you walk home in the evening? ....

6. Do you go by train to school/college/the office*? ....
   * Choose the most appropriate destination for you.

GRAMMAR

Possession in Hindi

There is no equivalent in Hindi for the English verb *to have*. Rather, possession is expressed using the verb होना *to be* with one of the following postpositions:

का *'s*
के पास *near*
को or में *in*

Which postposition is used depends on the nature of the object or person possessed, whether it is moveable or not, a person or part of the body, a concept or whether the possessor is inanimate (as in *this room has two doors*).

1. के पास *near* is used for the possession of movable objects and some abstract concepts.
2. का *'s* is used for immovable objects, animate beings, some abstract concepts and parts of the body.
3. का *'s* and में *in* are used for possession *by* inanimate objects.
4. में *in* and को are used for the possession of most abstract concepts, such as feelings, etc.

1. **Possession using the postposition के पास *near***

In cases where a person possesses inanimate objects that are movable (such as money), livestock or particular abstract concepts such as time, the postposition के पास *near* is employed. Literally, such things could be considered to be *near* a person.

क्या आपके पास मेरी क़लम है?
Do you have my pen?

उसके पास केवल पाँच रुपये थे।
He/she had only five rupees.

अंधों के देश में काने के पास सत्ता होती है।
In a land of blind people, the person with one eye has power.

हमारे पास बहुत ज़्यादा समय नहीं था।
We didn't have a lot of time.

It should be remembered that the postposition के पास *near* is also employed to indicate proximity as well as the destination of a verb of motion when it is a person:

वह महिला पेड़ के पास खड़ी है।
That woman is standing near a/the tree.

उसके पास गाड़ी है।
He/she has a car. *or* There is a car near her/him.

वह गाड़ी के पास है।
He/she is near a/the car.[1]

तुम अपने पिता जी के पास क्यों नहीं जाते?
Why don't you go to your father?

2. **Possession using the postposition का *'s***

The postposition का *'s* is employed to express possession of people (as in I *have a brother*), immovable objects (such as houses), parts of the body and some abstract concepts.

उस गाँव में हमारे कई मकान हैं।
We have several houses in that village.

ज़मींदार के दो गाँव थे।
The landowner had two villages.

---

1. When the postposition के पास governs an inanimate object, it can only mean *near*. Therefore, this sentence can only have one interpretation.

मेरी माँ की दो बहनें हैं।
My mother has two sisters.

मनुष्य के दो हाथ होते हैं।
A human being has two hands/arms.

Some speakers simply employ the invariable form के when referring to people/relatives or even to parts of the body.

राजा दशरथ के तीन रानियाँ थीं।
King Dasharatha had three queens.

हाथी के सूँड़ होती है।
An elephant has a trunk (*f*).

3. **Possession by inanimate objects using the postpositions का *'s* or में *in***
In cases where inanimate objects possess animate or inanimate objects, the postpositions का *'s* or में *in* are generally employed.

इस मकान में चार कमरे हैं।
This house has four rooms.

इस किताब में केवल चौबीस पाठ हैं।
This book has only twenty-four lessons.

अमरीका की जनसंख्या बहुत ज़्यादा है।
America has a very large population. (*America's population is very much*)

4. **The possession of abstract concepts using में and को**
The possession of abstract concepts, illness and feelings is generally expressed using the postpositions को and में.

पिता जी के सिर में बहुत दर्द था।
Father had a severe headache.

उसमें ताक़त नहीं है।
He/she doesn't have (the) strength.

उसके दिमाग़ में एक विचार आया।
He/she had a thought.

मेरे भाई को ज़ुकाम हुआ।
My brother had a cold.

मेरे दोस्त को बुख़ार है।
My friend has a fever.

उसे इस मामले में बहुत अनुभव है।
He/she has a lot of experience in this matter.

PRACTICE

📖 *Now turn to the Workbook and complete Activity 13.1.*

💿 **Do You Have Money, Kavita? क्या तुम्हारे पास पैसे हैं, कविता?**
Deepak and Kavita meet outside the library.

दीपक – कविता, क्या आज तुम्हारे पास पैसे हैं? अभी मुझे चाय चाहिये लेकिन मेरे पास पैसे नहीं हैं।

कविता – हाँ, मेरे पास चाय के लायक़ पैसे हैं। ठीक है, आज मैं तुम्हें चाय पिलाती हूँ। लेकिन दीपक, तुम्हारे पास कभी पैसे क्यों नहीं रहते?

दीपक – माफ़ करो। यह सच है कि तुम अक्सर चाय के पैसे देती हो। कल मुझसे इस के पैसे लेना।

कविता – ठीक है। आज तुम्हारे पास गाड़ी है?

दीपक – हाँ, मेरे पास गाड़ी है।

कविता – बहुत अच्छा। मुझे एक घंटे बाद घर तक छोड़ना।

दीपक – ठीक है। क्या तुम्हारे पास सेल है?

कविता – और क्या। तुम्हारे पास नहीं है?

दीपक – आज नहीं। मुझे अपना फ़ोन दो। मैं एक फ़ोन करता हूँ।

कविता – दीपक, अगर तुम्हारे पास पैसे और सेल रहते तो तुम बार-बार मुझसे नहीं माँगते।

दीपक – तो क्या हुआ।

कविता – ठीक है, कोई बात नहीं।

Glossary

अभी right now
x के लायक़ worthy of x
पिलाना to serve, make
  someone drink (v.t.)
माफ़ करना to forgive,
  to excuse (v.t.)
सच true

अक्सर often
देना to give (v.t.)
लेना to take (v.t.)
एक घंटे बाद after an hour
तक up till
छोड़ना to abandon, drop (v.t.)
सेल cell phone (m)

और क्या what else, of course!
फ़ोन करना to phone (v.t.)
बार-बार again and again
माँगना to demand, to ask
  (for something) (v.t.)
कोई बात नहीं (it's) no matter

Answer the following questions; then ask them of a partner.

1. आज क्या दीपक के पास पैसे हैं?

2. आज क्या आपके पास पैसे हैं?

3. आज क्या कविता के पास चाय के लायक़ पैसे हैं?

4. आज क्या दीपक कविता को चाय पिलाता है?

5. क्या आप अक्सर दोस्तों को चाय पिलाते हैं (पिलाती हैं?)

6. आज क्या दीपक के पास गाड़ी है?

7. क्या आपके पास गाड़ी है?

8. अगर दीपक के पास पैसे रहते तो क्या वह बार-बार कविता से माँगता?

GRAMMAR

The Gerund in Hindi

In addition to its use as a neutral imperative (see p. 64), the infinitive form of the verb is also employed as a noun (gerund) and as such it is considered to be masculine singular. In the negative it is preceded by न.

खाना *to eat* or *eating*
न खाना *to not eat* or *not eating*

a) As a verbal noun, it may be employed as the subject of the sentence.

ज़्यादा मिठाई खाना सेहत के लिये अच्छा नहीं है।

Eating too many sweets is not good for (one's) health.

अंदर आना मना है।

It is forbidden to come inside. (*to come inside is forbidden*)

In both of these examples, the verbal nouns (*eating, coming inside*) are the subjects of the verb.

b) The infinitive is also used with the verb चाहना *to want.*

हम हिन्दुस्तान जाना चाहते हैं।

We (*m*) want to go to India.

वह आप के साथ शहर में खाना खाना चाहती है।

She wants to eat food with you in the city.

आज रात को मैं एक फ़िल्म देखना चाहती हूँ।

I (*f*) want to see a movie tonight.

When expressing the desire to do something in the past using the infinitive and चाहना often the habitual past is employed.

आज सवेरे वह आपको फ़ोन करना चाहती थी।

This morning she wanted to phone you.

कल मेरी माँ आप से बात करना चाहती थीं।

Yesterday my mother wanted to talk to you.

c) The infinitive is governed by को *or* के लिये when used to express the purpose of an action. In such cases, as a masculine singular noun, it must be declined in the oblique. In most of these cases, the postposition may also be left unexpressed.

वे खाना खाने को शहर जाते हैं।

They (*m*) go to the city (in order) to eat food.

वे खाना खाने के लिये शहर जाते हैं।

They (*m*) go to the city (in order) to eat food.

वे खाना खाने शहर जाते हैं।

They (*m*) go to the city (in order) to eat food.

However, when an infinitive is employed as the purpose of the verb तैयार होना *to be/become ready*, the postposition is generally *not* omitted.

तैयार होना to be ready	वह आदमी ऐसी नौकरी करने को तैयार नहीं है। That man is not ready to do such a job.
तैयार होना to be ready	वह आदमी ऐसी नौकरी करने के लिये तैयार नहीं है। That man is not ready to do such a job.

An infinitive comprised of a noun and a verb (mostly the verb करना) may also be used in combination with other postpositions.

(x का) इंतज़ाम करना to arrange x	खाने का कुछ इंतज़ाम करो। Make some arrangement to eat.
(x से) इनकार करना to refuse x	वह चिट्ठी लिखने से इनकार करता है। He refuses to write a/the letter.
विश्वास करना to believe	अपनी आँखों से देखने पर भी मैंने विश्वास नहीं किया। Even upon seeing it with my own eyes I didn't believe it.

The Oblique Infinitive + लायक़ *capable, worthy*

The oblique form of the infinitive is used with the adjective लायक़ *capable, able, worthy* to give a sense of *worth x-ing*, where x is the action of the verb.

देखना to see, watch	दिल्ली में क्या-क्या देखने लायक़ है? What (all) is worth seeing in Delhi?
सुनना to listen, hear	क्या यह सी० डी० सुनने लायक़ है? Is this CD worth listening to?

लायक़ may be replaced by the adjective योग्य *capable, worthy, able* or the postposition के क़ाबिल *capable, able, worthy.*

PRACTICE

📖 *Now turn to the Workbook and complete Activity 13.2.*

💿 **What Is Worth Seeing in Delhi? दिल्ली में क्या-क्या देखने लायक़ है?**
Deepak and Kavita talk about the city they live in.

दीपक — कविता, मुझे बताओ कि तुम्हारे ख़्याल में दिल्ली में क्या-क्या देखने लायक़ है?

कविता — दीपक, तुम जानते हो कि दिल्ली में बहुत सारी चीज़ें देखने लायक़ हैं।

दीपक — हाँ, लेकिन आज मैं एक पुराने दोस्त को कुछ दिखाना चाहता हूँ।

कविता — तुम्हारा दोस्त कहाँ का रहनेवाला है?

दीपक — वह इलाहाबाद का रहनेवाला है। वह पहले कभी दिल्ली नहीं आया।

कविता — तुम्हारा दोस्त अभी कहाँ है?

दीपक — वह घर पर है। वह आराम करना चाहता था।

कविता — अच्छा। तो, दिल्ली में इंडिया गेट देखने लायक़ है। कुतुब मीनार देखने लायक़ है, और लाल क़िला देखने लायक़ है। और हाँ, बंगाली मार्केट में अपने दोस्त को खाना ज़रूर खिलाना।

दीपक — ठीक है। तुम भी आओ, खाने के लिये। आज शाम को छै बजे मेरे घर आना।

कविता — आज मेरा आना मुश्किल है। शाम को अपने दोस्त के साथ मेरे घर आना। हमारे साथ खाना खाना।

Glossary

बताना to tell (*v.t.*)
ख़्याल thought, idea, opinion (*m*)
लायक़ worthy, capable
जानना to know (*v.t.*)
सारा entire, all, whole
चीज़ thing (*f*)
पुराना old
दिखाना to show (*v.t.*)

चाहना to want (*v.t.*)
पहले previously
आराम करना to rest, relax (*v.t.*)
इंडिया गेट India Gate (*m*)
क़ुतुब मीनार Kutub Minar (*f*)
लाल क़िला Red Fort (*m*)
खाना खिलाना to feed food, to treat (*v.t.*)
ज़रूर certainly

भी also, as well
आना to come (*v.i.*)
मुश्किल difficult
ताज महल Taj Mahal (*m*)
आगरा Agra (*m*)
बाहर outside, out

Translate the following questions and ask a partner.

1. What things are worth seeing in Delhi? ....

2. Do you want to see the Red Fort in Delhi? ....

3. Is the Taj Mahal in Agra worth seeing? ....

4. Does Deepak want to show his (own) friend something in Delhi? ....

....

5. Do you want to go to eat at the Bengali Market in Delhi? ....

....

6. Do you want to go out to eat tonight (today at night)? ....

....

GRAMMAR

The Present Perfect Tense

In Lesson 12 the indicative past tense was introduced. It was explained that this tense is used when the action is complete but the time is not stated:

मैं आप के घर गया।
I (*m*) went to your home.

When the action is completed in the present, or there is some lingering effect of the action in the present, the present perfect tense is used. As the name suggests, the action is complete (perfect) in the present. The present perfect tense is formed using the perfect participle (see p. 96) together with the present tense of the verb होना *to be* (हूँ, है, हो, हैं).

मैं आप के घर आया हूँ।
I (*m*) have come to your home.

In this example the action is complete but in the present.

With masculine subjects:

Singular	Plural
मैं आया हूँ I have come	हम आये हैं we have come
तू आया है you have come	तुम आये हो you have come
	आप आये हैं you have come
यह आया है he/it/this has come	ये आये हैं he/they/these have come
वह आया है he/it/that has come	वे आये हैं he/they/those have come

With feminine subjects:

Singular	Plural
मैं आयी हूँ I have come	हम आयी हैं we have come
तू आयी है you have come	तुम आयी हो you have come
	आप आयी हैं you have come
यह आयी है she/it/this has come	ये आयी हैं she/they/these have come
वह आयी है she/it/that has come	वे आयी हैं she/they/those have come

मेरे भाई बंबई से आये हैं।
My brother has come from Bombay. (or, My brothers have come from Bombay.)

क्या आपने काम किया है?
Have you done the work?

उसने इस कमरे में क्या-क्या* देखा है?
What (things) has s/he seen in this room?
*The reduplication of क्या *what* gives a sense of plurality.

In the second example the perfect participle of a transitive verb is used, which means that the subject must be marked by the postposition ने (see p. 100). Therefore, the verb must agree with the object काम *work*, which is masculine singular.

In the third example, the verb is conjugated in masculine singular because there is no noun left un-marked by a postposition.

The Past Perfect Tense

In contrast to the present perfect, the past perfect is used to express actions that are complete (*perfect*) but the effect of which is no longer present (*past*). It is formed using the perfect participle together with the past form of the verb होना *to be* (था, थे, थी, थीं).

With masculine subjects:

Singular	Plural
मैं आया था I had come	हम आये थे we had come
तू आया था you had come	तुम आये थे you had come
	आप आये थे you had come
यह आया था he/it/this had come	ये आये थे he/they/these had come
वह आया था he/it/that had come	वे आये थे he/they/those had come

With feminine subjects:

Singular	Plural
मैं आयी थी I had come	हम आयी थीं we had come
तू आयी थी you had come	तुम आयी थीं you had come
	आप आयी थीं you had come
यह आयी थी she/it/this had come	ये आयी थीं she/they/these had come
वह आयी थी she/it/that had come	वे आयी थीं she/they/those had come

पिछले साल मैं हिन्दुस्तान गया था।
Last year I (*m*) had gone to India.

दो महीने पहले मैंने आपको एक चिट्ठी लिखी थी।
I had written you a letter two months ago.

In both of these examples, the actions took place at some point in the past and are no longer relevant to the present.

आज सुबह मैं आपके घर आया था लेकिन आप घर पर नहीं थे।
I (*m*) had come to your home this morning but you weren't there.

PRACTICE

 Now turn to the Workbook and complete Activities 13.3 and 13.4.

Have You Ever Been to America? How Many Times?
क्या आप कभी अमरीका गये? कितनी बार?

When asking whether a person has ever "been" to a particular place, the verb जाना *to go* is used with the adverb कभी *ever, sometime*. When asking the number of times, the word बार *time, turn* (f) is used. It is ordinarily used in the singular, even when referring to the plural.

कितनी बार? how many times?
पाँच बार five times

While sitting on the grass in Lodi Gardens, Deepak, Kavita and their friend Imran discuss traveling to America.

कविता	- कहो इमरान! क्या हाल है?
इमरान	- सब ठीक है। और तुम कैसी हो? नमस्ते दीपक, कैसे हो तुम?
दीपक	- बिल्कुल ठीक हूँ। इमरान, क्या तुम कभी अमरीका गये हो?
इमरान	- हाँ, मैं गया हूँ।
दीपक	- तुम कितनी बार गये हो?
इमरान	- मैं एक बार गया हूँ। मेरे बड़े भाई शिकागो में रहते हैं। कविता, क्या तुम कभी अमरीका गयीं?
कविता	- नहीं तो, मैं कभी नहीं गयी। लेकिन मैं बहुत जाना चाहती हूँ। मैंने सुना है कि न्यू यॉर्क देखने लायक़ शहर है।
इमरान	- हाँ, न्यू यॉर्क में बहुत चीज़ें करने और देखने लायक़ हैं। मैं अपने भाई के साथ वहाँ पाँच दिन के लिये रहा।

कविता – दीपक सोचता है कि अमरीका में कुछ देखने लायक़ नहीं है। क्यों, दीपक, सच कहती हूँ, न?

दीपक – मैंने ऐसा कभी नहीं कहा। मैं बस सोचता हूँ कि हिन्दुस्तान में इतनी अच्छी जगहें हैं कि अमरीका जाने की कोई ज़रूरत नहीं है। मैं विदेश जाने से पहले अपना देश देखना चाहता हूँ।

इमरान – दीपक की बात ठीक है, कविता।

Glossary

हाल state, condition (*m*)	कहना to say (*v.t.*)	विदेश foreign country (*m*)
बार time, turn (*f*)	न no; isn't it?	x से पहले before x
सुनना to listen, hear (*v.t.*)	ऐसा such, thus	देश country (*m*)
शहर city (*m*)	जगह place (*f*)	x के बारे में concerning, about x
चीज़ thing (*f*)	ज़रूरत necessity (*f*)	नहीं तो no (with emphasis)

Translate the following questions and ask a partner.

1. How many times has Imran been to America?

2. How many times have you been to India?

3. Has Kavita ever been to America?

4. Does Kavita want to go to America?

5. What has Kavita heard about New York?

6. Before going abroad (to a foreign country), what does Deepak want to do?

LESSON **14** चौदहवाँ पाठ

How Long Have You Been Learning Hindi?

What Do You Call This in Hindi? हिन्दी में इसे क्या कहते हैं?

The verb कहना *to say* is used in the expression "What do you call this?". The object is governed by the postposition को and the subject (you/people) is often omitted.

हिन्दी में इसे क्या कहते हैं?   What do (you/people) call this in Hindi?

हिन्दी में इसे पान कहते हैं।   In Hindi (you/people) call this *pān* (betel leaf).

My City Delhi मेरा शहर दिल्ली

Here Kavita talks a little about the city of Delhi, where she lives.

नमस्ते दोस्तो। आप लोग जानते हैं कि मैं दिल्ली की रहनेवाली हूँ। दो साल पहले मैं मुम्बई में अपने परिवार के साथ रहती थी। आजकल हम सब लोग दिल्ली में रहते हैं। कुछ लोग इस शहर को नई दिल्ली कहते हैं। बहुत लोग इस को सिर्फ़ दिल्ली कहते हैं। नई दिल्ली भारत की राजधानी है। दिल्ली बहुत बड़ा शहर है। हम डिफ़ेंस कॉलनी में रहते हैं। डिफ़ेंस कॉलनी दक्षिण दिल्ली में है। वह दिल्ली का एक बहुत अच्छा इलाक़ा है। मेरा और दीपक का कॉलेज उत्तर में दिल्ली विश्वविद्यालय के पास है। 'डी॰ यू॰' पुरानी दिल्ली के पास है। मेरे पास अपनी गाड़ी नहीं है तो मैं कभी-कभी अपने पिता जी की गाड़ी से कॉलेज जाती हूँ और कभी-कभी मेट्रो से। दिल्ली की मेट्रो नयी-नयी है। मेरी माँ ख़ान मार्केट के पास काम करती हैं। ख़ान मार्केट हमारे घर से बहुत दूर नहीं है।

Glossary

रहनेवाला resident	डिफ़ेंस कॉलनी Defence Colony	पुराना old
जानना to know (*v.t.*)		गाड़ी car (*f*)
पहले previously	दक्षिण south (*m*)	तो so, therefore
परिवार family (*m*)	इलाक़ा area, locality, territory (*m*)	मेट्रो metro (*f*)
कुछ लोग some people (*m*)		नया-नया new (*reduplication adds emphasis*)
नया new	उत्तर north (*m*)	
कहना to say, to state, to utter (*v.t.*)	विश्वविद्यालय university (*m*)	दूर far, remote, far away
राजधानी capital (*f*)	'डी॰ यू॰' D.U. (Delhi University)	देश country (*m*)

(icon) Translate the following questions and then answer them, or ask them of a partner.

1. What do many people call Kavita's city? ....

2. What is the name of your city? ....

3. Is Defence Colony in South Delhi? ....

4. Is Kavita's college near D.U.? ....

5. Is your house near a/the city? ....

6. What is the capital of India? ....

7. What is the capital of your country? ....

GRAMMAR

The Progressive Aspect

The progressive aspect is used to express an action that *is happening* or *was happening* at a particular time. It is also occasionally used to express an action that will take place in the immediate future or which is considered to have already begun, as in the statement *I am leaving this evening*.

The present progressive is formed using the stem of the main verb (this gives the meaning) together with the perfect form of the verb रहना *to stay/live* (indicating that the action is continuing) and the simple present tense of the verb होना *to be* (indicating that it is taking place in the present).

1. Take the stem of the main verb.
   जाना - जा
   to go – go

2. Add the perfect participle of रहना *to live/stay.*
   रहा/रहे/रही

3. Add to this the appropriate form of the simple present tense of होना *to be*.
   हूँ/है/हो/हैं

   | जाना | मैं अभी घर जा रहा हूँ। |
   | to go | I (*m*) am going home right now. |

The perfective form of रहना (रहा/रहे/रही) must agree in number and gender with the subject and the simple present tense of होना must agree with the subject in number and person.

With masculine subjects:

Singular	Plural
मैं जा रहा हूँ I am going	हम जा रहे हैं we are going
तू जा रहा है you are going	तुम जा रहे हो you are going
	आप जा रहे हैं you are going
यह जा रहा है he/it/this is going	ये जा रहे हैं he/these/they is/are going
वह जा रहा है he/it/that is going	वे जा रहे हैं he/those/they is/are going

With feminine subjects:

Singular	Plural
मैं जा रही हूँ I am going	हम जा रही हैं we are going
तू जा रही है you are going	तुम जा रही हो you are going
	आप जा रही हैं you are going
यह जा रही है she/it/this is going	ये जा रही हैं she/these/they is/are going
वह जा रही है she/it/that is going	वे जा रही हैं she/those/they is/are going

The regular place of the negative adverb नहीं in the present progressive is directly before the main verb. In the negative, the auxiliary verb होना may be omitted in spoken Hindi.

वह अभी दुकान में नहीं जा रही (है)।
She isn't going into the shop right now.

In negative sentences with a feminine plural subject, if the auxiliary verb होना *to be* has been omitted the nasalization is transferred to the perfective participle रही (रहीं).

ये लड़कियाँ अभी वह काम कर रही हैं।
These girls are doing that work right now.

ये लड़कियाँ अभी वह काम नहीं कर रही हैं।
These girls are not doing that work right now.

or

ये लड़कियाँ अभी वह काम नहीं कर रहीं।
These girls are not doing that work right now.

When using the pronoun हम, many women use the masculine plural verbal endings.

हम जा रहे हैं।   We (*f*) are going.

PRACTICE

📖 *Now turn to the Workbook and complete Activity 14.1 before continuing.*

How Long Have You Been Learning Hindi? आप कब से हिन्दी सीख रहे हैं?

An easy way to ask how long a person has been undertaking a particular action is to use the progressive together with कब से *since/from when*.

आप कब से दिल्ली में रह रहे हैं?   How long have you (*m*) been living in Delhi?
मैं दो साल से दिल्ली में रह रहा हूँ।   I (*m*) have been living in Delhi for two years.

💿 Here Kavita asks Deepak about how long he has been in Delhi.

कविता – दीपक, कैसे हो तुम?

दीपक – ठीक हूँ। तुम सुनाओ।

कविता – बस। तुम कब से दिल्ली में रह रहे हो?

दीपक – कविता, मैंने तुम्हें यह बताया था कि मैं यहाँ दो साल से रह रहा हूँ। मैं दो साल पहले जुलाई के महीने में यहाँ रहने के लिये आया था।

कविता – और मैं तुम्हें सिर्फ़ एक साल से जानती हूँ, न?

दीपक – हाँ। लेकिन उससे पहले मैंने तुम्हें कॉलेज में देखा था। बस तुमसे बात नहीं हुई थी।

कविता – तुम कब से गाड़ी चला रहे हो?

दीपक – तीन साल से। यहाँ आने से पहले इलाहाबाद में मैंने गाड़ी चलाना सीखा था।

कविता – मैं गाड़ी चलाना सीखना चाहती हूँ।

दीपक – तुम कब से अंग्रेज़ी सीख रही हो?

कविता – मैं बचपन से अंग्रेज़ी सीख रही हूँ, क्यों?

दीपक – क्योंकि मैं अंग्रेज़ी सीखना चाहता हूँ।

Glossary

बताना to tell (*v.t.*)
महीना month (*m*)
जानना to know (*v.t.*)
देखना to see, look (*v.t.*)

x की बात y से होना for x's
  conversation to take place with y (*v.i.*)
गाड़ी चलाना to drive a car (*v.t.*)
सीखना to learn (*v.t.*)

बचपन childhood (*m*)
क्योंकि because (*conj*)

Answer the following questions and then ask a partner.

1. दीपक दिल्ली में कब से रह रहा है? ⎯⎯⎯⎯⎯⎯⎯⎯⎯⎯⎯⎯⎯

2. क्या दिल्ली आने से पहले दीपक ने गाड़ी चलाना सीखा था? ⎯⎯⎯⎯⎯⎯

⎯⎯⎯⎯⎯⎯⎯⎯⎯⎯⎯⎯⎯⎯⎯⎯⎯⎯⎯⎯⎯⎯⎯⎯⎯⎯⎯⎯⎯⎯⎯⎯⎯⎯⎯⎯⎯⎯⎯

3. दीपक कविता को कितने साल से जानता है? ⎯⎯⎯⎯⎯⎯⎯⎯⎯⎯⎯⎯

4. कविता कब से अंग्रेज़ी सीख रही है? ⎯⎯⎯⎯⎯⎯⎯⎯⎯⎯⎯⎯⎯⎯⎯

5. आप कितने महीने से हिन्दी सीख रहे हैं? (सीख रही हैं) ⎯⎯⎯⎯⎯⎯⎯⎯

⎯⎯⎯⎯⎯⎯⎯⎯⎯⎯⎯⎯⎯⎯⎯⎯⎯⎯⎯⎯⎯⎯⎯⎯⎯⎯⎯⎯⎯⎯⎯⎯⎯⎯⎯⎯⎯⎯⎯

6. दीपक कितने साल से गाड़ी चला रहा है? ⎯⎯⎯⎯⎯⎯⎯⎯⎯⎯⎯⎯⎯

7. आप कब से इस शहर में रह रहे हैं? (रह रही हैं) ⎯⎯⎯⎯⎯⎯⎯⎯⎯

GRAMMAR

Formation of the Past Progressive

The past progressive is formed using the simple past tense of the verb होना *to be* (था, थे, थी, थीं) in place of the simple present tense. The past progressive is used only for actions that were taking place at a specific time in the past.

> क्या कल सुबह आप अपना काम कर रही थीं?
> Were you (*f*) doing your work in the morning yesterday?

In the negative, the auxiliary verb cannot be omitted.

> जी नहीं, कल सुबह मैं अपना काम नहीं कर रही थी।
> No, yesterday morning I (*f*) was not doing my work.

With masculine subjects:

Singular	Plural
मैं जा रहा था I was going	हम जा रहे थे we were going
तू जा रहा था you were going	तुम जा रहे थे you were going
	आप जा रहे थे you were going
यह जा रहा था he/it/this was going	ये जा रहे थे he/these/they was/were going
वह जा रहा था he/it/that was going	वे जा रहे थे he/those/they was/were going

With feminine subjects:

Singular	Plural
मैं जा रही थी I was going	हम जा रही थीं we were going
तू जा रही थी you were going	तुम जा रही थीं you were going
	आप जा रही थीं you were going
यह जा रही थी she/it/this was going	ये जा रही थीं she/these/they was/were going
वह जा रही थी she/it/that was going	वे जा रही थीं she/those/they was/were going

The present and past progressive are ordinarily not used to express such statements as *I am/was sitting on this chair*. In such cases, unless the act of sitting is actually taking place, the present progressive should not be employed.

बैठना
to sit

वह इस कुर्सी पर बैठ रहा है।
He is sitting down on this chair. (*in the act of sitting down*)

वह इस कुर्सी पर बैठा है।
He is sitting on this chair. (*is seated*)

पड़ना
to lie

आपकी किताब मेज़ पर पड़ी थी।
Your book was lying on the table. (*lay*)

PRACTICE

Now turn to the Workbook and complete Activity 14.2 before continuing.

GRAMMAR

Verbal Agreement

In Lesson 12 verbal agreement was briefly introduced (see p. 100). In Hindi the conjugation of the verb is influenced by the number, gender and often person of either the logical subject, the logical object or, if no word remains that is not governed by a postposition, by nothing.

1. **In subjectival construction**, the verb has the same number, person and gender as the logical subject (the agent) of the action.

बेचना   वे दुकानदार बहुत किताबें बेचते हैं।
to sell   Those shopkeepers (*m*) sell lots of books.

2. **In objectival construction,** the verb has the same number, person and gender as the logical object of the action.

उन दुकानदारों ने बहुत किताबें बेचीं।
Those shopkeepers sold lots of books.

3. **In neutral construction**, the verb is placed in the masculine singular.

उन दुकानदारों ने मुझे देखा।
Those shopkeepers saw me.

The logical subject of each of these sentences is *shopkeepers*. In the first example the verb is conjugated for this logical subject. In the second example the logical subject is governed by a postposition and so the verb is conjugated for *books*. In the third example there is no noun or pronoun that is not governed by a postposition. Therefore, the verb is in neutral construction. Verbs cannot agree with adverbs of any type.

सोमवार को सवेरे आठ बजे इस कमरे में मैंने उसी किताब को आराम से पढ़ा।
I comfortably read that very book in this room on Monday morning at eight o'clock.

When there are plural grammatical subjects, agreement can be summarized according to the following principles:

1. If the subjects are animate the verb is generally conjugated for masculine plural unless all the members are feminine.

रोज़ मेरे भाई-बहन, माँ, चाची और सहेलियाँ शहर जाते हैं।
My brothers and sisters, mother, aunty and friends (*f*) go to the city every day.

लड़के और लड़कियाँ बग़ीचे में खेलने के लिये गये।
The boys and girls went into the garden to play.

2. In the case of the verb होना *to be*, the verb may be conjugated for animate subjects that are closest to it in position.

उस आश्रम में महाराज के छै शिष्य और सात शिष्याएँ थीं।
In that ashram the Maharaj had six male disciples and seven female disciples.

3. Some female speakers will employ the masculine plural first person when talking about all female plural subjects.

हम वहाँ नौकरी नहीं करते।
We (*f*) do not work there.

4. When the plural subjects are inanimate, often the verb is conjugated for that which is closest to it in position. If there are masculine subjects the verb may also be conjugated in the masculine.

इस थैली में दो अंडे, पाँच अमरूद और तीन गोभियाँ थीं।
In this bag there were two eggs, five guavas and three cauliflowers.

मैंने मेज़ पर एक किताब, एक क़लम और एक लोटा रखा।
I placed a book (*f*), a pen (*f*) and a mug (*m*) on the table.

The Particles ही, भी, तक, तो

The particles ही, भी and तो have occasionally appeared in earlier lessons without being formally introduced. These are emphatic particles that stress the word that they follow. In addition to these three, the emphatic particle तक also emphasizes the preceding word. While ही and भी may *only* be used as emphatic particles (that is, they *must* follow a word), तो and तक may also be used in other functions. ही, भी and तक cannot begin a sentence in Hindi.

1. ही *just/only/merely* and भी *also/as well/even*.
   ही is restrictive (*just/only/merely*) and also stresses the preceding word. It may be used to emphasize almost any part of speech.

हम भारत ही जाते हैं।
We (*m*) go only to India. (nowhere else)

हमीं भारत जाते हैं। (हम + ही = हमीं)
Only we (*m*) go to India. (no one else)
(or *We* go to India.)

हम भारत जाते ही हैं।
We (*m*) *do go* to India.

When ही follows particular pronouns, adjectives and adverbs, it is incorporated into them.

Pronouns + ही in direct form

हम + ही = हमी or हमीं *We*, only we, just we, etc....
तुम + ही = तुम्ही or तुम्हीं *You*, only you, just you, etc....
यह + ही = यही *this very* (person, thing), only he/she, etc....
वह + ही = वही *that very* (person, thing), only he/she, etc....

Oblique Forms of Pronouns + ही

Oblique Pronoun + ही	**को**
मुझ + ही = मुझी	मुझी को Only (to) me (also मुझको ही or मुझे ही)
तुझ + ही = तुझी	तुझी को Only (to) you (also तुझको ही or तुझे ही)
इस + ही = इसी	इसी को Just (to) him/her/it/this (also इसको ही or इसे ही)
उस + ही = उसी	उसी को Just (to) him/her/it/that (also उसको ही or उसे ही)
इन + ही = इन्हीं	इन्हीं को Just (to) him/her/them/these (also इनको ही or इन्हें ही)
उन + ही = उन्हीं	उन्हीं को Just (to) him/her/them/those (also उनको ही or उन्हें ही)

Some Adverbs + ही

अब now + ही = अभी right now
तब then + ही = तभी right then
कब when + ही = कभी ever, sometime(s), at some time
कहाँ where + ही = कहीं somewhere
यहाँ here + ही = यहीं right here*
वहाँ there + ही = वहीं right there*

*These forms are very similar to the pronouns यह + ही = यही *this very (one)* and वह + ही = वही *that very (one)* and should not be confused.

Adjectives + ही

सब *all* + ही = सभी *every (one/thing)*
भी is inclusive in nature and is often translated as *also/as well/even*, etc. It emphasizes and includes the part of speech that it follows.

वे भी हिन्दी लिखते हैं।

They (*m*) also write Hindi. (as well as someone else)

वे हिन्दी भी लिखते हैं।

They (*m*) write Hindi as well. (as well as another language)

वे हिन्दी लिखते भी हैं।

They (*m*) also write Hindi. (as well as reading it, speaking it, etc.)

2. तो and तक

When it functions as an emphatic particle तो is difficult to translate. Often it merely stresses the word that it follows. (It is also used as a conjunction, where it may be translated as *so* or *then*.)

तुम तो हिन्दी में लिखते हो।

Of course you (*m*) write in Hindi.

वह तो है।

That is so. (Of course, everybody knows *that*)

बात तो यह है कि मेरी तनख़्वाह बहुत कम है।

The *thing* is my salary is not much at all. (very little)

Finally तक may function as an emphatic particle with a very similar force to भी. As a particle it is often translated as *even*.

मिलना

to be available, to find

वहाँ बैठने की जगह तक नहीं मिली।

There wasn't even a place to sit down there.

PRACTICE

📖 *Now turn to the Workbook and complete Activities 14.3, 14.4 and 14.5 before continuing.*

💿 I Too Want to Go to See the Film मैं भी फ़िल्म देखने जाना चाहता हूँ

Here Deepak, Kavita, Imran and Juhi discuss going to see a film in the evening.

इमरान	दीपक, क्या तुम आज शाम को फ़िल्म देखने आ रहे हो?
दीपक	हाँ। तुम आ रहे हो?
इमरान	हाँ, मैं भी आ रहा हूँ। कौन-सी फ़िल्म है?
दीपक	एक नयी फ़िल्म अभी निकली है। उस का नाम है, यह दोस्ती।
कविता	मैं भी आना चाहती हूँ। कितने लोग आ रहे हैं?
जुही	मैं तो आ रही हूँ। तुम भी आना कविता।
कविता	ठीक है। मैं खाना खाने को भी जाना चाहती हूँ।
इमरान	तुम खाना कहाँ खाना चाहती हो, कविता?
कविता	ख़ान मार्केट में।
दीपक	वह तो सिनेमा से बहुत दूर है। फ़िल्म दरियागंज में लगी है, डिलाइट में। मेरा भाई भी आना चाहता है, लेकिन उसने कहा कि वह खाना खाने जाना नहीं चाहता।
कविता	क्या मैं ही खाना खाने के लिए जाना चाहती हूँ?
इमरान	नहीं। मैं भी जाना चाहता हूँ। लेकिन फ़िल्म के बाद ही।
दीपक	मैं भी फ़िल्म के बाद ही खाना खाना चाहता हूँ। जुही, तुम?
जुही	हाँ मैं भी। दीपक, क्या हम सब लोग तुम्हारी गाड़ी से जा रहे हैं?
दीपक	हाँ जी।

Glossary

कौन-सा which
अभी right now
निकलना to emerge, come out (*v.i.*)
दोस्ती friendship (*f*)

खाना खाना to eat food (*v.t.*)
दूर far
दरियागंज Dariyaganj (a neighborhood of Delhi)
लगना to attach (*v.i.*)

डिलाइट Delite (name of a cinema in Delhi)
सिर्फ़ only
x के बाद after x

Create questions for the following answers and then ask them of a partner.

1. _____ जी हाँ, इमरान फ़िल्म देखने आ रहा है।
   [use क्या]

2. _____ जी हाँ, मैं भी आज शाम को फ़िल्म देखने
   जाना चाहता हूँ। (चाहती हूँ) [use क्या]

3. _____ जी हाँ, कविता भी फ़िल्म देखना चाहती
   है। [use क्या]

4. _____ इमरान फ़िल्म के बाद ही खाना खाना
   चाहता है। [use कब]

5. _____ जी नहीं, दीपक, इमरान और जुही भी
   खाना खाने के लिये जाना चाहते हैं। [use क्या]

6. _____ फ़िल्म देखने के बाद मैं घर जाना चाहता
   हूँ। (चाहती हूँ) [use क्या and करना in the infinitive form]

7. _____ फ़िल्म डिलाइट में लगी है। [use कहाँ]

LESSON **15** पंद्रहवाँ पाठ

Student Life in Delhi

Student Life in Delhi दिल्ली में छात्र की ज़िंदगी

Here Deepak talks about the life of a college student in Delhi.

नमस्ते दोस्तो! आप लोग जानते हैं कि मैं और कविता दोनों दिल्ली में छात्र हैं। छात्र का मतलब है विद्यार्थी या स्ट्यूडेंट। हम दोनों एक ही कॉलेज में पढ़ते हैं। हमारा कॉलेज दिल्ली विश्वविद्यालय का एक बहुत मशहूर कॉलेज है। वह डी० यू० के मेन कैम्पस से बहुत नज़दीक है लेकिन कविता के घर से काफ़ी दूर पड़ता है। वह मेरे घर से भी काफ़ी दूर है। मैं कविता के पास ही रहता हूँ लेकिन मैं डिफ़ेंस कॉलनी में नहीं, लाजपत नगर में रहता हूँ। हमारी कक्षाएँ लगभग रोज़ होती हैं। शाम को हम अक्सर दोस्तों के साथ फ़िल्म देखने या चाट खाने या किसी के घर पढ़ने के लिये जाते हैं। वीकेंड में हम अक्सर किसी पार्टी में जाते हैं। कभी कभी हम वीकेंड में लोदी गार्डन में भी घूमने जाते हैं। मैं शराब नहीं पीता। कविता भी नहीं पीती। लेकिन यहाँ हमारी उम्र के लोग भी शराब और सिगरेट पीते हैं।

Glossary

दोनों both
छात्र student (*m*)
विद्यार्थी student (*m*)
स्ट्यूडेंट student (*m*)
एक ही same
मशहूर famous
मेन कैम्पस (मुख्य परिसर)
  main campus (*m*)
नज़दीक close
काफ़ी दूर quite far
पड़ना to fall, lie (*v.i.*)

x के पास near x
लाजपत नगर Lajpat Nagar
  (a neighborhood of Delhi)
कक्षा class (*f*)
लगभग approximately
अक्सर often
चाट spicy fast food (*f*)
या or
वीकेंड weekend (*m*)
कोई some, any
शराब alcohol (*f*)

शराब पीना to drink alcohol (*v.t.*)
सिगरेट cigarette (*f*)
सिगरेट पीना to smoke
  cigarettes (*v.t.*)
लोदी गार्डन Lodi Gardens
  (a popular garden in South
  Delhi with tombs from the
  Lodi and Sayyed period,
  15–16th centuries)
घूमना to wander (*v.i.*)

Answer the following questions and then ask them of a partner.

1. क्या दीपक और कविता छात्र हैं? _____

2. क्या आप छात्र हैं?

3. क्या दीपक और कविता की कक्षाएँ लगभग रोज़ होती हैं?

4. क्या दीपक कविता के पास ही रहता है?

5. शाम को दीपक और कविता अक्सर क्या करते हैं?

6. शाम को आप अक्सर क्या करते हैं? (करती हैं)

7. क्या आप शराब पीते हैं? (पीती हैं)

8. क्या आप सिगरेट पीते हैं? (पीती हैं)

GRAMMAR

Contrary to Fact Statements

In Lesson 11 the expression of statements that are contrary to fact was discussed (see p. 88). It was explained that there are ordinarily two clauses, the first of which expresses a condition that is unrealized, making the second clause impossible. The first clause begins with अगर or यदि *if* (often omitted) and the second clause must begin with the conjunction तो *then*. The verb is restricted to the imperfect participle *without* the auxiliary verb होना.

ख़रीदना　　अगर आप दूध ख़रीदते तो वह चाय पिलाता।
to buy　　If you (*m*) had bought milk then he would have served tea.

पिलाना
to cause to drink

Because such statements are contrary to fact, they are classified as part of the subjunctive mood.[1]

Contrary-to-fact statements may also be expressed in the past tense (see p. 96), the present imperfect (see p. 67) and the progressive aspect (see p. 121). In such cases, the imperfect participle of होना (होता, होती, होते, होतीं) is employed in place of the tense marker (हूँ, है, हो, हैं) to indicate that the statement is contrary to fact.

1. **Past Tense**
ख़रीदना　　आज आपने दूध ख़रीदा।
to buy　　Today you bought milk.

Past Contrary to Fact
यदि आपने दूध ख़रीदा होता तो वह चाय पिलाता।
If you had bought milk, then he would have served tea.

1. The subjunctive mood comprises forms of the verb that express the action as a desire, hope, probability, unfulfilled condition, etc.

In this example only the first clause is expressed using the perfect participle and the imperfect form of होना. There is no significant difference in the meaning of the clauses, as the unrealized condition in the first clause means that the second action did not take place. This could have been expressed in the following manner with little difference:

यदि आपने दूध ख़रीदा होता तो उसने चाय पिलायी होती।

If you had bought milk, then he/she would have served tea.

2. **Imperfect Present Tense**
आप चाय के लिये दूध ख़रीदते हैं।
You (*m*) buy the milk for tea.

Imperfect Contrary to Fact
अगर आप कभी चाय के लिये दूध ख़रीदते होते तो अच्छा होता।
It would be good if you (*m*) bought milk for tea occasionally.

3. **Progressive Contrary to Fact**
Progressive Aspect
क्या आप दूध ख़रीदने दुकान में जा रहे हैं?
Are you (*m*) going into the shop to buy milk?

Progressive Contrary to Fact
अगर आप अभी दूध ख़रीदने दुकान में जा रहे होते तो मैं भी आता।
If you (*m*) were going to the shop to buy milk right now then I (*m*) would come too.

Finally, statements that are contrary to fact may be introduced by the exclamatory काश *if only*. The second clause is often omitted in such cases.

काश मैं भारत गयी होती!
If only I (*f*) had gone to India!

PRACTICE

📖 *Now turn to the Workbook and complete Activity 15.1 before continuing.*

I Tried to Call You मैंने आपको फ़ोन करने की कोशिश की

In Hindi many verbs are made up of a noun or adjective along with either the verb करना *to do*, or the verb होना *to be*. Often the nouns in such verbal phrases are linked to nouns or pronouns using का.

x की कोशिश करना *to try/endeavor to x*
x की मदद करना *to help x*
x का इंतज़ार करना *to wait for x*

 Deepak runs into Kavita outside the library on Monday.

दीपक – कविता, कल शाम को चार बजे तुम क्या कर रही थीं?

कविता – कल शाम को चार बजे? मैं पिता जी के साथ ख़ान मार्केट कुछ लेने जा रही थी। क्यों?

दीपक – मैं तुम्हें फ़ोन करने की कोशिश कर रहा था। मैं तुम्हें बुलाना चाहता था।

कविता – तुम किसलिये बुलाना चाहते थे?

दीपक – इमरान और एक-दो और दोस्तों के साथ मैं लोदी गार्डन गया था। अगर तुमने फ़ोन उठाया होता तो बहुत अच्छा होता। कई बार मैंने फ़ोन करने की कोशिश की।

कविता – मेरा सेल फ़ोन बंद था। तुम लोगों ने वहाँ क्या किया?

दीपक – बस, हमने बातें कीं। गपशप मारी। फिर चाट खाने गये।

कविता – अगर मैं उस वक़्त पिता जी के साथ नहीं जा रही होती तो मैं ज़रूर आती। उन्होंने मेरे लिये नया सेल फ़ोन लिया।

दीपक – कोई बात नहीं।

Glossary

लेना to take, to buy (*v.t.*)
फ़ोन करना to phone (*v.t.*)
x की कोशिश करना
  to try x (*v.t.*)
बुलाना to call, invite (*v.t.*)
किसलिये for what reason

फ़ोन उठाना to pick up the
  phone (*v.t.*)
कई बार several times
बंद होना to be closed,
  to be turned off (*v.i.*)
बात करना to talk (*v.t.*)

गपशप मारना to gossip (*v.t.*)
चाट spicy fast food (*f*)

Answer the following questions in Hindi.

1. कल शाम को चार बजे कविता कहाँ जा रही थी? ....

2. कल चार बजे कविता किस के साथ जा रही थी? ....

3. कल शाम कौन कविता को फ़ोन करने की कोशिश कर रहा था? _____

4. क्या कल दीपक बार बार कविता को फ़ोन करने की कोशिश कर रहा था? _____

5. क्या दीपक कल कविता को बुलाना चाहता था? _____

6. कल शाम को चार बजे क्या आप कविता के साथ जा रहे थे? (जा रही थीं) _____

7. कल अगर कविता अपने पिता के साथ नहीं जा रही होती तो क्या वह दीपक के साथ लोदी गार्डन जाती? _____

8. कल अगर कविता का फ़ोन बंद न होता तो क्या वह फ़ोन उठाती? _____

GRAMMAR

The Use of कोई and कुछ

कोई and कुछ are both indefinite pronouns and adjectives. When employed as pronouns they are clearly distinct. When employed as adjectives, however, they can be slightly more confusing.

1. कोई and कुछ as Pronouns

When कोई (someone, anyone, no one [negated]) is used as a pronoun, it refers to a single, animate being.

दफ़्तर में कोई आप का इन्तज़ार कर रहा है।
Someone is waiting in your office.

अभी उस कमरे में कोई नहीं है।
Right now there is no one in that room.

किसी ने कहा कि इस दफ़्तर में शाम को कोई नहीं रहता।
Someone said that no one remains in this office in the evening.

क्या किसी को चाय चाहिये?
Does anyone want tea?

To review the oblique forms of कोई see p. 53.

Some expressions using कोई
कोई और someone else
और कोई someone else
कोई भी anyone at all

आज कोई और आया।
Today someone else came.

जानना   क्या आप और किसी को जानती हैं?
to know   Do you (f) know anyone else?

अगर वहाँ कोई भी गया होता तो वह बहुत खुश होता।
If anyone at all had gone there, he would have been very happy.

When कुछ (something, anything, nothing [negated]) is used as a pronoun, it refers to inanimate objects.

हम भारत के बारे में कुछ तो जानते हैं।
We know something about India.

इस बोतल में कुछ नहीं है।
There is nothing in this bottle.

Some expressions using कुछ
सब कुछ everything
बहुत कुछ a lot
कुछ और some more, something else
और कुछ some more, something else
कुछ भी anything at all

उन्होंने पुलिस को सब कुछ बताया था।
They had told the police everything.

आप तो हिन्दुस्तान के बारे में बहुत कुछ जानते हैं।
You (m) know a lot about India.

क्या तुम्हें कुछ और चाहिये?
Do you want anything/something else?

क्या तुमको और कुछ चाहिये?
Do you want anything/something else?

2. कोई **and** कुछ **as Adjectives**
Ordinarily कोई is used with singular, countable nouns (as in *some man, any book*) and may be translated as *some, any, no* (when negated).

इंतज़ार करना	कोई आदमी दफ़्तर में आप का इंतज़ार कर रहा है।
to wait	Some man is waiting for you in the office.

पड़ना	कोई किताब मेज़ पर पड़ी है।
to lie, fall	There is some book lying on the table.

मिलना	किसी किताब में यह सूचना मिली।
to be obtained, meet	This information was obtained from some book.

दस आदमियों में से किन्हीं पाँच को पैसे दे।
Give money to any five of the ten men.

Some expressions using कोई as an adjective
कोई और some/any other
और कोई some/any other
कोई भी any at all

देना	कोई भी किताब मुझे दो।	मुझे और कोई किताब दीजिए।
to give	Give me any book at all.	Please give me some/any other book.

कोई is also used in front of numbers to indicate approximation. In this position, it is synonymous with लगभग, क़रीब and तक़रीबन *approximately, about.*

कोई दस लोग उस कमरे में इंतज़ार कर रहे हैं।
There are some ten people waiting in that room.

कोई पाँच क़लमें मुझे दीजिये।
Give me approximately five pens. *or* Give me any five pens.

As an adjective कुछ is generally translated as *some*. When it is used with a negative it simply translates as *no*. It is ordinarily employed with countable objects (both animate and inanimate) when they are in the plural and with uncountable objects in the singular.

इस गाँव में कुछ ठाकुर लोग भी रहते हैं।
Some Thakurs also live in this village.

क्या मेज़ पर कुछ किताबें पड़ी हैं?
Are there some books lying on the table?

उस कविता में कुछ रस नहीं है।
That poem has no flavor.

PRACTICE

 Now turn to the Workbook and complete Activity 15.2 before continuing.

GRAMMAR

The Use of पर

पर is employed as a conjunction and a postposition. As a conjunction it may be translated as *but* and as a postposition it may be rendered as *on*, *at* or *in*. It is also a masculine noun, where it is translated as *wing*, *feather*, or *plume*.

1. As a postposition पर means *on*, *at*, *in*.

   पाँच मिनट पहले मेरी माँ दरवाज़े पर खड़ी थीं।
   Five minutes ago my mother was standing at the door.

   मैंने मेज़ पर दो क़लमें रखी थीं।
   I had placed two pens on the table.

   भरोसा करना   उस पर भरोसा मत करो।
   to trust   Don't trust (on) him/her.

2. As a conjunction पर translates as *but*. Some other words in Hindi for this include किन्तु, परंतु, मगर, लेकिन.

   मैं जाना चाहता हूँ पर मेरे पास पैसे नहीं हैं।
   I (*m*) want to go but I don't have any money.

   वे आपके घर गये पर आप वहाँ नहीं थीं।
   They (*m*) went to your home but you (*f*) weren't there.

3. As a noun पर is translated as *wing, feather, plume*.

   फैलाना   चिड़िया ने पर फैलाये और हवा में उड़ी।
   to spread   A/the bird spread its wings and flew into the air.
   उड़ना
   to fly

The Absolutive कर

Two actions with the same logical subject may be combined in the same sentence using what is called "the absolutive कर" with the stem of the first verb. It is often translated as *having "verbed"* as in *Having finished my work I went to bed*. Depending on how closely one action follows the other कर may also be translated as *and*, as in *I finished my work and went to bed*. कर is invariable. It may be written attached to the verb stem or separately. The subject is only mentioned once.

उतारना
to take off,
to make descend
रखना
to place, put

कोट उतारकर उसने कुर्सी पर रखा।
Having taken off (his) coat, he placed (it) on a/the chair.
or, He took off his coat and placed it on a/the chair.

आप अंदर आकर बैठिये।
Please come in *and* sit down.

ओढ़ना
to wrap

राजा शानदार दोशाला ओढ़ कर दरबार में बैठते थे।
The king used to sit in the court draped in a magnificent shawl.
(*having wrapped a magnificent shawl...*)

मेरे भाई घर से निकलकर आये।
My brother(s) emerged from the house.
(*my brother having emerged from the house came*)

Occasionally कर is omitted, but is still understood to be present.

वह लड़का वहाँ से भाग ( ) आया था।
That boy had fled from there.
(*that boy having fled from there had come*)

वह हाथ-मुँह धो ( ) आया है।
He washed his hands and face before he came.
(*he having washed his hands and face has come*)

In the case of the stem of the verb करना, in place of कर the form के is employed. Colloquially के may be substituted for कर with other verbs as well.

नाश्ता करके हम स्कूल गये थे।
We (*m*) had eaten breakfast and gone to school.

When one or both of the actions are negated नहीं is ordinarily placed directly before the verb. Context will clarify which action is being negated or if both are being negated. If a negative adverb appears before the absolutive particle the form न is generally employed.

ऐसे कपड़े पहनकर वहाँ न जाओ।
Don't go there wearing those clothes.
(*having worn such clothes don't go there*)

वह अपना काम करके क्लास में नहीं आया।
He came to class without doing his work.

तुम अपना काम न कर के सारी दुनिया का काम करना चाहती हो।
You (f) want to do everyone else's work but your own.
(*you having not done your own work want to do the entire world's work*)

There are two common expressions that employ the absolutive कर. In both cases कर is often left unstated.

ले (कर) जाना to take away (*to take and go*)
ले (कर) आना to bring (*to take and come*)

दिखाना   मुझे ताज महल दिखाने के लिये भारत ले जाइये।
to show   Please take me to India to show me the Taj Mahal.

आप सभी लोगों के लिये भारत से क्या ले आयी हैं?
What have you (f) brought from India for everybody?

PRACTICE

📖 *Now turn to the Workbook and complete Activities 15.3 and 15.4.*

What Did You Do When You Got Home Yesterday Evening?
कल शाम को घर जाकर आपने क्या किया?

Here Kavita and Deepak discuss their previous evening.

दीपक – कविता, कल शाम को घर जा कर तुमने क्या किया?

कविता – घर जाकर मैंने थोड़ी पढ़ाई की, फिर खाना खाकर मैं जल्दी सोयी। घर जाकर तुमने क्या किया?

दीपक – घर जाकर मैंने मामी से बात की। उनसे बात करके मैंने कुछ खाना खाया। उन्होंने कल रात खीर बनायी।

कविता – खाना खा कर तुमने क्या किया?

दीपक – खाना खाकर मैंने एक डी० वी० डी० देखी। तुम इतनी जल्दी क्यों सोयीं?

कविता – घर में और कोई नहीं था। घर के सब लोग बाहर गये थे। करने को कुछ काम भी नहीं था।

दीपक – खाना खाकर क्या तुम टी० वी० देखना नहीं चाहती थीं?

कविता – नहीं। मैं कोई एक किताब और कल का अख़बार ले कर अपने कमरे में गई लेकिन मैंने कुछ नहीं पढ़ा। कल रात को डी० वी० डी० देख कर तुम बोर तो नहीं हुए?

दीपक – हुआ। असल में मैं तुम्हारे फ़ोन का इंतज़ार कर रहा था। लेकिन तुम्हारा फ़ोन नहीं आया।

कविता – ऐसे मत बनो। तुम बात करना चाहते थे तो तुमने ख़ुद फ़ोन क्यों नहीं किया?

Glossary

थोड़ा a little
फिर then, again
जल्दी quickly, early
सोना to sleep (*v.i.*)
x से बात करना to talk
  with x (*v.t.*)
खीर rice pudding (*f*)
डी॰ वी॰ डी॰ DVD (*f*)
इतना so much/many,
  this much/many
बाहर outside

अख़बार newspaper (*m*)
बोर होना to become bored (*v.i.*)
असल में in reality
x का इंतज़ार करना to wait for x (*v.t.*)
ऐसा such, thus
बनना to be made, become (*v.i.*)
ऐसे मत बनो don't put on an act
ख़ुद oneself (here yourself)
सुबह उठना to get up in the
  morning (*v.i.*)

पहुँचना to reach, arrive
  (*v.i.*)
पढ़ाई करना to study (*v.t.*)
नहाना to bathe (*v.t.* +
  v.i.)
कपड़े पहनना to put on
  clothes (*v.t.*)
पीना to drink (*v.t.*)
नाश्ता करना to eat
  breakfast (*v.t.*)

Translate the following questions and answer them or ask them of a partner.

1. Having got up what did you do yesterday morning?

2. Having reached college what did you do yesterday?

3. Having gone home what did you do yesterday evening?

4. Having done some study what did you do yesterday?

5. Having bathed what did you do yesterday morning?

6. Having put on clothes what did you do yesterday morning ?

7. Having eaten did you sleep last night (yesterday night)?

8. Having gone home did you watch television yesterday evening?

My Favorite Place in Delhi

My Favorite Place in Delhi दिल्ली में मेरी मनपसंद जगह

Here Kavita tells us what her favorite place is in Delhi.

नमस्कार मेरे दोस्तो! आज मैं आप लोगों को दिल्ली के बारे में कुछ और बताना चाहती हूँ। क्या आप जानना चाहते हैं कि दिल्ली में मेरी मनपसंद जगह कहाँ है? दिल्ली में मेरी मनपसंद जगह ख़ान मार्केट है। सी० पी० (कनॉट प्लेस) बहुत अच्छी जगह है। सी० पी० को अब राजीव चौक कहते हैं। पुरानी दिल्ली में ख़रीदने को बहुत कुछ मिलता है, लाल क़िला और जामा मस्जिद देखने में बहुत ही सुन्दर हैं, इंडिया गेट देखने लायक़ है, पर मेरी मनपसंद जगह ख़ान मार्केट ही है। वहाँ बहुत ही अच्छी दुकानें हैं। कपड़ों की अच्छी दुकानें हैं, किताबों की दुकानें हैं, खाने की जगहें हैं, वहाँ पान की दुकानें भी बहुत अच्छी हैं। ख़ान मार्केट के बाज़ार में रात को बहुत रौनक़ होती है। अक्सर मैं अपनी माँ के साथ वहाँ पैदल जाती हूँ। लोदी गार्डन भी वहाँ से बहुत नज़दीक है। अब आप बताइये। आपकी मनपसंद जगह कौन-सी है?

Glossary

x के बारे में concerning, about x
मनपसंद favorite
जगह place (*f*)
सी० पी० (कनॉट प्लेस) C.P. (Connaught Place; now known as Rajiv Chowk after Rajiv Gandhi)
राजीव चौक Rajiv Chowk (square)
पुराना old
ख़रीदना to buy (*v.t.*)
बहुत कुछ many things
मिलना to be available (*v.i.*)
लाल क़िला Red Fort (*m*)
जामा मस्जिद Jama Masjid (*f*) (the main mosque in Delhi)
सुन्दर beautiful
दुकान shop (*f*)
कपड़ा cloth (*m*)
कपड़े clothes (*m pl*)
रौनक़ color, gaiety, vibrancy (*f*)
नज़दीक close, near
इमारत building (*f*)
ऊँचा tall
कौन-सा which

Write a few sentences on your favorite place or city (शहर). Are there many shops there? Is it very colorful at night? Are there tall buildings there? What do people do there? Is it in India or America, or another country? Is there a lot (much) to buy (for buying) there (available)? What is worth seeing there? What do people do when they go there (having gone there)?

GRAMMAR

The Optative

The optative is the form of the verb that is used to express *doubt*, *possibility*, *probability*, *desire*, to give a *polite command* and to make a *suggestion*. It is also used when a secondary command (via another person) is given. The verb agrees in number and person (but not gender) with the logical subject. The optative is subsumed under the subjunctive mood. The optative is generally negated with न. However, नहीं may also be used.

The Formation of the Optative

The optative is formed by attaching the following suffixes to the stem of the verb:

ऊँ (for मैं)
ए (for तू, यह and वह)
ओ (for तुम)
एँ/यें (for हम, आप ये and वे)

Paradigm for the Verb देखना *to see/look*

Singular	Plural
मैं देखूँ I may/should see	हम देखें we may/should see
तू देखे you may/should see	तुम देखो* you may/should see
	आप देखें you may/should see
यह देखे he/she/it/this may/should see	ये देखें they/these/he/she may/should see
वह देखे he/she/it/that may/should see	वे देखें they/those/he/she may/should see

* This is the same as the familiar imperative form of the verb (see p. 62).

The verbs होना *to be/become/happen*, लेना *to take* and देना *to give* are irregular in the optative. Special attention should be given to their forms.

होना *to be, become, occur, take place, happen*

Singular	Plural
मैं होऊँ I may/should be, etc.	हम हों we may/should be, etc.
तू हो you may/should be, etc.	तुम हो(ओ) you may/should be, etc.
	आप हों you may/should be, etc.
यह हो he/she/it/this may/should be, etc.	ये हों they/these/he/she may/should be, etc.
वह हो he/she/it/that may/should be, etc.	वे हों they/those/he/she may/should be, etc.

देना *to give* (लेना *to take* will have the same form)

Singular	Plural
मैं दूँ I may/should give	हम दें we may/should give
तू दे you may/should give	तुम दो you may/should give
	आप दें you may/should give
यह दे he/she/it/this may/should give	ये दें they/these/he/she may/should give
वह दे he/she/it/that may/should give	वे दें they/those/he/she may/should give

The verbs जाना *to go* and आना *to come* have four alternative forms in written Hindi although their pronunciation does not change much:

जाये/जाए/जाय/जावे he/she may go   जायें/जाएँ/जायँ/जावें they/he/she may go
आये/आए/आय/आवे he/she may come   आयें/आएँ/आयँ/आवें they/he/she may come

The standard forms are: जाए, जाएँ, आए and आएँ.

Verbs the stem of which end in ई or ऊ shorten these vowels to इ and उ. Those that end in ई may also insert the semi-vowel य.

पीना *to drink*   पिऊँ/पियूँ I may drink   पिये/पिए he/she may drink
छूना *to touch*   छुऊँ I may touch   छुए he/she may touch

Uses of the Optative

The uses of the optative may be divided into seven broad categories:

1. The expression of a doubt, a possibility or uncertainty.
2. Polite requests, suggestions and seeking permission.
3. The expression of a desire.
4. The expression of blessings or well wishing.
5. Giving a secondary command (via another person).
6. Expressions involving the conjunction ताकि *so that*.

1. **The expression of a doubt, a possibility or uncertainty**

Expressions that convey a doubt, a possibility or uncertainty are ordinarily introduced by one of the following phrases:

a) शायद...   perhaps…
b) हो सकता है कि...[1]   it is possible that…
c) संभव/मुमकिन है कि...   it is possible that…[2]
d) यदि/अगर...   if…

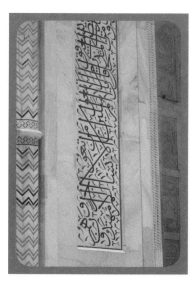

शायद हम हिन्दी सीखकर भारत भी जाएँ।
Perhaps we may even go to India after learning Hindi.

अगर आप हिन्दी सीखें तो भारत भी जाइये।
If you (may) learn Hindi then please go to India as well.

एक दिन शायद मैं अच्छी हिन्दी बोलूँ।
Perhaps one day I may speak good Hindi.

अगर तुम भारत जाना न चाहो तो मैं क्या करूँ?
What can I do if you don't want to go to India?

संभव है कि वह भारत न भी जाए।
It is possible that he/she may not even go to India.

---

1. This form is made up of the stem of the verb होना *to happen* etc., and a secondary verb सकना *to be able to*. It may be literally translated as "(it) is able to happen." For more on secondary verbs, see p. 184.

2. Due to the existence of a large lexicon that draws on a number of languages, there is often a choice of words for even common expressions such as these. Here, as in many cases, the synonymous words come from Sanskrit (यदि, संभव) and Persian or Arabic (मुमकिन, अगर). There are more literary forms of the word *perhaps* also, from Sanskrit (कदाचित्) and from Arabic (ग़ालिबन).

2. **Polite requests, suggestions and seeking permission**

This form of the verb is also employed to make a polite request, to make suggestions and to seek permission. The polite request is similar to an imperative (see p. 61) and may often be translated as *would you mind…* or *would you like to…*.

क्या अगले हफ़्ते मैं भी आप के साथ आऊँ?
Shall I also come with you next week?

टहलना to stroll	चलें, दीपक के साथ बाग़ में टहलने चलें? Come on, shall we go into the garden for a stroll with Deepak?

आज शाम को क्या मैं आप के लिये कुछ काम करूँ?
Can I do some work for you this evening?

पकाना to cook	आज रात को क्या मैं दाल पकाऊँ? Shall I cook lentils tonight?

x की मदद करना to help x	अगर आप के पास समय हो तो मेरी मदद करें। If you (may) have time then please help me.

जी, आप मेरे दफ़्तर में आकर बैठें।
Sir/Madam, would you please sit in my office.

तकलीफ़ उठाना to bother	आप यह तकलीफ़ न उठाएँ। Please don't bother (yourself).

3. **The expression of a desire**

The optative is also used to express a desire or a wish.

मेरी इच्छा है कि आप सब लोग हिन्दी सीखकर भारत जाएँ।
I wish that all of you would learn Hindi and go to India.

हम चाहते थे कि परीक्षा में सभी लोग पास हों।
We wanted everyone to pass in the exam.

मेरी एक ख़्वाहिश थी कि उर्दू सीखने लखनऊ जाऊँ।
It was my desire to go to Lucknow to learn Urdu.

4. **The expression of blessings or well wishing**

Expressions that bestow blessings, good wishes or seek protection are also generally formed using the optative.

नया साल आपको मुबारक हो!
Happy new year to you! (*may the new year be auspicious to you*)

आप का वैवाहिक जीवन सुखमय और मंगलमय हो।

May your married life be happy and auspicious.

(*may your married life be full of happiness and auspiciousness*)

रक्षा करना	भगवान उसकी रक्षा करे।
to protect	May god protect her/him.

हिफ़ाज़त करना	अल्लाह उसकी हिफ़ाज़त करे।
to protect	May god protect her/him.

इस साल दिवाली तेरे लिये शुभ हो।

May Diwali be auspicious for you this year.

(Diwali is an important Hindu festival celebrating the return of Lord Ram to Ayodhya.)

ईद मुबारक हो!

Happy Eid!

(Eid is an important Muslim festival celebrated at the end of the month of Ramadan.)

5. **Giving a secondary command (via another person)**

The optative is also employed to express a secondary command via another person.

कहना	उससे कहो कि फ़ोन करके मेरे पास आये।
to say	Tell her/him to phone and come to me.
	सबसे कई बार कहिये कि वे काम ठीक समय पर दें।
	Say to all of them several times to give their work on time.
	लड़के से कहो कि अपने भाई को न सताए।
	Tell the boy not to tease his brother.

6. **Expressions involving the conjunction ताकि *so that***

When the conjunction ताकि *so that*, *in order that* is used, the clause it introduces is ordinarily placed in the optative.

खेलना	जल्दी काम पूरा करो ताकि हम खेलने जायें।
to play	Hurry up and finish the work so that we can go and play.

मुझे कुछ पैसे दीजिये ताकि मैं कुछ किताबें खरीदूँ।

Please give me some money so I can buy some books.

There are a few other clauses that often introduce expressions where the verb is ordinarily placed in the optative. Here are three of the most common ones.

ज़रूरी/आवश्यक है कि...	It is necessary that...
आपको चाहिये कि...	You should...
मुनासिब/उचित है कि...	It is appropriate that...

हिन्दी बोलने के लिये ज़रूरी है कि आप लोग कुछ दिन हिन्दुस्तान जा कर रहें।
To speak Hindi it is necessary that you people stay in India for some time (days).

बिताना   आपको चाहिये कि आप एक साल हिन्दुस्तान में बिताएँ।
to pass/spend   You should spend a year in India.

PRACTICE

📖 *Now turn to the Workbook and complete Activity 16.1.*

💿 **I Want You to Talk to Vrinda मैं चाहता हूँ कि तुम वृंदा से बात करो**
Deepak and Kavita are sitting in the library.

दीपक   - कविता, मैं तुमसे एक बात करना चाहता हूँ।
कविता - क्या है? क्या हो रहा है?
दीपक   - मेरी बहन वृन्दा इलाहाबाद से मामा जी के घर आयी है। वह काफ़ी दुखी है। मैं
         चाहता हूँ कि तुम उससे बात करो।
कविता - अच्छा, क्या हुआ? वृंदा आम तौर पर बहुत खुश रहती है।
दीपक   - हाँ, लेकिन आजकल वह बहुत दुखी है। शायद पढ़ाई की कोई बात हो। माँ-बाप
         चाहते हैं कि वह इलाहाबाद के किसी कॉलेज में पढ़ाई करे लेकिन मैं सोचता हूँ कि
         वह दिल्ली आकर मेडिसिन पढ़ना चाहती है।
कविता - क्या उसकी इच्छा है कि वह डॉक्टर बने?
दीपक   - हाँ, शायद। बस उससे बात करो, न। तुम्हें बड़ी बहन मानती है।
कविता - ठीक है। मैं कब बात करूँ?
दीपक   - आज रात को मामा जी के घर आना, अगर तुम्हारे पास समय हो, तो।
कविता - ठीक है। अभी चाय पीने तुम जाना चाहते हो?
दीपक   - हाँ, चलो। एक कप चाय पी कर आते हैं।

Glossary

एक बात करना to say one thing (*v.t.*)   खुश happy   शायद perhaps

काफ़ी quite, enough   सोचना to think (*v.t.*)   x को y मानना to con-

दुखी sad, unhappy   इच्छा desire (*f*)   sider, think of x as y (*v.t.*)

आम तौर पर generally, ordinarily   बनना to become, to be made (*v.i.*)   तो then

Answer the following questions in Hindi and ask them of a partner.

1. वृन्दा कहाँ से आयी है? _____

2. वृन्दा किस के घर आयी है? _____

3. क्या दीपक चाहता है कि कविता वृन्दा से बात करे? _____

4. क्या वृन्दा की इच्छा है कि वह डॉक्टर बने? _____

5. आपकी क्या बनने की इच्छा है? _____

6. क्या आप चाहते हैं (चाहती हैं) कि वृन्दा डॉक्टर बने? _____

7. क्या अभी आप चाय पीने जाना चाहते हैं? (चाहती हैं) _____

GRAMMAR

The Potential

The optative form of the verb होना *to be/become* etc. (होऊँ, हो, हों) is also used to express *doubt, possibility* and *uncertainty* with the imperfect participle, the perfect participle and also with the progressive aspect. When used in this manner, it expresses a doubt etc. about an action that *may take place habitually, may have taken place,* and *may be taking place.*

शायद वह चाय के लिये दूध ख़रीदे।
Perhaps he/she may buy milk for the tea. (optative)

वह चाय के लिये दूध ख़रीदती है।
She buys milk for the tea. (imperfect present tense)

शायद वह चाय के लिये दूध ख़रीदती हो।
Perhaps she may buy milk for the tea. (imperfect potential, as a habit)

उसने चाय के लिये दूध ख़रीदा है।
He/she has bought milk for the tea. (present perfect)

शायद उसने चाय के लिये दूध ख़रीदा हो।
Perhaps she has bought milk for the tea. (perfect potential)

वह चाय के लिये दूध ख़रीद रही है।
She is buying milk for the tea. (present progressive)

शायद वह चाय के लिये दूध ख़रीद रही हो।
Perhaps she is buying milk for the tea. (progressive potential)

मुमकिन है कि वे लोग अभी एक फ़िल्म देखने जा रहे हों।
It is possible that those people may be going to see a film right now.

हो सकता है कि उसने ये तीन किताबें पढ़ी हों।
It is possible that he/she may have read these three books.

PRACTICE

📖 *Now turn to the Workbook and complete Activity 16.2 before continuing.*

GRAMMAR

Numbers and Counting
The Cardinal Numbers in Hindi
Most of the cardinal numbers from 1 to 20 have been introduced randomly in the earlier lessons of this book. In this lesson, the numbers from 1 to 50 are given as well as the divisions of ten up to 100. The remaining numbers to 100 are given in Appendix A at the end of the book. These are the standard forms of the numbers, but their forms and pronunciations do vary widely across the Hindi-speaking region.

एक one	बीस twenty	उनतालीस thirty-nine
दो two	इक्कीस twenty-one	चालीस forty
तीन three	बाईस twenty-two	इकतालीस forty-one
चार four	तेईस twenty-three	बयालीस forty-two
पाँच five	चौबीस twenty-four	तैंतालीस forty-three
छै/छह/छः six	पच्चीस twenty-five	चवालीस forty-four
सात seven	छब्बीस twenty-six	पैंतालीस forty-five
आठ eight	सत्ताईस twenty-seven	छियालीस forty-six
नौ nine	अट्ठाईस twenty-eight	सैंतालीस forty-seven
दस ten	उनतीस twenty-nine	अड़तालीस forty-eight
ग्यारह eleven	तीस thirty	उनचास forty-nine
बारह twelve	इकत्तीस thirty-one	
तेरह thirteen	बत्तीस thirty-two	पचास fifty
चौदह fourteen	तैंतीस thirty-three	साठ sixty
पंद्रह fifteen	चौंतीस thirty-four	सत्तर seventy
सोलह sixteen	पैंतीस thirty-five	अस्सी eighty
सत्रह seventeen	छत्तीस thirty-six	नब्बे ninety
अठारह eighteen	सैंतीस thirty-seven	सौ one hundred
उन्नीस nineteen	अड़तीस thirty-eight	

Below are given the symbols that represent the digits from 0 to 9. They are actually the basis of the "Arabic" numerals used in English. Both sets of numerals are commonly encountered in Hindi.

०	१	२	३	४	५	६	७	८	९
0	1	2	3	4	5	6	7	8	9

Other important numerals include:
सौ 100
एक सौ एक 101
दो सौ 200
हज़ार/सहस्र 1000
एक हज़ार एक 1001
दो हज़ार 2000
लाख 100,000 (written 1,00,000 in India)
एक लाख, एक हज़ार 101,000 (written 1,01,000)
करोड़ 10,000,000 (written 1,00,00,000)
एक करोड़, एक लाख 10,100,000 (written 1,01,00,000)
अरब 1,000,000,000

एक रुपये में सौ पैसे होते हैं।
There are one hundred paise in a rupee.

मेरे पास एक सौ एक रुपये हैं।
I have one hundred and one rupees.

Ordinal Numbers

Some of the first nine ordinal numbers are irregular. From the tenth onwards, however, ordinals are formed by attaching the suffix वाँ to the cardinal number. The ordinals function as आ ending adjectives (see pp. 20, 55).

पहला/प्रथम*	first	छठा	sixth
दूसरा/द्वितीय*	second	सातवाँ	seventh
तीसरा/तृतीय*	third	आठवाँ	eighth
चौथा/चतुर्थ*	fourth	नवाँ	ninth
पाँचवाँ	fifth	दसवाँ	tenth

 * The alternatives for the first four ordinals come from Sanskrit and are used in more formal
  Hindi. It is not uncommon to see the Sanskrit feminine form of these as well.

प्रथमा विभक्ति the nominative case (in Sanskrit)
द्वितीया कन्या the second girl

हमारा दफ़्तर तीसरी मंज़िल पर है।
Our office is on the third floor.

क्या आपने सातवाँ अभ्यास किया?
Have you done the seventh exercise?

Fractions

The most important fractions are listed below.

आधा half

एक तिहाई one third

एक चौथाई one quarter

तीन चौथाई three quarters

दसवाँ हिस्सा one tenth

पौन three quarters of

पौने less a quarter (with a number)

सवा one and a quarter/plus a quarter (with a number)

डेढ़ one and a half

ढाई two and a half

साढ़े plus a half (from and including 3½)

Aggregatives

दोनों both (all two)

तीनों all three

चारों all four

बीसों all twenty

बीसियों scores of

सैकड़ों hundreds of

हज़ारों thousands of

Days of the Week

The days of the week have occasionally appeared in earlier lessons in this book. There are at least two names for some of the days of the week, coming from different traditions.

सोमवार Monday (*m*) (the day of the moon)

मंगलवार Tuesday (*m*) (the day of Mars)

बुधवार Wednesday (*m*) (the day of Mercury)

गुरुवार/बृहस्पतिवार Thursday (*m*) (the day of Jupiter)

शुक्रवार Friday (*m*) (the day of Venus)

शनिवार/शनिश्चर Saturday (*m*) (the day of Saturn)

इतवार/रविवार Sunday (*m*) (the day of the Sun)

All of these except for the words for Monday and Sunday may also be abbreviated by eliding the word वार *day* at the end.

हम गुरु को अपने दोस्त के घर जाते हैं।
We go to our friend's home on Thursday.

There are further alternative names for the days of the week in the Urdu register, some of which are the same as those in Hindi. These are:

पीर Monday (*m*)

मंगल Tuesday (*m*)

बुध Wednesday (*m*)

जुमेरात Thursday (*f*)

जुमा Friday (*m*)

हफ़्ता Saturday (*m*)

इतवार Sunday (*m*)

Months of the Year

In India there are two important calendars: the Gregorian calendar, which is solar, and the *Vikramaditya* calendar, which is lunar. Here the names of the months according to the Gregorian calendar are given. For the *Vikramaditya* calendar, see Appendix A.

जनवरी	January	जुलाई	July
फ़रवरी	February	अगस्त	August
मार्च	March	सितम्बर	September
अप्रैल	April	अक्तूबर	October
मई	May	नवम्बर	November
जून	June	दिसंबर	December

The Use of से *from, by, with, than*

There are several verbs that involve communication (*speaking*, *saying*, *asking*, etc.), where the person addressed (indirect object) is marked by the postposition से.

x से बोलना to speak to x
x से कहना to say to x
x से पूछना to ask x
x से बात करना to talk with x
x से बातचीत करना to talk with x
x से वार्तालाप करना to converse with x
x से गुफ़्तगू करना to converse with x

Of the final four, it is possible to say that बात करना and बातचीत करना are perhaps more commonly employed and considered more informal. गुफ़्तगू करना is common to the Urdu register. All of these verbs are transitive, except for the verb बोलना, which may be both. बात, बातचीत and गुफ़्तगू are all feminine nouns.

क्या मैं आप से कुछ पूछूँ?
May I ask you something?

आजकल क्या आप उनसे बात करते हैं?
Do you (*m*) talk with them these days?

कल क्या तुमने उससे बात की?
Did you talk to him/her yesterday?

मैंने संजीव से पूछा था कि क्या हम फ़िल्म देखने चलें?
I asked Sanjeev, "Shall we go and see a film?"

मुझसे मत बोलो।
Don't speak to me.

भारतीय संस्कृति के बारे में वार्तालाप हुआ।
A discussion about Indian culture took place.

In the case of the the verb बताना *to tell*, however, the indirect object is governed by को.

उन छात्रों को बताना कि वे वहाँ खड़े न रहें।
Tell those students not to stand there.

PRACTICE

📖 *Now turn to the Workbook and complete Activity 16.3 before continuing.*

💿 **May I Ask You a Question? क्या मैं तुमसे एक सवाल पूछूँ?**
Sitting in a café in Khan Market, Vrinda and Kavita discuss Vrinda's problem.

कविता - वृन्दा, क्या मैं तुमसे एक सवाल पूछूँ?

वृन्दा, - हाँ, पूछो दीदी।

कविता - तुम इस वक़्त दिल्ली क्यों आयी हो?

वृन्दा, - ऐसे ही, कविता दीदी। मैं दो-एक दिन इलाहाबाद से बाहर निकलना चाहती थी।

कविता - क्या बात है? पढ़ाई अच्छी नहीं हो रही है? तुम्हारे माँ-बाप ने तुमसे कुछ कहा?

वृन्दा - मैं तुम्हें क्या बताऊँ? कोई इतनी बड़ी बात भी नहीं है।

कविता - फिर भी, मुझे बताओ, न।

वृन्दा - मैं तुमसे क्या कहूँ? माता-पिता चाहते हैं कि इलाहाबाद में ही रहकर आगे पढ़ूँ। लेकिन स्कूल के बाद मैं तो दीपक की तरह दिल्ली आकर पढ़ना चाहती हूँ।

कविता - तुम दिल्ली में क्यों पढ़ना चाहती हो?

वृन्दा - मैं दिल्ली में क्यों न पढ़ूँ? दीपक और संजीव दिल्ली में हैं। तुम भी हो। यहाँ के कॉलेज भी अच्छे हैं। आख़िर सब लोग दिल्ली आते हैं, न?

कविता - क्या तुमने अपने माँ-बाप से ये सब बातें की हैं?
वृन्दा - हाँ, दीदी। पर वे मेरी कहाँ सुनते हैं?
कविता - मैं फ़ोन कर के दीपक से इस की बात करूँ?
वृन्दा - अगर दीपक उनसे बात करे तो शायद वे मानें।

Glossary

सवाल question (*m*)

पूछना to ask (*v.t.*)

दीदी older sister (*f*)

निकलना to emerge, come out (*v.i.*)

बताना to tell (*v.t.*)

बड़ा big, major, important

फिर भी nevertheless

आगे ahead, in the future

x की तरह like x

आख़िर finally, in the end

बातें करना to talk (*v.t.*)

मेरी (बात) कहाँ सुनते हैं? where do they listen to me (my matter)?

मानना to accept, agree (*v.i.* + *v.t.*)

Make up questions for the following answers.

1. _____ जी हाँ, वह दो-एक दिन के लिये इलाहाबाद से बाहर निकलना चाहती थी। [use क्या]

2. _____ वे चाहते हैं कि स्कूल के बाद वृन्दा इलाहाबाद में रहे। [use क्या]

3. _____ वह दिल्ली में पढ़ना चाहती है क्योंकि दिल्ली के कॉलेज बहुत अच्छे हैं। [use क्यों]

4. _____ जी हाँ, उसके दोनों भाई दिल्ली में रहते हैं।
[use क्या]

5. _____ जी हाँ, वृन्दा ने ये सब बातें माँ-बाप से की हैं। [use क्या]

6. _____ जी हाँ, मैं चाहता हूँ (चाहती हूँ) कि वृन्दा दिल्ली आकर पढ़े। [use क्या]

LESSON **17** सत्रहवाँ पाठ

How Much Is That?

GRAMMAR

The Future Tense

The future tense is employed to talk about actions that will take place at any point in the future.

The Formation of the Future Tense

The future tense is formed simply by adding the appropriate future ending (गा/गे/गी) to the optative form of the verb.

क्या मैं यह काम करूँ? Shall I do this work?

मैं यह काम करूँगा। I (*m*) will do this work.

गा — masculine singular

गे — masculine plural

गी — feminine singular and plural

Hence, the paradigm for the future tense with the verb देखना *to see* is:

With masculine subjects:

Singular	Plural
मैं देखूँगा I will see	हम देखेंगे we will see
तू देखेगा you will see	तुम देखोगे you will see
	आप देखेंगे you will see
यह देखेगा he/this/it will see	ये देखेंगे he/these/they will see
वह देखेगा he/that/it will see	वे देखेंगे he/those/they will see

With feminine subjects:

Singular	Plural
मैं देखूँगी I will see	हम देखेंगी we will see
तू देखेगी you will see	तुम देखोगी you will see
	आप देखेंगी you will see
यह देखेगी she/this/it will see	ये देखेंगी she/these/they will see
वह देखेगी she/that/it will see	वे देखेंगी she/those/they will see

As in the optative, irregular forms for the verbs होना *to be, become,* etc., लेना *to take* and देना *to give* are used in the future tense. Hence, the paradigm for the verb होना in the future is:

With masculine subjects:

Singular	Plural
मैं हूँगा/होऊँगा I will be/become	हम होंगे we will be/become
तू होगा you will be/become	तुम होगे you will be/become
	आप होंगे you will be/become
यह होगा he/this/it will be/become	ये होंगे he/these/they will be/become
वह होगा he/that/it will be/become	वे होंगे he/those/they will be/become

With feminine subjects:

Singular	Plural
मैं हूँगी/होऊँगी I will be/become	हम होंगी we will be/become
तू होगी you will be/become	तुम होगी you will be/become
	आप होंगी you will be/become
यह होगी she/this/it will be/become	ये होंगी she/these/they will be/become
वह होगी she/that/it will be/become	वे होंगी she/those/they will be/become

The paradigm for देना *to give* (which is the same for लेना *to take*) is:

With masculine subjects:

Singular	Plural
मैं दूँगा I will give	हम देंगे we will give
तू देगा you will give	तुम दोगे you will give
	आप देंगे you will give
यह देगा he/this/it will give	ये देंगे he/these/they will give
वह देगा he/that/it will give	वे देंगे he/those/they will give

With feminine subjects:

Singular	Plural
मैं दूँगी I will give	हम देंगी we will give
तू देगी you will give	तुम दोगी you will give
	आप देंगी you will give
यह देगी she/this/it will give	ये देंगी she/these/they will give
वह देगी she/that/it will give	वे देंगी she/those/they will give

Verbs, the stems of which end in ई or ऊ, shorten these vowels to इ and उ. Those whose stems end in ई may also insert the semi-vowel य except in the first person.

पीना to drink   पिऊँगा/पियूँगा I will drink   पियेगी/पिएगी she will drink
छूना to touch   छुऊँगा I will touch   छुएगा he will touch

एक दिन मैं हिन्दुस्तान बसने के लिये जाऊँगी।
One day I (*f*) will settle down in India.

क्या अगले हफ़्ते तुम विश्वविद्यालय आओगे?
Will you (*m*) come to university next week?

शायद एक दिन हम समझेंगे कि गुस्सा होने से कोई फ़ायदा नहीं है।
Perhaps one day we (*m*) will understand there is no advantage in getting angry.

PRACTICE

📖 *Now turn to the Workbook and complete Activity 17.1 before continuing.*

How Much Is That? वह कितने का है?

There are several words for price in Hindi:

दाम (*m*)
कीमत (*f*)
भाव (*m*)

The most common ways of asking the price of something are:

इस का दाम क्या है? What is the price of this?
यह कितने (रुपये) का है? How much is this? (this is of how many [rupees]?)

In this expression, का will change to के/की depending on the gender of the item in question. For example:

यह क़लम कितने की है? How much is this pen (*f*)?

💿 Here Kavita and Deepak are in Khan Market. Kavita wants to buy something for Juhi's birthday.

कविता - दीपक, तुम 'अनोखी' की दुकान में मेरे साथ चलोगे?
दीपक - ठीक है। तुमको 'अनोखी' में क्या चाहिये?
कविता - कल जुही का जन्मदिन है। मैं उसके लिये कुछ लेना चाहती हूँ।
(दुकान में)
दीपक - क्या उस के लिये एक सलवार क़मीज़ ख़रीदोगी?
कविता - अभी मैं सिर्फ़ देख रही हूँ। भाई साहब, यह क़मीज़ कितने की है?
दुकानदार - वह ढाई सौ रुपये की है, मैडम।
दीपक - बहुत ही महँगी चीज़ है।

कविता	- दीपक, तुम चुप रहो। क़मीज़ सस्ती है। भाई साहब, इस कुरते का दाम क्या है?
दुकानदार	- वह साढ़े तीन सौ का है।
दीपक	- कविता, जुही के लिये तुम किताब क्यों नहीं लेतीं?
कविता	- तुम लो, न। जुही तुम्हारी दोस्त भी है। मैं एक क़मीज़ ही लूँगी।
दीपक	- ठीक है, मैं बग़ल में किताब की दुकान में जा रहा हूँ। मैं जुही को एक किताब दूँगा।
कविता	- ठीक है। किताब ख़रीदकर यहीं वापस आना। मैं इस दुकान में होऊँगी।

Glossary

अनोखी the name of a popular clothing store in Khan Market (अनोखा unique, peculiar)

जन्मदिन birthday (*m*)

सलवार क़मीज़ shalwar kameez (a loose fitting trouser and shirt) (*f*)

ढाई two and a half

सौ hundred

महँगा expensive

चुप रहना to remain silent, to shut up (*v.i.*)

सस्ता cheap

कुरता shirt (*m*)

साढ़े plus one half

बग़ल side, flank, armpit (*f*)

बग़ल में next door

यहीं right here

सोचना to think (*v.t.*)

कौन-सा which (*inter*)

किस दुकान में into which shop

Translate the following questions and then provide answers for them. Ask a partner the questions.

1. For whom does Kavita want to buy something? ....

2. Whose birthday is it tomorrow? ....

3. In(to) which shop does Kavita want to go? ....

4. How much is the shirt? ....

5. Does Deepak think that the shirt is expensive? ....

6. What will Deepak give Juhi? ....

7. What will Kavita buy? ....

GRAMMAR

The Presumptive

The presumptive is used to express the inferred or presumed certainty of a fact. In other words, it is assumed that an action must take place, must be taking place or must have taken place. It is formed by employing the future form of the verb होना *to be* with the imperfect participle, the perfect participle or in the progressive aspect.

वह इस के बारे में जानता है।
(imperfect present)
He knows about this/it.

वह इस के बारे में जानता होगा।
(imperfect presumptive)
He must know about this/it.

वे लड़कियाँ अभी विश्वविद्यालय आ रही हैं। (progressive aspect)
Those girls are coming to university right now.

वे लड़कियाँ अभी विश्वविद्यालय आ रही होंगी। (progressive presumptive)
Those girls must be on their way to university right now.

उसने अपना काम किया है। (present perfect)
He/she has done his/her (own) work.

उसने अपना काम किया होगा। (perfect presumptive)
He/she must have done his/her (own) work.

The use of the future form of होना with these verbal forms can also retain a sense of the future.

वह अभी आती होगी।   रात के साढ़े ग्यारह बजे हैं। वे सो रहे होंगे।
She must be on her way.   It is 11:30 P.M. He/They must/will be sleeping.

The presumptive form of होना *to be* is the same as the future form.

वे लोग अभी उस कमरे में होंगे।
Those people must be in that room right now.

कल वे लोग उस कमरे में होंगे।
Tomorrow those people will be in that room.

सोमवार को शिक्षक अपने दफ़्तर में होंगे।
The teacher will be/must be in his office on Monday. / The teacher must have been in his office on Monday.

PRACTICE

📖 *Now turn to the Workbook and complete Activity 17.2 before continuing.*

GRAMMAR

The Verbs लगना *to attach*, देना *to give* and पाना *to get, obtain*

When used with an infinitive in the oblique form, the verbs लगना, देना and पाना give a sense of *to begin to* (लगना), *to permit to* (देना) and *to be able to* (पाना).

जाने लगना *to begin to go*
जाने देना *to permit/allow to go*
जाने पाना *to be able to go*

1. लगना *to attach*

   चलने लगना   कीर्तन फिर से चलने लगा था।
   to begin to move   The devotional song began again.

   सताने लगना   उसे अपने बच्चों की याद सताने लगती थी।
   to begin to torment   The memory of her children would begin to torment her.

2. देना *to give*

   The person who is permitted to do an action is governed by the postposition को.

   उन्होंने हमें भारत जाने दिया था।
   They had allowed us to go to India.

   मुझे अभी परीक्षा देने दीजिये।
   Please let me take/sit the exam. (*please let me give the exam*)

   क्या उसने तुम्हें पत्र लिखने नहीं दिया?
   Didn't he/she let you write a/the letter?

   वहाँ तक तुम्हें पहुँचने कौन देगा?
   Who will let you get that far? (*who will let you reach up till there?*)

3. पाना *to get, obtain*

   पाना *to get, obtain* when employed with an oblique infinitive gives a sense of *to be able to*. When used in this manner, it functions as an intransitive verb. Its use is becoming less common in modern Hindi.

   वह हमारे लिये दाल नहीं बनाने पाया।
   He wasn't able to make dhal for us.

PRACTICE

📖 *Now turn to the workbook and complete Activity 17.3 before continuing.*

I Have Just Had Tea, Thanks मैं अभी चाय पीकर आया हूँ

When visiting someone's home in India you will most likely be asked if you would like a drink and often be asked to share a meal. When asked if you would like something to drink, the most polite response is to say that you have just had something (such as tea) before coming over. When asked to stay for a meal, you can say that you have just eaten.

मैं चाय पीकर आयी हूँ।   I (*f*) have just had tea.
मैं खाना खाकर आया हूँ।   I (*m*) have just eaten.

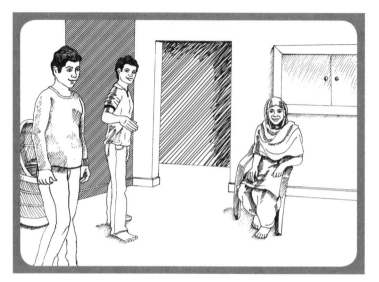

Deepak stops off at Imran's home in Old Delhi on his way home in the evening.

दीपक	– आदाब मिसेस ख़ान।
इमरान की माँ	– नमस्ते दीपक। तुम क्या लोगे, चाय या कॉफ़ी?
दीपक	– जी, मैं अभी चाय पीकर आया हूँ।
इमरान	– फिर भी, कम से कम चाय लो, दीपक। अम्मी, मैं भी चाय पियूँगा।
इमरान की माँ	– ठीक है। मैं चाय बनाती हूँ। तुम्हारे अब्बा अभी घर पहुँचते होंगे। दीपक, तुमने अभी तक रात का खाना तो नहीं खाया होगा?
दीपक	– जी, मैं तो खाना खाकर आया हूँ।
इमरान	– दिन में खाना खाया होगा। आज तुम हमारे साथ रात का खाना खाकर ही जाना, दीपक। मैं तुम्हें यहाँ से जाने नहीं दूँगा। खाने के बाद तुम और मैं फ़िल्म देखने चलेंगे।
दीपक	– इमरान, आज मैं घर जाकर खाना खाऊँगा। मामी रुकी होंगी। लेकिन कल शाम को आऊँगा। और कल हम ज़रूर फ़िल्म देखने जाएँगे। ठीक है?
इमरान	– ठीक है। अभी अपनी चाय लो और बताओ कि आज कविता से क्या बात हुई।

Glossary

आदाब greetings (*m*)	कम से कम at least	अभी तक by now
मिसेस Mrs.	अब्बा father (*m*)	रात का खाना dinner (*m*)
फिर भी nevertheless (*conj*)	पहुँचना to arrive, reach (*v.i.*)	रुकना to wait, stop (*v.i.*)

Answer the following questions and ask a partner.

1. क्या इमरान दीपक के पास आया है? _____

2. इमरान की माँ दीपक से क्या पूछती हैं? _____

3. क्या इमरान कॉफ़ी पीना चाहता है? ....

4. क्या इमरान के अब्बा अभी घर पहुँचते होंगे? ....

5. क्या आज दीपक इमरान के घर में खाना खाएगा? ....

6. क्या आज आप किसी दोस्त के घर खाना खाने जा रहे हैं? (जा रही हैं) ....

....

7. खाना खाने के बाद इमरान क्या करना चाहता है? ....

GRAMMAR

The Verb मिलना *to meet, find, acquire*

The verb मिलना *to meet, acquire, obtain, find, be mixed, encounter* is used in a variety of functions. The meaning conveyed depends on the particular postposition that is used in conjunction with this verb. मिलना is an intransitive verb and therefore, the logical subject is not governed by ने when the perfect participle is used.

1. **x से मिलना to meet x** (a planned meeting)

   When used to express a planned meeting, the person with whom one meets is marked by the postposition से. The postposition से is also used to express such things as resemblance in physical appearance or harmony.

   कल तुम मुझसे कक्षा के बाद मिलना।
   Meet with me after class tomorrow.

   आप से मिलकर मुझे बहुत ख़ुशी हुई।
   It was a pleasure to meet you. (*having met you a lot of happiness occurred to me*)

   इलाहाबाद में गंगा नदी यमुना से मिलती है।
   The Ganges meets the Yamuna in Allahabad.

   तेरी शक्ल तेरी माँ से बहुत मिलती है।
   You look a lot like your mother. (*your appearance meets with your mother*)

   इस विषय में भी हमारे विचार मिलते थे।
   Our thoughts used to be similar in this matter as well. (*in this subject also our thoughts used to meet*)

It is important to remember that the verb *to see* is frequently used in English in place of the verb *to meet*. The verb देखना *to see* is *not* employed in this manner in Hindi, except in such cases as inquiring about a person's state or condition.

मैं अपने बीमार दोस्त को देखने अस्पताल जा रहा हूँ।

I am going to see my sick friend in the hospital.

2. **मिलना to meet** (an accidental encounter)

When a meeting or encounter is *not planned* the logical subject is governed by को.

मुझे वह इत्तफ़ाक़ से सड़क में मिली थी।

I had bumped into her by chance in the street.

मुझे वे विश्वविद्यालय में कभी-कभी मिलते थे।

I used to bump into them/him occasionally at the university.

3. **मिलना to be available, to find, to obtain, to get**

The verb मिलना may also be used to express the availability of something, as in *Where does one get a newspaper around here?* If mentioned, the person who receives or obtains the object in question is governed by the postposition को.

रोज़ सवेरे इस कोने पर अख़बार मिलता है।

The newspaper is available on this corner every morning.

मुझे इस किताब में कुछ नहीं मिला।

I didn't find anything in this book.

शायद इस दुकान में अच्छी चाय मिले।

Perhaps we may get good tea in this shop.

क्या आप के देश में सब प्रकार के फल मिलते हैं।

Are all kinds of fruits available in your country?

आजकल डॉक्टरों को बहुत पैसा नहीं मिलता।

These days doctors don't receive a lot of money.

आपको यह नयी घड़ी कहाँ से मिली?

From where did you get this new watch?

PRACTICE

📖 *Now turn to the Workbook and complete Activities 17.4 and 17.5.*

Where Shall We Meet? हम कहाँ मिलेंगे?

Deepak phones Kavita to make plans for the evening.

दीपक	– हाय कविता, मैं दीपक बोल रहा हूँ।
कविता	– अरे दीपक, इस वक़्त कहाँ हो तुम?
दीपक	– मैं अभी कॉलेज में हूँ। क्या हम शाम को मिलें?
कविता	– तुम्हारा क्या ख़्याल है? हम क्या करेंगे?
दीपक	– तुम खाना खाने चलोगी?
कविता	– ठीक है। लेकिन कहाँ मिलेंगे?
दीपक	– आज 'करीम्स' जाने का मन हो रहा है। वहीं मिलें?
कविता	– नहीं। मैं मेट्रो से आ रही हूँ। मैं तुमसे चाँदनी चौक में मिलूँगी। गुरुद्वारे के पास।
दीपक	– हाँ, लेकिन उसके सामने ही। वहाँ एक पान की दुकान है। उस के सामने हम मिलेंगे।
कविता	– हाँ, जानती हूँ। उस दुकान की बग़ल में उर्दू की किताबें भी मिलती हैं। मैं अपनी एक सहेली के लिये एक उर्दू की किताब लेना चाहती हूँ।
दीपक	– हाँ, वहाँ बहुत अच्छी किताबें मिलती हैं। तो हम सात बजे मिलेंगे।
कविता	– ठीक है, हम शाम को मिलेंगे।
दीपक	– अच्छा, मैं फ़ोन रखता हूँ।

Glossary

x का मन होना to feel like x
  (the mind of x to happen) (*v.i.*)
वहीं right there
करीम्स (करीम होटल) Karim's
  (Karim Hotel) (a famous kabab
  restaurant in Old Delhi)

चाँदनी चौक Chandni Chowk
गुरुद्वारा Gurdwara (*m*)
x की बग़ल में next to x
फ़ोन रखना to place (put
  down) the phone (*v.t.*)

बुलाना to invite,
  summon, to call (*v.t.*)

Translate the following questions and answer them.

1. Are Deepak and Kavita talking on the phone? _____

2. Did Kavita phone Deepak? _____

3. Will Kavita meet Deepak in the evening? _____

4. Where will Kavita and Deepak meet in the evening? _____

5. Will Kavita come by the metro? _____

6. Where does Deepak want to meet with Kavita? _____

7. What time will they meet in the evening? _____

8. Are good books available in Chandni Chowk? _____

Now arrange with a friend to go out in the evening. Ask if he/she wants to go to eat, or see a film, or go to a shop. Where will you meet? What time will you meet? How will you go there? Does your friend want to invite someone else?

LESSON **18** अठारहवाँ पाठ

What Do You Like?

You Must Have Eaten Indian Food आपने हिन्दुस्तानी खाना खाया होगा

Here Kavita talks about Indian cuisine.

नमस्ते दोस्तो! आप लोगों ने हिन्दुस्तानी खाना खाया होगा। आप जानते होंगे कि उत्तर भारत में लोग रोटी, दाल-चावल और अलग-अलग सब्ज़ियाँ खाते हैं। कुछ लोग गोश्त भी खाते हैं। पहले भारत में इतने लोग गोश्त नहीं खाते थे पर आजकल बहुत लोग खाने लगे हैं। लोग ज़्यादातर मुर्ग़ी और बकरे का गोश्त खाते हैं। गाय का गोश्त बहुत ही कम लोग खाते हैं। मेरे परिवार में नाना-नानी गोश्त नहीं खाते। वे शुद्ध शाकाहारी हैं। मेरे माँ-बाप और भाई शाकाहारी नहीं हैं। मैं तो कभी-कभी गोश्त खाती हूँ। दीपक भी गोश्त खाता है लेकिन वह मुर्ग़ी ही खाता है। आप लोगों ने रोटी खायी होगी। लोग रोटी को चपाती भी कहते हैं। आपने अलग-अलग सब्ज़ियाँ खायी होंगी। दिन में और रात को हम घर में आलू की सब्ज़ी, मटर की सब्ज़ी, पालक, गोभी की सब्ज़ी, करेला, कद्दू, लौकी की सब्ज़ी, ऐसी चीज़ें खाते हैं, रोटी, दाल और चावल के साथ। शायद आपने लौकी नहीं खायी हो। हम गोश्त घर में नहीं खाते। अब आप लोग बताइये, आप क्या खाते हैं?

Glossary

उत्तर north (*m*)
रोटी roti, flat bread (*f*)
दाल lentils (*f*)
चावल rice (*m*)
अलग-अलग separate, different
सब्ज़ी vegetable (dish) (*f*)
गोश्त meat (*m*)

ज़्यादातर most
मुर्ग़ी chicken (*f*)
बकरा goat (*m*)
शुद्ध शाकाहारी pure vegetarian
पहले previously
आलू potato (*m*)
मटर peas (*m*)

पालक spinach (*m*)
गोभी cauliflower (*f*)
करेला bitter gourd (*m*)
कद्दू pumpkin (*m*)
लौकी gourd (*f*)

Answer the following questions. Then ask them of a partner.

1. उत्तर भारत में क्या लोग रोटी और चावल खाते हैं? _____

2. आजकल हिन्दुस्तान में कितने लोग गोश्त खाने लगे हैं? _____

3. क्या आप गोश्त खाते हैं? (खाती हैं) _____

4. क्या आप शाकाहारी हैं? _____

5. आप की मनपसंद सब्ज़ी क्या है? _____

6. क्या दीपक बकरे का गोश्त खाता है? _____

7. अपने घर में आप क्या खाते हैं? (खाती हैं) _____

GRAMMAR

को Verbs

In several expressions in Hindi the logical subject is marked by the postposition को. The first of these introduced earlier in this book involved the verbs चाहिये *needed/wanted* (see p. 56) and मिलना *to get, obtain* (see p. 165). In addition to these the expression of such things as physical sensations (such as injury, thirst, hunger, etc.), emotions (such as anger, love, enjoyment, etc.) as well as expressions concerning knowing or remembering and the possession of particular skills, all require the logical subject to be governed by को.

In this lesson six important को verbs are introduced.
1. मालूम होना to be known (to one), to find out, to seem
2. पता होना/चलना to be known (to one), to find out
3. आना to come (to know)
4. पसंद होना/आना to enjoy, to like
5. लगना to seem, to attach
6. होना to be

1. **मालूम होना to be known, to find out, to seem**

   The verb मालूम होना *to be known* can be construed in several ways, depending on the form of the verb. It is often translated as *to know* or *to seem*. It is *not* used when it is a person whom one knows. In such cases the verb जानना *to know* is employed. मालूम होना is restricted to the knowledge of information but not the acquisition of this knowledge.

   उसे मालूम है । He/she knows.
   उसे मालूम था । He/she knew.
   शायद उसे मालूम हो । Perhaps he/she may know.
   उसे मालूम हुआ । He/she found out.
   उसे मालूम होगा । He/she will find out *or* he/she must know.
   उसे मालूम होता है कि... It seems to him/her that...*
   उसे मालूम होता था कि... It seemed to him/her that...*
   *These can also be expressed using x को मालूम पड़ना *to seem to x.*

   क्या आपको मालूम है कि इंडिया जाने के टिकट का दाम क्या है?
   Do you know how much a ticket to India is?

   जी हाँ, मुझे मालूम है कि उसका पता क्या है ।
   Yes, I know what his/her address is.

   अच्छा! पहले यह मुझे मालूम नहीं था ।
   Really! I didn't know this before.

   कल उसे मालूम हुआ कि अगले साल उसकी नौकरी ख़त्म होगी ।
   He/she found out yesterday that next year his/her job will end.

   शायद उन्हें मालूम हो कि आप अभी जा रहे हैं ।
   Perhaps they (he/she) may know that you are going right now.

   उसे मालूम होगा कि हम यह काम कैसे करेंगे ।
   He/she will/must know how we will do this work.

   मुझे मालूम होता है कि हिन्दी सीखना इतना मुश्किल नहीं है ।
   It seems to me that it is not too difficult to learn Hindi.

   उसे आटे दाल का भाव मालूम पड़ेगा ।
   He/she will realize the harsh reality of life. (*he/she will find out the price of flour and dhal*)

   The adjective मालूम *known* may also be used with the verb करना *to do*, where it comes to mean *to find out*. Here the logical subject is not governed by को.

मालूम करना	कल मैंने मालूम किया कि टिकट का दाम क्या है ।
to find out	Yesterday I found out what the price of the ticket is.

2. पता होना/चलना/लगाना to be known (to one), to find out

These are similar in their use to मालूम होना *to know, find out* above. The verbs may be used interchangeably. पता as a noun means *address, whereabouts, information, knowledge*.

उसे इस जगह के बारे में कैसे पता चला?
How did he/she find out about this place?

मुझे पता है कि इसका जवाब क्या है।
I know what the answer to this is.

पता may also be combined with the verb करना *to do* or लगाना *to attach*. Here it means *to find out*. As with मालूम करना above, the logical subject in such cases is not marked by को.

पता करना   मैं इस के बारे में आपके लिये पता करने की कोशिश करूँगा।
to find out, discover   I (*m*) will try to find out about this for you.

3. आना to come (to know)

The verb आना *to come* is used with the logical subject marked by को to convey knowledge of a particular skill. It is also used to talk about some emotional and physical states, such as गुस्सा *anger* (*m*) and नींद *sleep* (*f*).

लड़के को थोड़ी-थोड़ी हिन्दी आती है।
The boy knows a little Hindi.

आजकल मेरी दोस्त को नींद नहीं आती।
These days my friend (*f*) can't sleep.

हिन्दुस्तान जाकर आपको हिन्दी आने लगेगी।
You will begin to pick up Hindi when you get to India.

क्या इसे देवनागरी लिपि में लिखना आता है?
Does he/she know how to write in the Devanagari script?

तुम्हें इतना गुस्सा क्यों आता है?
Why do you get so angry?

4. पसंद होना/आना to enjoy, to like

The word पसंद literally means *approved, liked, liking, choice, taste*. It is combined with the verbs होना *to be* and आना *to come*. When used with होना it often gives a general sense. With आना it often refers to a specific occasion or object.

मुझे हिन्दुस्तानी खाना बहुत पसंद है।
I like Indian food a lot.

मुझको यह खाना बहुत पसंद आया।
I liked this food a lot.

आपको यह किताब बहुत पसंद आएगी।
You will like this book a lot.

इस फ़िल्म में शाह रुख़ ख़ान ने काम किया होता तो उस लड़के को फ़िल्म और भी पसंद आती।
If Shah Rukh Khan had been in this film, that boy would have liked it even more.

प्रेमचंद की कहानियाँ किसको पसंद नहीं?
Who doesn't like Premchand's stories?

5. लगना **to seem, to attach, etc.**
The verb लगना is used in a variety of expressions where the logical subject is marked by को.

a) लगना to seem

आप (मुझे) परेशान लगते हैं।
You seem worried (to me).

आपको देखकर ऐसा लगता है कि आप के पास बहुत पैसे होंगे।
Looking at you, it seems (to me) that you must have a lot of money.

b) लगना to take, require (time etc.)
लगना *to attach* is also used to express the time or money required to perform a certain action, as in *It took me four hours to go to New York.* The logical subject is governed by को. The action, a verb in the infinitive form, is marked by में *in.*

मुझे यूनिवर्सिटी पहुँचने में दो घंटे लगते हैं।
It takes me two hours to reach the university. (*to me in reaching university two hours attach*)

उसे अपना काम करने में बहुत देर लगने लगी है।
It has begun to take him/her a long time to do his/her work.

मेधा को इतनी गरम चाय पीने में दो मिनट भी नहीं लगे।
It hardly took Medha two minutes to drink this very hot tea.

बौद्ध धर्म को चीन और जापान तक पहुँचने में कई हज़ार साल लगे थे।
It took Buddhism several thousand years to reach China and Japan.

हो सकता है कि हिन्दी सीखने में बहुत मेहनत नहीं लगे।
It may not take that much hard work to learn Hindi.

आपके घर में एक हफ़्ते में कितनी चाय लगती है?
How much tea do you go through in a week?

हवाई जहाज़ से इंग्लैंड जाने में बहुत पैसे लगते थे।
It used to take a lot of money to go to England by plane.

c) लगना to feel (physical sensations and emotional states)
The most common expressions in which लगना is used to express physical sensations and emotional states are:
x को भूख लगना x to feel hunger (*f*)
x को प्यास लगना x to feel thirst (*f*)
x को गर्मी लगना x to feel heat (*f*)
x को ठंड लगना x to feel cold (*f*)
x को चोट लगना x to sustain an injury (*f*)
x को डर लगना x to feel fear (*m*) (the object of the fear is governed by से *from, by, with*)

Ordinarily the present perfect tense of लगना is employed to express the sensation of hunger/thirst at the time of speaking (*I [etc.] feel hungry/thirsty*), and the progressive aspect to express the sensation of heat or cold (*I [etc.] feel hot/cold*).

उसे बहुत भूख लगी है।
He/she is very hungry. (*much hunger has attached to him/her*)

हमें बड़ी ठंड लग रही है।
We are feeling very cold.

बच्चों को अचानक भूख लगती है।
Children feel hungry all of a sudden.

अभी मुझे बहुत गर्मी लग रही है।
I am feeling very hot right now.

बीमारी से हमें बहुत डर लगता है।
We are very afraid of disease.

उस समय मेरी बहन को गाड़ियों से डर लगने लगा था।
Then (at that time) my sister had begun to be afraid of cars.

d) अच्छा/बुरा लगना to like/dislike (feel bad)
Earlier the expression *to like* was introduced using the verbs पसंद होना/आना (see p. 172).
अच्छा लगना *to seem good* is another very common way to express a fondness for something.
बुरा लगना *to feel bad* is often used to express sympathy for someone or something.

मुझे हिन्दुस्तान जाना अच्छा लगता है।
I like to go to India.

तुम्हें यह चाय अच्छी नहीं लगेगी।
You will not like this tea.

आपके बारे में ऐसी बात सुनकर मुझे बहुत बुरा लगा।
When I heard this about you I felt very bad.

6. होना **to be**

The verb होना is also employed to express involuntary actions as well as emotional states, where the logical subject is governed by को.

उसको बहुत पश्चाताप हुआ।
He/she became very remorseful. (*to her/him much remorse happened*)

यह ख़बर सुनकर उसे बहुत अफ़सोस हुआ।
After hearing this news he/she was very sorry.

आपको बहुत दुख हुआ, न।
You experienced a lot of sorrow, didn't you?

PRACTICE

Now turn to the Workbook and complete Activities 18.1 and 18.2 before continuing.

What Do You Like? आपको क्या अच्छा लगता है?

Here Kavita and Deepak discuss the various things they like and dislike.

कविता - दीपक, तुम्हें चाय ज़्यादा अच्छी लगती है या कॉफ़ी?

दीपक - मुझे चाय हमेशा से अच्छी लगती है, लेकिन कॉफ़ी अच्छी लगने लगी है। तुमको क्या अच्छा लगता है?

कविता - मुझे चाय और कॉफ़ी दोनों अच्छी लगती हैं। तुम्हें गोश्त अच्छा लगता है, न?

दीपक - तुम्हें मालूम है कि मुझे सिर्फ़ मुर्ग़ी खाना पसंद है। और तुम्हें?

कविता - पहले मुझे गोश्त खाना अच्छा नहीं लगता था लेकिन अब अच्छा लगने लगा है।

दीपक - तुम्हें हिन्दी फ़िल्में ज़्यादा पसंद हैं या अमरीकी फ़िल्में?

कविता - पहले मुझे हिन्दी फ़िल्में इतनी पसंद नहीं थीं। पर अब तुम्हारे साथ ज़्यादा देखने लगी हूँ। अब वे इतनी बकवास नहीं लगतीं। तुमने कोई भी अमरीकी फ़िल्म नहीं देखी होगी।

दीपक - यह तो सच नहीं है। तुम्हें मालूम नहीं है कि इलाहाबाद में मेरी ज़िंदगी कैसी होती थी। हम कभी-कभी अमरीकी फ़िल्में देखते थे। बस हम उनकी भाषा कम समझते थे।

Glossary

ज़्यादा more, most
हमेशा से (from) always
गोश्त meat (*m*)
अच्छा लगना to like (*v.i.*)
पसंद होना to like (*v.i.*)

या or
बकवास nonsense (*f*)
लगना to seem, appear (*v.i.*)
सच true
मालूम होना to be known (*v.i.*)

ज़िंदगी life (*f*)
भाषा language (*f*)
कम less
समझना to understand
(*v.i. + v.t.*)

Translate the following questions and then answer them. Try asking them of a partner.

1. Do you like tea or coffee more? _____

2. Do you like to watch Hindi films? _____

3. Has Kavita begun to like meat? _____

4. Do you like to watch American films? _____

5. Do you like to go to India? _____

6. Has Kavita begun to watch more Hindi films with Deepak? _____

7. Has Deepak seen an American film? _____

8. Do you like to eat Indian food? _____

GRAMMAR

Telling the Time

In order to learn how to tell the time in Hindi, some important numerical fractions need to be learned. Some of these were introduced in Lesson 16.

पौन *three-quarters of* (or quarter to one)
पौने *less one quarter* (from quarter to two onwards)
सवा *one and a quarter* (or plus one quarter)
डेढ़ *one and one half*
ढाई *two and one half*
साढ़े *plus one half* (from 3½ onwards)

Asking the Time

There are four common phrases that are used to ask "What time is it?" in Hindi.

बजना to strike   कितने बजे हैं/बज गये?[1] (*how many have struck?*)
टाइम क्या है? (*what time is?*)

1. This expression involves a compound verb that has not yet been introduced. In the verbal unit there are two verbs बजना *to strike* and जाना *to go*. In this combination, however, the verb जाना does not retain its meaning but instead, "colors" the meaning of the first verb बजना. For a discussion of compound verbs, see p. 188.

टाइम क्या हुआ? (*what time happened?*)
क्या बजा है? (*what has struck?*)

The verb बजना *to strike* is commonly employed in response to the question *what time is it?* It may be construed as *o'clock* in most responses.

दो बजे हैं। (बज गये)[2]
It is 2 o'clock. (*two have struck*)[3]

टाइम क्या है?
What is the time?

तीन बजे हैं।
It is 3 o'clock.

अभी क्या बजा होगा?
What must the time be now?
(*how many must have struck now*)

अभी सात बजे होंगे।
Now it must be 7 o'clock.

a) **Expressing time past the hour.**
   When expressing time after the hour the absolutive कर is used with बजना *to strike*.

दो बजकर बीस मिनट हुए हैं।
It is 20 past 2. (*having struck two twenty minutes have happened*)

तीन बजकर पच्चीस मिनट हुए हैं।
It is 25 past 3.

पाँच बज कर पैंतीस मिनट हुए हैं।
It is 5:35.

b) **Before the hour**
   To express time approaching the hour, the verb बजना *to strike* is used with the postposition में *in*. Sometimes the adjective बाक़ी *remaining* is also employed.

पाँच बजने में दस मिनट हैं।
It is 10 to 5. (*in striking five, there are ten minutes*)

---

2. Again we meet the same compound verb (see note above.)

3. This is also expressed as दो बज गये। This expression includes a compound verb जाना। For more on compound verbs, see p. 188.

पाँच बजने में दस मिनट बाक़ी हैं।
It is 10 to 5. (*in striking five ten minutes are remaining*)

c) **Quarter past…, half past…, quarter to…**
There exist particular phrases to express times such as *quarter past one*, *half past two*, etc., using the numerical divisions introduced above. Special attention should be paid to the expression of the times *half past one*, *half past two*, *a quarter past one* and *a quarter to one*.

सवा *one and a quarter*, or *a quarter past…*
सवा is an adjective, which on its own means *1¼*. When used with numbers from two onwards it adds one quarter to the number.

अभी सवा बजा है।
It is now a quarter past 1.

अभी सवा दो बजे हैं।
It is now a quarter past 2.

डेढ़ *half past one* (or *one and a half*)
ढाई *half past two* (or *two and a half*)
साढ़े *plus one half* (with a number from and including three to twelve)

अभी डेढ़ बजा है।
It is now half past 1.

अभी ढाई बजे हैं।
It is now half past 2.

अभी साढ़े तीन बजे हैं।
It is now half past 3.

पौन *three quarters* (*of one*)
पौने *a quarter to…* (*less a quarter*, with any number except one)

अभी पौन बजा है।
It is now a quarter to 1.

अभी पौने दो बजे हैं।
It is now a quarter to 2.

Finally, numbers up to and including one-and-a-half are considered singular.

2. **Adverbs involving clock times**

Clock times may be used adverbially as in the expression *Come at two o'clock*. In such cases, the verb बजना *to strike* is used adverbially (in the oblique). When a particular minute of the clock is specified, the postpositions पर *on*, *at* and पहले *before* are used.

अभी एक बजा है।
It is 1 o'clock.

कल एक बजे मुझसे मिलने आना।
Come to meet with me at 1 o'clock tomorrow.

दो बज कर बीस मिनट पर आप की परीक्षा शुरू होगी।
Your exam will begin at 20 past 2.

पाँच बजने से दस मिनट पहले आइये।
Come at 10 to 5.

A.M. and P.M. are expressed by employing the different words for various times of day.

सवेरे दस बजे 10 A.M. (also सुबह दस बजे)
दोपहर बारह बजे 12 P.M.
दिन में दो बजे 2 P.M.
शाम को पाँच बजे 5 P.M.
रात को ग्यारह बजे 11 P.M.

The day is traditionally divided into eight segments (पहर *a measure of time equal to three hours*). The four most important divisions of time in the day are:

सुबह/सवेरा *morning* (up till 12 P.M.)
दोपहर *midday* (from 12 P.M. until 4 P.M.)
शाम *evening* (from 4 P.M. until 8 P.M.)
रात *night* (from 8 P.M. until 12 A.M.)

कल सवेरे आठ बजे मुझसे मिलने आना।
Come and meet me at 8 A.M. tomorrow.

PRACTICE

📖 *Now turn to the Workbook and complete Activities 18.3 and 18.4.*

Pleased to Meet You आपसे मिलकर बहुत ख़ुशी हुई

In earlier chapters some greetings and expressions of farewell were introduced. There is one other expression that can be employed when introduced to a person or when parting:

आपसे मिलकर (मुझे) बहुत ख़ुशी हुई।
Pleased to meet you. (*having met you much happiness occurred [to me]*)

In response you can say:

मुझे भी। Likewise (*to me also*).

💿 Here Deepak meets Kavita's brother in Kavita's living room.

दीपक   - नमस्ते समीर। आप कैसे हैं?
समीर   - तुम दीपक होगे। नमस्ते। मैं मज़े में हूँ। तुम सुनाओ।
कविता - भैया, मैंने बताया, न, कि दीपक और मैं साथ साथ पढ़ते हैं।
समीर   - हाँ, हाँ। मुझे याद है। कविता ने तुम्हारे बारे में बहुत बताया है।
दीपक   - समीर, आप कितने दिन के लिये दिल्ली आये हैं?
समीर   - मुझे 'तुम' कहो। मैं चौदह दिन के लिये आया हूँ। इस वक़्त बहुत लंबी छुट्टी नहीं मिली मुझे।
दीपक   - तो क्या हम तीनों दो-तीन दिन के लिये कहीं घूमने चलें? क्या आपके पास... मुझे माफ़ करो, क्या तुम्हारे पास वक़्त है, समीर?

समीर - दो-तीन दिन के लिये जाने का मौक़ा मिलेगा। लेकिन कविता से पूछो। इन दिनों शायद उसे बहुत काम रहता होगा।

दीपक - कविता, क्या ख़्याल है?

कविता - मेरे लिये ठीक है।

दीपक - बहुत अच्छा है। अभी मैं चलता हूँ, लेकिन तुमसे मिलकर बहुत ख़ुशी हुई समीर।

समीर - हाँ, मुझे भी। कल मिलेंगे।

दीपक - ज़रूर।

Glossary

भैया brother (affectionate term) (*m*)

साथ साथ together

याद होना to remember (*v.i.*)

लंबा long

छुट्टी holiday (*f*)

तीनों all three

कहीं somewhere

घूमना to wander, take a trip (*v.i.*)

माफ़ करना to forgive (*v.t.*)

मौक़ा opportunity (*m*)

x को बहुत काम रहना much work to remain to x (to have a lot of work) (*v.i.*)

ख़्याल idea, thought, view, opinion (*m*)

मिलना to obtain, receive, get, to meet (*v.i.*)

मैं चलता हूँ I'm off

ख़ुशी happiness (*f*)

ज़रूर certainly

Answer the following questions and then ask a partner.

1. क्या कविता का भाई हिन्दुस्तान आया है? ....

2. कविता का भाई दिल्ली कितने दिन के लिये आया है? ....

....

3. इस वक़्त क्या समीर को लंबी छुट्टी मिली? ....

4. क्या कविता ने दीपक के बारे में समीर को बहुत बताया है? ....

....

5. क्या दीपक चाहता है कि वे तीनों कहीं घूमने जायें? ....

....

6. क्या आप कहीं घूमने के लिये जाना चाहते हैं? (चाहती हैं) ....

....

LESSON **19** उन्तीसवाँ पाठ

I Want to Leave at Five-Thirty

I Want to Leave at Five-Thirty मैं साढ़े पाँच बजे जाना चाहता हूँ
Here Kavita and Deepak discuss what time they should leave the library to go home.

कविता – अरे दीपक, आज तुम घर कितने बजे जाना चाहते हो?

दीपक – मैं साढ़े पाँच बजे जाना चाहता हूँ। और तुम?

कविता – पुस्तकालय सवा छै बजे बंद होता है। और मैं घर पौने सात बजे तक पहुँचना चाहती हूँ।

दीपक – ठीक है। मैं तुम्हें घर तक छोड़ूँ? अभी मेरे पास गाड़ी है। तो कितने बजे चलें?

कविता – पौने छै बजे तक हम चलें? अभी कितने बजे हैं?

दीपक – अभी तीन बजकर बीस मिनट हुए हैं। आज क्या तुमने दिन का खाना डेढ़ बजे खाया था या दो बजे?

कविता – ढाई बजे। मैं अभी-अभी वापस आयी हूँ। क्यों पूछते हो?

दीपक – क़रीब डेढ़ बजे मैं तुमको ढूँढने आया था लेकिन वहाँ तुम मिलीं नहीं।

कविता – तुम कितने बजे आये थे?

दीपक – शायद दो बजने में दस मिनट पर मैं आया होऊँगा।

कविता – ओह, उस वक़्त मैं एक किताब ढूँढने गयी थी।

दीपक – कोई बात नहीं। ठीक है, अभी हमारे पास ढाई घंटे हैं। मैं यहाँ बैठकर कुछ पढ़ाई करूँगा।

कविता – ठीक है।

Glossary

अरे hey

साढ़े plus a half (three and beyond)

पुस्तकालय library (*m*)

सवा one and a quarter; plus one quarter

बंद होना to be closed (*v.i.*)

पौने minus one quarter

छोड़ना to abandon, drop, leave (*v.t.*)

डेढ़ one and a half

ढाई two and a half

अभी-अभी right now

वापस आना to return (*v.i.*)

करीब approximately, close

ढूँढना to search (*v.t.*)

ओह Oh!

Answer the following questions and then ask them of a partner.

1. आज पुस्तकालय कितने बजे बंद होता है?

2. आज कविता कितने बजे घर जाना चाहती है?

3. आज दीपक कविता को ढूँढने कितने बजे आया था?

4. क्या आप रोज़ दिन का खाना दोपहर को डेढ़ बजे खाते हैं?

5. कविता शाम को कितने बजे तक घर पहुँचना चाहती है?

6. क्या आप रोज़ शाम के साढ़े छे बजे तक अपने घर पहुँचते हैं? (पहुँचती हैं)

7. आज दो बजने में दस मिनट पर कविता कहाँ गयी थी?

GRAMMAR

The Auxiliary Verbs सकना *to be able to*, पाना *to be able to, to obtain, acquire*, and चुकना *to be finished, completed*

1. सकना to be able to
2. पाना to be able to, to obtain
3. चुकना to be finished, to be spent

The three verbs सकना *to be able to*, पाना *to be able to, to obtain* and चुकना *to be finished, to be spent* are employed with the stem of a principal verb to give a sense of an ability (or inability) to perform an action (सकना, पाना) and the completion of an action (चुकना). For example, when used with the stem of the verb करना *to do* these give the following meanings:

कर सकना *to be able to do*
कर पाना *to be able to do*
कर चुकना *to have already done*

1. सकना **to be able to**

सकना *to be able to* cannot stand alone and must follow the stem of another verb. It gives a sense of the physical ability to perform an action. It is an intransitive verb, which means that when used in the past, ने will not govern the logical subject.

क्या तुम हिन्दी बोल सकते हो?
Can you (*m*) speak Hindi?

वे लड़कियाँ सवेरे जल्दी उठ
नहीं सकतीं ।
Those girls cannot get up early in
the morning.

हम पूरी फ़िल्म देख नहीं सकेंगे ।
We (*m*) will not be able to see the entire film.

मैं वह दवा पी नहीं सका ।
I (*m*) could not drink that medicine.

2. पाना **to be able to, to obtain**

पाना when used on its own means *to obtain*, *acquire*. It is transitive, and so ने will govern the logical subject when it is conjugated in the past tense.

उस देश में तुमने क्या पाया?
What did you acquire in that country?

When पाना is used with the stem of another verb, it indicates *to be able to*. It functions in a similar manner to सकना above, except that it is often used in the negative and indicates a desire to undertake an action but not the ability to do so. When used with the stem of another verb, it is intransitive.

रुकना	मुझे इतनी भूख लगी कि मैं रुक नहीं पाया ।
to wait, stop	I (*m*) was so hungry that I couldn't wait.
भरना	मज़दूरो! क्या तुम अपने बच्चों का पेट भर पाओगे?
to fill	Laborers! Will you (*m*) be able to fill your children's stomachs?

उठना   वह सवेरे जल्दी उठ नहीं पाता।
to get up, rise   He cannot get up early in the morning.

                      कल रात को मैं तुम्हारी पार्टी में आ नहीं पाऊँगी।
                      I (*f*) won't be able to come to your party tomorrow night.

3. **चुकना to be finished, to be spent**

   चुकना *to be finished*, *to be spent* when used with the stem of a verb gives a sense of finishing an action completely, often with no desire to repeat it. In English, it is often indicated by the use of the word *already*. It is an intransitive verb.

   मैंने यह फ़िल्म देखी है।
   I have seen this film.

   मैं यह फ़िल्म देख चुकी हूँ।
   I (*f*) have already seen this film.

   In the above example the use of the verb चुकना may indicate that the speaker has no desire to see the film again.

   शायद अब तक आप यह किताब पढ़ चुके हों।
   Perhaps you (*m*) have already read this book by now.

   क्या आप लोग खाना खा चुके हैं?
   Have you people (*m*) already eaten?

   कल तक मेरा काम हो चुका होगा।
   My work will have already been done by tomorrow.

   मैं तो अंगरेज़ी सीख चुकी, जी।
   I've (*f*) already learned English sir!

   In the final example, it is possible that चुकना is being used in a sarcastic manner to indicate that the speaker believes the action is beyond her capability.

PRACTICE

📖 *Now turn to the Workbook and complete Activity 19.1 before continuing.*

💿 The Weather in North India   उत्तर भारत का मौसम

Here Kavita talks about the seasons in north India throughout the year.

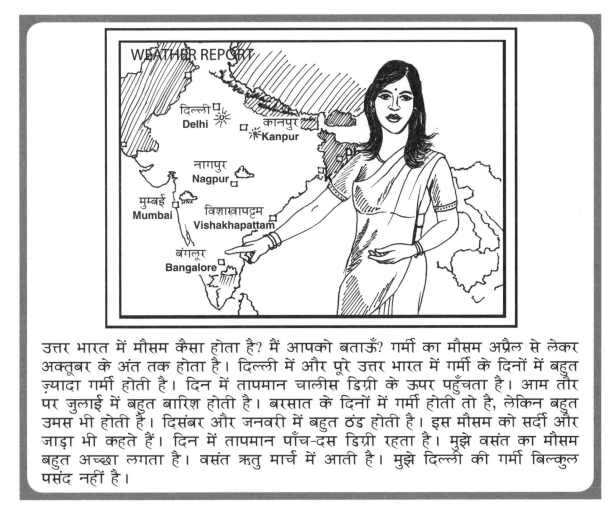

उत्तर भारत में मौसम कैसा होता है? मैं आपको बताऊँ? गर्मी का मौसम अप्रैल से लेकर अक्तूबर के अंत तक होता है। दिल्ली में और पूरे उत्तर भारत में गर्मी के दिनों में बहुत ज़्यादा गर्मी होती है। दिन में तापमान चालीस डिग्री के ऊपर पहुँचता है। आम तौर पर जुलाई में बहुत बारिश होती है। बरसात के दिनों में गर्मी होती तो है, लेकिन बहुत उमस भी होती है। दिसंबर और जनवरी में बहुत ठंड होती है। इस मौसम को सर्दी और जाड़ा भी कहते हैं। दिन में तापमान पाँच-दस डिग्री रहता है। मुझे वसंत का मौसम बहुत अच्छा लगता है। वसंत ऋतु मार्च में आती है। मुझे दिल्ली की गर्मी बिल्कुल पसंद नहीं है।

Glossary

उत्तर भारत north India (*m*)	तापमान temperature (*m*)	सर्दी cold, winter (*f*)
मौसम weather, season (*m*)	चालीस forty	जाड़ा cold, winter (*m*)
x से लेकर y तक from x until y	डिग्री degree (*f*)	वसंत spring (*m*)
अंत end (*m*)	x के ऊपर above x	ऋतु season (*f*)
पूरा entire, complete	आम तौर पर ordinarily	कौन-सा which (*inter*)
गर्मी heat, summer (*f*)	बारिश rain (*f*)	देश country (*m*)
गर्मी के दिन days of heat, summer (*m pl*)	बरसात rainy season (*f*)	बर्फ़ ice, snow (*f*)
	उमस humidity (*f*)	पड़ना to fall, lie (*v.i.*)
	ठंड cold, winter (*f*)	

Answer the following questions and ask them of a partner.

1. दिल्ली में गर्मी के दिन कब होते हैं? _____

2. दिल्ली में गर्मी के मौसम में तापमान कितना रहता है? _____
_____

3. आप के देश में गर्मी का मौसम कब होता है? _____

4. दिल्ली में बरसात किस महीने में होती है? _____

5. क्या कविता को दिल्ली की गर्मी अच्छी लगती है? _____

6. क्या आप कभी गर्मी के मौसम में हिन्दुस्तान गये हैं? (गई हैं) _____
_____

7. कविता को कौन-सा मौसम अच्छा लगता है? _____

8. आपके देश में ठंड का मौसम कब होता है? _____

Now write a short narrative about the weather where you live. From when until when is it hot? When is winter? Does it snow in winter? In which month is spring? Is it humid in summer? Which season (मौसम) do you like?

GRAMMAR

Compound Verbs: Coloring Verbs

Coloring verbs fall under the category of compound verbs. A compound verb is a verbal unit that is made up of two or more verbs. The first verb is the main verb and supplies the meaning. The verb (or verbs) that follows is considered subsidiary. Subsidiary verbs often provide such information as the tense, the mood, the aspect, or a shade of meaning.

> शायद वे लोग अभी चाय पीने को जा रहे हों।
> Perhaps those people may be going to drink tea right now.

In this example, the main verb is जाना *to go*. The subsidiary verbs are रहना *to stay/live* and होना *to be*. These verbs provide information about the aspect (रहना) and the tense or mood (होना). The progressive aspect was covered in Lesson 14.

The compound verbs introduced in this lesson are called coloring verbs. These are secondary verbs that are used with the stem of a main verb. These verbs do not retain their own meaning but add a shade of meaning, often an adverbial sense, to the meaning of the primary verb.

चिल्लाना   अचानक वह लड़की चिल्ला उठी ।
to scream   The girl suddenly screamed.
उठना
to rise

In this example, the coloring verb is उठना. When it is combined with a main verb (चिल्लाना *to scream*) it gives a sense of suddenness. Hence, चिल्ला उठना means *to scream suddenly*.

These are the most important coloring verbs:
1. जाना to go (*v.i.*)
2. लेना to take (*v.t.*)
3. देना to give (*v.t.*)
4. बैठना to sit (*v.i.*)
5. उठना to rise (*v.i.*)
6. पड़ना to fall, lie (*v.i.*)
7. डालना to put, pour, place, throw (*v.t.*)
8. रखना to put, place (*v.t.*)

Of these, the verbs that occur with the greatest frequency are the first three, that is, जाना, लेना and देना.

Using Coloring Verbs

It takes some time to acquire a sense of when to employ coloring verbs and when to avoid their use. At this stage, it is most important to be able to recognize them in the written and spoken forms of the language. There are some guidelines concerning their use that may be helpful.

1. Coloring verbs occur much less frequently in the negative.

2. The context is critical for the use of coloring verbs. Particular coloring verbs are used when there is a prior knowledge of the context on the part of both the speaker and the listener, or an action is undertaken for one's own benefit or the benefit of another person. Some coloring verbs are employed to give a sense of suddenness, or vehemence, or the completion of an action.

3. For the most part, the stem of an intransitive verb is used with an intransitive coloring verb, while a transitive stem is used with a transitive coloring verb.

    हो जाना *to become*, *happen*, *take place* (with a sense of completion)
    intransitive stem with intransitive coloring verb

    दे देना *to give* (for someone else's benefit)
    transitive stem with transitive coloring verb

    However, there are many exceptions to this.

    Now let's take a closer look at the most common coloring verbs.

1. **stem + जाना**

   a) The occurrence of the *stem of an intransitive verb* + जाना is relatively common and should be noted carefully. In most cases it rounds off the statement and gives a sense of completion. It is also used when both the speaker and the listener have a prior understanding of the context. It occurs frequently with the stem of होना.

पहुँचना to arrive	तीन बजे तक यहाँ ज़रूर पहुँच जाइये। Please reach here by three o'clock.
आना to come	नौ बजे मैं उस कोने पर आ जाऊँगी। I (*f*) will come to that corner at nine o'clock.
भूलना to forget	लखनऊ जाकर उसे भूल न जाना। Don't forget him/her when you go to Lucknow.
होना to become	भारत जाकर उस की हिन्दी बहुत अच्छी हो गयी। His/her Hindi became very good when he/she went to India.

   When the stem of the verb रहना is employed with जाना in the negative न/नहीं रह जाना, it gives a sense of total absence.

रहना to live, reside	उसने सोचा कि अब इस देश में मेरा कुछ नहीं रह गया। He/she thought, "Now I have nothing left in this country."

   b) When the *stem of a transitive verb* is employed with जाना, it may indicate a suddenness, a sense of completion and moving off, or even a lack of prior knowledge.

खोलना to open	मैं खिड़की खोल जाऊँ? Shall I open the window?
खाना to eat	वह सब समोसे खा गया। He devoured (ate) all of the samosas.

2. **लेना to take**

   a) The use of the *stem of a transitive verb* + लेना gives a sense of completion of an action for one's own benefit. It also indicates that both the speaker and the listener have a prior knowledge of the context of the discussion.

छूना to touch	प्रेमचंद की कहानियाँ सब का मन छू लेती हैं। Premchand's stories touch everyone's heart.
लड़ना to fight	तुम साथ होते तो मैं किसी से भी लड़ लेता। If you (*m*) were with me then I (*m*) could have taken on anyone.

b) The use of the *stem of an intransitive verb* + लेना is restricted to a few particular verbs such as होना *to be* and मिलना *to meet*. In such cases, it is treated as an intransitive verb and gives a sense of completion. In the combination साथ हो लेना it has a sense of *to accompany*.

होना	मैं उस के साथ हो लिया।
to be	I (*m*) accompanied him/her.

मिलना	कल उनसे मिल लीजिये।
to meet	Please meet with them tomorrow.

3. देना **to give**

a) The occurrence of a transitive verb + देना gives a sense of the undertaking of an action for the benefit of someone else. It also indicates a prior knowledge of the context of the action.

पढ़ाना	इन सब छात्रों को हम हिन्दी पढ़ा देंगे।
to teach	We (*m*) will teach all these students Hindi.

छोड़ना	यह बुरी आदत छोड़ दो।
to abandon	Give up this bad habit.

In this example it is not clear that the action is being undertaken for the benefit of another person:

समझाना	उसे समझा दीजिये कि वह अब यहाँ सिगरेट नहीं पी सकता।
to explain	Please explain to him that he cannot smoke here anymore.

b) When the *stem of a limited number of particular intransitive verbs* + देना occurs it generally denotes spontaneity. The most common verbs used in this way with देना include:

हँसना to laugh
रोना to cry
मुस्कराना to smile
चलना to move

When used with the stem of these verbs देना is treated as intransitive.[1]

रोना	मेरी कहानी सुनकर वह रो दी।
to cry	When she heard my story, she (suddenly) cried.

मुस्कराना	तुम्हारा काम देखकर कविता मुस्करा दी।
to smile	Kavita (suddenly) smiled when she saw your work.

चलना	आज सवेरे क़रीब आठ बजे मैं चल दिया।
to move	I (*m*) set off at approximately eight o'clock this morning.

---

1. If the verb देना is used as a transitive verb with the stem of such verbs as हँसना *to laugh*, रोना *to cry* and मुस्कराना *to smile*, it may contain a sense that the action was done in a forced or contrived manner.

4. **बैठना to sit**

The occurrence of the *stem of either a transitive or intrasitive verb* + बैठना gives a sense of suddenness, force and even an absence of thought. It may also indicate that the action is inappropriate in some manner.

झपटना	काला कुत्ता डाकिये पर झपट बैठा।
to pounce	The black dog suddenly pounced on the postman.
उठना	वह लड़की उठ बैठी।
to rise, get up	That girl suddenly got up.
मारना	ऐसा करोगे तो वह मार बैठेगी।
to beat, kill	If you do this (such) then she will beat/kill you.
पूछना	बच्चे कभी-कभी अजीब सवाल पूछ बैठते हैं।
to ask	Children sometimes suddenly ask strange questions.

5. **उठना to rise**

The occurrence of the *stem of either a transitive or an intransitive verb* + उठना gives a sense of a sudden undertaking. It is often employed with verbs that express emotions or momentum as well as verbs related to sound.

चिल्लाना	बच्चा मिठाई न मिलने पर चिल्ला उठा।
to scream	The child suddenly screamed when he didn't receive a sweet.
चौंकना	आपको देखकर वह ज़रूर चौंक उठेगी।
to be startled	When she sees you she certainly will be startled.
लजाना	दुल्हन शायद लजा उठे।
to be shy	Perhaps the bride may become shy.
झूमना	संगीत सुनकर उसका मन झूम उठा।
to sway	Hearing the music his/her heart began to sway.

6. **पड़ना to fall, lie**

The occurrence of the *stem of an intransitive verb* + पड़ना indicates the suddenness of an action or a chance happening. There is a lack of prior knowledge of the action and it often involves a downward momentum.

लगना	उसे बुरा लग पड़ा।
to seem, appear	He/she suddenly felt bad.
खुलना	उसी समय हवा से पालकी का पर्दा खुल पड़ा।
to open	Right then the curtain of the palanquin suddenly opened with the wind.
आना	तभी वह कमरे में आ पड़ी।
to come	Right then she suddenly entered the room.

7. डालना **to put, pour, place, throw**

The occurrence of the *stem of a transitive verb* + डालना indicates completion with vehemence and within a short time. It may also denote an absence of hesitation and an effort to finish off an action.

लूटना
to rob, steal

लगता है कि डाकू तो सारा गाँव लूट डालेंगे।
It seems that the bandits will rob the entire village.

मारना
to kill, beat

अरे बचाओ! इसने तो मुझे मार डाला।
Hey save (me)! He/she has killed/beaten me.

करना
to do

यह शुभ कार्य तुम्हीं कर डालो।
You do this auspicious task.

पीना
to drink

यह दवा बहुत मीठी है, बच्चा एक साँस में पी डालेगा।
This medicine is very sweet, a child will drink it in one gulp.

8. रखना **to put, place**

The occurrence of a transitive verb + रखना indicates priority or precedence in time.

कहना
to say

मैंने अपने दोस्त से कह रखा है कि हम आज शाम को छै बजे मिलेंगे।
I have said to my friend that we will meet this evening at 6 P.M.

लगाना
to attach

उसने तुम्हारे लिये खाना लगा रखा है।
He/she has put the food out for you.

PRACTICE

Now turn to the Workbook and complete Activity 19.2 before continuing.

It's So Hot! I'm So Thirsty! बहुत गर्मी लग रही है! मुझे बहुत प्यास लगी है!

When talking about feeling hot or cold, the following verbs (introduced in Lesson 18) are ordinarily used:

गर्मी (*f*) लगना to feel heat
ठंड (*f*) लगना to feel cold

Most often they are used in the progressive aspect when you want to say "I'm feeling hot/cold."

मुझे बहुत गर्मी लग रही है। I am feeling very hot. (*much heat is attaching to me*)
मुझे बहुत ठंड लग रही है। I am feeling very cold. (*much cold is attaching to me*)

When talking about feeling hungry or thirsty the following verbs are used:

भूख (*f*) लगना hunger to attach
प्यास (*f*) लगना thirst to attach

It is best to use them in the present perfect when you want to say, "I am hungry/thirsty."

मुझे बहुत भूख लगी है। I am very hungry. (*much hunger has attached itself to me*)
मुझे बहुत प्यास लगी है। I am very thirsty. (*much thirst has attached itself to me*)

Deepak and Kavita try to avoid the heat in Delhi in April.

कविता - दीपक, आज बहुत ज़्यादा गर्मी हो रही है। अब मैं पढ़ भी नहीं सकती। मुझे बहुत प्यास भी लगी है।

दीपक - हाँ, मुझे भी बहुत ज़्यादा गर्मी लग रही है। क्या तापमान होगा?

कविता - मुझे मालूम नहीं। चालीस के आसपास होगा। हम क्या करें? आज तुम्हारे पास गाड़ी है?

दीपक - नहीं, आज मैं मेट्रो से कॉलेज आया हूँ। कहीं ए० सी० में बैठकर खाना खाएँ?

कविता - मुझे भूख बिल्कुल नहीं लगी। गर्मी के दिनों में मुझे भूख नहीं लगती। अगर तुम आज गाड़ी से आये होते तो हम अभी मेरे घर जा सकते।

दीपक - हाँ। तो क्या हम सी० पी० जा कर फ़िल्म देखें? मेट्रो से जा सकते हैं। सिनेमाहाल में ए० सी० भी है।

कविता - वह तो है, लेकिन मेरे पास अभी तीन घंटे नहीं हैं। मुझे इतनी प्यास लगी है कि मैं क्या बताऊँ।

दीपक - मुझे भी बहुत प्यास लगी है। चलो, अभी कैंटीन में कुछ ठंडा पियें और फिर मेट्रो से सी० पी० चलेंगे। वहाँ तय करेंगे कि क्या करें।

कविता - ठीक है।

Glossary

गर्मी heat (f)
प्यास लगाना to feel thirsty (v.i.)
गर्मी लगाना to feel hot (v.i.)
तापमान temperature (m)
चालीस forty
x के आसपास around x
मेट्रो metro (f)

ए॰ सी॰ A.C.
बैठना to sit (v.i.)
भूख लगाना to feel hungry (v.i.)
गर्मी के दिन summer (the days of heat) (m)
बिल्कुल absolutely
सी॰ पी॰ C.P. (Connaught Place)

वह तो है that's true
घंटा hour (m)
ठंडा cold
तय करना to decide, settle (v.t.)
सोचना to think (v.t.)
साल year (m)

Translate the following questions into Hindi. Then ask them of a partner.

1. Does Kavita think that it is very hot today? _____

2. Do Kavita and Deepak feel very thirsty? (has much thirst attached to Deepak and Kavita) _____

3. Does Kavita feel hungry in the summer? _____

4. Do you feel hungry in the summer? _____

5. Does Kavita have three hours to watch a film today? _____

6. Has Deepak come to college by car today? _____

7. If Deepak had come to college by car, where could they have gone? _____

8. Will you go to India during the summer? _____

9. Are you hungry right now? _____

10. Are you feeling hot right now? _____

GRAMMAR

The Comparative/Superlative
The Comparative

Two or more objects are compared in Hindi by employing the postposition से *than, with, by, from.* से governs the noun or pronoun that is the object of the comparison. The adjective of comparison then follows.

वह मुझसे लम्बा है।
He is taller than I.

यह लड़की तुमसे बहुत होशियार है।
This girl is much smarter than you.

मुम्बई दिल्ली से बड़ा शहर है।
Mumbai is a bigger city than Delhi.

मेरा घर तुम्हारे घर से बड़ा है।
My house is bigger than your house.

पुरुष स्त्री से बलवान होता है।
Men are stronger than women. (*man is stronger than woman*)

लड़कियाँ लड़कों से होशियार होती हैं।
Girls are smarter than boys.

In the case of the comparison of ages, the adjectives बड़ा *big* and छोटा *small* are used to express the idea of being *older* and *younger*.

क्या आप की बहन आपसे बड़ी है?
Is your sister older than you?

जी नहीं, वह मुझसे छोटी है।
No, she is younger than I.

The Superlative
The superlative (biggest, tallest, fastest, etc.) is formed by employing the phrase सबसे *from all* and then the adjective.

सबसे बड़ा biggest/oldest (from *all* big/old)
सबसे तेज़ sharpest (from *all*)

भारत में सब से ज़्यादा लोग हिन्दी बोलते हैं।
The greatest number of people (most people) in India speak Hindi.

दुनिया में चीन की आबादी सब से अधिक है।
The population of China is the largest in the world.

एशिया दुनिया का सब से बड़ा महाद्वीप है।
Asia is the largest continent in the world.

इस कमरे में कौन सब से लंबा है?
Who is the tallest in this room?

Other words frequently employed with the comparative and superlative include the following:

काफ़ी enough   काफ़ी बड़ा big enough, quite big
बहुत much   बहुत बड़ा very big
थोड़ा a little   थोड़ा बड़ा a little bigger

थोड़ा बहुत some	थोड़ा बहुत बड़ा somewhat bigger
ज़्यादा much	ज़्यादा बड़ा much bigger*
अधिक much	अधिक बड़ा much bigger*
कम less	कम बड़ा not as big

*Both of these may also be translated simply as *bigger*.

Sanskrit and Persian comparative and superlative suffixes are also encountered occasionally in Hindi. The Sanskrit endings only occur with Sanskrit adjectives, while the Persian endings are only employed with adjectives of Persian origin.

Sanskrit Comparative/Superlative Endings

-तर -er
-तम -est

उच्च high   उच्चतर higher   उच्चतम highest

Persian Comparative/Superlative Endings

-तर -er
तरीन -est

बद bad   बदतर worse   बदतरीन worst

PRACTICE

 Now turn to the Workbook and complete Activities 19.3 and 19.4.

LESSON **20** बीसवाँ पाठ

I Can't Come On Tuesday

I Can't Come on Tuesday मैं मंगल को नहीं आ पाऊँगा

Here Deepak and Kavita discuss going out on Tuesday on the phone.

दीपक	– हाय कविता, मैं दीपक बोल रहा हूँ। क्या हाल है?
कविता	– अरे दीपक, कल तुम कॉलेज क्यों नहीं आये थे?
दीपक	– कल मेरी तबीयत ठीक नहीं थी।
कविता	– अफ़सोस की बात है। आज तुम्हारी तबीयत कैसी है?
दीपक	– अब तो तबीयत ठीक हो गयी है।
कविता	– अच्छी बात है। मंगल को तुम क्या कर रहे हो?
दीपक	– मंगल को किस समय?
कविता	– शाम को। जुही के यहाँ एक पार्टी होगी।
दीपक	– मंगल की शाम को मैं आ नहीं पाऊँगा। मुझे कुछ काम है।
कविता	– पार्टी में चलो, न। बहुत मज़ा आयेगा।
दीपक	– सचमुच मैं जा नहीं पाऊँगा। लेकिन क्या तुम बुध को फ़िल्म देखने जा सकोगी?
कविता	– कौन-सी फ़िल्म?
दीपक	– "माँ, तुझे सलाम"।
कविता	– वह तो मैं देख चुकी हूँ। मुझे इतनी अच्छी नहीं लगी।
दीपक	– फिर भी मैं देखना चाहता हूँ। तो मैं और इमरान जाएँगे। क्या हम कल मिल पाएँगे?
कविता	– ठीक है। अगर तुम जुही की पार्टी में नहीं आ सकोगे तो हम कल मिलेंगे।

Glossary

अरे say, hey
तबीयत health, disposition (*f*)
किस समय at what time (*inter*)
x के यहाँ at x's place
पार्टी party (*f*)

मुझे कुछ काम है । I have work to do.
मज़ा आना (for) enjoyment to
 come, to be enjoyable (*v.i.*)
सचमुच really
कौन-सा which (*inter*)

"माँ, तुझे सलाम"
 "Salaam to you, Mother"
फिर भी nevertheless

Answer the following questions, then ask them of a partner.

1. क्या दीपक जुही के यहाँ जा पाएगा? ....

2. क्या कविता चाहती है कि दीपक पार्टी में आए? ....

3. क्या कविता "माँ तुझे सलाम" देख चुकी है? ....

4. क्या उसे फ़िल्म बहुत अच्छी लगी? ....

5. मंगल की शाम को क्या हो रहा है? ....

6. क्या दीपक और कविता कल मिलेंगे? ....

7. दीपक किस के साथ फ़िल्म देखने जाएगा? ....

8. क्या आप किसी दोस्त के साथ आज रात को फ़िल्म देखना चाहते हैं? (चाहती हैं) ....

GRAMMAR

Expressing Obligation

In Hindi different degrees of obligation (moral, mild, strong) to undertake or not undertake an action are expressed using the infinitive together with one of three verbs:

चाहिये *wanted/needed* (moral obligation)
होना *to be* (mild obligation)
पड़ना *to lie, fall* (strong obligation)

To form expressions of obligation:

1. The logical subject (the person who should, must, ought to perform the action) is governed by को.

2. The verb expressing the action appears in the infinitive form.

3. चाहिये (moral obligation), होना (mild obligation), or पड़ना (strong obligation) is employed with the infinitive.

4. The infinitive is treated as an adjective and thus agrees with the number and gender of a preceding noun or pronoun. होना and पड़ना are also conjugated for the number and gender of a noun or pronoun that preceeds the infinitive.

a) चाहिये (moral obligation)

When चाहिये is used with the infinitive form of a verb the statement may be translated as *should* as in, *you should go home*.

दीपक को जाना चाहिये ।
Deepak should go.

कविता को चाय पीनी चाहिये ।
Kavita should drink tea (*f*).

दीपक को चार समोसे नहीं खाने चाहिये ।
Deepak should not eat four samosas (*m pl*).

कविता को ये पाँच किताबें पढ़नी चाहिये ।
Kavita should read these five books (*f pl*).

To place this in the past, the simple past tense of the verb होना (था, थे, थी, थीं) is employed. This often gives a sense of an action that should have been undertaken but was not.

दीपक को जाना चाहिये था ।
Deepak should have gone.

कविता को चाय पीनी चाहिये थी ।
Kavita should have drunk tea.

दीपक को चार समोसे नहीं खाने चाहिये थे ।
Deepak should not have eaten four samosas.

कविता को ये पाँच किताबें पढ़नी चाहिये थीं ।
Kavita should have read these five books.

मुझे दो घंटे पहले घर जाना चाहिये था ।
I should have gone home two hours ago.

आज तक उसे अपना काम कर लेना चाहिये था ।
He/she should have done his/her work by today.

b) infinitive + होना (mild obligation)

A mild obligation to undertake an action is expressed by employing the infinitive with होना *to be*. This may be translated as *have to*, but it can also be thought of as simply expressing an intention to undertake an action.

मुझे अभी घर जाना है।
I have to go home right now. (I am off home now)

मुझे चाय पीनी है।
I have to drink tea. (I need a cup of tea)

क्या तुम्हें यह किताब पढ़नी है?
Do you have to read this book? (Do you want to read this book?)

कल रात को दस बजे उसे घर जाना था।
Last night at ten P.M. he/she had to go home.

आज शाम को तुम्हें वहाँ जाकर उससे बात करनी होगी।
You will have to go there this evening and talk to him/her.

आजकल गुरुवार के दिन शिक्षक को क्लास के लिये जल्दी जाना होता है।
These days the teacher has to leave early for class on Thursdays.

अगर मुझे रोज़ एक फ़िल्म देखनी होती तो मैं पागल हो जाता।
If I had to watch a film every day, I would go crazy.

c) infinitive + **पड़ना** *to fall, lie* (strong obligation)

In cases where the infinitive is used with **पड़ना** *to fall, lie* it conveys a strong obligation to undertake an action, perhaps with a sense of reluctance as well as an external compulsion. It may be translated into English as *must* or *have to*. It should not be confused with the presumptive (see p. 161).

गर्मी के दिनों में शायद मुझे अमरीका में रहना पड़े।
Perhaps I will have to remain in America in the summer.

अपनी किताब छपवाने के बाद रुशदी को छुपना पड़ा।
After publishing his book Rushdie had to hide.

अगले हफ़्ते मुझे किराया देना पड़ेगा।
Next week I must pay my rent.

To express the strongest sense of obligation in the immediate future, the future form of **पड़ना** is employed.

मुझे अभी घर जाना ही पड़ेगा।
I just must go home right now.

The use of the imperfect present indicates a strong obligation as a habit in the present.

हर छै तारीख़ को उसे किराया देना पड़ता है।
On the sixth of every month he/she must pay his/her rent.

Some Further Aspects of Obligation

1. In expressions such as *I have to give him money*, both the logical subject and the indirect object are governed by को. In such circumstances, there is the possibility of an ambiguity arising over what is the logical subject.

> मुझे आपको दस डॉलर देने हैं।
> I have to give you ten dollars.
> or, You have to give me ten dollars.

Often context will clarify such an ambiguity. In colloquial speech some speakers employ ने in place of को with the logical subject to further clarify this.

> मैंने आपको दस डॉलर देने हैं।
> I have to give you ten dollars.

2. Occasionally, when the logical subject does not denote a particular animate being, it is not governed by को. This is often the case when the verbs होना and रहना are employed.

> भारत में ऐसी स्थिति नहीं होनी चाहिये।
> Such a situation shouldn't occur in India.

> उस खाते में इतने पैसे रहने चाहिये।
> This much money should remain in that account.

PRACTICE

Now turn to the Workbook and complete Activity 20.1 before continuing.

Kavita Is Smarter Than I Am कविता मुझसे होशियार है
Here Deepak talks about Kavita.

कविता बहुत अच्छी लड़की है। वह मुझसे होशियार है, इसमें कोई शक नहीं है। उसे हमेशा इम्तहान में बहुत अच्छे नम्बर मिलते हैं। वह मुझसे पढ़ाई में बहुत ज़्यादा मेहनत भी करती है। हो सकता है कि हमारे दोस्तों में से कविता सबसे होशियार छात्र हो। इमरान भी बहुत होशियार है। लेकिन मेरे ख़्याल में कविता सबसे मेहनती और होशियार है। इमरान सबसे बड़ा है और जुही सबसे छोटी है, उम्र में। लेकिन मैं इमरान से लंबा हूँ। दुनिया के बारे में कविता को सबसे ज़्यादा मालूम है। इमरान को भी बहुत मालूम है क्यों कि वह अमरीका जा चुका है। उन्हें कम से कम दुनिया के बारे में मुझसे ज़्यादा मालूम है। लेकिन मुझे इलाहाबाद के बारे में उनसे ज़्यादा मालूम है। हो सकता है कि हम लोगों में से जुही के पास सबसे ज़्यादा पैसे हों, लेकिन मुझे ठीक से मालूम नहीं क्योंकि हम दोस्त इस बारे में कभी बात नहीं करते। जुही के माँ-बाप के पास बहुत पैसे होंगे। पिछले साल उन्होंने जुही को एक नयी गाड़ी दी थी।

Glossary

होशियार smart, intelligent

इसमें कोई शक नहीं है।
  There is no doubt about (in) this.

इम्तहान examination (*m*)

नम्बर grade, mark, number (*m*)

मेहनत करना to work hard (*v.t.*)

हो सकता है (it) could be,
  is possible

मेरे ख़्याल में in my opinion

मेहनती hardworking,
  industrious

बड़ा big, old

छोटा small, young

उम्र में in age

लंबा tall

मालूम होना to be known (*v.i.*)

ठीक से properly,
  correctly, accurately

इस बारे में about this

बात करना to talk (*v.t.*)

दुनिया के बारे में
  about the world

Provide questions for the following statements.

1. _____ दीपक के ख़्याल में कविता उससे होशियार है। [use कौन]

2. _____ जी हाँ, उम्र में जुही सब से छोटी है। [use क्या]

3. _____ दीपक को इलाहाबाद के बारे में सब से ज़्यादा मालूम है।
   [use कौन]

4. _____ इमरान अमरीका जा चुका है। [use कहाँ]

5. _____ कविता को दुनिया के बारे में सबसे ज़्यादा मालूम है। [use
   किसके बारे में]

6. _____ इमरान सबसे लंबा है। [use कौन]

7. _____ जी नहीं दीपक कविता से ज़्यादा मेहनती नहीं है। [use
   क्या]

8. _____ जी हाँ, पिछले साल उन्होंने जुही को एक नयी गाड़ी दी
   थी। [use क्या, जुही के माँ-बाप]

GRAMMAR

Uses of वाला and को

वाला is a very commonly employed suffix that may be attached to nouns, pronouns, adjectives, adverbs and the infinitive form of verbs. When वाला is attached to nouns, pronouns and adverbs, it singles one thing out from many things. When it is attached to the infinitive form of a verb, it may either denote a person who performs the action of the verb or indicate that the action is about to take place. Words formed by attaching वाला are considered adjectival in nature. In the written language वाला may be attached to the word it follows or written separately.

Use of वाला

1. With nouns and infinitives

   When वाला is used with nouns and infinitives, these are placed in the oblique.

   कमरेवाला *the matter/person connected to the room*
   कमरोंवाला *the matter/person connected to the rooms*
   करनेवाला *the person who does/is about to do*

2. With adjectives and the demonstrative pronouns

   Adjectives and demonstrative pronouns remain in the direct case when followed by वाला, unless the resultant adjective is governed by a postposition.

   > छोटा वाला *the small one*
   > यह वाला *this one*
   > छोटे वाले कमरे में *in the small room* (as opposed to some other room)
   > इस वाले कमरे में *in this room* (as opposed to some other room)

   > नीली वाली किताब मुझे दे दो।
   > Give me the blue book.

   > नीचे वाला फ़्लैट उसको बहुत पसंद आया।
   > He/she really liked the apartment below.

   > शराब पीनेवाले आदमी को भूख नहीं लगती।
   > The man who drinks alcohol doesn't feel hungry.

   > वह लाहौर की रहनेवाली है।
   > She is a resident of Lahore. (*she is Lahore's liver*)

   > वह वाली फ़िल्म मुझे काफ़ी अच्छी लगी।
   > I liked that film quite a lot.

3. With infinitive forms of verbs

   When वाला is employed with the infinitive form of a verb, it may indicate someone who undertakes a particular action, or may indicate that someone is about to undertake an action.

   > वह चाय बनानेवाला है।
   > He is about to make tea.
   > He is a/the tea maker.

   > मेरी माँ चाय पीनेवाली हैं।
   > My mother is about to drink tea.
   > My mother is a tea drinker.

ये लोग हिन्दी सीखनेवाले हैं।
These people are about to learn Hindi.
These people are students of Hindi.

In most cases there is no ambiguity.

ऐसा लगता है कि बारिश होनेवाली है।
It seems that it is about to rain.

भारत के प्रधानमंत्री अमरीका आनेवाले हैं।
India's Prime Minister is about to come to the U.S.

मैं अभी विश्वविद्यालय जानेवाली हूँ।
I (*f*) am about to go to university.

4. The idea that an action is about to take place may also be expressed through the use of the oblique infinitive of the verb + को.

ऐसा लगता है कि बारिश होने को है।
It seems that it is about to rain.

भारत के प्रधानमंत्री अमरीका आने को हैं।
India's Prime Minister is about to come to the U.S.

मैं अभी विश्वविद्यालय जाने को हूँ।
I am about to go to university.

PRACTICE

Now turn to the Workbook and complete Activities 20.2 and 20.3 before continuing.

How Long Does It Take You to Get Home from College?
कॉलेज से घर जाने में कितनी देर लगती है?

Here Kavita asks Deepak how long it takes him to get home from college.

कविता - दीपक, गाड़ी से कॉलेज से घर जाने में तुम्हें कितनी देर लगती है?

दीपक - अक्सर मुझे जाने में बहुत देर लगती है। पुरानी दिल्ली में बहुत भीड़ रहती है। सुबह से शाम को ज़्यादा देर लगती है। क्यों?

कविता - अभी कितनी देर लगेगी? मुझे जल्दी घर जाना है। अगर मैं मेट्रो से जाऊँ तो कम से कम एक घंटा लगेगा।

दीपक - इस वक़्त गाड़ी से जाने में शायद इससे कम समय लगे। बस से जाने में सबसे ज़्यादा वक़्त लगेगा। शायद तुम्हें गाड़ी से ही जाना चाहिये। अभी घर क्यों जाना है?

कविता - पिता जी ने अभी फ़ोन किया है। उन्हें आज रात को मुम्बई हवाई जहाज़ से जाना पड़ेगा। उन्होंने कहा कि जाने से पहले उन्हें मुझसे एक बात करनी है।

दीपक - अच्छा, हवाई जहाज़ से मुम्बई जाने में कितने घंटे लगते हैं?

कविता - मुझे ठीक से पता नहीं लेकिन मैं सोचती हूँ कि शायद दो घंटे लगते हों।

दीपक - ठीक है। चलो, अगर इतनी जल्दी पहुँचना हो तो मैं तुमको गाड़ी से छोड़ दूँगा। शायद कम समय लगेगा क्योंकि स्टेशन से तुम्हें ऑटो से भी जाना पड़ेगा, न?

कविता - शुक्रिया दीपक।

Glossary

देर लगना to take time (delay) (*v.i.*)	घंटा hour (*m*)	छोड़ देना to leave,
अक्सर often	हवाई जहाज़ airplane (*m*)	abandon, to drop (*v.t.*)
भीड़ crowd (*f*)	ठीक से properly	शुक्रिया thank you
जल्दी quickly	पता होना to be known (*v.i.*)	
कम से कम at least	पहुँचना to arrive (*v.i.*)	

Translate the following questions into Hindi and then answer them or ask a partner.

1. Does it take Deepak a long time (much delay) to go home from college? _____

2. How long does it take you to go to the office/college/school*? _____
   *Choose the most appropriate destination for you.

3. Does Kavita have to go home quickly right now? _____

4. How many hours does it take to go from America to India by plane? _____

5. Who must go to Mumbai tonight? _____

6. Should Kavita go home by the metro or by car? _____

7. Will it take Kavita longest to go home by bus? _____

8. Does it take you longer (much delay) to go home by bus or train? _____

9. Will Deepak drop (छोड़ देना) Kavita at home? _____

LESSON 21 इक्कीसवाँ पाठ

Forgive Me, I Was Delayed

Forgive Me, I Was Delayed माफ़ कीजिये, मुझे देर हुई

When asking forgiveness, the verb माफ़ करना *to forgive* is ordinarily employed. When attracting someone's attention, the verb सुनना *to listen* should be used.

माफ़ करना
to forgive

मुझे माफ़ कीजिये। मुझसे ग़लती हुई।
Please forgive me. I made a mistake. (*by me a mistake occurred*)

सुनना
to listen, hear

भाई साहब, सुनिये। क्या आपको मालूम है कि लाल क़िला कहाँ है?
Excuse me (please listen), Sir. Do you know where the Red Fort is?

Here Kavita apologizes for being late to meet Deepak at Lodi Gardens.

कविता - हाय दीपक। माफ़ करो, मुझे आने में देर हुई।

दीपक - हाय कविता। क्या हुआ? आधे घंटे की देर हुई। मैं जानेवाला ही था।

कविता - मैं आ रही थी। फिर याद आया कि मुझे ख़ान मार्केट में पिता जी का एक काम करना था। मैंने सोचा था कि वह पाँच मिनट का काम होगा। काम करने में बहुत देर लग गयी।

दीपक - तुम फ़ोन तो कर सकती थीं, मुझे।

कविता - मैं तुम्हें फ़ोन करने ही वाली थी लेकिन मैंने देखा कि मेरा फ़ोन मर गया था।

दीपक - हाँ, मैंने भी तुम्हें फ़ोन करने की कोशिश की। मैं पाँच मिनट और तुम्हारा इंतज़ार करनेवाला था। अगर तुम नहीं आतीं तो मैं घर जाता।

कविता - चलो, मैं तुम्हें ख़ान मार्केट में बरिस्ता में चाय पिलाऊँगी। आज बाहर बहुत गर्मी लग रही है।

दीपक - हाँ, लेकिन हम ऑटो से चलेंगे। मैं ऑटोवाले को बुलाता हूँ।

कविता - दीपक, ऑटोवाले इतनी कम दूर नहीं जाएँगे। हमको पैदल जाना पड़ेगा।

Glossary

माफ़ करना to forgive (*v.t.*)
(x को) देर होना delay, to happen (to x) (*v.i.*), to be delayed
(x को) याद आना x to remember (*v.i.*)
(x को) देर लगना delay to, attach (to x), to take time (*v.i.*)

मर जाना to die (*v.i.*)
और more, and
x का इंतज़ार करना to wait for x (*v.t.*)
बरिस्टा Barista (a chain of coffee shops)
ऑटो auto (three-wheeled transportation) (*m*)

इतनी कम दूर such a little distance
पैदल जाना to walk (*v.i.*)
क्योंकि because
बाद after

Translate the following questions into Hindi and then answer them or ask a partner.

1. आज किसको देर हुई है? _____

2. कविता को कितनी देर हुई है? _____

3. दीपक कितनी देर और इंतज़ार करनेवाला था? _____

4. कविता ने दीपक को फ़ोन क्यों नहीं किया? _____

5. आज कॉलेज/दफ़्तर आने में क्या आपको देर हुई? _____

6. पाँच मिनट बाद दीपक क्या करनेवाला था? _____

7. अगर कविता नहीं आती तो दीपक क्या करता? _____

GRAMMAR

The Passive Voice

The passive voice is used when the focus of the sentence is the logical object of the action rather than the logical subject. The logical subject is often left unexpressed and the verb shows agreement for the gender and number of the logical object, unless it is governed by a postposition.

The government passed a bill in parliament. (active voice)
A bill was passed in parliament. (passive voice)

The passive is formed from the perfect participle of a transitive verb together with the verb जाना *to go*.

खाना to eat	उसने दो समोसे खाये। He/she ate two samosas. (active voice) दो समोसे खाये गये। Two samosas were eaten. (passive voice)	
पीना to drink	मेरी माँ यहाँ चाय पियेगी। My mother will drink tea here. (active voice) यहाँ चाय पी जाएगी। Tea will be drunk here. (passive voice)	

The passive voice may be employed with the majority of verbal forms.

यह काम उस दफ़्तर में किया जाता है । (imperfect present tense)
This work is done in that office.

यह काम उस दफ़्तर में किया जाता था । (habitual past tense)
This work used to be done in that office.

यह काम पूरा किया गया (है/था) । (perfective tense)
This work was (has/had been) completed.

कल तक यह काम पूरा किया जाएगा । (future tense)
This work will be completed by tomorrow.

शायद कल तक यह काम पूरा किया जाये । (optative)
Perhaps this work will (may) be completed by tomorrow.

कल तक इस काम को पूरा किया जाए । (optative)
This work should be completed by tomorrow.

यह काम कल पूरा किया गया होगा । (presumptive)
This work must have been completed yesterday.

शायद कल तक यह काम पूरा किया गया हो । (potential)
Perhaps this work was completed yesterday.

शायद कल यह काम पूरा किया जा सके । (optative, compound verb)
Perhaps this work may possibly be completed by tomorrow.

कल तक यह काम पूरा किया जाना चाहिये था । (moral obligation)
This work should have been completed by yesterday.

यह काम कल पूरा कर दिया गया । (coloring verb)
This work was done yesterday.

If the logical subject of the action is mentioned, it is governed either by the postposition के द्वारा *by the agency of*, or by the phrase के हाथ/हाथों *by the hand/s of*. (Some people also employ से *by*.)

लिखना	यह कहानी प्रेमचंद के द्वारा लिखी गयी ।
to write	This story was written by Premchand.

मारना	बहादुर बादशाह अंग्रेज़ों के हाथों मारे गये ।
to kill	The brave king was killed by (the hand of) the British.

The Use of को with the Logical Object in the Passive Voice

You will recall that when the logical direct object of an action is animate and denotes a particular being (see p. 65), it is governed by the postposition को.

मारना	हमारी फ़ौज ने शत्रु को मार डाला।
to kill, strike	Our army killed the enemy. (active voice)

Because the logical object is the focus of the sentence in the passive, it does not have to be governed by को.

शत्रु मार डाला गया।
The enemy was killed. (passive voice)

However, को may still be employed with the logical object in the passive voice. If the logical direct object is a particular being and is perhaps an unwilling participant in the action, it may be governed by को.

कोई औरत बुलायी गयी है।
Some woman has been called.

आप की माँ को बुलाया गया है।
Your mother has been called.

मैं हिन्दी सीखने के लिये भारत भेजी गयी हूँ।
I (*f*) have been sent to India to study Hindi.

मुझे हिन्दी सीखने के लिये भारत भेजा गया है।
I have been sent to India to study Hindi. (perhaps unwillingly)

If the verb takes two objects (for example, देना *to give*), the indirect object is still governed by को in the passive voice.

इन्हें दो किताबें दी जाएँ।
She/he/they should be given two books.

उसको पाँच संतरे बेचे गये।
He/she was sold five oranges.

The intransitive verbs ले (कर) जाना *to take away* and लाना *to bring* may also be used in the passive voice. In the case of ले जाना the perfect participle of जाना is exceptional in its form.

perfect participle of जाना —	गया, गए/गये, गई/गयी, गईं/गयीं
perfect participle of जाना in the passive voice —	जाया, जाए/जाये, जाई/जायी

तुम्हारी किताब यहाँ से ले जायी गयी होगी।
Your book must have been taken away from here.

There exist in Hindi some verbs that are considered *naturally passive*. That is to say, there is no need to use the passive voice with them. Below is a list of some of these verbs.

Naturally Passive		**Active**	
बनना	*to be made*	बनाना	*to make*
कटना	*to be cut*	काटना	*to cut*
खुलना	*to be opened*	खोलना	*to open*
बँधना	*to be tied*	बाँधना	*to tie*
टूटना	*to break (be broken)*	तोड़ना	*to break*

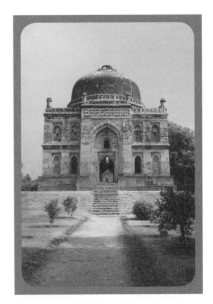

यह दरवाज़ा अपने-आप खुलता है ।
This door opens by itself. (naturally passive)

गाड़ियाँ इस शहर में बनती थीं ।
Cars used to be made in this city. (naturally passive)

गाड़ियाँ इस शहर में बनायी जाती थीं ।
Cars used to be made in this city. (passive voice)

PRACTICE

📖 *Now turn to the Workbook and complete Activity 21.1 before continuing.*

GRAMMAR

The Passive of Inability

There is another important application of the passive voice. When the passive voice is used in the *negative*, it may convey the sense of an *inability to perform an action*. This is sometimes called the feasibility construction. In such cases, the logical subject is often mentioned and governed by the postposition से.

यह काम मुझसे किया नहीं गया ।
I couldn't do this work. (*this work was not done by me*)

This could also be expressed using सकना *to be able to* or पाना *to be able to* with the stem of the verb (see p. 184).

मैं यह काम नहीं कर पाया ।
I (*m*) couldn't do this work.

The passive of inability may also be used with intransitive verbs.

आज सुबह मुझसे उठा नहीं गया ।
I could not get up this morning. (*today by me [it] was not risen*)

उस की हालत मुझसे देखी नहीं जा रही थी।

I couldn't bear to see his/her condition.*

> * When employed in the passive of inability the verb देखना *to see, watch* quite often has the sense of inability to look at something/someone because of a feeling of unpleasantness or pity.

इतनी ठंडी चाय मेरे प्रियतम से पी नहीं जाएगी।

My beloved (*m*) won't be able to drink such cold tea.

कल रात चिन्ता के मारे माँ से सोया नहीं गया।

Last night my mom couldn't get to sleep because she was worried.

PRACTICE

📖 *Now turn to the Workbook and complete Activities 21.2 and 21.3.*

I Think That ...   मैं सोचता हूँ कि ...

In Hindi there are several ways to express your opinion on any particular matter involving either the verb सोचना *to think* or the nouns विचार/ख़्याल (*m*) *thought, idea, opinion.*

मैं सोचता हूँ कि ... I (*m*) think that…
मेरे ख़्याल में ... In my opinion/thought…
मेरे विचार में ... In my opinion/thought…
मेरा ख़्याल यह है कि ... It is my opinion/thought that…

When asking someone else's view, the following common expression may be used:
(इस मामले में) आपका क्या विचार/ख़्याल है? What do you think (about this matter)?

💿 Here Kavita and Deepak discuss what Vrinda should do after school.

दीपक - कविता, तुमने नहीं बताया कि वृन्दा से तुम्हारी क्या बात हुई?

कविता - ओह, कल मैं तुमसे बात करने को ही थी लेकिन फिर मैं भूल गयी।

दीपक - तो क्या बात हुई?

कविता - वृन्दा स्कूल पूरा होने के बाद दिल्ली आना चाहती है। मेरे ख़्याल में अच्छा होगा अगर तुम्हारे माँ-बाप उसे आने दें।

दीपक - तुम ऐसा क्यों सोचती हो?

कविता - वृंदा सोचती है कि इलाहाबाद में उस के लिये कुछ नहीं रखा है। मेरे ख़्याल में उसकी यह बात बिल्कुल सच है।

दीपक - वह तो है, पर अगर वह दिल्ली आये तो माँ-बाप अकेले हो जाएँगे।

कविता - मैं यह समझती हूँ, लेकिन उन्होंने तुमको दिल्ली आने दिया था, न? और तुम्हारा भाई भी यहाँ आकर नौकरी कर रहा है।

दीपक - तो तुम्हारा क्या ख़्याल है? क्या मुझे माँ-बाप से इस मामले में बात करनी चाहिये?

कविता - मैं ऐसा सोचती हूँ। दिल्ली में वृन्दा को ज़्यादा मौक़े मिलेंगे। और अगर वह डॉक्टर न भी बने तो कम से कम उसे कुछ और करने का मौक़ा मिलेगा। यही मेरा विचार है।

दीपक - ठीक है, मैं आज रात को उन्हें फ़ोन कर के बात करूँगा।

Glossary

ओह Oh!

फिर then

भूल जाना to forget (*v.i.*)

पूरा complete

ख़्याल idea, thought, opinion (*m*)

कुछ नहीं रखा है। nothing is left (placed)

सच true

वह तो है that's so, true

अकेला alone

समझना to understand (*v.i. + v.t.*)

इस मामले में about (in) this matter

मामला matter, issue (*m*)

मौक़ा opportunity (*m*)

मिलना to receive, to obtain (*v.i.*)

विचार idea, thought, opinion (*m*)

x से बात करना to talk to x (*v.t.*)

Translate the following questions. Answer them, and then ask them of a partner.

1. Do you think that Vrinda should remain in Allahabad? _____

2. Is it your thought/opinion that Vrinda should come to Delhi and study? (having come to Delhi)

3. Did Deepak's parents allow Deepak to come to Delhi? _____

4. Should Deepak's parents allow Vrinda to come to Delhi? _____

5. In your opinion are more opportunities available (मिलना) in Delhi than Allahabad?

6. Do you think that Deepak should talk to his parents? _____

LESSON **22** बाईसवाँ पाठ

Do You Know Urdu?

Do You Know Urdu? क्या आपको उर्दू आती है?

When discussing a knowledge of languages and other things, it is always best to be modest about your abilities. For this reason, the adjective थोड़ा *a little*, *some*, *meager* is often used and occasionally reduplicated (थोड़ा-थोड़ा).

> क्या आपको हिन्दी आती है? Do you know Hindi?
> जी हाँ, मुझे थोड़ी-थोड़ी हिन्दी आती है। Yes, I know a little Hindi.

Here Kavita, Deepak and Imran discuss the languages they know.

कविता – इमरान, क्या मैं तुमसे कुछ पूछूँ?

इमरान – ज़रूर कविता। तुम्हें क्या पूछना है?

कविता – क्या तुम्हें उर्दू आती है?

इमरान – हाँ, मुझे थोड़ी उर्दू आती है। क्यों?

दीपक – हिन्दी और उर्दू में क्या फ़र्क़ है, इमरान?

इमरान – यह बहुत मुश्किल सवाल है, दीपक।

कविता – दीपक, इमरान को बोलने दो। इमरान, मुझे उर्दू पढ़ना सिखा दो।

इमरान - मुझे उर्दू पढ़ना तो आता है, लेकिन लिखना मुझे बहुत अच्छी तरह नहीं आता। तुमको उर्दू क्यों सीखनी है?

कविता - अलग-अलग भाषाएँ सीखने का शौक़ है मुझे। मुझे थोड़ी अंग्रेजी आती है, और अब मैं उर्दू भी सीखना चाहती हूँ।

इमरान - उर्दू इतनी मुश्किल ज़बान नहीं है। और उर्दू हिन्दी के बहुत क़रीब है। लेकिन लिखना थोड़ा मुश्किल है।

दीपक - तो इमरान, क्या सिर्फ़ उनकी लिपियों में फ़र्क़ है? या दोनों के बीच में इससे ज़्यादा फ़र्क़ है?

इमरान - लिपियों में फ़र्क़ तो है। हिन्दी देवनागरी में लिखी जाती है और उर्दू नस्तालिक़ में लिखी जाती है। लेकिन कुछ शब्द भी अलग होते हैं।

Glossary

ज़रूर certainly
उर्दू Urdu (a language predominantly used in the north of the subcontinent) (f)
थोड़ा a little
फ़र्क़ difference (m)
मुश्किल difficult

अच्छी तरह well, in a good manner
अलग-अलग different, separate
भाषा language (f)
x को y का शौक़ होना x to have the interest/hobby of y (v.i.)
ज़बान language (f)
x के क़रीब close to x

लिपि script (f)
x के बीच में between x
देवनागरी Devanagari (Hindi script) (f)
नस्तालिक़ Nastaliq (Urdu script) (f)
शब्द word (m)

Answer the following questions. Then ask them of a partner.

1. क्या इमरान को उर्दू आती है?

2. क्या आपको हिन्दी आती है?

3. क्या इमरान को उर्दू लिखना आता है?

4. क्या आपको हिन्दी लिखना आता है?

5. क्या कविता को भाषा सीखने का शौक़ है?

6. क्या आपको ज़बान सीखने का शौक़ है?

7. आपको कितनी हिन्दी आती है?

8. क्या आपको हिन्दी लिखना अच्छी तरह आता है?

GRAMMAR

Compound Verbs

In Lesson 19 compound verbs involving the stem and a coloring verb were introduced (see p. 188). In such compounds the secondary verb adds a shade of meaning to the principal meaning of the stem. In this chapter compound verbs are introduced in which the principal verb occurs in the imperfect participle (see p. 66) or perfect participle (see p. 96) together with particular secondary verbs. Such compounds express the continuity of an action either as a habit or a state.

In this chapter the following combinations of verbs are introduced.
1. Imperfect/Perfect Participle + रहना *to stay, live*
2. Imperfect/Perfect Participle + जाना *to go*
3. Perfect Participle + करना *to do*
4. Imperfect Participle + आना *to come*
5. Imperfect Participle + बनना *to be made*

1. **Imperfect/Perfect Participle + रहना *to stay, live***

    The use of रहना *to stay, to live* with imperfect and perfect participles expresses the continuation of an action as a state. Both verbs show agreement in the *number* and *gender* of the subject. In cases where the principal verb occurs in the imperfect participle, the action is incomplete.

पढ़ना   पढ़ता
to read   *reading* (imperfect participle)

वह पढ़ती रहती है।
She keeps on reading.

मेरी बहन दिन-भर पढ़ती रहती है।
My sister reads all day. (continues to read)

तुम अपना काम करते रहो।
You (*m*) continue doing your work.

वह लड़का इस बारे में सोचता रहा।
That boy continued to think about this.

तालिबे इल्म रात को बारह बजे तक अपनी पढ़ाई करता रहा।
The student continued to study until twelve o'clock at night.

When the principal verb occurs in the perfect participle, the action is complete but the state is ongoing.

उनकी दोस्ती हमेशा के लिये बनी रहेगी।
They will remain friends forever. (*their friendship will remain made forever*)

इतवार को दिन-भर मैं सोया रहा।
I (*m*) slept the entire day Sunday.
  (*I remained asleep all day Sunday*)

मेरे फ़्लैट में फ़र्श पर मेरी सब किताबें पड़ी रहती हैं।
All my books are always lying on the floor of
  my apartment.

PRACTICE

📖 *Now turn to the Workbook and complete Activities 22.1 and 22.2, employing the compound verb* रहना *to live, stay* to give a sense of the continuity of a state*.

GRAMMAR

2. **Imperfect/Perfect Participle +** जाना *to go*
   When the imperfect participle of the principal verb occurs with the verb जाना *to go*, it gives a sense of the continuation of an action with a fluctuation in the degree (either increasing or decreasing).

बढ़ना
to increase

भारत की जनसंख्या बढ़ती ही जा रही है।
India's population just keeps on growing.

उतरना
to descend, go down

उसका बुख़ार धीरे-धीरे उतरता जा रहा है।
His/her fever is slowly subsiding.

मैं पागल होता जा रहा हूँ।
I am going crazy. (*continuing to go crazy*)

The perfect participle is combined with जाना to give several meanings. It is either combined with the perfect participle of intransitive verbs (i.e., सोया *slept*) or the oblique perfect participle of both transitive and intransitive verbs (i.e., सोए *slept*, देखे *saw*).

a) The perfect participle of intransitive verbs + जाना *to go*
   When the perfect participle of an intransitive verb is combined with जाना *to go* it gives a sense of *going to* or *about to*.

फटना
to burst

मेरा सिर दर्द से फटा जा रहा है।
My head is going to burst from pain.

उमड़ना
to overflow

उस के मन में प्रेम का सागर उमड़ा जा रहा था।
An ocean of love was surging in his/her heart.

चलना
to move

हम सूर्योदय से पहले चले गये।
We set off before dawn.*

* The verb चला जाना is extremely common and should be noted carefully. It literally means *to go away* and combines the two verbs चलना and जाना. This combination *never* has a passive sense.

b) The oblique perfect participle of transitive and intransitive verbs + जाना *to go*

When the oblique form of the perfect participle is combined with जाना *to go* it most often denotes *continuity*, or the *imminent completion* of an action.

बोलना to speak	वह आदमी बोले जाता है। That man speaks incessantly.
लिखना to write	लेखक सरकार के ख़िलाफ़ लेख लिखे जा रहा था। The writer was writing articles against the government.
करना to do	अपना काम किए जाओ। Continue to do your (own) work.
ख़त्म होना to finish	दुकान में संतरे ख़त्म हुए जा रहे हैं। In the shop the oranges are almost gone. (*in the shop the oranges are about to be finished*)

Take care not to confuse this with the passive voice (see p. 209).

The following chart will help you to distinguish the two forms.

Passive Voice	**Oblique perfect participle + जाना**
the principal verb is transitive (it can be intransitive in passive of inability)	principal verb may be *either* transitive *or* intransitive
principal verb and जाना show agreement	the two verbs do not necessarily show agreement
the logical subject *ordinarily* is not mentioned	the logical subject is mentioned

3. **Perfect Participle + करना** *to do*

The perfect participle is employed with करना *to do* to express the undertaking of an action as a habit. Importantly, the perfect participle occurs in the masculine singular form. करना is conjugated for the *number, gender* and *person* of the subject.

करना to do	अपना काम किया करो। Do your work. (as a habit)
पढ़ाई करना to do study	रोज़ कम से कम दो घंटे हिन्दी की पढ़ाई किया करो। Study Hindi for at least two hours every day.
पढ़ना to read	वह लड़की अखबार पढ़ा करती है। That girl reads the newspaper. (as a habit)

आना | हमारे यहाँ आया कीजिये।
to come | Please come to our place. (regularly)

होना | उस कोने पर एक दुकान हुआ करती थी।
to be | There used to be a shop on that corner.

The verb जाना *to go* takes an exceptional form (जाया) when used as the principal verb with करना.

हम हर साल हिन्दुस्तान जाया करते हैं।
We go to India every year. (as a habit)

पिछले साल हर हफ़्ते तुम अजायबघर जाया करती थीं।
Last year you (*f*) used to go to the museum every week. (as a habit)

PRACTICE

📖 *Now turn to the Workbook and complete Activity 22.3, employing the compound verb* करना *to do to indicate that the action takes place as a habit.*

GRAMMAR

4. **Imperfect Participle +** आना *to come*
   When an imperfect participle is employed with the verb आना *to come* it denotes the continuation of an action as a state from some time in the past into the present and perhaps into the future.

   मेरा परिवार इस गाँव में पीढ़ियों से रहता आया है।
   My family has lived in this village for generations.

5. **Imperfect Participle +** बनना *to be made*
   When an imperfect participle is employed in the masculine plural with बनना *to be made*, it denotes the capacity to undertake an action. It is generally used in negative expressions, where the logical subject is governed by the postposition से.

   आज मुझसे विश्वविद्यालय जाते नहीं बना।
   Today I couldn't bring myself to go to university.

   Expressions involving the imperfect participle + आना and बनना are less frequently encountered than the other combinations described in this lesson.

PRACTICE

📖 *Now turn to the Workbook and complete Activity 22.4.*

I Can't Tell You How Tired I Am मैं इतना थक गया कि मैं क्या बताऊँ

Kavita and Deepak are sitting in Deepak's uncle's home in Delhi when Deepak's brother, Sanjeev, comes in.

कविता	—	नमस्ते संजीव, बहुत दिनों से आपसे मुलाक़ात नहीं हुई। आप कैसे हैं?
संजीव	—	हाय कविता। हाँ, मुझे बहुत काम करना पड़ता है। रोज़ मैं रात को बहुत देर से घर आया करता हूँ। दिन भर मैं काम करता रहता हूँ। और मेरा दफ़्तर यहाँ से बहुत दूर भी है।
कविता	—	तो आपको कभी छुट्टी नहीं मिलती?
संजीव	—	बहुत कम। रोज़ घर आने तक मैं इतना थक जाता हूँ कि मैं क्या बताऊँ। वीकेंड तक मुझे इतनी थकान हो जाती है कि मुझसे उठा भी नहीं जाता।
कविता	—	आप रात को कितने बजे घर पहुँचते हैं?
संजीव	—	कभी बारह बजे, कभी डेढ़ बजे रात को। दिन भर नींद लगी रहती है। एक दिन मेज़ पर भी मुझे नींद आ गयी।
कविता	—	संजीव, यह तो कोई ज़िंदगी नहीं है। मौज-मस्ती करने का मौक़ा भी चाहिये।
संजीव	—	हाँ, लेकिन दो महीने बाद मेरी नयी नौकरी लग जाएगी। शायद तब थोड़ा आराम मिलेगा।
कविता	—	तो आप काम करते रहते हैं और दीपक और मैं सिर्फ़ मज़े करते रहते हैं।
दीपक	—	यह तो सच नहीं है, कविता। तुम तो पढ़ाई करती रहती हो।
कविता	—	लेकिन मुझे ऐसा लगता है कि संजीव की ज़िंदगी हमारी ज़िंदगी से बहुत ज़्यादा मुश्किल है।
संजीव	—	शायद, लेकिन ऐसी नौकरी के लिये आजकल बहुत अच्छी तनख़्वाह भी मिलने लगी है। और तुम तो डॉक्टर बनने ही वाली हो। डॉक्टर बन जाने पर तुम्हें आटे दाल का भाव मालूम होगा।

Glossary

x से y की मुलाक़ात होना
  y to meet with x (*v.i.*)

छुट्टी holiday, vacation (*f*)

थक जाना to become tired (*v.i.*)

x को थकान हो जाना
  x to become tired (*v.i.*)

डेढ़ one and a half

x को नींद लगना x to feel
  sleepy (*v.i.*)

x को नींद आ जाना x to fall
  asleep (*v.i.*)

ज़िंदगी life (*f*)

मौज-मस्ती करना to enjoy,
  have fun (*v.t.*)

मौक़ा opportunity (*m*)

नौकरी लग जाना to start a
  job (*v.i.*)

आराम rest (*m*)

मज़े करना to enjoy,
  have fun (*v.t.*)

तनख़्वाह salary (*f*)

आटे दाल का भाव मालूम
  होना to discover a harsh
  truth (*v.i.*)

कभी ever, sometime

Translate the following questions. Answer them, and then ask them of a partner.

1. Does Sanjeev have to do a lot of work? _____

2. Does Sanjeev ever get (receive) a vacation/holiday? _____

3. When do you get (receive) a vacation/holiday? _____

4. What time does Sanjeev reach home at night? _____

5. Do you get very tired at night? _____

6. Does it seem to Kavita that Sanjeev's life is more difficult then hers? _____

LESSON **23** तेईसवाँ पाठ

Delhi Just Keeps Growing

Delhi Just Keeps Growing दिल्ली बढ़ती जा रही है
Here Kavita talks more about her city.

आज मैं आपको दिल्ली के बारे में थोड़ा बहुत और बताना चाहती हूँ। आप लोगों को मालूम तो है कि दिल्ली बहुत बड़ा शहर है। आपको यह भी मालूम होगा कि दिल्ली के उत्तर में डी॰ यू॰ स्थित है। दक्षिण में जवाहरलाल नेहरू विश्वविद्यालय है। ज़्यादातर लोग उसे जे॰ एन॰ यू॰ कहते हैं। दोनों विश्वविद्यालय बहुत मशहूर हैं। दक्षिण में, बहुत दूर कुतुब मीनार स्थित है। सी॰ पी॰ बिल्कुल बीच में है। सी॰ पी॰ को अंग्रेज़ लोगों ने बनवाया था। सी॰ पी॰ के उत्तर में पुरानी दिल्ली है। पुरानी दिल्ली शाहजहाँ ने बनवायी थी। पश्चिम में हवाई अड्डा और गुड़गाँव हैं। कुछ सालों से गुड़गाँव बहुत विकसित होता जा रहा है। वहाँ बहुत मॉल हो गये हैं और बहुत लोग रहने लगे हैं। पूर्व में यमुना नदी है। मेरा घर सी॰ पी॰ से बहुत दूर नहीं है। यह दिल्ली का नक़्शा है। दिन-ब-दिन दिल्ली की आबादी बढ़ती जा रही है। लोग सारे देश से आकर यहाँ बसने लगे हैं। कुछ साल बाद दिल्ली का शहर कैसा होगा, यह हम कह नहीं सकते।

Glossary

थोड़ा बहुत और a little bit more
उत्तर north (*m*)
स्थित situated
दक्षिण south (*m*)
जवाहरलाल नेहरू Jawaharlal
   Nehru (India's first Prime
   Minister)
ज़्यादातर most
मशहूर famous
कुतुब मीनार Kutub Minar (a
   minaret built in the 12th century)

सी० पी० C.P. (Connaught
   Place)
बनवाना to have built (*v.t.*)
शाहजहाँ Shah Jahan (17th
   century Mughal emperor)
पश्चिम west (*m*)
हवाई अड्डा airport (*m*)
गुड़गाँव Gurgaon (a suburb
   of Delhi close to the airport)
विकसित होना to become
   developed (*v.i.*)

मॉल mall (*m*)
पूर्व east (*m*)
यमुना नदी Yamuna River
   (*f*)
नक़्शा map (*m*)
दिन-ब-दिन day by day
आबादी population (*f*)
बढ़ना to increase,
   to grow (*v.i.*)
बसना to settle,
   inhabit (*v.i.*)

Answer the following questions. Then ask them of a partner.

1. क्या दिल्ली की आबादी बढ़ती जा रही है? _____

2. क्या आपके शहर की आबादी बढ़ती जा रही है? _____

3. डी० यू० उत्तर दिल्ली में स्थित है या दक्षिण दिल्ली में? _____

_____

4. दिल्ली का हवाई अड्डा कहाँ स्थित है? _____

5. सी० पी० कहाँ है? _____

6. लोग कहाँ से आकर दिल्ली में बसने लगे हैं? _____

7. क्या कविता का घर सी० पी० से बहुत दूर है? _____

GRAMMAR

Relative/Correlative Clauses

In Lesson 7 all of the forms of the pronouns with different postpositions were introduced (see p. 53). At the time all of these except the relative pronoun were explained. Hindi has only one relative pronoun, जो, which corresponds to *who, what, which, that* in English. The relative pronoun is employed in a subordinate clause to refer to a noun or pronoun in a main clause. In Hindi the clause that contains the relative pronoun, the relative or subordinate clause, ordinarily precedes the main clause.

जो लड़की किताब पढ़ रही है, वह मेरी दोस्त है।
The girl who is reading the book is my friend.
(*which girl is reading a book, she is my friend*)

In this example the initial clause is subordinate, that is, it cannot stand alone:

जो लड़की किताब पढ़ रही है which girl is reading a book

The second clause is the main or independent clause. This means that it is a complete sentence.

वह मेरी दोस्त है । She is my friend.

The word order of relative and correlative clauses in Hindi is relatively flexible. The example above could be expressed in the following way.

वह लड़की मेरी दोस्त है, जो वहाँ किताब पढ़ रही है ।
That girl is my friend, who is reading a book over there.

जिसने रेडियो में भाषण दिया उसको तीन भाषाएँ आती हैं ।
The person who gave a speech on the radio knows three languages.
(*who gave a speech on the radio, to her/him three languages come*)

जिस में भी हिम्मत हो, वह ज़रूर अपना लक्ष्य प्राप्त करेगा ।
Whoever has courage will certainly achieve his/her aim.*

> * When the gender of the subject is not specified, in subjectival construction the verb is conjugated in the masculine singular.

वह लड़की जो हिन्दी बोलती है, अगले हफ़्ते कक्षा में आएगी ।
The girl who speaks Hindi will come to the class next week.

मेरा जो धर्म है, उसे मैं समझने की कोशिश करूँगी ।
I (*f*) will try to understand my duty.
(*which is my duty, I will try to understand it*)

जो with the Different Postpositions

In Lesson 7 the different forms of the pronouns were introduced with various postpositions. Here जो is repeated with the postpositions का, को, and ने.

	+ का *'s*	+ को	+ ने
जो (sing)	जिसका *whose*	जिसको or जिसे *to whom/whom*	जिसने *who*
जो (pl)	जिनका *whose* (pl)	जिनको or जिन्हें *to whom/whom* (pl)	जिन्होंने *who*

जिन्होंने मुझे हिन्दी सिखायी थी वे हिन्दी बहुत अच्छी तरह* जानती हैं ।
The person (*f*) who taught me Hindi knows the language very well.
> * अच्छी तरह *in a good manner, well*

जिसे उसका नाम नहीं मालूम हो, उसे पूछना चाहिये ।
Whoever doesn't know his/her name should ask.
(*who may know his/her name he/she should ask*)

In addition to the relative pronoun, there are also relative adjectives and adverbs. Below are listed all of these with the equivalent correlative forms.

Relative	Correlative (far)	Correlative (near)	Interrogative (?)
जो *which, who, that*	वह *he/she, that, it*	यह *he/she, this, it*	कौन/क्या *who, what*
जो *which, who* (pl)	वे *he/she, they, those*	ये *he/she, they, these*	कौन *who*
जब *when*	तब *then*	अब *now*	कब *when*
जहाँ *where*	वहाँ *there*	यहाँ *here*	कहाँ *where*
जिधर *where*	उधर *there*	इधर *here*	किधर *where*
जैसा *of which sort*	वैसा *such, thus*	ऐसा *such, thus*	कैसा *how, what sort of*
जैसे *in which manner*	वैसे *in that manner*	ऐसे *in this/such a manner*	कैसे *in which manner*
जितना *as much, many*	उतना *that/so much, many*	इतना *this/so much, many*	कितना *how much, many*

जब आप हिन्दुस्तान जाएँगे, तब क्या मेरी याद आएगी?
Will you (*m*) remember me when you go to India?

जब आप हमसे बात करना चाहें तब हमारे पास आइये।
Come and see me/us when you want to talk to me/us.
(*when you may want to talk, then come near me/us*)

जहाँ वे जाएँ वहाँ मैं भी जाऊँगा।
I (*m*) will go where he/she/they may go.

जैसा आप कहें।
As you say.
(*As you may say*)

जितनी नींद मुझे आती है, उतनी ही नींद आपको भी आती है।
You become as sleepy as I do.
(*as much sleep as comes to me, just that much sleep comes to you as well*)

जो घड़ी उस आदमी के पास है वह आपकी होगी।
That must be your watch that that man has.

The insertion of भी *also*, *even*, *as well* makes relative clauses less specific.

जो भी *whatever/whoever/whichever*

जो भी भारत जाना चाहे उसे मेरे पास आना चाहिये।

Whoever wants to go to India should come to me.

जब भी *whenever*

जब भी तुम निश्चय करो तभी मुझे बताओ।

Tell me whenever you decide.

(*whenever you may decide, right then tell me*)

जिधर/जहाँ भी *wherever*

जहाँ भी वह बसे वहीं उसकी माँ भी बसेगी।

His/her mother will settle wherever he/she does.

(*wherever he/she may settle, right there his/her mother will settle*)

जैसा भी *however*

जैसा भी मुझे बताया जाए मुझे वैसा ही करना चाहिये।

I should do exactly as I am told.

(*however I may be told, I should do that manner*)

जितना भी *however much*

जितने भी पैसे हम इकट्ठे कर सकें उतने हम आपको दे देंगे।

We will give you as much money as we can collect.

(*however much money we may be able to gather that much we will give you*)

PRACTICE

📖 *Now turn to the Workbook and complete Activity 23.1, using the different forms of the relative and correlative pronouns, adjectives and adverbs to complete the sentences.*

Shall We Go via Bengali Market? क्या हम बंगाली मार्केट से होकर जाएँ?

The term "via" may be expressed in Hindi in two ways:

x से हो कर *via x*

x के रास्ते *via x (by x's way/path)*

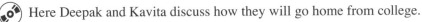 Here Deepak and Kavita discuss how they will go home from college.

कविता – दीपक, क्या हम आज शाम को बंगाली मार्केट से हो कर घर जा सकते हैं?

दीपक – बंगाली मार्केट से हो कर क्यों? क्या तुम्हें कुछ काम है वहाँ?

कविता – हाँ, मुझे कुछ मिठाई लेनी है।

दीपक – बंगाली मार्केट में सचमुच मिठाई ख़रीदने की ज़रूरत है? ख़ान मार्केट में अच्छी मिठाई नहीं मिलती क्या?

कविता – दीपक, तुम्हें मालूम है कि बंगाली मार्केट में जितनी अच्छी मिठाई मिलती है उतनी अच्छी ख़ान मार्केट में नहीं मिलती।

दीपक – ठीक है, लेकिन इस वक़्त बंगाली मार्केट में बहुत गाड़ियाँ होंगी। वहाँ पार्किंग कहीं नहीं मिलेगी। क्या मिठाई कहीं और नहीं मिलेगी?

कविता – अच्छी मिठाई की दुकानें और कहीं हैं दिल्ली में?

दीपक – ठीक है, हम बंगाली मार्केट से हो कर घर जाएँगे। मिठाई किस के लिये है?

कविता – माँ ने मँगवायी है। तुम्हें याद नहीं है कि आज हमारे घर कुछ लोग रात को खाने को आनेवाले हैं?

Glossary

बंगाली मार्केट Bengali Market	x की ज़रूरत होना the necessity	कहीं और anywhere else
मिठाई sweet(s) (*f*)	(*f*) of x to happen (*v.i.*)	मँगवाना to have ordered (*v.t.*)
	पार्किंग parking (*f*)	

Translate the following questions. Answer them, and then ask them of a partner.

1. Via where does Kavita want to go home? ....

2. What does Kavita want to buy in the Bengali Market? ....

3. Why does Deepak not want to go to Bengali Market? _____

4. Who has ordered the sweets? _____

5. Do you like sweets? _____

6. Are such good sweets available in Khan Market as are available in Bengali Market?

GRAMMAR

As long as / Until / By the time... By then...

When the relative and correlative adverbs जब *when* and तब *then* are employed with the postposition तक *by*, *until* they indicate that one action continues until another begins, or that one action does not begin until another is completed. Such statements are often translated into English as *by the time*, *until*, *as long as*.

Use of जब तक... तब तक...

1. The order of the clauses is the opposite of the English order.
2. The possible combinations of verb tenses and moods are limited in the two clauses and should be noted carefully.
3. The negative adverb नहीं/न/ना is often employed in the first clause (जब तक...) to indicate that no change takes place in the action in the second clause until the action in the first clause is completed.

1. As with other relative-correlative clauses, the regular order of the clauses in a statement employing जब तक... तब तक... is the opposite of the English order.

> जब तक आप मेहनत करते रहेंगे तब तक आपको जीवन में सफलता मिलती रहेगी।
> You will continue to obtain success in life as long as you work hard. (*As long as you continue to work hard, you will continue to obtain success in life.*)

2. The possible combinations of verb tenses and moods are limited in the two clauses and should be noted carefully. It is advisable to have both clauses *either* in the perfective tense, *or* in the present, *or* the future/optative when employing जब तक... तब तक... .

> जब तक आप आये थे तब तक फ़िल्म शुरू हो चुकी थी।
> The film had already started by the time you arrived.

> जब तक वह यहाँ रहती है तब तक वह हमारे साथ ही रहती है।
> While she's here she lives with us.

जब तक कविता दिल्ली में रहेगी तक तब दीपक कहीं नहीं जाएगा।

Deepak will not go anywhere as long as Kavita lives in Delhi.

जब तक काम हो तब तक मैं करता रहूँगा।

I (*m*) will continue to work as long as there is work.

जब तक मुझे नौकरी मिलेगी तब तक मेरे सब पैसे ख़त्म हो जाएँगे।

By the time I get a job all my money will be gone.

3. The negative adverb नहीं/न/ना is often employed in the first clause (जब तक...) to indicate that no change takes place in the action in the second clause until the action in the first clause is completed.

जब तक रेलगाड़ी न चले तब तक हम प्लैटफ़ार्म पर रुके रहेंगे।

We will wait on the platform until the train goes.

(*as long as the train may not go, until then we will wait right here on the platform*)

जब तक तुम कमरे में नहीं आये थे तब तक माहौल बहुत ख़राब रहा।

The atmosphere was very bad until you came into the room.

(*as long as you didn't come into the room, until then the atmosphere remained very bad*)

जब तक मेरी मदद न करो तब तक मैं तुम्हें सताता रहूँगा।

I will continue to harass you until you help me.

(*as long as you don't do my help, until then I will continue to harass you*)

जब तक किसी देश की भाषा न सीखें तब तक उस देश के बारे में कुछ जान नहीं सकते।

You can't learn about any country until you learn its language.

(*as long as you may not learn some country's language, until then you cannot learn about that country*)

जब तक गर्मी का मौसम नहीं आया था तब तक हम जूते पहने रहते थे।

We used to wear shoes until the hot weather came.

(*as long as the hot weather didn't come, until then we used to wear shoes*)

PRACTICE

📖 *Now turn to the Workbook and complete Activities 23.2 and 23.3.*

I Am Quite Worried about the Exams

PRACTICE

I Am Quite Worried about the Exams
मुझे इम्तहान की काफ़ी फ़िक्र हो रही है

When talking about anxiety the following expressions are often employed:

फ़िक्र worry, anxiety, concern, care (*f*)

(The synonym चिंता *worry, anxiety, concern, care* (*f*) can be used in place of this.)

फ़िक्र होना	मुझे x की फ़िक्र है। I am worried about x.
	मुझे x की फ़िक्र हो रही है। I am worried about x.
फ़िक्र करना	मैं x की फ़िक्र करता हूँ। I worry about x.

Here Deepak and Kavita discuss their upcoming exams.

दीपक — कविता, आजकल इम्तहान सिर पर हैं। मुझे इसकी बहुत फ़िक्र हो रही है।

कविता — इतनी फ़िक्र क्यों हो रही है?

दीपक — जितने अच्छे नंबर तुम्हें हर बार मिलते हैं उतने अच्छे नंबर मुझे कहाँ मिलते हैं?

कविता — फ़िक्र मत करो। तुम अच्छे इम्तहान दोगे। मुझे तुम पर पूरा भरोसा है।

दीपक — हाँ, लेकिन जब मुझे बहुत फ़िक्र होती है तब मैं पढ़ाई पर ध्यान नहीं दे सकता।

कविता — थोड़ी सी फ़िक्र होनी चाहिये। जिसे फ़िक्र नहीं होती वह इंसान नहीं होता।

दीपक — तुम ठीक कहती हो कविता। क्या तुम्हें इम्तहान देने से पहले फ़िक्र होती है?

कविता — और क्या! पर जितनी फ़िक्र तुमको होती है, उतनी फ़िक्र मुझे नहीं होती।

दीपक — कविता, तुम्हारा पहला इम्तहान कब है?

कविता — मेरा पहला इम्तहान परसों है। तुम्हारा पहला इम्तहान कब है?

दीपक — मेरा भी परसों है। कितने बजे?

कविता — ढाई बजे। क्या हम साथ-साथ चलें?

दीपक — ठीक है। अब मैं कुछ पढ़ाई करूँगा।

Glossary

इम्तहान (x के) सिर
  पर होना (x's) exams to be
  imminent (*v.i.*)

x की फ़िक्र होना to be
  worried about x (*v.i.*)

हर बार every time

x को y पर पूरा भरोसा होना
  x to have complete confidence
  in y (*v.i.*)

x पर ध्यान देना to concentrate
  on x (*v.t.*)

थोड़ा सा a little-ish

इंसान human (*m*)

और क्या! what else!

परसों the day before yesterday;
  the day after tomorrow

साथ-साथ together

Answer the following questions. Then ask them of a partner.

1. आजकल दीपक को किस बात की फ़िक्र हो रही है? _____

2. जब आपको इम्तहान देने पड़ते हैं तब क्या आपको फ़िक्र होती है? _____

_____

3. जिसको कभी फ़िक्र नहीं होती, उसके बारे में कविता क्या सोचती है? _____

_____

4. जब दीपक को फ़िक्र होती है, क्या वह पढ़ाई पर ध्यान दे सकता है? _____

_____

5. जब आपको फ़िक्र होती है, क्या आप पढ़ाई पर ध्यान दे सकते हैं? (दे सकती हैं)

_____

6. क्या दीपक कविता से इम्तहान की ज़्यादा फ़िक्र करता है? _____

7. कविता का पहला इम्तहान कब है? _____

8. क्या आपके सिर पर इम्तहान हैं? _____

GRAMMAR

The imperfect and the perfect participles are frequently used as nouns, adjectives and adverbs. The imperfect participle is used to indicate that an action is incomplete (i.e., the *reading* boy) whereas the perfect participle is employed to indicate that the action is complete (i.e., the *read* boy *or* the "educated" boy).

Participles as Adjectives

The imperfect participle was introduced in Lesson 9 (see p. 66). It indicates that the action is incomplete. The perfective participle was introduced in Lesson 12 (see p. 96). It indicates that the action is complete.

Infinitive	Imperfect participle	Perfect participle
खाना *to eat*	खाता *eating*	खाया *eaten*
पढ़ना *to read*	पढ़ता *reading*	पढ़ा *read*

As an adjective, the imperfect and the perfect participles decline like ordinary आ ending adjectives (see p. 20). They may be placed before the noun they qualify (attributive) or may occur as a part of the predicate (predicative). The verb होना in the perfective form (हुआ, हुए, हुई) is often (but not necessarily) employed with these participles to clarify their use as adjectives. This does not perceivably change the meaning and is often left unexpressed.

Imperfect Participle

रोटी खाता (हुआ) लड़का	a/the roti eating boy (*m sing*, direct case)
रोटी खाते (हुए) लड़के	(the) roti eating boys (*m pl*, direct case)
रोटी खाते (हुए) लड़के को	to a/the roti eating boy (*m sing*, oblique case)
रोटी खाते (हुए) लड़कों को	to (the) roti eating boys (*m pl*, oblique case)
किताबें पढ़ती (हुई) लड़की	a/the books reading girl (*f sing*, direct case)
किताबें पढ़ती (हुई) लड़कियाँ	(the) books reading girls (*f pl*, direct case)
किताबें पढ़ती (हुई) लड़की को	to a/the books reading girl (*f sing*, oblique case)
किताबें पढ़ती (हुई) लड़कियों को	to (the) books reading girls (*f pl*, oblique case)

चलती (हुई) गाड़ी से मत उतरना
Don't get down from a moving train.

दिल्ली में मैंने अंग्रेज़ी बोलते (हुए) लोग देखे।
In Delhi I saw people who speak English.
(*in Delhi I saw English speaking people*)

दौड़ती (हुई) लड़की गिर पड़ी।
The girl who was running suddenly fell over.
(*the running girl suddenly fell over*)

भागते (हुए) चोर को पकड़ लिया गया।
The thief was caught as he was fleeing.
(*the fleeing thief was caught*)

Perfect Participle

बैठा (हुआ) लड़का	a/the seated boy (*m sing*, direct case)
बैठे (हुए) लड़के	(the) seated boys (*m pl*, direct case)
बैठे (हुए) लड़के को	to a/the seated boy (*m sing*, oblique case)
बैठे (हुए) लड़कों को	to a/the seated boys (*m pl*, oblique case)
बैठी (हुई) लड़की	a/the seated girl (*f sing*, direct case)
बैठी (हुई) लड़कियाँ	(the) seated girls (*f pl*, direct case)
बैठी (हुई) लड़की को	to a/the seated girl (*f sing*, oblique case)
बैठी (हुई) लड़कियों को	to (the) seated girls (*f pl*, oblique case)

वह खोयी निगाहों से मेरी ओर देखने लगा।
He began to look in my direction with a lost gaze.
(*with lost glances*)

मेज़ पर पड़े (हुए) काग़ज़ उठा कर लाना।
Bring the papers lying on the table. (*pick up the papers lying on the table and bring*)

यह मेरी पढ़ी (हुई) किताब है।
I have read this book.
(*this is my read book*)

मैंने वहाँ बैठी (हुई) लड़कियों से बात की थी।
I spoke to the girls who are seated over there.

खुले हुए दरवाज़े से अंदर जाइए।
Go in through the open door.

एक आदमी आप से मिलने के लिये आया (हुआ) है।
A man has come to meet you.

हम भी पढ़े-लिखे आदमी हैं।
I am / We are also educated.
(*we are also read and written men*)

PRACTICE

📖 *Now turn to the Workbook and complete Activity 24.1.*

 **Where Are You Going for the Summer?** गर्मी के दिनों में आप कहाँ जानेवाले हैं?
Deepak and Kavita discuss what they are going to do in the summer after their exams.

दीपक - कविता, इम्तहान ख़त्म होने के बाद तुम क्या करनेवाली हो?

कविता - मैं और मेरी माँ पहाड़ों में जानेवाले हैं, गर्मी से बचने के लिये। अभी भी मुझे बहुत ज़्यादा गर्मी लग रही है।

दीपक - हाँ, और अभी तक जून का महीना शुरू भी नहीं हुआ। कितने दिन जाने की सोच रही हो?

कविता - कम से कम एक महीने जाएँगे। मेरी माँ अल्मोड़ा की है तो हम वहाँ जाकर रहेंगे। तुम क्या करनेवाले हो?

दीपक - मैंने सोचा था कि मैं इलाहाबाद जाऊँगा। अब पढ़ाई पूरी होने को है। इसके बाद मैं क्या करूँ, मुझे मालूम नहीं। नौकरी की तलाश करनी होगी। नौकरी शुरू करने से पहले माँ-बाप और वृन्दा के पास जाने की सोची थी।

कविता - तुम हमारे साथ क्यों नहीं चलते? मेरी माँ को अच्छा लगेगा।

दीपक - तुम्हें अच्छा नहीं लगेगा?

कविता - दीपक, मुझे सब कुछ साफ़-साफ़ कहना पड़ेगा, क्या?

दीपक - अच्छा, मैं माँ-बाप से बात कर के तुम्हें जवाब दूँगा।

Glossary

ख़त्म होना to be finished (*v.i.*)
पहाड़ mountain (*m*)
बचना to be saved (*v.i.*)
शुरू होना to be commenced (*v.i.*), to begin

x की (बात) सोचना to think of x (*v.t.*)
अल्मोड़ा Almora (a town in the foothills of the Himalayas)
x की तलाश करना to search for x (*v.t.*)

साफ़-साफ़ कहना to say clearly (*v.t.*)
x का सफ़र करना to travel to x (*v.t.*)
कहीं somewhere

Answer the following questions. Then ask them of a partner.

1. पढ़ाई पूरी होने के बाद दीपक कहाँ जानेवाला है? _____

2. पढ़ाई पूरी होने के बाद कविता कहाँ जानेवाली है? _____

3. कविता किसके साथ जानेवाली है? _____

4. कविता कितने दिन के लिये जानेवाली है? _____

5. दीपक कहाँ जाने की सोच रहा है? _____

6. क्या दीपक को जल्दी नौकरी की तलाश करनी पड़ेगी? _____

7. क्या दीपक को मालूम है कि पढ़ाई पूरी होने पर वह क्या करेगा? _____

Write a short narrative about what you are about to do after you finish studying or at the end of the year. Are you going to take a trip somewhere? Are you going to search for a job? Will you go somewhere with a friend? Will you go in the summer or the winter? For how long will you go?

GRAMMAR

Participles as Adverbs

The imperfect and perfect participles are also employed as adverbs in a number of ways. When employed as adverbs, they *always* appear in the oblique form. The masculine, oblique form of होना (हुए) may also be used for clarity.

1. **Imperfect Participle as an Adverb**

   When the imperfect participle is employed as an adverb, it generally provides information about the manner or the time of the principal action. There are four forms that these adverbs may take.

   a) The oblique imperfect participle + हुए
   b) The oblique reduplicated imperfect participle
   c) The oblique imperfect participle + समय/वक़्त
   d) The oblique imperfect participle + ही

   a) the oblique imperfect participle + हुए

   The use of the imperfect participle + हुए gives a sense of *while…*, as in *while running*. The oblique form of होना is employed for clarity but may be left unexpressed.

   मैंने लड़की को दौड़ते हुए देखा।
   I saw the girl running. (*while running*)*
   * There is some ambiguity here about who was running.

   लड़का किताब पढ़ते (हुए) सो गया।
   The boy fell asleep while reading.

   हम बात करते (हुए) चलते रहे।
   We talked as we went.
   (*while talking we continued to move*)

   b) The oblique reduplicated imperfect participle

   The participle may be reduplicated with very little difference in meaning from (a) above. Occasionally this gives a sense of one action interrupting another.

   वह लड़का पढ़ते-पढ़ते सो गया।
   That boy fell asleep while reading.

   घर पहुँचते-पहुँचते अंधेरा हो जाएगा।
   It will be dark by the time (we) arrive home.

   सड़क में चलते-चलते वह फेरीवाले के सामने रुक गया।
   While going along in the street he stopped in front of the hawker.

   c) The oblique imperfect participle + समय/वक़्त

   The imperfect participle may be combined with समय/वक़्त *time* with little difference in meaning. It may be translated as *at the time of…*, *while* or *when*.

   चाय बनाते-समय गर्म पानी ध्यान से कप में डालना।
   When you are making the tea, pour the hot water into the cup carefully.

नौकरी करते-वक़्त मुझे बहुत मज़ा आता है।
I really enjoy myself when I work.

d) The oblique imperfect participle + ही
The combination of the imperfect participle + ही gives a sense of *as soon as….*

घर जाते ही वह लड़का सो गया।
As soon as he got home the boy went to sleep.

काम पूरा करते ही वह घर छोड़कर बाहर चली गयी।
As soon as she had finished work she left the house and went outside.

खाना खाते ही हमें महसूस हुआ कि कोई चीज़ सड़ गयी होगी।
As soon as we ate we felt that something must have been off.

It is important to remember that the subject of both clauses must be the same. If there is a different subject in the first clause, it must be marked by the invariable postposition के.

हमारे घर पहुँचते-पहुँचते अंधेरा हो जाएगा।
It will be dark by the time we arrive home.

ज्योति के भारत पहुँचते ही काम अच्छी तरह चलने लगा।
As soon as Jyoti arrived in India the work began to go well.

रेलगाड़ी के चलते ही मेरा मन शान्त हो गया।
As soon as the train departed, my heart became tranquil.

उसके भारत जाते-समय दूसरे छात्र परीक्षा दे रहे थे।
When he/she was going to India, the other students were doing their exam.

उसके बस से उतरते-वक़्त किसी ने बटुए की चोरी कर ली।
Someone stole (his/her) wallet as he/she was getting down from the bus.

PRACTICE

📖 *Now turn to the Workbook and complete Activity 24.2.*

GRAMMAR

2. **Perfect Participle as an Adverb**
The perfect participle is also employed as an adverb. It takes the oblique form and हुए may be employed for clarity. It may also be reduplicated in particular cases.

आज वह लड़की बहुत ख़ूबसूरत कपड़े पहने (हुए) है।
That girl is wearing very beautiful clothes today.

मेरा दोस्त मेरी किताब लिये हुए मेरे यहाँ आ गया।
My friend (*m*) came to my place with my book.

मैं सारे दिन बैठे-बैठे थक गयी।
I (*f*) became tired sitting down all day.

The Perfect Participle + बिना/बग़ैर *without*

The postposition के बिना/बग़ैर *without* is employed with the oblique perfect participle to give the meaning of *without x-ing*. In these cases, के is omitted and बिना/बग़ैर may appear either before or after the participle.

काम किये बिना क्लास में मत आना।
Don't come to class without doing (your) work.

बिना काम किये कक्षा में मत आना।
Don't come to class without doing (your) work.

हिन्दुस्तान बग़ैर गये आप अच्छी हिन्दी कैसे सीख पाएँगे?
How will you (*m*) be able to learn good Hindi without going to India?

Special expressions using the imperfect and perfect participles

Oblique imperfect and perfect participles are used in expressions that indicate how long an action has been taking place (imperfect) and how long it has been since an action has taken place (perfect).

1. Expressing the duration of an action that is taking place.

   Formation:
   a) The logical subject is governed by को
   b) The oblique imperfect participle is used (हुए may be employed for clarity)
   c) कितना *how much/many* is employed with a time word (in questions)
   d) The verb होना is employed

   subject + को   oblique imperfect participle (हुए)   कितना (time word)   होना

   आपको हिन्दी सीखते हुए कितने साल हो गये?
   For how many years have you been studying Hindi?
   मुझे सीखते (हुए) छै साल हो गये।
   I have been learning for six years.
   अमरीका में रहते (हुए) उसे क़रीब बीस वर्ष हुए हैं।
   He/she has been living in America for approximately twenty years.

2. Expressing the duration since an action has taken place.
   In these expressions, the perfect participle in the oblique form is used instead of the imperfect participle. The rest remains the same.

subject + को   oblique perfect participle (हुए)   कितना (time word)   होना

मुझे हिन्दी सीखे (हुए) छै साल हो गये।
It is six years since I learned Hindi.

आप को हिन्दुस्तान गये (हुए) कितने बरस हो गये?
How many years is it since you have been in India?

Participles as Nouns

Imperfect and perfect participles may also function as nouns.

वह रोतों को हँसा सकता है।
He is able to make the crying laugh.

पानी में डूबते को बचाओ।
Save the one who is drowning in the water.

दिल चीज़ क्या है, आप मेरी जान लीजिये।
बस एक बार मेरा कहा मान लीजिये।
What is the heart, take my life as well.
But just once accept what I say.
(From the film *Umrao Jan*)

PRACTICE

📖 *Now turn to the Workbook and complete Activities 24.3 and 24.4.*

APPENDIX A
Numbers, Dates, Seasons and Money

Numbers

The Numbers from 1 to 100		
एक one	पैंतीस thirty-five	उनहत्तर sixty-nine
दो two	छत्तीस thirty-six	सत्तर seventy
तीन three	सैंतीस thirty-seven	इकहत्तर seventy-one
चार four	अड़तीस thirty-eight	बहत्तर seventy-two
पाँच five	उनतालीस thirty-nine	तिहत्तर seventy-three
छै/छह/छः six	चालीस forty	चौहत्तर seventy-four
सात seven	इकतालीस forty-one	पचहत्तर seventy-five
आठ eight	बयालीस forty-two	छिहत्तर seventy-six
नौ nine	तैंतालीस forty-three	सतहत्तर seventy-seven
दस ten	चवालीस forty-four	अठहत्तर seventy-eight
ग्यारह eleven	पैंतालीस forty-five	उनासी seventy-nine
बारह twelve	छियालीस forty-six	अस्सी eighty
तेरह thirteen	सैंतालीस forty-seven	इक्यासी eighty-one
चौदह fourteen	अड़तालीस forty-eight	बयासी eighty-two
पंद्रह fifteen	उनचास forty-nine	तिरासी eighty-three
सोलह sixteen	पचास fifty	चौरासी eighty-four
सत्रह seventeen	इक्यावन fifty-one	पचासी eighty-five
अठारह eighteen	बावन fifty-two	छियासी eighty-six
उन्नीस nineteen	तिरपन fifty-three	सत्तासी eighty-seven
बीस twenty	चौवन fifty-four	अठासी/अट्ठासी eighty-eight
इक्कीस twenty-one	पचपन fifty-five	नवासी eighty-nine
बाईस twenty-two	छप्पन fifty-six	नब्बे ninety
तेईस twenty-three	सत्तावन fifty-seven	इक्यानवे ninety-one
चौबीस twenty-four	अट्ठावन fifty-eight	बानवे/बयानवे ninety-two
पच्चीस twenty-five	उनसठ fifty-nine	तिरानवे ninety-three
छब्बीस twenty-six	साठ sixty	चौरानवे ninety-four
सत्ताईस twenty-seven	इकसठ sixty-one	पचानवे ninety-five
अट्ठाईस twenty-eight	बासठ sixty-two	छियानवे ninety-six
उनतीस twenty-nine	तिरसठ sixty-three	सत्तानवे ninety-seven
तीस thirty	चौंसठ sixty-four	अट्ठानवे ninety-eight
इकत्तीस thirty-one	पैंसठ sixty-five	निन्यानवे ninety-nine
बत्तीस thirty-two	छियासठ sixty-six	सौ one hundred
तैंतीस thirty-three	सड़सठ sixty-seven	
चौंतीस thirty-four	अड़सठ sixty-eight	

Days of the Week

There are at least two names for some of the days of the week, coming from different traditions.

सोमवार Monday (*m*) (the day of the moon)
मंगलवार Tuesday (*m*) (the day of Mars)
बुधवार Wednesday (*m*) (the day of Mercury)
गुरुवार/बृहस्पतिवार Thursday (*m*) (the day of Jupiter)
शुक्रवार Friday (*m*) (the day of Venus)
शनिवार/शनिश्चर Saturday (*m*) (the day of Saturn)
इतवार/रविवार Sunday (*m*) (the day of the Sun)

Urdu: पीर Monday (*m*)
Urdu: मंगल Tuesday (*m*)
Urdu: बुध Wednesday (*m*)
Urdu: जुमेरात Thursday (*f*)
Urdu: जुमा Friday (*m*)
Urdu: हफ़्ता Saturday (*m*)
Urdu: इतवार Sunday (*m*)

Dates

Dates in India are worked out according to either the Gregorian calendar or one of the Indian dating systems. The most common of these is called the Vikramaditya system, which was named after King Vikramaditya. This is roughly 57 years ahead of the Gregorian calendar. Dates in the Vikramaditya system are prefixed by the Sanskrit word संवत् *year, era* (*m*), whereas dates in the Gregorian calendar are prefixed by the Arabic word सन् *year*.

Dates are expressed in the following manner:

दो जून को on 2 June
पहली तारीख़ को on the first (date)
मार्च की दूसरी तारीख़ को on 2 March
सन् दो हज़ार दस में in the year 2010
सन् उन्नीस सौ बयानबे में in the year 1992
इस साल दिसम्बर में in this December
अगले साल सितम्बर के महीने में next year in the month of September
दो साल पहले two years ago
दो साल बाद after two years

Months of the Year According to the Hindu Calendar

The Hindu calendar is mostly used in religious ceremonies. The months are based on the lunar months but the years are solar. The months are divided into two halves: the bright half (शुक्ल पक्ष) and the dark half (कृष्ण पक्ष). The months do not correspond exactly to the months of the Gregorian calendar and often begin approximately halfway through the Gregorian month. The new year begins in the month of चैत on the first day of the light half of the month. All of the months are masculine.

Hindi Name	Sanskrit Name	Gregorian Month	
माघ	माघ	जनवरी	January
फागुन	फाल्गुन	फ़रवरी	February
चैत	चैत्र	मार्च	March
बैसाख	वैशाख	अप्रैल	April
जेठ	ज्येष्ठ	मई	May
असाढ़	आषाढ़	जून	June
सावन	श्रावण	जुलाई	July
भादों	भाद्रपद	अगस्त	August

क्वार	आश्विन	सितम्बर	September
कार्तिक	कार्तिक	अक्तूबर	October
अगहन	अग्रहायण	नवम्बर	November
पूस	पौष	दिसंबर	December

The Seasons in Hindi

While मौसम (*m*) is commonly employed for "weather" as well as "season" in Hindi, when the Sanskrit terms for the seasons are used, the word ऋतु *season* (*f*) is preferred. There are traditionally six seasons in Hindi:

वसंत spring (*m*) (March–May)
ग्रीष्म summer (*m*) (May–July)
वर्षा rains (*f*) (July–September)
शरद autumn (*f*) (September–November)
हेमंत winter (*m*) (November–January)
शिशिर cool season (*m*) (January–March)

The other common words for the seasons are:
गर्मी का मौसम summer (weather/season of heat)
गर्मी के दिन summer (days of heat)
जाड़ा cold, winter (*m*)
जाड़े का मौसम winter (weather/season of cold)
जाड़े के दिन winter (days of cold)
जाड़ों के दिन winter (days of cold)
ठंड cold, winter (*f*)
ठंड का मौसम winter (weather/season of cold)
सर्दी/सरदी cold, winter (*f*)
सर्दी का मौसम winter (weather/season of cold)
बरसात rain, the rainy season (*f*)
बरसात का मौसम rainy season
बसंत spring (*m*)
बहार spring (*f*)
बारिश rain, rainy season (*f*)

Money

The currency of India is the Rupee, which is divided into one hundred *paise*. The paisa itself has become almost obsolete in India. However, the word remains and is used to mean "money" in general. The word रुपया can also be used for "money."

रुपया rupee (*m*)   पैसा paisa (*m*)

Sums of money are represented in the following manner:

A single rupee:
1 रु or 1/- (Re 1)

and

Plural rupees:
250 रु or 250/- (Rs 250)

The Hindi numerals introduced in Lesson 16 are also encountered.

२५० रु or २५०/-
(Rs 250)

Some Common Postpositions

This list of common postpositions in Hindi is by no means exhaustive. It merely illustrates what sorts of words function as postpositions.

Single-word Postpositions	
का *'s* (possessive postposition) को *to* (object marker) तक *until, by* ने *past tense marker*	पर *on, at, in* में *in* से *from, with, by*

Postpositional Phrases	
x की अपेक्षा *in comparison with x*	x के दरमियान *in the middle of x, during x*
x की ओर *towards, in the direction of x*	x के दौरान *during x*
x की जगह में *in place of x*	x के द्वारा *by, through the agency of x*
x की तरह *like x*	x के नज़दीक *near x*
x की तरफ़ *towards, in the direction of x*	x के निकट *near x*
x की तुलना में *in comparison with x*	x के नीचे *beneath, below, under x*
x की/के बगल में *next to x*	x के पश्चात *after x*
x की भाँति *like x*	x के/से पहले *before x*
x की वजह से *because of x*	x के पार *beyond x*
x के अंदर *inside x*	x के पास *near x* (also substitutes for the verb
x के अतिरिक्त *in addition to x*	*to have*)
x के अनुकूल *befitting, suitable for x*	x के पीछे *behind x*
x के अनुसार *according to x*	x के प्रति *towards x*
x के अलावा *besides x*	x के प्रतिकूल *opposed, contrary to x*
x के आगे *ahead of x*	x के फलस्वरूप *as a result of x*
x के आसपास *near about, around x*	x के बग़ैर *without x*
x के उपरान्त *after x*	x के बजाय *instead of x*
x के ऊपर *above x*	x के बदले (में) *in place of, in lieu of x*
x के क़रीब *near x*	x के बराबर *equal to, like x*
x के कारण *because of x*	x के बाद *after x*
x के किनारे *on the side/bank of x*	x के बारे में *about, concerning x*
x के ख़िलाफ़ *opposed to x*	x के बावजूद *in spite of x*
x के चारों ओर/तरफ़ *all around x, in all four*	x के बाहर *outside x*
directions	x के बिना *without x*
x के जैसे *like x*	x के बीच *in the middle of x*

x के भीतर inside x	x के वास्ते for, for the sake of x
x के मारे because of x	x के विपरीत opposed, contrary to x
x के मुताबिक़ according to x	x के विरुद्ध against x
x के मुक़ाबले in comparison with x	x के समय at the time of x
x के यहाँ at x's place	x के समान like, equal to x
x के योग्य worthy of x	x के सहारे with the support of x
x के लायक़ worthy of x	x के साथ with x
x के लिये for, for the sake of x	x के सामने in front of x
x के वक़्त at the time of x	x के सिवा(य) except, apart from x

There are four postpositions that can be reversed and used as prepositions before the noun or pronoun as in English.

x के बिना without x

वह मेरे बिना भारत गया।
वह बिना मेरे भारत गया।
He went to India without me.

x के बग़ैर without x

मैं दोस्तों के बग़ैर हिन्दी नहीं पढ़ता।
मैं बग़ैर दोस्तों के हिन्दी नहीं पढ़ता।
I (m) don't study Hindi without my friends.

x के मारे because of x

बीमारी के मारे मैंने काम नहीं किया।
मारे बीमारी के मैंने काम नहीं किया।
I didn't do the work because of illness.

x के सिवा(य) apart from x

तुम्हारे सिवा सभी लोग गये।
सिवा तुम्हारे सभी लोग गये।
Everybody went apart from you.

APPENDIX C

Countries, Nationalities and Regional Indian Identities

Often nationalities are followed by लोग "people," as in:
अमरीकी लोग Americans (American people)

Afghanistan अफ़ग़ानिस्तान	Afghani अफ़ग़ानी
America अमरीका	American अमरीकी, अमरीकन
Andhra Pradesh आंध्र प्रदेश	Andhra आंध्र
Assam असम	Assamese असमी
Australia ऑस्ट्रेलिया	Australian ऑस्ट्रेलियाई, ऑस्ट्रेलियन
Bangladesh बंग्लादेश	Bangladeshi बंग्लादेशी
Bengal बंगाल	Bengali बंगाली
Bhutan भूटान	Bhutanese भूटानी
Canada कैनाडा	Canadian कैनेडियन
China चीन	Chinese चीनी
England इंग्लैंड	English अंग्रेज़, इंग्लिश, इंग्लिस्तानी, विलायती
Europe यूरोप	European यूरोपीय, यूरोपीयन
France फ़्रांस	French फ़्रांसीसी
Germany जर्मनी	German जर्मन
Haryana हरियाणा	Haryana हरियाणवी
India भारत, हिन्दुस्तान, इंडिया	Indian भारतीय, हिन्दुस्तानी
Japan जापान	Japanese जापानी
Kannada कन्नड़	Kannada कन्नड़
Kashmir कश्मीर	Kashmiri कश्मीरी
Kerala केरल	Keralite केरल
Maharashtra महाराष्ट्र	Maratha मराठा
Myanmar म्यानमार	Myanmar म्यानमार
Nepal नेपाल	Nepalese नेपाली
Orissa उड़ीसा	Orissi उड़िया
Pakistan पाकिस्तान	Pakistani पाकिस्तानी
Portugal पुर्तगाल	Portuguese पुर्तगाली
Punjab पंजाब	Punjabi पंजाबी
Russia रूस	Russian रूसी
Spain स्पेन	Spanish स्पेनिश, स्पेनी
Sri Lanka श्री लंका	Sri Lankan श्री लंकन
Tamil Nadu तमिल नाडु	Tamil तमिल

APPENDIX **D**
Family Relations

There are more precise terms for particular relations in Hindi than in English. While words such as "aunty" and "uncle" are gaining a certain popularity among particular Hindi-speaking groups and being used sometimes to address elders who are not necessarily family relations, the words below are all still commonly used.

Here terms are given according to the relationship to "self."

पिता Father	
दादा - दादी	paternal grandfather - grandmother
चाचा - चाची	father's younger brother - his wife
ताऊ - ताई	father's older brother - his wife
फूफी (बुआ) - फूफा	father's sister - her husband
चचेरा भाई - चचेरी बहन	male cousin - female cousin (father's side)
माता Mother	
नाना - नानी	maternal grandfather - grandmother
मामा - मामी	mother's brother - his wife
मौसी - मौसा	mother's sister - her husband
ममेरा भाई - ममेरी बहन	male cousin - female cousin (mother's side)
भाई - भाभी	brother - his wife
भतीजा - भतीजी	brother's son - daughter (nephew, niece)
बहन - बहनोई	sister - her husband
भानजा - भानजी	sister's son - daughter (nephew, niece)
बेटा - बहू	son - his wife (daughter-in-law)
पोता - पोती	grandson - granddaughter (son's side)
बेटी - दामाद	daughter - her husband (son-in-law)
नाती - नातिन	grandson - granddaughter (daughter's side)
पति Husband - पत्नी Wife	
ससुर - सास	father-in-law - mother-in-law
साला - सलहज	wife's brother - his wife
साली - साढू	wife's sister - her husband
There are some additional terms for the female subject:	
जेठ - जेठानी	husband's elder brother - his wife
देवर - देवरानी	husband's younger brother - his wife
ननद - ननदोई	husband's sister - her husband

There are a few variations that are used in addition to some of these terms. It should be noted that the terms साला *brother-in-law* and साली *sister-in-law* should be used with caution as they are also strong terms of abuse.

APPENDIX E
The Verbal Unit

Perhaps the most important part of the verbal unit is the participle. Hindi has two participles: the imperfect participle and the perfect participle.

The imperfect participle indicates that *the action is incomplete*.

The perfect participle indicates that *the action is complete*.

Auxiliary verbs provide further information about the tense, mood and aspect in the verbal unit.

This is a list of all of the possible verbal constructions for a masculine subject using the verb जाना *to go*.

जाना *to go*

Imperfect participle — जाता *goes*:
वह जाता है he goes (imperfect present)

वह जाता था he used to go (habitual past)

शायद वह जाता हो perhaps he goes (potential)

वह जाता होगा he must go (presumptive)

जाता हुआ going (adjective)

अगर वह जाता तो… if he went then … (contrary to fact)

वह जाता रहता है he keeps on going (imperfect participle + रहना)

Perfect participle — गया *gone*:
वह गया he went (past)

वह गया है he has gone (present perfect)

वह गया था he had gone (past perfect)

शायद वह गया हो perhaps he may have gone (past potential)

वह गया होगा he must have gone (past presumptive)

अगर वह गया होता तो… if he had gone then …

गया हुआ gone (adjective)

वह जाया करता है he goes as a habit (perfective participle masc. singular + करना)[1]

बिना गये/गये बिना without going (oblique perfect participle + बिना)

Future Tense
वह जाएगा he will go (future)

Imperatives
जा, जाओ, जाइये, जाना, जाइयेगा (please) go (imperative)

Optative
शायद वह जाए perhaps he may go (optative)

---

1. The form of जाना is irregular in this construction.

Stem Form

वह जा सकता है he can go (stem + सकना)
वह जा पाता है he can go (stem + पाना)
वह जा चुका है he has already gone (stem + चुकना)
वह जा रहा है he is going (present progressive)
वह जा रहा था he was going (past progressive)
शायद वह जा रहा हो he may be going (potential progressive)
वह जा रहा होगा he must be going (presumptive progressive)
अगर वह जा रहा होता तो … if he had been going then … (progressive contrary to fact)

Infinitive Form

उसे जाना है he has to go (obligation)
उसे जाना चाहिये he should go (obligation)
उसे जाना पड़ता है he is compelled to go (obligation)
वह जाना चाहता है he wants to go (infinitive + चाहना)
वह जाना शुरू करता है he begins to go (infinitive + शुरू करना)

Oblique Infinitive Form

वह जाने देता है he allows to go (oblique infinitive + देना)
वह जाने लगता है he begins to go (oblique infinitive + लगना)
वह जानेवाला है he is about to go, he is a "goer" (oblique infinitive + वाला)
वह जाने को है he is about to go (oblique infinitive + को)

Absolutive

जाकर having gone (absolutive)

Adverbial Use

जाते हुए going (adverbial use)[2]
गये हुए gone (adverbial use)[2]

The verb जाना is also used as a secondary verb in the following ways:

वह बोले जाता है। He keeps on speaking. (perfect participle in oblique form + जाना)
मेरा सिर फटा जा रहा है। My head is about to explode. (perfect participle in oblique form + जाना)
काम हो गया है। The work is finished. (verb stem + जाना)
भारत की आबादी बढ़ती जा रही है। The population of India just keeps growing. (imperfect participle + जाना)

Use of ने

With transitive verbs in the perfective form the postposition ने governs the logical subject of the sentence. The verb will then either agree with the logical object (if it is not governed by a postposition)—objectival construction; or will agree with nothing—neutral construction.

वह कहती है। She says. (subjectival construction)
उसने बात की। He/she talked. (objectival construction)
उसने कहा। He/she said. (neutral construction)

---

2. These can also be masculine plural/oblique adjectives.

Answer Key to Practice Exercises

Meeting Kavita

Hello. My name is Kavita. What is your name? I am an Indian girl. Are you Indian? Are you American? Who is this? This is my friend. His name is Deepak. This is my home. My home is in Delhi. My home is big. This is my book. My book is blue.

1. लड़की का नाम क्या है? लड़की का नाम कविता है। The girl's name is Kavita.
2. आपका नाम क्या है? मेरा नाम… है। My name is … .
3. क्या कविता हिन्दुस्तानी लड़की है? जी हाँ, कविता हिन्दुस्तानी लड़की है। Yes, Kavita is an Indian girl.
4. क्या आप हिन्दुस्तानी हैं? जी हाँ, मैं हिन्दुस्तानी हूँ। जी नहीं, मैं हिन्दुस्तानी नहीं हूँ। Yes, I am Indian. No, I am not Indian.
5. क्या आप अमरीकी हैं? जी हाँ, मैं अमरीकी हूँ। जी नहीं, मैं अमरीकी नहीं हूँ। Yes, I am American. No, I am not American.
6. लड़का कौन है? लड़का दीपक है। The boy is Deepak.
7. क्या कविता की किताब लाल है? जी नहीं, कविता की किताब नीली है। No, Kavita's book is blue.
8. क्या कविता का घर बड़ा है? जी हाँ, वह बड़ा है। Yes, it is big.
9. क्या आपका घर बड़ा है? जी हाँ, वह बड़ा है। जी नहीं, वह बड़ा नहीं है। No, it is not big.

For 8 you can also respond जी हाँ, कविता का मकान बड़ा है। Yes, Kavita's house is big.
For 9, you can also respond जी हाँ, मेरा मकान बड़ा है। Yes, my house is big. (This can also be expressed in the negative.)

More about Deepak

Hello. I am Deepak. I am from Allahabad but these days I am in Delhi. Are you American or Indian? Who is Kavita? Kavita is my friend. Where is my parents' home? My parents' home is in Allahabad. My parents and my sister are in Allahabad. One of my uncles is in Delhi. This is his home. His name is Kripa Lal. I have a lot of friends in Delhi.

1. यह लड़का कौन है? यह लड़का दीपक है। Who is this boy? This boy is Deepak.
2. क्या दीपक दिल्ली का है? जी नहीं, दीपक दिल्ली का नहीं है। वह इलाहाबाद का है। Is Deepak from Delhi? No, Deepak is not from Delhi. He is from Allahabad.
3. क्या आप दिल्ली के/की हैं? जी नहीं, मैं दिल्ली का/की नहीं हूँ। (जी हाँ, मैं दिल्ली का/की हूँ।) Are you from Delhi? No, I am not from Delhi. (Yes, I am from Delhi.)
4. दीपक का घर कहाँ है? दीपक का घर इलाहाबाद में है। Where is Deepak's home? Deepak's home is in Allahabad.
5. तुम्हारा घर कहाँ है? मेरा घर… में है। Where is your home? My home is in …
6. क्या आप अमरीकी हैं? जी हाँ, मैं अमरीकी हूँ। (जी नहीं, मैं अमरीकी नहीं हूँ।) Are you American? Yes, I am American. (No, I am not American.)

7. क्या दिल्ली में दीपक के बहुत दोस्त हैं? जी हाँ, दिल्ली में उस के बहुत दोस्त हैं। Does Deepak have a lot of friends in Delhi? Yes, he has a lot of friends in Delhi.

Lesson 5

Meeting Kavita's Family

This is my family. This is my older brother. His name is Sameer. These are my parents. My mother's name is Sunita and my father's name is Amitabh. And these are my (maternal) grandparents. "Nani" means mother's mother. "Nana" means mother's father. My (paternal) grandparents are not in Delhi. They are in Mumbai.

1. क्या कविता का भाई है? जी हाँ, उसका भाई है।
2. क्या आपका भाई है? जी हाँ, मेरा भाई है। जी नहीं मेरा कोई भाई नहीं है।
3. समीर कौन है? समीर कविता का भाई है।
4. क्या कविता के नाना-नानी दिल्ली में हैं? जी हाँ, वे दिल्ली में हैं।
5. क्या कविता के दादा-दादी दिल्ली में हैं? जी नहीं, वे मुम्बई में हैं।
6. क्या आपके नाना-नानी/दादा-दादी ... में हैं? (the name of your city) जी हाँ, वे ...में हैं।
7. नाना-नानी का मतलब क्या है? नाना-नानी का मतलब maternal grandparents है।

How Are You? How's the Weather?

Kavita : Hello Deepak, how are you?

Deepak : I am completely fine (at perfect ease). You tell (me).

Kavita : Fine. I am fine. How were you yesterday?

Deepak : Yesterday I was sick. How were you yesterday?

Kavita : Yesterday I was well. How was yesterday's weather?

Deepak : Yesterday's weather was charming. Today's weather is bad.

Kavita : Today the weather is not bad, Deepak.

1. आप कैसे/कैसी हैं? मैं ठीक हूँ। How are you? I am okay.
2. कल आप कैसे थे (कैसी थीं)? कल मैं ठीक था/थी। (कल मैं बीमार था/थी।) How were you yesterday? Yesterday I was okay. (Yesterday I was sick.)
3. आज का मौसम कैसा है? आज का मौसम अच्छा/ख़राब है। How is the weather today? The weather today is good/bad.
4. क्या आज का मौसम बहुत ख़राब है? जी नहीं, आज का मौसम बहुत ख़राब नहीं है। Is the weather today very bad? No, the weather today is not very bad.
5. कल का मौसम कैसा था? कल का मौसम सुहावना था। How was the weather yesterday? The weather yesterday was charming.
6. क्या कल का मौसम बहुत अच्छा था? जी हाँ, कल का मौसम बहुत अच्छा था। Was yesterday's weather very good? Yes, yesterday's weather was very good.

Lesson 6

Meeting Deepak's Family

This is my family. This is my sister. Her name is Vrinda. And I have an older brother. His name is Sanjeev. These are my (paternal) grandparents. My parents are in Allahabad. And this is my uncle. I am twenty-two years old. And Kavita is twenty-two years of age. What is your age? Kavita is a good friend of mine. Kavita does not have a sister.

1. दीपक की बहन का नाम क्या है? दीपक की बहन का नाम वृन्दा है। Deepak's sister's name is Vrinda.
2. क्या आपकी बहन है? जी हाँ, मेरी बहन है। (जी नहीं, मेरी कोई बहन नहीं है।) Yes, I have a sister. (No, I don't have any sister.)
3. उसकी उम्र क्या है? उसकी उम्र … साल की है। She is … years of age.
4. दीपक की क्या उम्र है? दीपक की उम्र बाईस साल की है। Deepak is twenty-two years of age.
5. कविता कितने साल की है? कविता बाईस साल की है। Kavita is twenty-two years of age.
6. आपकी उम्र क्या है? मेरी उम्र …की है। My age is … .
7. आपके कितने अच्छे दोस्त हैं? मेरे बहुत अच्छे दोस्त हैं। I have many friends.

Lesson 7

Outside the Library

Deepak : Hello Kavita, how are you today?

Kavita : I am absolutely fine today. You tell (me).

Deepak : Fine, everything's fine. How is your brother these days?

Kavita : He is okay. How is your sister these days?

Deepak : She is well. Hey, Imran, greetings. How are you?

Imran : I am very well. How are both of you?

Deepak : Fine. Imran, today is your mother's birthday, right?

Imran : Yes, today mum is very happy.

Kavita : Really. How old is she?

Imran : She is fifty.

Deepak : Wow, that's great.

1. आज कविता कैसी है? आज कविता बिल्कुल ठीक है। How is Kavita today? Today Kavita is absolutely fine.
2. आज क्या दीपक ठीक है? जी हाँ, आज दीपक ठीक है। Is Deepak okay today? Yes, today Deepak is fine.
3. आज कौन मज़े में है? आज इमरान मज़े में है। Who is in fine spirits today? Today Imran is in fine spirits.
4. आज तुम्हारा क्या हाल है? आज मैं मज़े में हूँ। (मैं ठीक हूँ।) How are you today? Today I am in fine spirits. (I am fine.)
5. क्या इमरान दीपक और कविता का दोस्त है? जी हाँ, वह उनका दोस्त है। Is Imran Deepak and Kavita's friend? Yes, he is their friend.
6. आज इमरान की माँ क्यों खुश हैं? आज इमरान की माँ खुश हैं क्योंकि आज उनका जन्मदिन है। Why is Imran's mother happy today? Today Imran's mother is happy because today (it) is her birthday.
7. क्या आज तुम्हारी माँ का जन्मदिन है? जी नहीं, आज मेरी माँ का जन्मदिन नहीं है। (जी हाँ, आज मेरी माँ का जन्मदिन है।) Is (it) your mother's birthday today? No, (it) is not my mother's birthday today. (Yes, [it] is my mother's birthday today.)
8. क्या आज तुम्हारे पिता जी का जन्मदिन है? जी नहीं, आज मेरे पिता जी का जन्मदिन नहीं है। (जी हाँ, आज मेरे पिता जी का जन्मदिन है।) Is (it) your father's birthday today? No, (it) is not my father's birthday today. (Yes, [it] is my father's birthday today.)

What Does Kavita Want?

Hello friends. In reality my life is very good. I do not want much. I want good grades in my exam. And yes, I want tea right now. My brother wants a lot of money. And he wants a new car. What do you want? Money? Peace? Who doesn't want peace in life? Everyone wants peace in the world, right? Enough, I don't want much.

1. क्या कविता को बहुत पैसे चाहिए? जी नहीं, कविता को बहुत पैसे नहीं चाहिए। No, Kavita does not want/need a lot of money.
2. क्या आपको बहुत पैसे चाहिए? जी हाँ, मुझको बहुत पैसे चाहिए। Yes, I want/need a lot of money.
3. क्या कविता के भाई को नयी गाड़ी चाहिए? जी हाँ, कविता के भाई को नयी गाड़ी चाहिए। Yes, Kavita's brother wants/needs a new car.
4. क्या दुनिया में सब लोगों को शांति चाहिये? जी हाँ, दुनिया में सब लोगों को शांति चाहिये। Yes, all the people in the world want/need peace.
5. अभी कविता को कॉफ़ी चाहिये या चाय? अभी उसे चाय चाहिये। Right now she wants tea.
6. परीक्षा में किसे अच्छे नंबर चाहिये? परीक्षा में कविता को अच्छे नंबर चाहिये। Kavita wants good grades in the exam.

Lesson 8

How Many Brothers and Sisters Do You Have?

We are two siblings. I have one brother, Sameer. These days he is in Australia. Previously, all of the people in my family were in Bombay. My father has two brothers. One of my father's brothers has two boys, and the other brother has two girls. Deepak has two siblings. How many brothers and sisters do you have? What are your brothers' names? What are your sisters' names?

1. कविता के कितने भाई-बहन हैं? उसके एक भाई हैं। How many brothers and sisters does Kavita have? She has one brother.
2. आजकल कविता के भाई कहाँ हैं? आजकल वे ऑस्ट्रेलिया में हैं। Where is Kavita's brother these days? These days he is in Australia.
3. क्या पहले कविता के परिवार के सब लोग बंबई में थे? जी हाँ, पहले कविता के परिवार के सब लोग बंबई में थे। Were all the people in Kavita's family previously in Bombay? Yes, all the people in Kavita's family were previously in Bombay.
4. आप के कितने भाई-बहन हैं? मेरे दो भाई-बहन हैं। (मेरा कोई भाई-बहन नहीं है। मेरी दो बहनें हैं।) How many brother and sisters do you have? I have two brothers and sisters. (I have no brothers and sisters. I have two sisters.)
5. आपके भाइयों और बहनों के नाम क्या हैं? मेरे भाई का नाम ... है। (मेरे भाइयों के नाम ... और ... हैं।) मेरी बहन का नाम ... है। (मेरी बहनों के नाम ... और ... हैं।) What are the names of your brothers and sisters? My brother's name is ... . (The names of my brothers are ... and ... .) My sister's name is ... . (The names of my sisters are ... and ... .)
6. कविता के पिता जी के भाइयों के कितने लड़के-लड़कियाँ हैं? कविता के पिता जी के एक भाई के दो लड़के हैं और दूसरे भाई की दो लड़कियाँ हैं। How many boys and girls do Kavita's father's brothers have? One of Kavita's father's brothers has two boys and the other brother has two girls.

What Does Deepak Want?

Hello my friends. How are you? What did my friend Kavita want? Do you remember? Yes, she wanted good grades in her exam. What do I want? I don't want just one thing. I want many things. I want a good job after (my) studies. I wanted two books from the library yesterday. My sister wants a new mobile phone and my brother wanted a lot of money but now he wants nothing. Enough, we want just this much.

1. कविता को क्या चाहिये था? उसे परीक्षा में अच्छे नंबर चाहिये थे। She had wanted/needed good grades in the exam.
2. दीपक को क्या चाहिये? दीपक को बहुत चीज़ें चाहिए। Deepak wants/needs many things.
3. क्या दीपक को बहुत चीज़ें चाहिए? जी हाँ, दीपक को बहुत चीज़ें चाहिए। Yes, Deepak wants/ needs many things.
4. कल दीपक को क्या चाहिये था? कल दीपक को लाइब्रेरी से दो किताबें चाहिये थीं। Yesterday Deepak wanted/needed two books from the library.
5. क्या दीपक की बहन को बहुत पैसे चाहिए? जी नहीं, उसे नया फ़ोन चाहिए। No, she wants/ needs a new phone.

Lesson 9

What Do You Do?

Kavita and Deepak are both students. They study in a college in Delhi. Kavita's father is in the army and her mother is a doctor. These days they live in Delhi. Deepak's mother and father live in Allahabad. Deepak's father works for (in) Indian Railways and his mother is a school teacher. Deepak lives in Delhi with an uncle. Deepak's sister lives in Allahabad. She comes to Delhi occasionally. Deepak's brother works in Delhi in IT. These days Kavita's brother lives in Australia. He studies there. Now you tell, where do you live and what do you do?

1. दिल्ली में कौन रहता है? दिल्ली में कविता, कविता के माँ-बाप, दीपक, दीपक का भाई और दीपक के मामा-मामी रहते हैं। Who lives in Delhi? Kavita, Kavita's parents, Deepak, Deepak's brother and Deepak's uncle and aunty live in Delhi.
2. दिल्ली के कॉलेज में कौन पढ़ता है? दिल्ली के कॉलेज में दीपक और कविता पढ़ते हैं। Who studies in a Delhi college? Deepak and Kavita study in a Delhi college.
3. क्या आप कॉलेज में पढ़ते हैं? (पढ़ती हैं) जी हाँ, मैं कॉलेज में पढ़ता हूँ। (पढ़ती हूँ) जी नहीं, मैं कॉलेज में नहीं पढ़ता। (नहीं पढ़ती) Do you study in college? Yes, I study in college. No, I don't study in college.
4. आप क्या करते हैं? (करती हैं) मैं कॉलेज में पढ़ता हूँ। (पढ़ती हूँ) or मैं दफ़्तर में काम करता हूँ। What do you do? I study in college. *or* I work in an office.
5. क्या दीपक के पिता सेना में हैं? जी नहीं, दीपक के पिता सेना में नहीं हैं। कविता के पिता सेना में हैं। Is Deepak's father in the army? No, Deepak's father in not in the army. Kavita's father is in the army.
6. क्या कविता की माँ डॉक्टर है? जी हाँ, कविता की माँ डॉक्टर है। Is Kavita's mother a doctor? Yes, Kavita's mother is a doctor.
7. क्या कविता का भाई दिल्ली में आई० टी० में काम करता है? जी नहीं, दीपक के भाई दिल्ली में आई० टी० में काम करते हैं। Does Kavita's brother work in IT in Delhi? No, Deepak's brother works in IT in Delhi.
8. क्या आप छात्र हैं? जी हाँ, मैं छात्र हूँ। जी नहीं, मैं छात्र नहीं हूँ। Are you a student? Yes, I am a student. No, I am not a student.

9. क्या आप नौकरी करते हैं? (करती हैं) जी नहीं, मैं नौकरी नहीं करता। (करती) Do you work?
No, I do not work.

What Do You Do on Monday?

Kavita : Tomorrow is Monday. What do you do on Monday(s)?

Deepak : On Monday(s) I go to college early, why?

Kavita : Then what do you do?

Deepak : After college I go back to my uncle's home. On Monday I make dinner with my aunty. What
do you do?

Kavita : I go to my mother. Mum works late at the surgery on Monday(s). I help her on Monday(s).
After that, we go to Khan Market. Come to the market with us tomorrow.

Deepak : Great.

1. क्या सोमवार को दीपक जल्दी कॉलेज जाता है? जी हाँ, वह जल्दी कॉलेज जाता है। Yes,
he goes to college early.

2. क्या कविता सोमवार को माँ की मदद करती है? जी हाँ, वह सोमवार को माँ की मदद करती
है। Yes, she helps her mother.

3. क्या आप सोमवार को कॉलेज जाते हैं? (जाती हैं) जी हाँ, मैं सोमवार को कॉलेज जाता हूँ।
(जाती हूँ) जी नहीं मैं सोमवार को कॉलेज नहीं जाता। (नहीं जाती) Yes, I go to college on
Monday. No, I don't go to college on Monday.

4. क्या आप मंगलवार को जल्दी घर जाते हैं? (जाती हैं) जी हाँ, मैं मंगलवार को जल्दी घर
जाता हूँ। (जाती हूँ) जी नहीं, मैं मंगलवार को जल्दी घर नहीं जाता। (नहीं जाती) Yes, I go
home early on Tuesday. No, I don't go home early on Tuesday.

5. क्या आप शनिवार को सुपर मार्केट जाते हैं? (जाती हैं) जी हाँ, मैं शनिवार को सुपर मार्केट
जाता हूँ। (जाती हूँ) जी नहीं, मैं शनिवार को सुपर मार्केट नहीं जाता। (नहीं जाती) Yes, I
go to the supermarket on Saturday. No, I don't go to the supermarket on Saturday.

6. क्या आप बुधवार को रात का खाना बनाते हैं? (बनाती हैं) जी हाँ, मैं बुधवार को रात का
खाना बनाता हूँ। (बनाती हूँ) जी नहीं, मैं बुधवार को रात का खाना नहीं बनाता। (नहीं
बनाती) Yes, I cook on Wednesday. No, I don't cook on Wednesday.

Lesson 10

What Time Do You …?

Kavita gets up every day at seven o'clock. She bathes and then at eight o'clock she eats breakfast. On
Monday she goes to college at 9 A.M. At four o'clock she goes to her mother at the surgery. There she
helps her mother. At six o'clock she and her mother go to the market. On Monday Kavita's father has dinner prepared. On Wednesday she goes to college at twelve o'clock. On Thursday she remains in college
the entire day. Deepak gets up at eight o'clock every day. He eats dinner at eight o'clock. Deepak goes
to class on Monday, Tuesday and Thursday. On Wednesday and Friday he studies the entire day in the
library. Kavita occasionally studies with Deepak in the library on Friday.

1. रोज़ मुबह आठ बजे कौन उठता है? रोज़ मुबह आठ बजे दीपक उठता है। Who gets up every
morning at eight o'clock? Deepak gets up at eight o'clock every day.

2. कविता रोज़ नाश्ता कितने बजे करती है? कविता रोज़ नाश्ता आठ बजे करती है। What time
does Kavita eat breakfast every day? Kavita eats breakfast at eight o'clock every day.

3. सोमवार को कविता कितने बजे माँ के पास जाती है? सोमवार को कविता चार बजे माँ के पास जाती है। What time does Kavita go to her mother on Monday? Kavita goes to her mother at four o'clock on Monday.

4. दीपक और कविता कॉलेज कितने दिन जाते हैं? दीपक पाँच दिन और कविता चार दिन कॉलेज जाती है। How many days do Deepak and Kavita go to college? Deepak goes to college five days and Kavita goes four days. (हफ़्ते में *during the week*)

5. आप रोज़ कितने बजे उठते हैं? (उठती हैं) मैं रोज़ सात बजे उठता हूँ। (उठती हूँ) What time do you get up every day? I get up every day at seven o'clock.

6. क्या कविता कभी दीपक के साथ पुस्तकालय में पढ़ती है? जी हाँ, वह कभी दीपक के साथ पुस्तकालय में पढ़ती है। Does Kavita study with Deepak sometimes in the library? Yes, she sometimes studies with Deepak in the library.

7. दीपक रात का खाना कितने बजे खाता है? वह रात का खाना आठ बजे खाता है। What time does Deepak eat dinner? He eats dinner at eight o'clock.

8. आप रात का खाना कितने बजे खाते हैं (खाती हैं)? मैं रात का खाना सात बजे खाता हूँ। (खाती हूँ) What time do you eat dinner? I eat dinner at seven o'clock.

Where Did Kavita and Deepak Use to Live?

Deepak : Kavita, where did you use to live two years ago?

Kavita : We used to live in Bombay. We lived with (my) (paternal) grandparents. Now we live with (my) (maternal) grandparents. My brother and I studied in school in Bombay. Now my brother studies in college in Australia and we live in Delhi. Previously, you used to live in Allahabad, right?

Deepak : Yes, my parents and my sister still live in Allahabad but now my brother and I live in Delhi with (our) uncle. My sister occasionally comes to Delhi. You know, don't you, that my brother works in IT.

Kavita : Yes, and where do your (paternal) grandparents live?

Deepak : They live in Allahabad, with my parents. And my (maternal) grandparents live in Benaras. They used to live in Allahabad.

An example response:

दो साल पहले मैं अमरीका में रहता था। पाँच साल पहले मैं हिन्दुस्तान में रहता था। पाँच साल पहले मैं माँ-बाप के साथ रहता था। अब मैं माँ-बाप के साथ नहीं रहता। मैं हिन्दुस्तान में स्कूल जाता था। मैं दोस्तों के साथ नहीं रहता था। मैं पत्नी के साथ नहीं रहता था। पाँच साल पहले मैं भाइयों के साथ रहता था। मेरी कोई बहन नहीं है। अभी मैं नौकरी नहीं करता। मैं पढ़ता हूँ।

Two years ago I used to live in America. Five years ago, I used to live in India. Five years ago I used to live with my parents. Now I don't live with my parents. I used to go to school in India. I didn't use to live with friends. I didn't live with (my) wife. Five years ago I lived with my brothers. I have no sister. Right now I do not work. I study.

Whose Cell Phone? Whose Friends?

Kavita : Let's go. Let's go to the canteen before class. (We will) drink tea.

Deepak : I don't want tea. I drink more coffee these days.

Kavita : Okay, baba. If you want coffee, then drink coffee. It doesn't matter to me. Where is my mobile? I will call some friends.

Deepak : Your friends or my friends?

Kavita : My friends, of course. Every Wednesday I drink tea with my friends in the canteen before class.
Deepak : Okay. Give me your mobile for a minute. I will make a call.
Kavita : Don't you have your own mobile?
Deepak : Yes, but it is at home today. Every Wednesday I eat with my brother in town.
Kavita : Phone quickly. Give me your book. I will look at it in the meantime.
Deepak : Okay. Take the book and give me the phone.

1. क्या कविता अपने दोस्तों को बुलाती है? जी हाँ, वह अपने दोस्तों को बुलाती है। Does Kavita invite her friends? Yes, she invites her friends.
2. क्या दीपक कविता के भाई को फ़ोन करता है? जी नहीं, वह अपने भाई को फ़ोन करता है। Does Deepak phone Kavita's brother? No, he phones his (own) brother.
3. हर बुध को दीपक किस के साथ शहर में खाना खाता है? हर बुध को वह अपने भाई के साथ शहर में खाना खाता है। With whom does Deepak eat every Wednesday in the city? Every Wednesday he eats in the city with his brother.
4. क्या दीपक कविता को कविता की किताब देता है? जी नहीं, वह कविता को अपनी किताब देता है। Does Deepak give Kavita her book? No, he gives Kavita his (own) book.
5. क्या कविता दीपक से अपनी किताब लेती है? जी नहीं, वह दीपक से दीपक की किताब लेती है। Does Kavita take her own book from Deepak? No, she takes Deepak's book from Deepak.
6. आज दीपक का सेल कहाँ है? आज दीपक का सेल घर पर है। Where is Deepak's cell phone today? Deepak's cell phone is at home today.
7. कविता को चाय चाहिये या कॉफ़ी? कविता को चाय चाहिये। Does Kavita want tea or coffee? Kavita wants tea.

Lesson 11

What Do You Study?
Deepak : Kavita, do you study (by) yourself?
Kavita : Yes, I always study (by) myself. What do you do?
Deepak : I do my history studies myself. But in economics a friend helps me.
Kavita : I study English (by) myself but practice English with a friend. In Hindi economics is *arth-shastra*, isn't it?
Deepak : Yes. Do you study biology yourself?
Kavita : You mean, biology? No, I study with two girl friends. Deepak, do you drive a car yourself?
Deepak : Yes, these days I drive myself. Previously I used to drive with (my) uncle.

1. क्या दीपक अपने-आप (खुद) इतिहास पढ़ता है? जी हाँ, वह अपने-आप (खुद) इतिहास पढ़ता है। Yes, he studies history himself.
2. क्या आप हमेशा अपने-आप पढ़ते हैं? (पढ़ती हैं) जी हाँ, मैं हमेशा अपने-आप पढ़ता हूँ। (पढ़ती हूँ) Yes, I always study (by) myself.
3. क्या दीपक खुद गाड़ी चलाता है? जी हाँ, वह खुद गाड़ी चलाता है। Yes, he drives a car himself.
4. क्या पहले दीपक खुद गाड़ी चलाता था? जी नहीं वह अपने मामा के साथ चलाता था। No, he used to drive with his uncle.
5. क्या कविता सचमुच हमेशा अपने-आप पढ़ती है? जी नहीं, वह कभी कभी दोस्तों के साथ पढ़ती है। No, she sometimes studies with friends.

6. क्या कविता जीव-विज्ञान अपने दोस्तों के साथ पढ़ती है? जी हाँ, वह दो दोस्तों के साथ पढ़ती है। Yes, she studies with two friends.

7. क्या आप अपने आप हिन्दी पढ़ते हैं? (पढ़ती हैं) जी हाँ, मैं अपने आप पढ़ता हूँ। (पढ़ती हूँ) जी नहीं, मैं दोस्तों के साथ पढ़ता हूँ। (पढ़ती हूँ) Yes, I study by myself. No, I study with friends.

If I Were a Rich Man…

Deepak : Kavita, if you were very wealthy, where would you live?

Kavita : If I were very wealthy, I would live in New York.

Deepak : Why would you live in New York?

Kavita : I don't know. New York is such a big city and many types of people live there. It would certainly be a lot of fun there. Where would you live?

Deepak : If I were wealthy I would still live in Delhi.

Kavita : Why would you live in Delhi? What is so special about Delhi?

Deepak : Delhi is a very good city. There is everything here.

Kavita : If you were very wealthy, would you study in college?

Deepak : That is a very good question. If I were really wealthy, then perhaps I would not study in college. I don't know. Would you study? Would you become a doctor?

Kavita : Yes, if I were very wealthy, even then I would study.

Deepak : If you were very wealthy, would you buy a new car?

Kavita : I would not buy (one) for myself, but for my parents.

Example responses:

1. अगर आप बहुत अमीर होते (होतीं) तो आप कहाँ रहते (रहतीं)? अगर मैं बहुत अमीर होता (होती) तो मैं हिन्दुस्तान में रहता। (रहती) If you were very wealthy, where would you live? If I were very wealthy I would live in India.

2. अगर आप बहुत अमीर होते (होतीं) तो क्या आप दिल्ली में रहते (रहतीं)? जी नहीं, अगर मैं बहुत अमीर होता (होती) तो मैं दिल्ली में नहीं रहता (रहती), मैं पहाड़ों में रहता। (रहती) If you were very wealthy, would you live in Delhi? If I were very wealthy, I would not live in Delhi, I would live in the mountains.

3. अगर आप बहुत अमीर होते (होतीं) तो आप क्या ख़रीदते? (ख़रीदतीं) अगर मैं बहुत अमीर होता (होती) तो मैं नयी घड़ी ख़रीदता (ख़रीदती)। If you were very wealthy, what would you buy? If I were very wealthy I would buy a new watch (घड़ी watch (*f*)).

4. अगर आप बहुत अमीर होते (होतीं) तो क्या आप नयी गाड़ी ख़रीदते? (ख़रीदतीं) जी हाँ, अगर मैं बहुत अमीर होता (होती) तो मैं नयी गाड़ी ख़रीदता। (ख़रीदती) If you were very wealthy, would you buy a new car? Yes, if I were very wealthy, I would buy a new car.

5. अगर आप बहुत अमीर होते (होतीं) तो क्या आप कभी नौकरी करते? (करतीं) जी नहीं, अगर मैं बहुत अमीर होता (होती) तो मैं कभी नौकरी नहीं करता। (करती) If you were very wealthy, would you ever work? No, if I were very wealthy I would never work.

6. अगर आप बहुत अमीर होते (होतीं) तो आप किसको पैसे देते? (देतीं) अगर मैं बहुत अमीर होता (होती) तो मैं अपनी माँ को पैसे देता। (देती) If you were very wealthy, to whom would you give money? If I were very wealthy I would give my mother money.

Lesson 12

What's Your Daily Routine?

What is my daily routine? Do you people remember? I get up daily in the morning at seven o'clock. I bathe and then I eat breakfast. On Monday one of my classes takes place in the morning (On Monday I have a morning class). I reach college in the morning at nine o'clock. On Monday evening I go to my mum at four o'clock. She works in her surgery three days a week. There I help her for two hours. On that day father has dinner prepared. On Tuesday I don't have class. I go to the library in the afternoon. Often Deepak is there. We often watch a Hindi film in the cinema on Tuesday evening. On Wednesday I go to the canteen with my friends before class and drink tea there. On Thursday I stay in college the entire day. We eat dinner every day at nine o'clock. Sometimes mother cooks and sometimes father has it prepared. At night I study for two hours. Then I sleep. Now you tell (me), what time do you get up every day? What time do you eat breakfast? What time do you go to college? What time do you sleep at night?

Example responses:

1. आप रोज़ कितने बजे उठते हैं? (उठती हैं) मैं रोज़ छे बजे उठता हूँ। (उठती हूँ) I get up daily at six o'clock.

2. रोज़ सुबह आप कितने बजे नाश्ता करते हैं? (करती हैं) रोज़ सुबह मैं सात बजे नाश्ता करता हूँ। (करती हूँ) I eat breakfast every day in the morning at seven o'clock.

3. रोज़ सुबह आप कितने बजे नहाते हैं? (नहाती हैं) रोज़ सुबह मैं आठ बजे नहाता हूँ। (नहाती हूँ) I bathe every day in the morning at eight o'clock.

4. मंगलवार की सुबह आप कितने बजे कॉलेज/दफ़्तर जाते हैं? (जाती हैं) मंगलवार की सुबह मैं नौ बजे कॉलेज/दफ़्तर जाता हूँ। (जाती हूँ) I go to college/the office on Tuesday morning at nine o'clock.

5. बुधवार की दोपहर को आप कितने बजे दिन का खाना खाते हैं? (खाती हैं) बुधवार की दोपहर को मैं एक बजे दिन का खाना खाता हूँ। (खाती हूँ) I eat lunch at one o'clock in the afternoon on Wednesday.

6. बृहस्पतिवार की शाम को आप कितने बजे घर जाते हैं? (जाती हैं) बृहस्पतिवार की शाम को मैं पाँच बजे घर जाता हूँ। (जाती हूँ) I go home on Thursday('s) evening at five o'clock.

7. शुक्रवार की रात को आप कितने बजे खाना खाते हैं? (खाती हैं) शुक्रवार की रात को मैं आठ बजे खाना खाता हूँ। (खाती हूँ) I eat dinner at eight o'clock on Friday('s) night.

8. शनिवार की रात को आप कितने बजे सोते हैं? (सोती हैं) शनिवार की रात को मैं ग्यारह बजे सोता हूँ। (सोती हूँ) I sleep at eleven o'clock on Saturday('s) night.

9. रोज़ आप कितने घंटे टेलीविज़न देखते हैं? (देखती हैं) रोज़ मैं दो घंटे टी० वी० देखता हूँ। (देखती हूँ) I watch television for two hours a day.

Where Were You Born? Where Did You Grow Up?

Kavita : Deepak, where were you born?

Deepak : I was born in Allahabad. Where were you born?

Kavita : I was born in Delhi. Where was your sister born?

Deepak : She and my brother were both born in Allahabad. All three of us grew up in Allahabad. But you used to live in Bombay, right?

Kavita : Yes, I grew up in Bombay. We lived in Bombay for many years, with my (paternal) grand-parents. Prior to that, my parents used to live in Delhi. My father comes from Delhi and my mother was born in the mountains of Uttarakhand. If my mother had not come to Delhi to study, then perhaps they would not have met.

1. दीपक कहाँ पैदा हुआ? दीपक इलाहाबाद में पैदा हुआ । Deepak was born in Allahabad.
2. कविता कहाँ पैदा हुई? कविता दिल्ली में पैदा हुई । Kavita was born in Delhi.
3. कविता कहाँ बड़ी हुई? कविता बंबई में बड़ी हुई । Kavita gew up in Bombay.
4. दीपक, उस का भाई और उस की बहन कहाँ बड़े हुए? दीपक, उस का भाई और उस की बहन इलाहाबाद में बड़े हुए । Deepak, his brother and his sister grew up in Allahabad.
5. आप कहाँ पैदा हुए? (हुई) मैं ... में पैदा हुआ । (हुई) I was born in ... .
6. आप कहाँ बड़े हुए? (बड़ी हुई) मैं ... में बड़ा हुआ । (बड़ी हुई) I grew up in ... .
7. क्या आप भारत में बड़े हुए? (बड़ी हुई) जी हाँ, मैं भारत में बड़ा हुआ । (बड़ी हुई) Yes, I grew up in India. जी नहीं, मैं भारत में बड़ा नहीं हुआ (बड़ी नहीं हुई), मैं ... में बड़ा हुआ (बड़ी हुई) । No, I didn't grow up in India, I grew up in ... .

Did You Watch the Film Last Night?

Kavita   : Hey Deepak, how are you?

Deepak   : I am fine. What about you? What did you do last night?

Kavita   : I saw a film on TV last night and then I read a book. What did you do?

Deepak   : I did nothing. Which film did you watch?

Kavita   : I watched an old Shah Rukh Khan film, *DDLJ*. The film came on Zee TV. You didn't watch?

Deepak   : No. I slept early last night. I wasn't feeling well.

Kavita   : What happened?

Deepak   : I had a headache. I slept at around eight o'clock. Which book did you read?

Kavita   : I read a novel. It is Amitav Ghosh's new book.

Deepak   : Really. How is the book?

Kavita   : It's very good. So, did you eat dinner (food) last night?

Deepak   : No. Because of the headache I didn't eat dinner (food).

1. कल रात क्या कविता ने एक फ़िल्म देखी? जी हाँ, कल रात उसने एक फ़िल्म देखी । Did Kavita watch a film last night? Yes, she watched a film.
2. कविता ने फ़िल्म कहाँ देखी? उसने फ़िल्म टी० वी० में देखी । Where did she see the film? She saw it on TV.
3. कल रात दीपक की तबीयत कैसी थी? कल रात दीपक की तबीयत ठीक नहीं थी । How was Deepak's health last night? Last night Deepak's health was not okay.
4. कल रात दीपक की तबीयत क्यों ठीक नहीं थी? क्योंकि उसके सिर में दर्द था । Why was Deepak's health not okay last night? Because he had a headache (there was pain in his head).
5. कल रात कविता ने क्या पढ़ा? कल रात उसने एक उपन्यास पढ़ा । What did Kavita read last night? Last night she read a novel.
6. कल रात क्या दीपक ने खाना खाया? जी नहीं, उसने खाना नहीं खाया । Did Deepak eat dinner (food) last night? No, he did not eat dinner (food).
7. कल रात दीपक कितने बजे सोया? कल रात वह लगभग आठ बजे सोया । What time did Deepak sleep last night? Last night he slept at approximately eight o'clock.

Lesson 13

How Do You Go to College?

Kavita   : Deepak, how do you come to college?

Deepak   : I sometimes come by car and sometimes by metro. How do you come?

Kavita   : I mostly come by metro. On Wednesday morning I come with my father by car.

Deepak : And how do you go to your mother's surgery on Monday evening?
Kavita : Mum's surgery is near Khan Market. I go there by auto. And then mum and I walk up to Khan Market. From there we walk back to the surgery and then go home by car.

1. दीपक कॉलेज कैसे जाता है? दीपक कभी गाड़ी से कॉलेज जाता है, कभी मेट्रो से जाता है।
   Deepak goes to college sometimes by car, sometimes by the metro.
2. कविता कॉलेज कैसे जाती है? कविता ज़्यादातर मेट्रो से कॉलेज जाती है। बुधवार की सुबह वह अपने पिता के साथ गाड़ी से जाती है। Kavita goes to college mostly by the metro. On Wednesday morning she goes with her father by car.
3. आप स्कूल/कॉलेज/दफ़्तर कैसे आते हैं? (आती हैं) मैं ट्रेन से कॉलेज आता हूँ। (आती हूँ) (Example:) I come to college by train.
4. सोमवार को कविता और उस की माँ ख़ान मार्केट कैसे जाती हैं? सोमवार को कविता और उस की माँ ख़ान मार्केट पैदल जाती हैं। Kavita and her mother walk to Khan Market on Monday.
5. क्या आप शाम को घर पैदल जाते हैं? (जाती हैं) जी नहीं, मैं गाड़ी से जाता हूँ। (जाती हूँ) जी हाँ, मैं पैदल जाता हूँ। (जाती हूँ) (Example:) No, I go by car. Yes, I walk.
6. क्या आप ट्रेन से स्कूल/कॉलेज/दफ़्तर जाते हैं? (जाती हैं) जी नहीं, मैं कॉलेज पैदल जाता हूँ। (जाती हूँ) (Example:) No, I walk to college.

Do You Have Money, Kavita?
Deepak : Kavita, do you have money today? I want tea right now but I don't have money.
Kavita : Yes, I have enough (appropriate) money for tea. Okay, I will buy you (make you drink) tea today. But Deepak, why don't you ever have money?
Deepak : Forgive me. It is true that you often pay for (the) tea. Take the money for it from me tomorrow.
Kavita : Okay. Do you have a car today?
Deepak : Yes, I have a car.
Kavita : Great. Drop me home after an hour.
Deepak : Okay. Do you have a cell (phone)?
Kavita : Of course. Don't you?
Deepak : Not today. Give me your phone. I (will) make a call.
Kavita : Deepak, if you had money and a phone, you would not ask from me again and again.
Deepak : So, what's the big deal (what happened)?
Kavita : Okay, it's nothing.

1. आज क्या दीपक के पास पैसे हैं? जी नहीं, आज उसके पास पैसे नहीं हैं। Does Deepak have money today? No, he doesn't have money today.
2. आज क्या आपके पास पैसे हैं? जी हाँ, आज मेरे पास पैसे हैं। Do you have money today? Yes, I have money today. जी नहीं, आज मेरे पास पैसे नहीं हैं। No, I don't have money today.
3. आज क्या कविता के पास चाय के लायक़ पैसे हैं? जी हाँ, आज उसके पास चाय के लायक़ पैसे हैं। Does Kavita have enough money for tea today? Yes, she has enough money (worthy) for tea today.
4. आज क्या दीपक कविता को चाय पिलाता है? जी नहीं, आज दीपक कविता को चाय नहीं पिलाता, कविता दीपक को चाय पिलाती है। Does Deepak buy (serve) Kavita tea today? No, Deepak does not buy (serve) Kavita tea today, Kavita buys Deepak tea.

5. क्या आप अक्सर दोस्तों को चाय पिलाते हैं (पिलाती हैं?) जी हाँ, मैं अक्सर दोस्तों को चाय पिलाता हूँ। (पिलाती हूँ) जी नहीं मैं कभी दोस्तों को चाय नहीं पिलाता। (नहीं पिलाती) Do you often buy (serve) tea for friends? Yes, I often buy (serve) friends tea. No, I never buy (serve) friends tea.

6. आज क्या दीपक के पास गाड़ी है? जी हाँ, आज उसके पास गाड़ी है। Does Deepak have a/the car today? Yes, he has a/the car today.

7. क्या आपके पास गाड़ी है? जी हाँ, मेरे पास गाड़ी है। जी नहीं, मेरे पास गाड़ी नहीं है। Do you have a car? Yes, I have a car. No, I don't have a car.

8. अगर दीपक के पास पैसे रहते तो क्या वह बार-बार कविता से माँगता? जी नहीं, अगर उसके पास पैसे रहते तो वह बार-बार कविता से नहीं माँगता। If Deepak had money, would he demand it again and again from Kavita? No, if he had money, he would not demand (ask) it again and again from Kavita.

What Is Worth Seeing in Delhi?

Deepak : Kavita, tell me, in your opinion what is worth seeing in Delhi?

Kavita : Deepak, you know that there are many things worth seeing in Delhi.

Deepak : Yes, but today I want to show an old friend.

Kavita : Where is your friend from?

Deepak : He is from Allahabad. He has never come to Delhi before.

Kavita : Where is your friend right now?

Deepak : He is at home. He wanted to rest.

Kavita : Good. So, in Delhi India Gate is worth seeing. The Kutub Minar is worth seeing and the Red Fort is worth seeing. And yes, certainly take your friend out to eat at Bengali Market.

Deepak : Okay. You come to eat as well. Come to my place at six o'clock this evening.

Kavita : It is difficult for me to come today. Come to my place with your friend in the evening. Have dinner with us.

1. दिल्ली में क्या-क्या देखने लायक़ है? दिल्ली में बहुत सारी चीज़ें देखने लायक़ हैं। दिल्ली में इंडिया गेट देखने लायक़ है। कुतुब मीनार देखने लायक़ है। और लाल क़िला देखने लायक़ है। Many things are worth seeing in Delhi. India Gate is worth seeing. The Kutub Minar is worth seeing. And the Red Fort is worth seeing.

2. क्या आप दिल्ली में लाल क़िला देखना चाहते हैं? (चाहती हैं) जी हाँ, मैं लाल क़िला देखना चाहता हूँ। (चाहती हूँ) दिल्ली में मैं कुछ देखना नहीं चाहता। (नहीं चाहती) Yes, I want to see the Red Fort. I don't want to see anything in Delhi.

3. क्या आगरा में ताज महल देखने लायक़ है? जी हाँ, आगरा में ताज महल देखने लायक़ है। Yes, the Taj Mahal in Agra is worth seeing.

4. क्या दीपक अपने दोस्त को दिल्ली में कुछ दिखाना चाहता है? जी हाँ, वह अपने दोस्त को दिल्ली में कुछ दिखाना चाहता है। Yes, he wants to show his (own) friend something in Delhi.

5. क्या आप दिल्ली के बंगाली मार्केट में खाना खाने के लिये जाना चाहते हैं? (चाहती हैं) जी हाँ, मैं दिल्ली के बंगाली मार्केट में खाना खाने को जाना चाहता हूँ। (चाहती हूँ) Yes, I want to go to eat at the Bengali Market in Delhi. जी नहीं, मैं दिल्ली के बंगाली मार्केट में खाना खाने को जाना नहीं चाहता। (चाहती) No, I don't want to go to the Bengali Market in Delhi to eat.

6. आज रात को क्या आप खाना खाने को बाहर जाना चाहते हैं? (चाहती हैं) जी हाँ, मैं आज रात को खाना खाने को बाहर जाना चाहता हूँ। (चाहती हूँ) जी नहीं, मैं आज रात को खाना खाने घर जाना चाहता हूँ। (चाहती हूँ) Yes, I want to go out to eat tonight. No, I want to go home to eat tonight.

Have You Ever Been to America? How Many Times?

Kavita   : Say, Imran. How are you?

Imran   : Everything is fine. And how are you? Hello Deepak, how are you?

Deepak : I am absolutely fine. Imran, have you ever been to America?

Imran   : Yes, I have been.

Deepak : How many times have you been?

Imran   : I have been once. My older brother lives in Chicago. Kavita, have you ever been to America?

Kavita   : No, I have never been. But I really want to go. I have heard that New York is a city worth seeing.

Imran   : Yes, there are lots of things worth doing and seeing in New York. I stayed there for five days with my brother.

Kavita   : Deepak thinks that there is nothing worth seeing in America. I am speaking the truth, aren't I Deepak?

Deepak : I never said such. I just think that there are so many good places in India that there is no need to go to America. I want to see my own country before seeing a foreign country.

Imran   : Deepak is right, Kavita. (Deepak's matter is right)

1. इमरान अमरीका कितनी बार गया है? इमरान एक बार गया है। Imran has been once.
2. आप कितनी बार हिन्दुस्तान गये हैं? (गयी हैं) मैं एक बार गया हूँ। (गई हूँ) or मैं कभी हिन्दुस्तान नहीं गया। (गयी) I have been once. *or* I have never been to India.
3. क्या कविता कभी अमरीका गयी है? जी नहीं, वह कभी अमरीका नहीं गयी। No, she has never been to America.
4. क्या कविता अमरीका जाना चाहती है? जी हाँ, वह जाना चाहती है। Yes, she wants to go.
5. कविता ने न्यू यॉर्क के बारे में क्या सुना है? उसने सुना है कि न्यू यॉर्क देखने लायक़ है। She has heard that New York is worth seeing.
6. विदेश जाने से पहले दीपक क्या करना चाहता है? विदेश जाने से पहले दीपक अपना देश देखना चाहता है। Before going abroad, Deepak wants to see his own country.

Lesson 14

My City Delhi

Hello friends. You know that I am a resident of Delhi. Two years ago I used to live in Mumbai with my family. These days we all live in Delhi. Some people call this city New Delhi. Many people just call it Delhi. New Delhi is the capital of India. Delhi is a very big city. We live in Defence Colony. Defence Colony is in South Delhi. It is a very good area of Delhi. Deepak and my college is in the north near Delhi University. "D.U." is near old Delhi. I don't have a car, so I sometimes go to college by my father's car and sometimes by the metro. The metro in Delhi is very new. My mother works near Khan Market. Khan Market is not far from our home.

1. बहुत लोग कविता के शहर को क्या कहते हैं? बहुत लोग कविता के शहर को सिर्फ़ दिल्ली कहते हैं। Many people simply call Kavita's city Delhi.
2. आप के शहर का नाम क्या है? मेरे शहर का नाम बॉस्टन है। (Example:) The name of my city is Boston.
3. क्या डिफ़ेंस कॉलनी दक्षिण दिल्ली में है? जी हाँ, वह दक्षिण दिल्ली में है। Yes, it is in South Delhi.
4. क्या कविता का कॉलेज डी॰ यू॰ के पास है? जी हाँ, वह डी॰ यू॰ के पास है। Yes, it is near D.U.
5. क्या आपका घर शहर के पास है? जी नहीं वह शहर से बहुत दूर है। No, it is very far from the city.

6. भारत की राजधानी क्या है? भारत की राजधानी नई दिल्ली है । The capital of India is New Delhi.

7. आपके देश की राजधानी क्या है? मेरे देश की राजधानी वॉशिंगटन डी॰ सी॰ है । (Example:) The capital of my country is Washington D.C.

How Long Have You Been Learning Hindi?

Kavita   : Deepak, how are you?

Deepak : I am fine. And you?

Kavita   : Fine. How long have you been living in Delhi?

Deepak : Kavita, I told you that I have been living here for two years. I came here to live two years ago in July.

Kavita   : And I have known (know) you for only one year, right?

Deepak : Yes. But before that I saw you in college. Only I didn't speak to you. (conversation didn't happen with you)

Kavita   : How long have you been driving a car?

Deepak : For three years. Before coming here I learned to drive a car in Allahabad.

Kavita   : I want to learn to drive a car.

Deepak : How long have you been learning English?

Kavita   : I have been learning English since childhood, why?

Deepak : Because I want to learn English.

1. दीपक दिल्ली में कब से रह रहा है? वह वहाँ दो साल से रह रहा है । How long has Deepak been living in Delhi? He has been living there for two years.

2. क्या दिल्ली आने से पहले दीपक ने गाड़ी चलाना सीखा था? जी हाँ, उसने दिल्ली आने से पहले गाड़ी चलाना सीखा था । उसने गाड़ी चलाना इलाहाबाद में सीखा था । Had Deepak learned to drive a car before coming to Delhi? Yes, he learned to drive a car before coming to Delhi. He learned to drive a car in Allahabad.

3. दीपक कविता को कितने साल से जानता है? वह कविता को एक साल से जानता है । How long has Deepak known Kavita? He has known her for one year.

4. कविता कब से अंग्रेज़ी सीख रही है? वह बचपन से अंग्रेज़ी सीख रही है । How long has Kavita been learning English? She has been learning since childhood.

5. आप कितने महीने से हिन्दी सीख रहे हैं? (सीख रही हैं) मैं दो-तीन महीने से सीख रहा हूँ । (सीख रही हूँ) How long have you been learning Hindi? (Example:) I have been learning for two or three months.

6. दीपक कितने साल से गाड़ी चला रहा है? वह तीन साल से गाड़ी चला रहा है । How long has Deepak been driving a car? He has been driving a car for three years.

7. आप कब से इस शहर में रह रहे हैं? (रह रही हैं) मैं बहुत सालों से इस शहर में रह रहा हूँ । (रह रही हूँ) मैं सिर्फ़ दो साल से इस शहर में रह रहा हूँ । (रह रही हूँ) How long have you been living in this city? I have been living in this city for many years. I have been living in this city for only two years.

I Too Want to Go to See the Film

Imran   : Deepak, are you coming to see the film this evening?

Deepak : Yes. Are you coming?

Imran   : Yes. I am also coming. Which film is it?

Deepak : A new film just came out. Its name is यह दोस्ती (*This Friendship*).

Kavita : I also want to come. How many people are coming?

Juhi : I am coming. You also come, Kavita.

Kavita : Okay. I also want to go to eat.

Imran : Where do you want to eat, Kavita?

Kavita : In Khan Market.

Deepak : That is far from the cinema. The film is showing in Dariyaganj at the Delite. My brother also wants to come. But he said that he doesn't want to go to eat.

Kavita : Do only I want to go to eat?

Imran : No. I too want to go. But only after the film.

Deepak : I too want to eat only after the film. Juhi, you?

Juhi : Yes, me too. Deepak, is everyone going by your car?

Deepak : Yes.

1. क्या इमरान फ़िल्म देखने आ रहे हैं? जी हाँ, इमरान फ़िल्म देखने आ रहे हैं। Is Imran coming to watch the film? Yes, Imran is coming to watch the film.

2. क्या आप भी आज शाम को फ़िल्म देखने जाना चाहते हैं? (चाहती हैं) जी हाँ, मैं भी आज शाम को फ़िल्म देखने जाना चाहता हूँ। (चाहती हूँ) जी नहीं, मैं आज शाम को फ़िल्म देखने जाना नहीं चाहता। (नहीं चाहती) Do you also want to go to watch a film this evening? Yes, I too want to go to watch a film this evening. No, I don't want to go to watch a fim this evening.

3. क्या कविता भी फ़िल्म देखना चाहती है? जी हाँ, कविता भी फ़िल्म देखना चाहती है। Does Kavita also want to watch a film? Yes, Kavita also wants to watch a film.

4. इमरान खाना कब खाना चाहता है? इमरान फ़िल्म के बाद ही खाना खाना चाहता है। When does Imran want to eat food? Imran wants to eat only after the film.

5. क्या कविता ही खाना खाने के लिये जाना चाहती है? जी नहीं, दीपक, इमरान और जुही भी खाना खाने के लिये जाना चाहते हैं। Does only Kavita want to go to eat? No, Deepak, Imran and Juhi also want to go to eat.

6. फ़िल्म देखने के बाद आप क्या करना चाहते हैं? (चाहती हैं) फ़िल्म देखने के बाद मैं घर जाना चाहता हूँ। (चाहती हूँ) What do you want to do after seeing the film? I want to go home after seeing the film.

7. फ़िल्म कहाँ लगी है? वह डिलाइट में लगी है। Where is the film showing (attached)? It is showing at the Delite.

Lesson 15

Student Life in Delhi

Hello friends! You know that Kavita and I are both students in Delhi. The meaning of *chatra* is *vidyarthi* or student. We both study at the same college. Our college is a famous college of Delhi University. It is very close to the main campus of D.U. but quite far from Kavita's home. It is also quite far from my home. I live just near Kavita, but I don't live in Defence Colony, I live in Lajpat Nagar. We have classes almost daily. In the evening we often go with friends to see a film or to eat *chat* or to study at someone's home. On the weekend we often go to a party. Sometimes on the weekend we also go for a stroll in Lodi Gardens. I don't drink alcohol. Kavita also does not drink alcohol. But here people our age do drink alcohol and smoke cigarettes.

1. Are Deepak and Kavita students? जी हाँ, वे छात्र हैं। Yes, they are students.
2. Are you a student? जी हाँ, मैं छात्र हूँ। जी नहीं, मैं छात्र नहीं हूँ। Yes, I am a student. No, I am not a student.
3. Do Deepak and Kavita's classes take place almost every day? जी हाँ, उनकी कक्षाएँ लगभग रोज़ होती हैं। Yes, their classes take place almost every day.
4. Does Deepak live just near Kavita? जी हाँ, वह कविता के पास ही रहता है। Yes, he lives just near Kavita.
5. What do Deepak and Kavita often do in the evening? शाम को वे अक्सर दोस्तों के साथ फ़िल्म देखने के लिये जाते हैं। (या चाट खाने, या किसी के घर पढ़ने जाते हैं) In the evening they often go to see a film with friends. (or go to eat *chat*, or to study at someone's house)
6. What do you often do in the evening? शाम को मैं अक्सर टी॰ वी॰ देखता हूँ। (देखती हूँ) (या फ़िल्म देखने जाता हूँ, या बाहर खाना खाता हूँ) (जाती हूँ, खाती हूँ) Often I watch TV in the evening. (or go to see a film, or eat out)
7. Do you drink alcohol? जी हाँ, मैं शराब पीता हूँ। (पीती हूँ) जी नहीं, मैं शराब नहीं पीता। (नहीं पीती) Yes, I drink alcohol. No, I don't drink alcohol.
8. Do you smoke cigarettes? जी हाँ, मैं सिगरेट पीता हूँ। (पीती हूँ) जी नहीं, मैं सिगरेट नहीं पीता। (नहीं पीती) Yes, I smoke cigarettes. No, I don't smoke cigarettes.

I Tried to Call You

Deepak : Kavita, what were you doing yesterday evening at four o'clock?

Kavita : Yesterday evening at four o'clock? I was going with my father to buy something in Khan Market. Why?

Deepak : I was trying to phone you. I wanted to invite you.

Kavita : For what did you want to invite me?

Deepak : I went with Imran and one or two friends to Lodi Gardens. It would have been good if you had picked up the phone. I tried to phone you several times.

Kavita : My cell was switched off. What did you do there?

Deepak : Just talked. And gossiped. And went to eat *chat*.

Kavita : If I was not going with my father at that time, I would certainly have come. He bought a new cell phone for me.

Deepak : Not a problem.

1. कल शाम को चार बजे कविता कहाँ जा रही थी? कल शाम को वह ख़ान मार्केट कुछ लेने जा रही थी। Where was Kavita going yesterday at four o'clock in the evening? She was going to buy something from Khan Market.
2. कल चार बजे कविता किस के साथ जा रही थी? कल चार बजे वह अपने पिता के साथ जा रही थी। With whom was Kavita going at four o'clock yesterday? She was going with her father at four o'clock yesterday.
3. कल शाम कौन कविता को फ़ोन करने की कोशिश कर रहा था? कल शाम को दीपक उसको फ़ोन करने की कोशिश कर रहा था। Who was trying to phone Kavita yesterday in the evening? Deepak was trying to phone her yesterday in the evening.
4. क्या कल दीपक बार बार कविता को फ़ोन करने की कोशिश कर रहा था? जी हाँ, कल वह बार बार कविता को फ़ोन करने की कोशिश कर रहा था। Was Deepak trying to phone Kavita again and again yesterday? Yes, he was trying to phone Kavita again and again.

5. क्या दीपक कल कविता को बुलाना चाहता था? जी हाँ, वह कल कविता को बुलाना चाहता था। Did Deepak want to invite Kavita yesterday? Yes, he wanted to invite Kavita yesterday.

6. कल शाम को चार बजे क्या आप कविता के साथ जा रहे थे? (जा रही थीं) जी नहीं, मैं कविता के साथ नहीं जा रहा था। (जा रही थी) कविता के पिता जी उस के साथ जा रहे थे। Yesterday evening at four o'clock were you going with Kavita? No, I was not going with Kavita. Kavita's father was going with her.

7. कल अगर कविता अपने पिता के साथ नहीं जा रही होती तो क्या वह दीपक के साथ लोदी गार्डन जाती? जी हाँ, कल अगर वह अपने पिता के साथ नहीं जा रही होती तो वह दीपक के साथ लोदी गार्डन जाती। If Kavita had not been going with her father yesterday then would she have gone with Deepak to Lodi Gardens? Yes, if Kavita had not been going with her father yesterday then she would have gone with Deepak to Lodi Gardens.

8. कल अगर कविता का फ़ोन बंद न होता तो क्या वह फ़ोन उठाती? जी हाँ, कल अगर उसका फ़ोन बंद न होता तो वह फ़ोन उठाती। If Kavita's phone had not been switched off yesterday, would she have answered it (picked up)? Yes, if her phone had not been switched off yesterday, she would have answered it.

What Did You Do When You Got Home Yesterday Evening?

Deepak : Kavita, what did you do when you got home last night?

Kavita : After getting home I studied a bit, then after eating dinner I slept early. What did you do when you got home?

Deepak : After I got home I talked with my aunty. After talking with her I ate. She made kheer last night.

Kavita : What did you do after eating?

Deepak : After eating I watched a DVD. Why did you sleep so early?

Kavita : No one else was at home. Everyone had gone out. There also was nothing to do.

Deepak : You didn't want to watch TV after eating?

Kavita : No. I took a book and yesterday's newspaper and went into my room but I didn't read anything. After you watched the DVD last night, did you not get bored?

Deepak : I did get bored. In reality I was waiting for you to call (for your call). But you didn't call.

Kavita : Don't act like this (don't become such). If you wanted to talk then why didn't you phone yourself?

Example responses:

1. कल सुबह उठकर आपने क्या किया? कल सुबह उठकर मैंने नहाया। (मैं नहाया/नहायी)
   Yesterday morning I got up and bathed.

2. कल कॉलेज पहुँचकर आपने क्या किया? कल कॉलेज पहुँचकर मैं क्लास में गया/गयी।
   Yesterday, having reached college I went into class.

3. कल शाम को घर जाकर आपने क्या किया? कल शाम को घर जाकर मैंने टेलीविज़न देखा।
   I went home yesterday evening and watched television. (Having gone home yesterday evening I watched television.)

4. कल कुछ पढ़ाई करके आपने क्या किया? कल कुछ पढ़ाई कर के मैं सोया (सोयी)। कल कुछ पढ़ाई करके मैंने खाना खाया। Yesterday I did some study and slept. (Having done some study yesterday, I slept.) Yesterday I did some study and ate. (Having done some study yesterday, I ate.)

5. कल सुबह नहाकर आपने क्या किया? कल सुबह नहाकर मैंने नाश्ता किया। कल सुबह नहाकर मैंने चाय/कॉफ़ी पी। Yesterday morning, I bathed and ate breakfast. (Yesterday morning, having bathed I ate breakfast.) Yesterday morning I bathed and drank tea/coffee. (Yesterday morning, having bathed I drank tea/coffee.)

6. कल सुबह कपड़े पहनकर आपने क्या किया? कल सुबह कपड़े पहनकर मैं कॉलेज गया। (गयी) Yesterday morning I put on my clothes and went to college.

7. कल रात खाना खाकर क्या आप सोये? (सोयीं) जी हाँ, कल रात खाना खाकर मैं सोया। (सोयी) जी नहीं, कल रात खाना खाकर मैंने टी॰ वी॰ देखा। Yes, I ate and slept last night. No, I ate and watched TV last night.

8. कल शाम को घर जाकर क्या आपने टेलीविज़न देखा? जी हाँ, कल शाम को घर जाकर मैंने टेलीविज़न देखा। जी नहीं, कल शाम को घर जाकर मैंने खाना खाया। Yes, yesterday evening I went home and watched TV. No, yesterday evening I went home and ate.

Lesson 16

My Favorite Place in Delhi

Hello my friends! Today I want to tell you some more about Delhi. Do you want to know where my favorite place is in Delhi? My favorite place in Delhi is Khan Market. C.P. (Connaught Place) is a very good place. Now C.P. is called Rajiv Chawk. There is much to buy in Old Delhi and the Red Fort and the Jama Masjid are very beautiful to look at. India Gate is worth seeing, but my favorite place is Khan Market. There are very good shops there. There are good clothes shops, bookshops, eating places, and the *pān* shops are good too. At night Khan Market is very colorful. Often I walk there with my mum. Lodi Gardens is also very close by (to there). Now you tell (me). Where is your favorite place?

An example response:

मेरा मनपसंद शहर न्यू यॉर्क है। न्यू यॉर्क अमरीका में है। न्यू यॉर्क में बहुत ज़्यादा दुकानें हैं। ऊँची ऊँची इमारतें भी हैं। वहाँ बहुत लोग रहते हैं और काम भी करते हैं। रात को बहुत रौनक़ होती है। न्यू यॉर्क में बहुत ख़रीदने को मिलता है। बहुत करने के लिये भी है। वहाँ बहुत संग्रहालय (museums) भी हैं। वहाँ मैनहैटन देखने लायक़ है। लोग वहाँ जाकर चीज़ें ख़रीदते हैं और घूमते भी हैं।

My favorite city is New York. New York is in America. There are many stores in New York. There are also many tall buildings. Many people live there and also work there. There is much color at night as well. There is a lot to buy in New York. There is a lot to do as well. There are also many museums there. Manhattan is worth seeing. People go there to buy things and also to stroll (around).

I Want You to Talk to Vrinda

Deepak : Kavita, I want to talk to you.

Kavita : What is it? What is happening?

Deepak : My sister Vrinda has come to my uncle's home from Allahabad. She is quite upset. I want you to talk to her.

Kavita : Really, what happened? Vrinda is ordinarily very happy.

Deepak : Yes, but these days she is very sad. Perhaps it is a matter of her studies. My parents want her to study in a college in Allahabad, but I think that she wants to study medicine in Delhi.

Kavita : Does she want to become a doctor?

Deepak : Yes, maybe. Just talk to her, won't you? She thinks of you as an older sister.

Kavita : Okay. When should I talk to her?

Deepak : Come to my uncle's home tonight, if you have time, that is (then).
Kavita : Okay. Do you want to go to drink tea right now?
Deepak : Yes, let's go (and) have a cup of tea and come back.

1. वृन्दा कहाँ से आयी है? वह इलाहाबाद से आयी है। From where has Vrinda come? She has come from Allahabad.
2. वृन्दा किस के घर आयी है? वह अपने मामा के घर आयी है। To whose home has Vrinda come? She has come to her uncle's home.
3. क्या दीपक चाहता है कि कविता वृन्दा से बात करे? जी हाँ, वह चाहता है कि कविता वृन्दा से बात करे। Does Deepak want Kavita to talk to Vrinda? Yes, he wants Kavita to talk to Vrinda.
4. क्या वृन्दा की इच्छा है कि वह डॉक्टर बने? जी हाँ, उस की इच्छा है कि वह डॉक्टर बने। Is it Vrinda's desire to become a doctor? Yes, it is her desire to become a doctor.
5. आपकी क्या बनने की इच्छा है? मेरी वकील बनने की इच्छा है। What do you want to become? (Example:) I want to become a lawyer.
6. क्या आप चाहते हैं (चाहती हैं) कि वृन्दा डॉक्टर बने? जी हाँ, मैं चाहता हूँ (चाहती हूँ) कि वृन्दा डॉक्टर बने। Yes, I want Vrinda to become a doctor.
7. क्या अभी आप चाय पीने जाना चाहते हैं? (चाहती हैं) जी हाँ, अभी मैं चाय पीने जाना चाहता हूँ। (चाहती हूँ) Do you want to go to drink tea right now? Yes, I want to go to drink tea right now.

May I Ask You a Question?
Kavita : Vrinda, may I ask you a question?
Vrinda : Yes, ask *didi*.
Kavita : Why have you come to Delhi at this time?
Vrinda : No reason, Kavita didi. I wanted to get out of Allahabad for one or two days.
Kavita : What is the matter? Are your studies not going well? Did your parents say something to you?
Vrinda : What can I tell you? It is not such a big deal.
Kavita : Nevertheless, tell me, won't you?
Vrinda : What may I say to you? My parents want me to stay in Allahabad and study further. But after school I want to come and study in Delhi.
Kavita : Why do you want to study in Delhi?
Vrinda : Why shouldn't I study in Delhi? Deepak and Sanjeev are here. You are also here. The colleges here are good. In the end everyone comes to Delhi, don't they?
Kavita : Did you talk to your parents about these things?
Vrinda : Yes, didi. But where do they listen to me?
Kavita : May I phone Deepak and talk to him about this?
Vrinda : If Deepak talks to them then they may agree.

1. क्या वृन्दा दो-एक दिन के लिये इलाहाबाद से बाहर निकलना चाहती थी? जी हाँ, वह दो-एक दिन के लिये इलाहाबाद से बाहर निकलना चाहती थी। Did Vrinda want to get out of Allahabad for one or two days? Yes, Vrinda wanted to get out of Allahabad for one or two days.
2. वृन्दा के माँ-बाप क्या चाहते हैं? वे चाहते हैं कि स्कूल के बाद वृन्दा इलाहाबाद में रहे। What do Vrinda's parents want? They want Vrinda to remain in Allahabad after school.
3. वृन्दा दिल्ली में क्यों पढ़ना चाहती है? वह दिल्ली में पढ़ना चाहती है क्योंकि दिल्ली के कॉलेज बहुत अच्छे हैं। Why does Vrinda want to study in Delhi? She wants to study in Delhi because Delhi colleges are very good.

4. क्या वृन्दा के दोनों भाई दिल्ली में रहते हैं? जी हाँ, उसके दोनों भाई दिल्ली में रहते हैं।
   Do both of Vrinda's brothers live in Delhi? Yes, both of her brothers live in Delhi.

5. क्या वृन्दा ने ये सब बातें माँ-बाप से की हैं? जी हाँ, वृन्दा ने ये सब बातें माँ-बाप से की हैं। Has Vrinda talked to her parents about all of these things? Yes, Vrinda has talked to her parents about all of these things.

6. क्या आप चाहते हैं (चाहती हैं) कि वृन्दा दिल्ली आकर पढ़े? जी हाँ, मैं चाहता हूँ (चाहती हूँ) कि वृन्दा दिल्ली आकर पढ़े। Do you want Vrinda to come to Delhi and study? Yes, I want Vrinda to come to Delhi and study.

Lesson 17

How Much Is That?

Kavita	: Deepak, will you go with me into the shop Anokhi?
Deepak	: Okay. What do you want/need in Anokhi?
Kavita	: It is Juhi's birthday tomorrow. I want to get something for her. (in the shop)
Deepak	: Will you buy a shalwar kameez for her?
Kavita	: I am just looking right now. Sir, how much is this shirt?
Shopkeeper	: It is two hundred and fifty rupees, Madam.
Deepak	: That's a really expensive thing.
Kavita	: Shut up, Deepak. The shirt is cheap. Sir, what is the price of this shirt?
Shopkeeper	: That is three hundred and fifty.
Deepak	: Kavita, why don't you get a book for Juhi?
Kavita	: You get one, why don't you? Juhi is your friend too. I am going to buy a shirt.
Deepak	: Okay, I am going into the shop next door. I am going to give Juhi a book.
Kavita	: Okay. Buy your book and come back right here. I will be in this shop.

1. कविता किस के लिये कुछ ख़रीदना चाहती है? वह जुही के लिये कुछ ख़रीदना चाहती है। She wants to buy something for Juhi.

2. कल किसका जन्मदिन है? कल जुही का जन्मदिन है। It is Juhi's birthday tomorrow.

3. कविता किस दुकान में जाना चाहती है? वह 'अनोखी' में जाना चाहती है। She wants to go into Anokhi.

4. क़मीज़ कितने की है? क़मीज़ ढाई सौ की है। The shirt is Rs 250.

5. क्या दीपक सोचता है कि वह क़मीज़ महँगी है? जी हाँ, वह सोचता है कि वह महँगी है। Yes, he thinks that it is expensive.

6. दीपक जुही को क्या देगा? वह जुही को एक किताब देगा। He will give her a book.

7. कविता क्या ख़रीदेगी? वह एक क़मीज़ ख़रीदेगी। She will buy a shirt.

I Have Just Had Tea, Thanks

Deepak	: Greetings Mrs. Khan.
Imran's mother	: Hello Deepak. What will you take, tea or coffee?
Deepak	: I have just had tea.
Imran	: Nevertheless, at least have tea, Deepak. Mother, I too will drink tea.
Imran's mother	: Okay. I will make tea. Your father will be home soon. Deepak, you haven't eaten yet have you.
Deepak	: Yes, I have just eaten.

Imran	: You must have eaten during the day. Eat with us tonight, Deepak. I won't allow you to go. After eating we will go to see a film.
Deepak	: Imran, I will eat at home today. My aunt must be waiting. But I will come tomorrow evening. And we will certainly go to see a film tomorrow. Okay?
Imran	: Okay. Now take your tea and tell me what you talked about with Kavita today.

1. क्या इमरान दीपक के पास आया है? जी नहीं, इमरान दीपक के पास नहीं आया है। दीपक इमरान के पास आया है। Has Imran come to Deepak? No, Imran has not come to Deepak. Deepak has come to Imran.

2. इमरान की माँ दीपक से क्या पूछती हैं? इमरान की माँ दीपक से पूछती हैं कि "तुम क्या लोगे, चाय या कॉफ़ी"? What does Imran's mother ask Deepak? Imran's mother asks Deepak, "What will you take, tea or coffee?"

3. क्या इमरान कॉफ़ी पीना चाहता है? जी नहीं, वह चाय पीना चाहता है। Does Imran want to drink coffee? No, he wants to drink tea.

4. क्या इमरान के अब्बा अभी घर पहुँचते होंगे? जी हाँ, वे अभी घर पहुँचते होंगे। Must Imran's father be about to arrive home? Yes, he must be about to arrive home.

5. क्या आज दीपक इमरान के घर में खाना खाएगा? जी नहीं, आज वह इमरान के घर में खाना नहीं खाएगा। Will Deepak eat at Imran's home today? No, he will not eat at Imran's home today.

6. क्या आज आप किसी दोस्त के घर खाना खाने जा रहे हैं? (जा रही हैं) जी हाँ, मैं किसी दोस्त के घर खाना खाने जा रहा हूँ। (जा रही हूँ) जी नहीं, मैं किसी दोस्त के घर खाना खाने नहीं जा रहा हूँ। (जा रही हूँ) Are you going to some friend's home to eat today? Yes, I am going to some friend's home to eat today. No, I am not going to some friend's home to eat today.

7. खाना खाने के बाद इमरान क्या करना चाहता है? खाना खाने के बाद इमरान फ़िल्म देखने जाना चाहता है। What does Imran want to do after eating? After eating Imran wants to go to see a film.

Where Shall We Meet?

Deepak	: Hi Kavita, I am Deepak speaking. (It's Deepak here.)
Kavita	: Hey Deepak, where are you at the moment?
Deepak	: I am at college right now. Shall we meet this evening?
Kavita	: What is your idea? (What do you think?) What shall we do?
Deepak	: Will you go to eat?
Kavita	: Okay. But where shall we meet?
Deepak	: I feel like going to Karim's today. Shall we meet there?
Kavita	: No. I am coming by metro. I will meet you in Chandni Chowk. Near the Gurudwara.
Deepak	: Yes, but in front of it. There is a *pān* shop. Let's meet in front of it.
Kavita	: Yes, I know. One can get Urdu books next door to that shop. I want to buy a book for my friend.
Deepak	: Yes, there are good books available there. So we will meet at seven o'clock.
Kavita	: Okay. We will meet in the evening.
Deepak	: I put down the phone. (Okay, bye.)

1. क्या दीपक और कविता फ़ोन में बात कर रहे हैं? जी हाँ, वे फ़ोन में बात कर रहे हैं। Yes, they are talking on the phone.

2. क्या कविता ने दीपक को फ़ोन किया? जी नहीं, दीपक ने कविता को फ़ोन किया। No, Deepak phoned Kavita.

3. क्या कविता दीपक से शाम को मिलेगी? जी हाँ, वह उससे शाम को मिलेगी। Yes, she will meet him in the evening.

4. शाम को दीपक और कविता कहाँ मिलेंगे? वे चाँदनी चौक में गुरुद्वारे के सामने मिलेंगे। They will meet in Chandni Chowk in front of the Gurudwara.

5. क्या कविता मेट्रो से आएगी? जी हाँ, वह मेट्रो से आएगी। Yes, she will come by the metro.

6. दीपक कविता से कहाँ मिलना चाहता है? वह करीम्स में मिलना चाहता है। He wants to meet with her at Karim's.

7. वे शाम को कितने बजे मिलेंगे? वे शाम को सात बजे मिलेंगे। They will meet in the evening at 7 o'clock.

8. क्या चाँदनी चौक में अच्छी किताबें मिलती हैं? चाँदनी चौक में उर्दू की अच्छी किताबें मिलती हैं। Do you get good books in Chandni Chowk? In Chandni Chowk good Urdu books are available.

An example response:

(फ़ोन पर) नमस्ते दोस्त। अभी तुम क्या कर रहे हो? शाम को क्या करोगे? क्या बाहर जाना चाहते हो? क्या फ़िल्म देखने हम चलें? या खाना खाने चलें? तुम कहाँ जाना चाहते हो? तुम क्या करना चाहते हो? चलो, हम दुकान में जाएँगे। कुछ जूते (shoes) ख़रीद कर हम फ़िल्म देखने चलेंगे फिर खाना खाने जाएँगे। कौन-सी फ़िल्म देखना चाहते हो? हम कितने बजे मिलेंगे? छै बजे? ठीक है। हम कहाँ मिलेंगे? क्या हम सिनेमाघर के सामने मिलें? अच्छा, दुकान के सामने मिलें? नहीं, मैं वहाँ मिलना नहीं चाहता। मेरा एक दोस्त वहाँ रहता है, मैं नहीं चाहता कि वह मुझे देखे। तुम कैसे आओगे? बस से? ठीक है। क्या तुम किसी और को बुलाना चाहते हो? नहीं, उसे मत बुलाओ। ठीक है, शाम को छै बजे मिलेंगे। अच्छा, नमस्ते।

(On the phone) Hello friend. What are you doing right now? What will you do in the evening? Do you want to go out? Shall we go to watch a film? Or to eat? Where do you want to go? What do you want to do? Okay, we will go to the shop. We will buy some shoes and go to watch a film. Then we will go to eat. Which film do you want to watch? What time will we meet? Six o'clock? Okay. Where will we meet? Shall we meet in front of the movie theater? Okay, shall we meet in front of the store? No, I don't want to meet there. One of my friends lives there and I don't want him to see me. How will you come? By bus? Okay. Do you want to invite someone else? No, don't invite him/her. Okay, we will meet at six o'clock. Okay, bye.

Lesson 18

You Must Have Eaten Indian Food

Hello friends! You must have eaten Indian food. You must know that people in north India eat roti, rice and lentils and different vegetables. Some people eat meat also. Previously in India very few people ate meat but these days many people have begun to eat (it). People eat mostly chicken and goat. Very few people eat beef. In my family, my grandparents don't eat meat. They are pure vegetarians. My parents and my brother are not vegetarians. I also eat meat occasionally. Deepak also eats meat, but he only eats chicken. You must have eaten roti. People also call this chapati. You must have eaten different vegetables. For lunch and dinner at home we eat things like potatoes, peas, spinach, cauliflower, bitter gourd, pumpkin and gourd with rice and roti and lentils. Perhaps you may not have eaten gourd. We don't eat meat at home. Now it's your turn. Tell me what you eat.

1. उत्तर भारत में क्या लोग रोटी और चावल खाते हैं? जी हाँ, उत्तर भारत में लोग रोटी और चावल खाते हैं। Do people eat roti and rice in North India? Yes, people eat roti and rice in North India.

2. आजकल हिन्दुस्तान में कितने लोग गोश्त खाने लगे हैं? आजकल हिन्दुस्तान में बहुत लोग गोश्त खाने लगे हैं। These days how many people have begun eating meat in India? These days many people have begun eating meat in India.

3. क्या आप गोश्त खाते हैं? (खाती हैं) जी हाँ, मैं गोश्त खाता हूँ। (खाती हूँ) जी नहीं, मैं शाकाहारी हूँ। Do you eat meat? Yes, I eat meat. No, I am a vegetarian.

4. क्या आप शाकाहारी हैं? जी हाँ, मैं शाकाहारी हूँ। जी नहीं, मैं गोश्त खाता हूँ। (खाती हूँ) Yes, I am a vegetarian. No, I eat meat.

5. आप की मनपसंद सब्ज़ी क्या है? मेरी मनपसंद सब्ज़ी बैंगन है। (Example:) My favorite vegetable is eggplant.

6. क्या दीपक बकरे का गोश्त खाता है? जी नहीं, वह सिर्फ़ मुर्ग़ी खाता है। Does Deepak eat goat's meat? No, he only eats chicken.

7. अपने घर में आप क्या खाते हैं? (खाती हैं) घर में मैं रोटी, चावल, अलग-अलग सब्ज़ियाँ, गोश्त और दाल खाता हूँ। (खाती हूँ) What do you eat at home? (Example:) At home I eat roti, rice, different vegetables, meat, and dhal.

What Do You Like?

Kavita : Deepak, do you like tea or coffee more?

Deepak : I have always liked tea, but am beginning to like coffee. What do you like?

Kavita : I like both tea and coffee. You like meat, don't you?

Deepak : You know that I only like chicken. And you?

Kavita : Previously I did not like to eat meat, but now I am starting to like it.

Deepak : Do you prefer Hindi films more, or American?

Kavita : Previously I didn't like Hindi films so much. But now I have begun to watch them more with you. They don't seem such nonsense. You must not have seen an American film.

Deepak : That's not true. You don't know how my life was in Allahabad. We used to watch American films occasionally. We just couldn't understand their language well. [*Here Deepak is perhaps using the first person plural pronoun to refer to himself. This is common in north India.*]

(Example responses:)

1. आपको चाय ज़्यादा पसंद है या कॉफ़ी? मुझे चाय ज़्यादा अच्छी लगती है। I like tea more.

2. क्या आपको हिन्दी फ़िल्में देखना अच्छा लगता है? जी हाँ, मुझे हिन्दी फ़िल्में देखना पसंद है। Yes, I like to watch Hindi films.

3. क्या कविता को गोश्त अच्छा लगने लगा है? जी हाँ, कविता को गोश्त अच्छा लगने लगा है। Yes, Kavita has begun to like meat.

4. क्या आपको अमरीकी फ़िल्में देखना अच्छा लगता है? जी नहीं, मुझे अमरीकी फ़िल्में देखना अच्छा नहीं लगता। No, I do not like to watch American films.

5. क्या आपको भारत जाना अच्छा लगता है? जी हाँ, मुझे भारत जाना अच्छा लगता है। Yes, I like to go to India.

6. क्या कविता दीपक के साथ ज़्यादा हिन्दी फ़िल्में देखने लगी है? जी हाँ, कविता दीपक के साथ ज़्यादा हिन्दी फ़िल्में देखने लगी है। Yes, Kavita has begun to watch more Hindi films with Deepak.

7. क्या दीपक ने कोई अमरीकी फ़िल्म देखी? जी हाँ, उसने कुछ अमरीकी फ़िल्में देखी हैं।
   Yes, Deepak has seen some American films.

8. क्या आपको भारतीय खाना खाना अच्छा लगता है? जी हाँ, मुझे हिन्दुस्तानी खाना खाना पसंद है।   Yes, I like to eat Indian food.

Pleased to Meet You

Deepak : Hello Sameer. How are you?

Sameer : You must be Deepak. Hello. I am fine. And you?

Kavita : Brother, I told you, didn't I, that Deepak and I study together.

Sameer : Yes, yes. I remember. Kavita has told me a lot about you.

Deepak : Sameer, for how many days have you come to Delhi?

Sameer : Call me "tum." I have come for fourteen days. I didn't get a very long holiday this time.

Deepak : So shall the three of us go for a trip somewhere for two or three days? Do "you"… forgive me, do "you" have time, Sameer?

Sameer : I will get the opportunity to go for two or three days. But ask Kavita. She must have a lot of work these days.

Deepak : Kavita, what do you think? (what is your thought)

Kavita : It is fine by (for) me.

Deepak : (That's) great! I am off, but it was a pleasure to meet you Sameer.

Sameer : Likewise. See you tomorrow.

Deepak : Certainly.

1. क्या कविता का भाई हिन्दुस्तान आया है? जी हाँ, वह हिन्दुस्तान आया है।   Has Kavita's brother come to India? Yes, he has come to India.

2. कविता का भाई दिल्ली कितने दिन के लिये आया है? वह चौदह दिन के लिये आया है।
   For how many days has Kavita's brother come to Delhi? He has come for fourteen days.

3. इस वक़्त क्या समीर को लंबी छुट्टी मिली? जी नहीं, इस वक़्त उसे लंबी छुट्टी नहीं मिली।
   Did Sameer get a long holiday at this time? No, he did not receive a long break at this time.

4. क्या कविता ने दीपक के बारे में समीर को बहुत बताया है? जी हाँ, उसने दीपक के बारे में समीर को बहुत बताया है।   Has Kavita told Sameer a lot about Deepak? Yes, she has told Sameer a lot about Deepak.

5. क्या दीपक चाहता है कि वे तीनों कहीं घूमने जायें? जी हाँ, वह चाहता है कि वे तीनों घूमने जायें।   Does Deepak want the three of them to go for a trip? Yes, he wants them to go for a trip.

6. क्या आप कहीं घूमने के लिये जाना चाहते हैं? (चाहती हैं) जी हाँ, मैं कहीं घूमने के लिये जाना चाहता हूँ। (चाहती हूँ) Do you want to go wandering anywhere? Yes, I want to go wandering somewhere। जी नहीं, मैं कहीं घूमने के लिये जाना नहीं चाहता। (चाहती) No, I don't want to go wandering anywhere.

Lesson 19

I Want to Leave at Five-Thirty

Kavita : Hey Deepak, what time do you want to go home today?

Deepak : I want to go at 5:30. And you?

Kavita : The library closes at 6:15. And I want to get home by quarter to seven.

Deepak : Okay, shall I drop you home? I have my car. So what time should we leave?

Kavita : Shall we leave at a quarter to six? What is the time now?

Deepak : Right now it is twenty past three. Did you have lunch today at 1:30? Or at two?

Kavita : I had lunch at 2:30. I have only just returned. Why do you ask?

Deepak : I came to search for you at 1:30 but didn't find you.

Kavita : What time did you come?

Deepak : I must have come at 10 minutes to 2.

Kavita : Oh, I went to look for a book at that time.

Deepak : It's no matter. Okay, we have two and a half hours. I will sit here and do some study.

Kavita : Okay.

1. आज पुस्तकालय कितने बजे बंद होता है? आज पुस्तकालय सवा छै बजे बंद होता है। What time does the library close today? The library closes at 6:15 today.

2. आज कविता कितने बजे घर जाना चाहती है? आज वह पौने छै बजे घर जाना चाहती है। What time does Kavita want to go home today? She wants to go home at a quarter to six today.

3. आज दीपक कविता को ढूँढने कितने बजे आया था? आज वह कविता को ढूँढने डेढ़ बजे आया था। What time did Deepak come looking for Kavita today? Today he came looking for Kavita at 1:30.

4. क्या आप रोज़ दिन का खाना दोपहर को डेढ़ बजे खाते हैं? जी नहीं, मैं रोज़ दिन का खाना दोपहर को साढ़े बारह बजे खाता हूँ। (खाती हूँ) Do you eat lunch every day at 1:30? (Example:) No, I eat lunch every day at 12:30.

5. कविता शाम को कितने बजे तक घर पहुँचना चाहती है? वह शाम को पौने सात बजे तक घर पहुँचना चाहती है। By what time does Kavita want to reach home? She wants to reach home by quarter to seven.

6. क्या आप रोज़ शाम के साढ़े छै बजे तक अपने घर पहुँचते हैं? (पहुँचती हैं) जी हाँ, मैं रोज़ शाम के साढ़े छै बजे तक अपने घर पहुँचता हूँ। (पहुँचती हूँ) Do you get home at 6:30 in the evening every day? (Example:) Yes, I get home at 6:30 in the evening every day.

7. आज दो बजने में दस मिनट पर कविता कहाँ गयी थी? आज दो बजने में दस मिनट पर वह एक किताब ढूँढने गयी थी। Where had Kavita gone today at ten minutes to two? Today at ten minutes to two she had gone to search for a book.

The Weather in North India

How is the weather in North India? Shall I tell you? Summer occurs from April until the end of October. In Delhi and in all of North India it is very hot in summer. During the day the temperature reaches above forty degrees. Generally it rains a lot in July. During the rainy season it is still hot, but it is also very humid. It is very cold in December and January. This season is also called *sardi* and *jaaraa*. During the day the temperature is five to ten degrees. I like spring very much. Spring occurs in March. I don't like the heat in Delhi at all.

1. दिल्ली में गर्मी के दिन कब होते हैं? दिल्ली में गर्मी के दिन अप्रैल से लेकर अक्तूबर के अंत तक होते हैं। When does summer take place in Delhi? Summer takes place in Delhi from April until the end of October.

2. दिल्ली में गर्मी के मौसम में तापमान कितना रहता है? दिल्ली में गर्मी के मौसम में तापमान चालिस डिग्री के ऊपर पहुँचता है। How hot (much) does the temperature become in summer in Delhi? In Delhi in summer the temperature reaches above forty degrees.

3. आपके देश में गर्मी का मौसम कब होता है? मेरे देश में गर्मी का मौसम जून से लेकर अगस्त तक होता है। When does summer occur in your country? In my country summer takes place from June until August.

4. दिल्ली में बरसात किस महीने में होती है? दिल्ली में बरसात जुलाई में होती है। In which month does the rainy season occur in Delhi? In Delhi the rainy season takes place in July.

5. क्या कविता को दिल्ली की गर्मी अच्छी लगती है? जी नहीं, उसे दिल्ली की गर्मी अच्छी नहीं लगती। Does Kavita like summer in Delhi? No, she does not like summer in Delhi.

6. क्या आप कभी गर्मी के मौसम में हिन्दुस्तान गये हैं? (गई हैं) जी हाँ, मैं गर्मी के मौसम में हिन्दुस्तान गया हूँ। (गई हूँ) जी नहीं, मैं कभी गर्मी के मौसम में हिन्दुस्तान नहीं गया। (नहीं गई) Have you ever been to India in the summer? Yes, I have been to India in the summer. No, I have never been to India in the summer.

7. कविता को कौन-सा मौसम अच्छा लगता है? उसे वसंत का मौसम बहुत अच्छा लगता है। What season does Kavita like? Kavita likes the spring season a lot.

8. आपके देश में ठंड का मौसम कब होता है? मेरे देश में ठंड का मौसम दिसंबर में होता है। When does winter take place in your country? (Example:) In my country, winter takes place in December.

I'm So Hot! I'm So Thirsty!

Kavita : Deepak, it is so hot today. I can't even study now. I am also so thirsty.

Deepak : Yes, I too am feeling very hot. What must the temperature be?

Kavita : I don't know. It must be around forty. What should we do? Do you have your car today?

Deepak : No, today I have come to college by the metro. Shall we sit somewhere in the A.C. (in an air-conditioned place) and eat?

Kavita : I don't feel hungry at all. I don't feel hungry at all in summer. If you had come by car today, then we could have gone to my home right now.

Deepak : Yes. So shall we go and see a film in C.P.? We can go by the metro. There is A.C. in the theatre as well.

Kavita : That's true, but I don't have three hours at the moment. I can't tell you how thirsty I am. (I am so thirsty that what may I tell you)

Deepak : I too am very thirsty. Okay, let's get something cold to drink from the canteen and then go by metro to C.P. We can decide there what we should do.

Kavita : Okay.

1. क्या कविता सोचती है कि आज बहुत गर्मी हो रही है? जी हाँ, वह सोचती है कि आज बहुत गर्मी हो रही है। Yes, she thinks that it is very hot today.

2. क्या कविता और दीपक को बहुत प्यास लगी है? जी हाँ, उन्हें बहुत प्यास लगी है। Yes, they feel very thirsty.

3. क्या कविता को गर्मी के दिनों में बहुत भूख लगती है? जी नहीं, उसे गर्मी के दिनों में बहुत भूख नहीं लगती। No, she doesn't feel hungry in the summer.

4. क्या आपको गर्मी के दिनों में बहुत भूख लगती है? जी नहीं, मुझे गर्मी के दिनों में बहुत भूख नहीं लगती। No, I don't feel very hungry in summer. जी हाँ, गर्मी के दिनों में मुझे बहुत भूख लगती है। Yes, I feel very hungry in summer.

5. क्या आज फ़िल्म देखने के लिये कविता के पास तीन घंटे हैं? जी नहीं, आज फ़िल्म देखने को उसके पास तीन घंटे नहीं हैं। No, she doesn't have three hours to watch a film today.

6. क्या आज दीपक गाड़ी से कॉलेज आया है? जी नहीं आज वह गाड़ी से नहीं आया। No, he did not come by car today.

7. अगर आज दीपक गाड़ी से कॉलेज आया होता तो वे कहाँ जा सकते? अगर वह गाड़ी से आया होता तो वे कविता के घर जा सकते। If Deepak had come to college by car, then they could have gone to Kavita's home.

8. क्या आप गर्मी के दिनों में हिन्दुस्तान जाएँगे? (जाएँगी) जी हाँ, मैं गर्मी के दिनों में भारत जाऊँगा। (जाऊँगी) Yes, I will go to India during the summer. जी नहीं, मैं गर्मी के दिनों में हिन्दुस्तान नहीं जाऊँगा। (जाऊँगी) No, I will not go to India in the summer.

9. क्या आपको अभी भूख लगी है? जी नहीं, अभी मुझे भूख नहीं लगी। No, I am not hungry right now. जी हाँ, मुझे अभी भूख लगी है। Yes, I am hungry right now.

10. क्या आपको अभी गर्मी लग रही है? जी नहीं, अभी मुझे गर्मी नहीं लग रही है। जी हाँ, मुझे अभी गर्मी लग रही है। No, I am not feeling hot right now. Yes, I am feeling hot right now.

Lesson 20

I Can't Come on Tuesday

Deepak : Hi Kavita, it's Deepak. How are you?
Kavita : Hey Deepak, why didn't you come to college yesterday?
Deepak : My health was not okay yesterday.
Kavita : That's a shame. How is your health today?
Deepak : It is better today.
Kavita : That's good. What are you doing on Tuesday?
Deepak : What time on Tuesday?
Kavita : In the evening. Juhi is having a party.
Deepak : I can't come on Tuesday evening. I have some work.
Kavita : Come to the party, won't you. It will be fun.
Deepak : Really, I will not be able to go. But can you go to see a film on Wednesday?
Kavita : Which film?
Deepak : *Greetings to You, Mother.*
Kavita : I have already seen it. I didn't like it that much.
Deepak : Really? Nevertheless, I want to see it so Imran and I will go. So will you and I be able to meet tomorrow?
Kavita : Okay. If you can't come to Juhi's party then let's meet tomorrow.

1. क्या दीपक जुही के यहाँ जा पाएगा? जी नहीं, वह जा नहीं पाएगा। Will Deepak be able to go to Juhi's place? No, he will not be able to go.

2. क्या कविता चाहती है कि दीपक पार्टी में आए? जी हाँ, वह चाहती है कि दीपक पार्टी में आए। Does Kavita want Deepak to come to the party? Yes, she wants Deepak to come to the party.

3. क्या कविता "माँ तुझे सलाम" देख चुकी है? जी हाँ, वह देख चुकी है। Has Kavita already seen *Greetings to You, Mother*? Yes, she has seen it.

4. क्या उसे फ़िल्म बहुत अच्छी लगी? जी नहीं, उसे फ़िल्म बहुत अच्छी नहीं लगी। Did she like the film? No, she didn't like it much.

5. मंगल की शाम को क्या हो रहा है? मंगल की शाम को जुही के यहाँ पार्टी होगी। What is happening on Tuesday evening? On Tuesday evening Juhi is having a party.

6. क्या दीपक और कविता कल मिलेंगे? जी हाँ, वे कल मिलेंगे। Will Deepak and Kavita meet tomorrow? Yes, they will meet tomorrow.

7. दीपक किस के साथ फ़िल्म देखने जाएगा? दीपक इमरान के साथ फ़िल्म देखने जाएगा। With whom will Deepak go to watch the film? Deepak will go with Imran to watch the film.

8. क्या आप किसी दोस्त के साथ आज रात को फ़िल्म देखना चाहते हैं? (चाहती हैं) जी हाँ, मैं आज रात को किसी दोस्त के साथ फ़िल्म देखना चाहता हूँ। (चाहती हूँ) Do you want to watch a film tonight with some (a) friend? Yes, I want to watch a film tonight with some (a) friend. जी नहीं, मैं आज रात को किसी दोस्त के साथ फ़िल्म देखना नहीं चाहता। (चाहती) No, I don't want to watch a film tonight with some (a) friend.

Kavita Is Smarter Than I Am

Kavita is a very good girl. She is smarter than I am; there is no doubt about this. She always receives good grades in her exam. She works harder in her studies than I do as well. It is possible that Kavita is the smartest student among our friends. Imran is also very smart. But in my opinion, Kavita is the smartest and most industrious. Imran is the oldest and Juhi is the youngest, in age. But I am taller than Imran. Kavita knows most about the world. Imran also knows a lot because he has been to America. At least the two of them know more about the world than I do. But I know more about Allahabad than them. It is possible that from among our friends Juhi has the most money, but I don't know for sure because we friends never talk about this. Juhi's parents must have a lot of money. Last year they gave Juhi a new car.

1. दीपक के ख़्याल में कौन उससे होशियार है? दीपक के ख़्याल में कविता उससे होशियार है। In Deepak's opinion, who is smarter than he is? In Deepak's opinion, Kavita is smarter than he.
2. क्या उम्र में जुही सब से छोटी है? जी हाँ, उम्र में जुही सब से छोटी है। Is Juhi the youngest? Yes, Juhi is the youngest.
3. इलाहाबाद के बारे में सब से ज़्यादा किसे मालूम है? दीपक को इलाहाबाद के बारे में सब से ज़्यादा मालूम है। Who knows most about Allahabad? Deepak knows most about Allahabad.
4. इमरान कहाँ जा चुका है? इमरान अमरीका जा चुका है। Where has Imran already been? Imran has already been to America.
5. कविता को किस के बारे में सबसे ज़्यादा मालूम है? कविता को दुनिया के बारे में सबसे ज़्यादा मालूम है। About what does Kavita know the most? Kavita knows the most about the world.
6. कौन सबसे लंबा है? दीपक सबसे लंबा है। Who is the tallest? Deepak is the tallest.
7. क्या दीपक कविता से ज़्यादा मेहनती है? जी नहीं, दीपक कविता से ज़्यादा मेहनती नहीं है। Is Deepak more hardworking than Kavita? No, Deepak is not more hardworking than Kavita.
8. क्या पिछले साल जुही के माँ-बाप ने जुही को एक नयी गाड़ी दी थी? जी हाँ, पिछले साल उन्होंने जुही को एक नयी गाड़ी दी थी। Had Juhi's parents given her a new car last year? Yes, they had given Juhi a new car last year.

How Long Does It Take You to Get Home from College?

Kavita : Deepak, how long does it take you to go home by car from college?

Deepak : Often it takes me a long time. It is so crowded in Old Delhi. It takes longer to go in the evening than in the morning. Why?

Kavita : How long will it take now? I have to go home quickly. If I (may) go by metro, then it will take at least an hour.

Deepak : At this time it could be faster to go by car. It will take the longest time to go by bus. Perhaps you should go by car. Why do you have to go home right now?

Kavita : My father just called. He has to go to Mumbai by plane and he wants to talk to me before he goes.

Deepak : Really. How many hours does it take to go to Mumbai by plane?

Kavita : I don't know for sure, but I think that perhaps it takes two hours.

Deepak : Okay. Let's go. If you have to get there so quickly, then I will drop you by car. Perhaps it will take less time because you will have to go by auto(rickshaw) from the station, won't you?

Kavita : Thanks, Deepak.

1. क्या दीपक को कॉलेज से घर जाने में बहुत देर लगती है? अक्सर उसे घर जाने में बहुत देर लगती है। Often it takes him a long time to go home.

2. आपको दफ़्तर/स्कूल/कॉलेज जाने में कितनी देर लगती है? मुझे दफ़्तर जाने में आधा घंटा लगता है। (Example:) It takes me half an hour to go to the office.

3. क्या अभी कविता को जल्दी घर जाना है? जी हाँ, अभी उसे जल्दी घर जाना है। Yes, she has to go home quickly right now.

4. अमरीका से हवाई जहाज़ से हिन्दुस्तान जाने में कितने घंटे लगते हैं? हवाई जहाज़ से अमरीका से हिन्दुस्तान जाने में कम से कम चौदह घंटे लगते हैं। It takes at least fourteen hours to go from America to India by plane.

5. आज रात को किसको मुम्बई जाना पड़ेगा? आज रात को कविता के पिता जी को मुम्बई जाना पड़ेगा। Kavita's father must go to Mumbai tonight.

6. कविता को मेट्रो से घर जाना चाहिये या गाड़ी से? कविता को गाड़ी से घर जाना चाहिये। Kavita should go home by car.

7. क्या कविता को बस से घर जाने में सब से ज़्यादा देर लगेगी? जी हाँ, उसे बस से घर जाने में सब से ज़्यादा देर लगेगी। Yes, it will take Kavita longest to go home by bus.

8. आपको घर जाने में बस से ज़्यादा देर लगती है या ट्रेन से? मुझे बस से घर जाने में ज़्यादा देर लगती है। (Example:) It takes me longer to go home by bus.

9. क्या दीपक कविता को घर पर छोड़ देगा? जी हाँ, वह कविता को घर पर छोड़ देगा। Yes, Deepak will drop Kavita at home.

Lesson 21

Forgive Me, I Was Delayed

Kavita : Hi Deepak. Forgive me! I am late.

Deepak : Hi Kavita. What happened? You are half an hour late. I was about to go.

Kavita : I was coming. Then I remembered that I had to do something for my father in Khan Market. I thought that it was only a five-minute task. It took a long time to do it.

Deepak : You could have phoned me.

Kavita : I was about to phone you but I saw that my phone was dead.

Deepak : Yes, I too tried to call you. I was going to wait five minutes more for you. If you had not come, then I would have gone home.

Kavita : Okay, I will buy you a cup of tea in Barista in Khan Market. Today it feels so hot outside.

Deepak : Yes, but let's go by auto. I will call an autowallah.

Kavita : Deepak, autowallahs will not go such a short distance. We will have to walk.

1. आज किसको देर हुई है? आज कविता को देर हुई है। Who is late today? Today Kavita is late.

2. कविता को कितनी देर हुई है? उसको आधे घंटे की देर हुई है। How late is Kavita? She is half an hour late.

3. दीपक कितनी देर और इंतज़ार करनेवाला था? वह पाँच मिनट और इंतज़ार करनेवाला था। How much longer was Deepak about to wait? He was about to wait for five minutes more.

4. कविता ने दीपक को फ़ोन क्यों नहीं किया? उसने दीपक को फ़ोन नहीं किया क्योंकि उसका फ़ोन मर गया था। Why did Kavita not phone Deepak? She didn't phone Deepak because her phone had died.

5. आज कॉलेज/दफ़्तर आने में क्या आपको देर हुई? जी नहीं, आज कॉलेज आने में मुझे देर नहीं हुई। Were you late to college/the office today? (Example:) No, I was not late to college today.

6. पाँच मिनट बाद दीपक क्या करनेवाला था? पाँच मिनट बाद दीपक घर जानेवाला था। What was Deepak about to do after five minutes? After five minutes Deepak was about to go home.

7. अगर कविता नहीं आती तो दीपक क्या करता? अगर कविता नहीं आती तो दीपक घर जाता। If Kavita had not come, what would Deepak have done? If Kavita had not come, Deepak would have gone home.

I Think That…

Deepak : Kavita, you didn't tell me what Vrinda said to you.

Kavita : Oh, I was about to talk to you yesterday but then I forgot.

Deepak : So what did you talk about? (what talk happened)

Kavita : Vrinda wants to come to Delhi after she completes school. In my opinion it would be good if your parents would let her come.

Deepak : Why do you think that (such)?

Kavita : Vrinda thinks that there is nothing left for her in Allahabad. In my opinion, she is right.

Deepak : That's true, but if she may come to Delhi, then (our) parents will be alone.

Kavita : I understand this, but they let you come to Delhi, didn't they? And your brother came here and is working.

Deepak : So what do you think? Should I talk to my parents about this matter?

Kavita : I think so (such). Vrinda will have more opportunities in Delhi. And if she doesn't become a doctor, then at least she will have the opportunity to do something else. This is my thought.

Deepak : Okay, I will phone them tonight and talk about it.

1. क्या आप सोचते हैं कि वृन्दा को इलाहाबाद में रहना चाहिये? जी नहीं, मैं सोचता हूँ (सोचती हूँ) कि उसे दिल्ली आना चाहिए। जी हाँ, मैं सोचता हूँ (सोचती हूँ) कि उसको इलाहाबाद में रहना चाहिये। No, I think that she should come to Delhi. Yes, I think that she should stay in Allahabad.

2. क्या आपका यह ख़्याल है कि दिल्ली आकर वृंदा को पढ़ना चाहिये? जी हाँ, मेरा यह ख़्याल है कि दिल्ली आकर वृंदा को पढ़ना चाहिये। जी नहीं, मेरा यह ख़्याल है कि इलाहाबाद में रहकर वृंदा को पढ़ना चाहिये। Yes, it is my thought that Vrinda should come to Delhi and study. No, it is my thought that Vrinda should stay in Allahabad and study.

3. क्या दीपक के माता-पिता ने दीपक को दिल्ली आने दिया? जी हाँ, दीपक के माता-पिता ने दीपक को दिल्ली आने दिया। Yes, Deepak's parents allowed Deepak come to Delhi.

4. क्या दीपक के माँ-बाप को वृंदा को दिल्ली आने देना चाहिये? जी हाँ, दीपक के माँ-बाप को वृंदा को दिल्ली आने देना चाहिये। Yes, Deepak's parents should let Vrinda come to Delhi.

5. क्या आपके ख़्याल में इलाहाबाद से दिल्ली में ज़्यादा मौक़े मिलते हैं? जी हाँ, मेरे ख़्याल में इलाहाबाद से दिल्ली में ज़्यादा मौक़े मिलते हैं। Yes, in my opinion, there are more opportunities in Delhi than in Allahabad.

6. क्या आप सोचते हैं (सोचती हैं) कि दीपक को अपने माँ-बाप से बात करनी चाहिये? जी हाँ, मैं सोचता हूँ (सोचती हूँ) कि उसको अपने माँ-बाप से बात करनी चाहिये। जी नहीं, मैं नहीं सोचता (नहीं सोचती) कि उसको अपने माँ-बाप से बात करनी चाहिये। Yes, I think that he should talk to his parents. No, I don't think that he should talk to his parents.

Lesson 22

Do You Know Urdu?

Kavita : Imran, can I ask you something?

Imran : Certainly, Kavita. What do you have to ask?

Kavita : Do you know Urdu?

Imran : Yes, I know a little Urdu. Why?

Deepak : What's the difference between Hindi and Urdu, Imran?

Imran : This is a difficult question, Deepak.

Kavita : Deepak, let Imran speak. Imran, teach me to read Urdu.

Imran : I know how to read Urdu, but I don't know how to write it well. Why do you have to learn Urdu?

Kavita : I am interested in learning different languages. I know a little English and now I want to learn Urdu as well.

Imran : Urdu is not such a difficult language. And Hindi and Urdu are very close. But writing it is a little difficult.

Deepak : So is there only a difference in their scripts? Or is there more difference than this between them?

Imran : There is certainly a difference in their scripts. Hindi is written in Devanagari and Urdu is written in Nastaliq. But some words are different also.

1. क्या इमरान को उर्दू आती है? जी हाँ, इमरान को थोड़ी उर्दू आती है। Does Imran know Urdu? Yes, Imran knows a little Urdu.

2. क्या आपको हिन्दी आती है? जी हाँ, मुझको थोड़ी हिन्दी आती है। Do you know Hindi? Yes, I know a little Hindi.

3. क्या इमरान को उर्दू लिखना आता है? इमरान को उर्दू लिखना अच्छी तरह नहीं आता। Does Imran know how to write Urdu? Imran doesn't know (how) to write Urdu well.

4. क्या आपको हिन्दी लिखना आता है? जी हाँ, मुझे हिन्दी लिखना थोड़ा आता है। Do you know how to write Hindi? Yes, I know (how) to write Hindi a bit.

5. क्या कविता को भाषा सीखने का शौक़ है? जी हाँ, उसे भाषा सीखने का शौक़ है। Is Kavita interested in learning languages? Yes, she is interested in learning languages.

6. क्या आपको ज़बान सीखने का शौक़ है? जी हाँ, मुझे भाषा सीखने का शौक़ है। Are you interested in learning languages? Yes, I am interested in learning languages.

7. आपको कितनी हिन्दी आती है? मुझे थोड़ी हिन्दी आती है। How much Hindi do you know? I know a little Hindi.

8. क्या आपको हिन्दी लिखना अच्छी तरह आता है? जी नहीं, मुझे हिन्दी लिखना अच्छी तरह नहीं आता। Do you know how to write Hindi well? No, I don't know (how) to write Hindi well.

I Can't Tell You How Tired I Am

Kavita : Hello Sanjeev, it's been a long time. (a meeting with you for many days has not happened) How are you?

Sanjeev : Hi Kavita. Yes, I have to do a lot of work. I come home from work very late at night. I just work all day. And my office is very far from here as well.

Kavita : Don't you ever get a holiday?

Sanjeev : Rarely (very little). I can't tell you how tired I get by the time I come home. By the weekend I am so tired that I can't get up.

Kavita : What time do you arrive home at night?

Sanjeev : Sometimes 12 A.M., sometimes 1:30 A.M. I am sleepy all day. One day I even fell asleep at my desk.

Kavita : This is no life. You need an opportunity to enjoy (life) as well.

Sanjeev : Yes, but in two months I am going to start a new job. Perhaps then I will get a bit of a rest.

Kavita : So you constantly work and Deepak and I simply enjoy ourselves.

Deepak : That's not true, Kavita. You study all the time.

Kavita : But it seems to me that Sanjeev's life is more difficult than our lives.

Sanjeev : Perhaps, but good salaries are now available for such jobs nowadays. And you are going to become a doctor. Then you will discover the painful reality.

1. क्या संजीव को बहुत काम करना पड़ता है? जी हाँ, संजीव को बहुत काम करना पड़ता है। Yes, Sanjeev has to do a lot of work.

2. क्या कभी संजीव को छुट्टी मिलती है? संजीव को बहुत कम छुट्टी मिलती है। Sanjeev receives very little holiday.

3. आपको छुट्टी कब मिलती है? मुझे (जून के महीने) में छुट्टी मिलती है। I get a holiday in (the month of June).

4. रात को संजीव कितने बजे घर पहुँचता है? रात को संजीव कभी बारह बजे, कभी डेढ़ बजे घर पहुँचता है। Sanjeev reaches home sometimes at 12 A.M., sometimes at 1:30 A.M.

5. रात को क्या आपको बहुत थकान होती है? जी हाँ, रात को मुझे बहुत थकान होती है। Yes, I get very tired at night.

6. क्या कविता को ऐसा लगता है कि संजीव की ज़िंदगी उसकी ज़िंदगी से मुश्किल है? जी हाँ, कविता को ऐसा लगता है कि संजीव की ज़िंदगी उसकी ज़िंदगी से मुश्किल है। Yes, it seems to Kavita that Sanjeev's life is more difficult than hers.

Lesson 23

Delhi Just Keeps Growing

Hello my friends! Today I want to tell you a little more about Delhi. You know that Delhi is a very big city. You must also know that D.U. is situated in north Delhi. Jawaharlal Nehru University is in the south. Most people call this J.N.U. Both universities are very famous. The Kutub Minar is very far off in the south. C.P. is in the middle. The English built C.P. To the north of C.P. is Old Delhi. Shah Jahan built Old Delhi. To the west is the airport and Gurgaon. For the past few years Gurgaon has continued to develop. Many malls have sprung up and a lot of people have begun to live there. In the east is the Yamuna River. My house is not far from C.P. This is the map of Delhi. The population of Delhi is growing more every day. People are coming here and settling from the entire country. We can't say how Delhi will be in a few years.

1. क्या दिल्ली की आबादी बढ़ती जा रही है? जी हाँ, वह बढ़ती जा रही है। Is the population of Delhi just continuing to grow? Yes, it is continuing to grow.

2. क्या आपके शहर की आबादी बढ़ती जा रही है? जी हाँ, मेरे शहर की आबादी बढ़ती जा रही है। जी नहीं, वह नहीं बढ़ रही है। Is the population of your city continuing to grow? Yes, my city's population is continuing to grow. No, it is not growing.

3. डी॰ यू॰ उत्तर दिल्ली में स्थित है या दक्षिण दिल्ली में? वह उत्तर दिल्ली में स्थित है। Is D.U. situated in north or south Delhi? It is in north Delhi.

4. दिल्ली का हवाई अड्डा कहाँ स्थित है? दिल्ली का हवाई अड्डा पश्चिम में स्थित है। Where is Delhi's airport? Delhi's airport is in the west.

5. सी० पी० कहाँ है? सी० पी० बीच में है। C.P. is in the middle.

6. लोग कहाँ से आकर दिल्ली में बसने लगे हैं? लोग सारे देश से आकर दिल्ली में बसने लगे हैं। Where have people begun to come from and settle in Delhi? People have begun to come from the entire country and settle in Delhi.

7. क्या कविता का घर सी० पी० से बहुत दूर है? जी नहीं, उसका घर सी० पी० से बहुत दूर नहीं है। जी नहीं उसका घर सी० पी० के बहुत पास है। Is Kavita's home very far from C.P.? No, her home is not very far from C.P. No, her home is very close to C.P.

Shall We Go via Bengali Market?

Kavita : Deepak, can we go home this evening via the Bengali Market?

Deepak : Why via the Bengali Market? Do you have some work there?

Kavita : Yes, I have to buy some sweets.

Deepak : Do you really need to go to the Bengali Market to buy sweets? You can't get good sweets in Khan Market?

Kavita : Deepak, you know that you can't get as good sweets in Khan Market as in the Bengali Market.

Deepak : Okay, but there will be many cars in the Bengali Market at this time. We won't find parking anywhere. Can't we get sweets anywhere else?

Kavita : Where are the other good sweet shops in Delhi?

Deepak : Okay, we will go home via the Bengali Market. For whom are the sweets?

Kavita : My mother has asked (for them). Don't you remember that some people are coming to our home this evening for dinner?

1. कविता कहाँ से होकर घर जाना चाहती है? कविता बंगाली मार्केट से होकर घर जाना चाहती है। Via where does Kavita want to go home? Kavita wants to go home via the Bengali Market.

2. बंगाली मार्केट में कविता क्या ख़रीदना चाहती है? बंगाली मार्केट में कविता मिठाई ख़रीदना चाहती है। What does Kavita want to buy from the Bengali Market? Kavita wants to buy sweets in the Bengali Market.

3. दीपक बंगाली मार्केट क्यों जाना नहीं चाहता? दीपक बंगाली मार्केट जाना नहीं चाहता क्योंकि वहाँ बहुत गाड़ियाँ होंगी। Why does Deepak not want to go to the Bengali Market? Deepak does not want to go to Bengali Market because there will be many cars there.

4. किसने मिठाई मँगवायी है? कविता की माँ ने मिठाई मँगवायी है। Who has ordered the sweets? Kavita's mother has ordered the sweets.

5. क्या आपको मिठाई अच्छी लगती है? जी हाँ, मुझे मिठाई अच्छी लगती है। Do you like sweets? Yes, I like sweets.

6. बंगाली मार्केट में जितनी अच्छी मिठाई मिलती है, क्या ख़ान मार्केट में उतनी अच्छी मिठाई मिलती है? जी नहीं, बंगाली मार्केट में जितनी अच्छी मिठाई मिलती है, ख़ान मार्केट में उतनी अच्छी मिठाई नहीं मिलती। Can such good sweets be obtained in Khan Market as can be found in Bengali Market? No, such good sweets cannot be obtained in Khan Market as can be found in Bengali Market.

Lesson 24

I Am Quite Worried about the Exams

Deepak : Kavita, these days the exams are imminent. I am quite worried about this.

Kavita : Why are you so worried?

Deepak : Where do I obtain the sort of grades that you obtain every time?

Kavita : Don't worry. You will give good exams. I have every confidence in you.

Deepak : Yes, but when I worry a lot I can't concentrate on my studies.

Kavita : A little bit of anxiety should occur. He who doesn't worry is not human.

Deepak : You are right, Kavita. Do you worry before (giving) exams?

Kavita : Of course! But not as much as you.

Deepak : When is your first exam, Kavita?

Kavita : My first exam is in two days. When is your first exam?

Deepak : Mine is also the day after tomorrow. What time (is yours)?

Kavita : Two-thirty. Shall we go together?

Deepak : Okay. I will do some study now.

1. आजकल दीपक को किस बात की फ़िक्र हो रही है? आजकल उसे इम्तहान की फ़िक्र हो रही है। What is Deepak worried about these days? He is worried about the exam these days.

2. जब आपको इम्तहान देने पड़ते हैं तब क्या आपको फ़िक्र होती है? जी हाँ, जब मुझे इम्तहान देने पड़ते हैं तब मुझे फ़िक्र होती है। Do you worry when you have to take an exam? Yes, I worry when I have to take an exam.

3. जिसको कभी फ़िक्र नहीं होती, उसके बारे में कविता क्या सोचती है? जिसको कभी फ़िक्र नहीं होती, उसके बारे में वह सोचती है कि वह इंसान नहीं है। What does Kavita think about those who don't worry? She things that those who don't worry are not human.

4. जब दीपक को फ़िक्र होती है, क्या वह पढ़ाई पर ध्यान दे सकता है? जी नहीं, जब दीपक को फ़िक्र होती है, तब वह पढ़ाई पर ध्यान नहीं दे सकता। Can Deepak concentrate on his studies when he is worried? No, he can't concentrate on his studies when he is worried.

5. जब आपको फ़िक्र होती है, क्या आप पढ़ाई पर ध्यान दे सकते हैं? (दे सकती हैं) जी नहीं, जब मुझको फ़िक्र होती है, तब मैं पढ़ाई पर ध्यान नहीं दे सकता। (नहीं दे सकती) जी हाँ, जब मुझको फ़िक्र होती है, तब भी मैं पढ़ाई पर ध्यान दे सकता हूँ। (दे सकती हूँ) Can you concentrate on your studies when you are worried? No, I can't concentrate on my studies when I am worried. Yes, even when I am worried I can concentrate on my studies.

6. क्या दीपक कविता से इम्तहान की ज़्यादा फ़िक्र करता है? जी हाँ, वह कविता से इम्तहान की ज़्यादा फ़िक्र करता है। Does Deepak worry more than Kavita about the exam? Yes, he worries more than Kavita about the exam.

7. कविता का पहला इम्तहान कब है? उसका पहला इम्तहान परसों है। When is Kavita's first exam? Her first exam is the day after tomorrow.

8. क्या आपके सिर पर इम्तहान हैं? जी हाँ, मेरे सिर पर इम्तहान हैं। Are your exams imminent? Yes, they are imminent.

Where Are You Going for the Summer?

Deepak : Kavita, what are you going to do after the exams are over?

Kavita : My mother and I are going to go to the mountains, to avoid (be saved from) the heat. Even now I am feeling really hot.

Deepak : Yes, and the month of June hasn't even begun yet. For how many days are you thinking of going?

Kavita : We will go for at least a month. My mother is from Almora, so we will go and stay there. What are you going to do?

Deepak : I thought that I would go to Allahabad. College is almost over. After this I don't know what
I should do. I will have to look for a job. I thought that I would go and see mum and dad and
Vrinda before I start a job.

Kavita : Why don't you go with us? My mother will like it.

Deepak : You won't like it?

Kavita : Deepak, do I have to make everything so clear?

Deepak : Okay, I will talk to my parents and give you an answer.

1. पढ़ाई पूरी होने के बाद दीपक कहाँ जानेवाला है? पढ़ाई पूरी होने के बाद वह इलाहाबाद
जानेवाला है। या शायद वह कविता के साथ अल्मोड़ा जाएगा। Where is Deepak going to go
after (his) studies are complete? After (his) studies are complete, he is going to go to Allahabad. Or
perhaps he will go with Kavita to Almora.

2. पढ़ाई पूरी होने के बाद कविता कहाँ जानेवाली है? वह पहाड़ों में जानेवाली है। Where is
Kavita going to go after (her) studies are complete? She is going to go to the mountains.

3. कविता किसके साथ जानेवाली है? वह अपनी माँ के साथ जानेवाली है। With whom is Kavita
going to go? She is going to go with her (own) mother.

4. कविता कितने दिन के लिये जानेवाली है? वह कम से कम एक महीने के लिये जानेवाली
है। For how long is Kavita going to go? She is going to go for at least one month.

5. दीपक कहाँ जाने की सोच रहा है? वह इलाहाबाद जाने की सोच रहा है। Where is Deepak
thinking of going? He is thinking of going to Allahabad.

6. क्या दीपक को जल्दी नौकरी की तलाश करनी पड़ेगी? जी हाँ, उसे जल्दी नौकरी की तलाश
करनी पड़ेगी। Will Deepak have to search for a job quickly? Yes, he will have to search for a job
quickly.

7. क्या दीपक को मालूम है कि पढ़ाई पूरी होने पर वह क्या करेगा? जी नहीं उसे मालूम नहीं है
कि पढ़ाई पूरी होने पर वह क्या करेगा। Does Deepak know what he will do on the completion
of his studies? No, he doesn't know what he will do on the completion of his studies.

An example response:

इस साल के अंत में मैं हिन्दुस्तान जानेवाली हूँ। पढ़ाई पूरी होने पर मैं हिन्दुस्तान जानेवाली हूँ।
मैं हिन्दुस्तान घूमने जानेवाली हूँ। मैं भारत तीन महीने के लिये जाऊँगी। उसके बाद मैं नौकरी
की तलाश करना शुरू करूँगी। नौकरी की तलाश करने से पहले मैं एक दोस्त के साथ घूमने
जानेवाली हूँ। मैं गर्मी के दिनों में जानेवाली हूँ। मैं यूरोप से होकर हिन्दुस्तान जाऊँगी।

At the end of this year I am going to go to India. On the completion of my studies I am going to go to
India. I am going to go traveling in India. I will go to India for three months. After that I will begin to
search for a job. Before searching for a job I will go traveling with a friend. I am going to go in summer.
I am going to go to India via Europe.

Hindi-English Glossary

The words in this glossary are arranged according to the order of the Hindi syllabary. The information in the first set of parentheses provides the first occurrence of the word in the Textbook (T). The information in the second set provides the page number of the glossary or glossaries in which the word occurs in the Workbook (W). The final set of parentheses indicates the lesson in the Textbook in which any relevant grammatical information is located (GR).

(T1, p. 4) = Textbook, Lesson 1, p. 4
(W1, p. 3) = Workbook, Lesson 1 Glossary, p. 3
(GR 8) = Grammar, Textbook Lesson 8

अ

अंक (*m*) number, numeral, figure (T6, p. 46)
अंगूठी (*f*) a ring (T6, p. 46)
अंग्रेज़ी (*f*) English (T6, p. 46)
अंचल (*m*) the outward fringe of the sari, region, frontier (T6, p. 46)
अंडा (*m*) egg (T6, p. 44)
अंत (*m*) end (W13, p. 70)
अंतर्मुखी (*adj*) introvertive (W6, p. 25)
अंदर (*adv*) inside (T13, p. 111) (W6, p. 28)
अंधा (*adj*) blind, irrational, unenlightened (T13, p. 108)
अंधेरा (*adj*) dark, black (T24, p. 235) (W22, p. 125)
अकेला (*adj*) alone (W22, p. 125)
अकेले (*adv*) alone (W23, p. 130)
अकखड़ (*adj*) headstrong, rude and rough (W6, p. 25)
अक्तूबर (*m*) October (T16, p. 154)
अक्षर (*m*) letter (of the alphabet), character, symbol (W6, p. 26)
अक्सर (*adv*) often (T11, p. 91) (W9, 22 pp. 48, 124)
अख़बार (*m*) newspaper (T5, p. 36) (W4, p. 18)
अगर (*conj*) if (T10, p. 83) (W11, p. 60)
अगला (*adj*) next, following
अगली बार (*adv*) next time (T11, p. 93) (W15, p. 85)
अगले हफ़्ते (*adv*) next week (T11, p. 92) (W7, p. 35)
अगस्त (*m*) August (T16, p. 154)
अचानक (*adv*) suddenly (T18, p. 174) (W19, p. 110)
अच्छा (*adj*) good (T5, p. 32) (W4, p. 18)
(x को) अच्छा लगना (*v.i.*) (x) to like (T18, p. 174) (W18, p. 104) (GR 18)
अच्छी तरह (*adv*) well, in a good manner (T22, p. 215) (W23, p. 130)
अजायबघर (*m*) museum (T22, p. 219)

अजीब (*adj*) strange, peculiar (T19, p. 192)
अट्ठाईस (*adj*) twenty-eight (T16, p. 151)
अट्ठारह/अठारह (*adj*) eighteen (T16, p. 151)
अट्ठारहवाँ (*adj*) eighteenth (T18, p. 168) (W12, p. 65)
अड़तालीस (*adj*) forty-eight (T16, p. 151)
अड़तीस (*adj*) thirty-eight (T16, p. 151)
अतः hence, therefore, thus (T5, p. 33)
अधिक (*adj*) more, too much (T19, p. 196) (W10, p. 54)
अधिकारी (*m*) official, officer (W10, p. 54)
अध्यापक (*m*) teacher, educator, lecturer (T6, p. 43) (W17, p. 98)
अनुभव (*m*) experience (T13, p. 110)
अनोखी (*f*) Anokhi (name of a popular clothing store in Khan Market) (अनोखा (*adj*) unique, peculiar) (T17, p. 160)
अपना (*adj*) one's own (T10, p. 82) (W10, p. 54) (GR 10)
अपने-आप (*adv*) (by) oneself (T11, p. 85) (W11, p. 60) (GR 11)
अपने ढंग से (*adv*) independently
अपने मन का (*adj*) independent, of one's own mind (W10, p. 54)
अपने लिये (*adv*) for oneself (T11, p. 90)
अप्पू (*m*) Appu (name) (T11, p. 88)
अप्रैल (*m*) April (month) (T16, p. 154)
अफ़सर (*m*) officer (T4, p. 26)
अफ़सोस (*m*) sorrow, grief (T18, p. 175)
(x को) अफ़सोस होना (*v.i.*) (x) to feel sorrow (T18, p. 175)
अब (*adv*) now (T8, p. 66) (W4, p. 18)
अभी (*adv*) right now (अब + ही) (T17, p. 57) (T14, p. 128) (W6, 8 pp. 28, 41) (GR 14)

अभी-अभी (*adv*) right now (W13, p. 71)

अभी भी (*adv*) even now (T10, p. 80)

अभ्यास (*m*) practice (T6, p. 43) (W23, p. 130)

(x) (का) अभ्यास करना (*v.t.*) to practice (x) (T11, p. 86)

अमरीका (*m*) America (T4, p. 29)

अमरीकी (*adj*) American (T3, p. 22)

अमरूद (*m*) guava (T3, p. 21)

अमिताव घोष (*m*) Amitav Ghosh (name, of a famous Indian author) (T12, p. 103)

अमीर (*adj*) wealthy (T11, p. 85)

अम्मी जान (*f*) mother dear (T7, p. 50)

अय्यर (*m*) Ayyar (name) (T6, p. 43)

अरब (*adj*) a billion; (*m*) Arab (T16, p. 152)

अरी (*f voc*) hey! (T7, p. 55)

अरे (*m voc*) hey! (T7, p. 55) (W4, p. 18)

अरे वाह (*voc*) Oh wow! (T7, p. 50)

अर्थशास्त्र (*m*) economics (T11, p. 86)

अलग (*adj*) different (T11, p. 89)

अलग-अलग (*adj*) separate, different (T11, p. 89)

अली Ali (name) (T1, p. 5)

अल्मोड़ा (*m*) Almora (name of a town in the foothills of the Himalayas) (T24, p. 234)

अल्लाह (*m*) Allah, God (T16, p. 146)

असल (*adj*) real, true (W7, p. 35)

असल में (*adv*) in reality (W7, p. 35)

असलियत (*f*) reality (W18, p. 104)

अस्पताल (*m*) hospital (W15, 21 pp. 85, 119)

अस्सलाम अलैकुम Peace be upon you! (a greeting) (T7, p. 51)

अस्सी (*adj*) eighty (T16, p. 151)

आ

आँख (*f*) eye (T5, p. 20)

आँगन (*m*) courtyard (W8, p. 41)

आँधी (*f*) storm, dust-storm (T6, p. 47)

आइना (*m*) mirror (W11, p. 60)

आओ (*v.i.*) come (imperative form with तुम) (W4, p. 18)

आख़िर (*m*) the end; (*adv*) finally, in the end (T16, p. 155)

आगरा (*m*) Agra (name of a city in U.P.) (T13, p. 115)

आगे (*adv*) ahead, in front, before, in the future (T16, p. 155)

आज (*m + adv*) today (T2, p. 13) (W3, p. 13)

आजकल (*adv*) these days (T4, p. 29) (W2, p. 8)

आज्ञा (*f*) command, order (W8, p. 41)

आटा (*m*) flour (T18, p. 171) (W18, p. 104)

आटे दाल का भाव मालूम होना (*v.i.*) to discover a harsh truth (T18, p. 171)

ऑटो(रिक्शा) (*m*) auto(rickshaw) (T13, p. 105)

आठ (*adj*) eight (T10, p. 77)

आठवाँ (*adj*) eighth (T8, p. 59)

आदत (*f*) habit (T19, p. 191)

आदत पड़ना (*v.i.*) a habit to form

आदत छोड़ना (*v.t.*) to abandon a habit

आदमी (*m*) man (T2, p. 13) (W2, p. 8)

आदर (*m*) respect, esteem, honor

(x का) आदर करना (*v.t.*) to respect (x)

आदाब (*m*) manners, salutation ("greetings") (T7, p. 50)

आधा (*adj*) one half (T16, p. 153) (W14, 23 pp. 78, 129)

आना (*v.i.*) to come (T1, p. 5) (W9, p. 48) (GR 22)

आप (*pro*) you (plural polite) (T2, p. 14) (GR 4)

आप ही (*adv*) (by) oneself (T11, p. 85) (GR 11)

आपका (*adj*) your (T2, p. 14) (GR 4)

आपको (*pro*) oblique form of आप + को (T7, p. 53) (GR 7)

आपत्ति (*f*) objection (W16, p. 91)

आपने (*pro*) you (oblique form of आप + ने) (T7, p. 53) (GR 7, 12)

आफ़ताब (*m*) the sun; Aftab (name) (T7, p. 57)

आबादी (*f*) population (T19, p. 196) (W11, p. 60)

आम (*m*) mango (T1, p. 7) (W1, p. 3)

आम (*adj*) general, ordinary (T1, p. 7)

आम तौर पर (*adv*) generally (W10, p. 54)

आय (*f*) income (T1, p. 6)

आराम (*m*) rest, relaxation

आराम करना (*v.t.*) to relax (W12, p. 65)

आराम से (*adv*) comfortably (T14, p. 126)

आराम-प्रिय (*adj*) loving relaxation (T10, p. 77)

ऑर्डर (*m*) order (W8, p. 41)

आलू (*m*) potato (T7, p. 54) (W3, 13 pp. 13, 71)

आवश्यक (*adj*) necessary (T5, p. 33)

आवाज़ (*f*) voice, noise (W2, p. 8)

आशा (*f*) hope (T5, p. 33)

(x को) आशा होना (*v.i.*) (x) to hope (W18, p. 104)

आश्रम (*m*) ashram (hermitage) (T6, p. 46)

आसपास (*adv*) nearby, near about (T19, p. 194) (W7, p. 35)

आसफ़ुद्दौला (*m*) Asaf-ud-Daula (name) (W12, p. 65)

आसान (*adj*) easy (W3, p. 13)

ऑस्ट्रेलिया (*m*) Australia (T8, p. 61)

ऑस्ट्रेलियन (*adj*) Australian (T10, p. 77)

आसपास (*adv*) nearby, around (T19, p. 194) (W7, p. 35)

इ

इंग्लैंड (*m*) England (T18, p. 174)

इंडिया (*m*) India (T18, p. 171)

इंडिया गेट (*m*) India Gate (T13, p. 114)

इंतज़ाम (*m*) arrangement (T13, p. 113)

(x का) इंतज़ाम करना (*v.t.*) to arrange (x) (T13, p. 113)

इंतज़ार (*m*) waiting (T15, p. 134)

(x का) इंतज़ार करना (*v.t.*) to wait (for x) (T15, p. 134) (W22, p. 125)

इंदिरा (*f*) Indira (name) (W10, p. 54)

इंशाअल्लाह! (*voc*) God willing!

इंसान (*m*) human being (T24, p. 230)

इकट्ठा (*adj*) collected, gathered (T23, p. 226)

इकट्ठा करना (*v.t.*) to collect, gather (T23, p. 226)

इकतालीस (*adj*) forty-one (T16, p. 151)

इक्तीस (*adj*) thirty-one (T16, p. 151)

इक्कीस (*adj*) twenty-one (T16, p. 151) (W10, p. 54)

इक्कीसवाँ (*adj*) twenty-first (T21, p. 206)

इच्छा (*f*) desire (T16, p. 147) (W8, 20 pp. 41, 114)

इतना (*adj*) this much, so much, so (T8, p. 66) (W3, 21 pp. 13, 119) (GR 23)

इतनी कम दूर (*adv*) such a little distance (T21, p. 207)

इतवार (*m*) Sunday (T11, p. 94) (W9, p. 48) (GR 16)

इतिहास (*m*) history (T11, p. 86)

इत्तफ़ाक़ (*m*) concurrence, agreement, coincidence, assent, consent (T17, p. 166)

इत्तफ़ाक़ से (*adv*) by chance (T17, p. 166)

इधर (*adv*) here, this side, over here (T23, p. 225) (W7, p. 35) (GR 23)

इन (*pro*) oblique form of ये (T2, p. 14) (GR 7)

इनका (*adj*) his/her/their (T2, p. 14) (GR 2, 4)

(x से) इनकार करना (*v.t.*) to refuse, to deny (x) (T13, p. 113)

इन्हीं (*pro*) इन + ही (T14, p. 128) (GR 14)

इन्हें/इनको (*pro*) oblique form of ये + को (T7, p. 53) (GR 7)

इन्होंने (*pro*) he/she/they/these (oblique form of ये + ने) (T7, p. 53) (GR 7, 12)

इमारत (*f*) building (T2, p. 13) (W12, p. 65)

इम्तहान (*m*) examination (T20, p. 202) (W15, 19 pp. 85, 109)

इम्तहान (x के) सिर पर होना (*v.i.*) (x's) exams to be imminent (T24, p. 230)

इरादा (*m*) intention (W9, p. 48)

इलाक़ा (*m*) area, locality, territory (T14, p. 120)

इलाज (*m*) remedy, treatment (W13, p. 71)

इलाहाबाद (*m*) Allahabad (name of a city in U.P.) (T4, p. 29) (W2, p. 8)

इस (*pro*) oblique form of यह (T2, p. 14) (GR 7)

इस तरह (*adv*) in this way (W11, p. 60)

इस बारे में (*adv*) about this (T20, p. 202)

इस बीच (*adv*) meanwhile (W12, p. 65)

इस मामले में (*adv*) about (in) this matter (T13, p. 110)

इसका (*adj*) his/her/its (T2, p. 14) (GR 2, 4)

इसने (*pro*) he/she/it/this (oblique form of यह + ने) (T7, p. 53) (GR 7, 12)

इसमें कोई शक नहीं है । There is no doubt about (in) this. (T20, p. 202)

इसलिये (*conj*) therefore (W10, p. 54)

इसी (*pro*) इस + ही (T14, p. 128) (GR 14)

इसे/इसको (*pro*) oblique form of यह + को (T7, p. 53) (GR 7)

ई

ईकनॉमिक्स (*m*) economics (T11, p. 86)

ईद (*f*) the festival of Eid (T16, p. 148) (W12, p. 65)

ईद-उज़-जुहा (*f*) name of Eid (W15, p. 85)

ईद-उल-अज़हा (*f*) name of Eid (W15, p. 85)

ईमान (*m*) faith, belief, integrity (T1, p. 7)

ईश्वर/ईश्वर (*m*) God (T5, p. 32)

उ

उचित (*adj*) proper, appropriate (T16, p. 148)

उठना (*v.i.*) to rise, get up (T1, p. 76) (W9, p. 48) (GR 19)

उठाना (*v.t.*) to get up, make rise (T15, p. 135) (W24, p. 137)

उड़ना (*v.i.*) to fly (T15, p. 139)

उड़ाना (*v.t.*) to make fly

उतरना (*v.i.*) to descend, come off (T22, p. 217) (W19, p. 110)

उतारना (*v.t.*) to get down, make descend (T15, p. 140)

उत्तर (*m*) north (T14, p. 120)

उत्तर प्रदेश (*m*) Uttar Pradesh (North Province) (a state in north India) (W21, p. 120)

उत्तर भारत (*m*) north India (T19, p. 187)

उत्तराखंड (*m*) Uttarakhand (a state to the northwest of Uttar Pradesh) (T12, p. 99)

उदार (*adj*) generous (W10, p. 54)

उदास (*adj*) sad, dejected, gloomy (T2, p. 13)

उधर (*adv*) there, over there (T23, p. 225)

उन (*pro*) oblique form of वे (T2, p. 14) (GR 7)

उनका (*adj*) his/her/their (T2, p. 14) (GR 2, 4)

उनचास (*adj*) forty-nine (T16, p. 151)

उनतालीस (*adj*) thirty-nine (T16, p. 151)

उनतीस (*adj*) twenty-nine (T16, p. 151)

उन्नति (*f*) progress, rise, promotion, improvement, development (W6, p. 25)

उन्तीस (*adj*) nineteen (T12, p. 104)

उन्तीसवाँ (*adj*) nineteenth (T19, p. 183)

उन्हीं (*pro*) उन + ही (T14, p. 128) (GR 14)

उन्हें/उनको (*pro*) oblique form of वे + को (T7, p. 53) (GR 7)

उन्होंने (*pro*) he/she/they/those (oblique form of वे + ने) (T7, p. 53) (GR 7, 12)

उपन्यास (*m*) novel (T12, p. 103)

उपवास (*m*) fast (not eating) (W24, p. 137)

उमर (*f*) see उम्र

उमड़ना (*v.i.*) to surge, swell, to flood, to gust (T22, p. 217)

उमस (*f*) humidity (T19, p. 187)

उम्मीद (*f*) hope, expectation (W21, p. 120)

उम्र (*f*) age (T6, p. 48) (W10, p. 54)

उर्दू (*f*) Urdu (language) (T17, p. 167) (W21, p. 120)

उस (*pro*) oblique form of वह (T2, p. 14) (GR 7)

उसका (*adj*) his/her/its (T2, p. 14) (GR 2, 4)

उसने (*pro*) oblique form of वह + ने (T7, p. 53) (GR 7, 12)

उसी (*pro*) उस + ही (T14, p. 126) (GR 14)

उसे/उसको (*pro*) oblique form of वह + को (T7, p. 53) (GR 7)

ऊ

ऊँचा (*adj*) high (T3, p. 20) (W5, p. 23)

ऊँट (*m*) camel (T6, p. 47)

ऋ

ऋतु (*f*) season (T10, p. 78)

ए

ए॰ सी॰ (*f*) A.C. (T19, p. 194)

एक (*adj*) one (T4, p. 29) (W2, p. 8)

एक घंटे बाद (*adv*) after an hour (T13, p. 110)

एक तिहाई (*adj*) one-third (T16, p. 153)

एक चौथाई (*adj*) one-quarter (T16, p. 153)

एक दिन (*adv*) one day (T11, p. 91)

एक बात करना (*v.t.*) to say one thing (T16, p. 149)

एक बार (*adv*) once, one time (T13, p. 118)

एक साथ (*adv*) together (W10, p. 54)

एक ही (*adj*) same (T15, p. 132)

एकदम (*adv*) immediately, suddenly, in one breath, completely; (*adj*) perfect (T11, p. 91)

एक्सप्रेस (*adj*) express (W14, p. 78)

एशिया (*m*) Asia (T19, p. 196)

ऐ

ऐंद्रिय (*adj*) sensual (W6, p. 25)

ऐ O! (*voc*) (T1, p. 5)

ऐतिह्य (*m*) tradition (W6, p. 25)

ऐनक (*f*) spectacles (T1, p. 7)

ऐश्वर्य (*m*) opulence, prosperity, glory and grandeur (W6, p. 25)

ऐसा (*adj*) such, of this type (T11, p. 89) (W4, p. 18) (GR 23)

ऐसी कोई बात नहीं It's not like that (lit: such any matter isn't) (W4, p. 18)

ऐसे मत बनो don't put on an act (T15, p. 141)

ऐसे ही (*adv*) no reason, just such (W6, 7 pp. 28, 35) (GR 14)

ओ

ओ (*voc*) O! (T7, p. 55) (W3, p. 13)

ओढ़ना (*v.t.*) to cover, drape, wrap (one's own body) (T15, p. 140)

ओर (*f*) direction (T3, p. 20)

ओह (*voc*) oh! (W5, p. 23)

औ

और (*adj/adv/conj*) and, more (T3, p. 20) (W7, p. 35)

और क्या what else, of course! (T9, p. 70)

औरत (*f*) woman (T3, p. 21)

क

कंघी (*f*) comb (T6, p. 43)

कंजूस (*adj*) miserly, miser (W11, p. 60)

कंबल (*m*) blanket (T6, p. 44)

कई (*adj*) several (T13, p. 108) (W5, 15 pp. 23, 85)

कई बार (*adv*) several times (T15, p. 135)

कक्षा (*f*) class (T6, p. 46) (W10, p. 54)

कचहरी (*f*) court (W17, p. 98)

कटना (*v.i.*) to be cut (T21, p. 211)

कठिन (*adj*) difficult (T5, p. 33)

कथा (*f*) story (W10, p. 54)

कद्दू/कद्दू (*m*) pumpkin (T6, p. 44)

कन्या (*f*) girl, daughter, virgin (T16, p. 152)

कप (*m*) cup (T24, p. 235)

कपड़ा (*m*) cloth (T16, p. 144) (W7, p. 35)

कपड़े (*m*) clothes (T15, p. 140)

कपड़े पहनना (*v.t.*) to put on clothes (T15 p. 140)

कब (*adv*) when (T11, p. 91) (W9, p. 48) (GR 23)

कब की बात when's matter (when did it happen)
  (W6, p. 28)

कब से since when, for how long (W6, p. 28)

कभी (*adv*) ever, sometime (कब + ही) (T5, p. 33)
  (W12, p. 65) (GR 14)

कभी-कभी (*adv*) sometimes (T9, p. 70) (W9, p. 48)

कम (*adj*) less, too little (T1, p. 5) (W1, p. 3)

कम से कम (*adj*) at least (T17, p. 164)

कमरा (*m*) room (T2, p. 13) (W2, p. 8)

कमल (*m*) lotus (T1, p. 7) (W1, p. 3)

कमीज़ (*f*) shirt (T2, p. 13)

कर (*invar*) absolutive कर (T15, p. 140) (GR 15)

करना (*v.t.*) to do, to perform, to complete, to act,
  to execute (T8, p. 63) (GR 22)

क़रीब (*adv*) near (T15, p. 138) (W11, 15 pp. 60, 85)

क़रीम्स (*m*) Karim's (a famous kabab restaurant in
  Old Delhi) (T17, p. 168)

करेला (*m*) bitter gourd (T18, p. 169)

करोड़ (*adj*) ten million (T16, p. 152)

कल (*m*) yesterday, tomorrow (T1, p. 5) (W5, p. 23)

कल रात (*adv*) last night (T11, p. 94) (W12, p. 65)
  (GR 11)

क़लम (*f*) pen (T1, p. 7) (W1, p. 3)

कलकल (*m*) sweet and soft sound (of a flowing stream)
  (T1, p. 6)

कला (*f*) art (T1, p. 5)

कविता (*f*) poem, Kavita (name) (T3, p. 22)
  (W2, 8 pp. 8, 41)

क़व्वाली (*f*) qawwali (a genre of devotional song)
  (W11, p. 60)

कष्ट (*m*) suffering, pain, hardship, distress
  (T6, p. 43)

(x से) कहना (*v.t.*) to say (to x) (T1, p. 1)
  (W9, 11 pp. 48, 60) (GR 16)

(x को) (y) कहना (*v.t.*) to call (x) (y) (T14, p. 120)

कहाँ (*inter*) where (T4, p. 28) (W2, p. 8)

कहाँ का (*adj*) of where (T4, p. 28) (W7, p. 35)

कहानी (*f*) story (T2, p. 13) (W1, p. 3)

कहीं (*adv*) somewhere (कहाँ + ही) (T14, p. 128)

कहीं और (*adv*) anywhere/somewhere else
  (T23, p. 227)

काँच (*m*) glass (W4, p. 18)

का (*pp*) 's (T1, p. 5) (GR 2)

कागज़ (*m*) paper (T4, p. 26) (W10, p. 54)

काटना (*v.t.*) to cut, to chop, to bite (T21, p. 211)

कान (*m*) ear (W1, p. 3)

काना (*adj*) one-eyed (T13, p. 108)

क़ानून (*m*) law, regulation (W21, p. 120)

कॉनसर्ट (*m*) concert (W11, p. 60)

कापी (*f*) notebook (W1, p. 3)

काफी (*adj*) enough, quite (T4, p. 26) (W4, p. 18)

कॉफ़ी (*f*) coffee (T10, p. 83) (W6, 7 pp. 28, 35)

क़ाबिल (*adj*) able, worthy, capable (T13, p. 113)

काम (*m*) work, business (T8, p. 63) (W1, p. 3)

काम करना (*v.t.*) to work (T9, p. 70) (W9, p. 48)

कार्य (*m*) work, business

कॉलेज (*m*) college (T9, p. 70) (W5, p. 23)

काश (*voc*) Alas!; if only (T15, p. 134) (GR 15)

किंतु (*conj*) but (T15, p. 139)

कि (*conj*) that, for (T10, p. 83) (GR 12)

कितना (*adj*) how much, many (T5, p. 36) (W3, p. 13)
  (GR 5)

कितने बजे (*adv*) at what time (T10, p. 76)
  (W12, p. 65)

किताब (*f*) book (T2, p. 13) (W2, p. 8)

किनका (*inter adj*) whose (oblique form of कौन [*pl*])
  (T4, p. 28) (GR 4, 7)

किन्हीं का (*adj*) some (people)'s (oblique form of कोई
  [*pl*]) (T7, p. 53) (GR 7)

किन्हीं को (*pro pl*) oblique form of कोई + को
  (T7, p. 53) (GR 7)

किन्हींने (*pro pl*) oblique form of कोई + ने (T7, p. 53)
  (GR 7, 12)

किन्होंने (*pro pl*) oblique form of कौन + ने (T7, p. 53)
  (GR 7, 12)

किराया (*m*) rent (T20, p. 201) (W7, p. 35)

किस दुकान में (*adv*) in(to) which shop (T17, p. 161)

किस समय (*inter*) at what time (T20, p. 198)

किसका (*inter adj*) whose (oblique form of कौन) (T4, p. 28) (W4, p. 18) (GR 4)

किसके लिये (*inter adv*) for whom (T7, p. 53) (W4, 7 pp. 18, 35)

किसको/किसे (*inter pro*) (to) whom (oblique form of कौन + को) (T7, p. 53) (GR 7, 11)

किसने (*pro*) oblique form of कौन + ने (T7, p. 53) (GR 7, 12)

किसलिये (*inter*) for what reason, why (T15, p. 135)

किसान (*m*) farmer, peasant (W10, p. 54)

किसी का (*adj*) someone's, anyone's (T4, p. 28) (GR 4)

किसी को (*pro*) (to) someone, anyone, oblique form of कोई + को (T7, p. 53) (GR 7)

किसीने (*pro sing*) someone/anyone/some/any (oblique form of कोई + ने) (T7, p. 53) (GR 7, 12)

किसे/किसको (*pro*) oblique form of कौन + को (T7, p. 53) (GR 7)

(x) की ओर (*pp*) in the direction of (x) (T24, p. 232) (W17, p. 98)

(x) की जगह (*pp*) in place of (x) (W24, p. 137)

(x) की तरह (*pp*) like (x) (T16, 155) (W11, p. 60)

(x) की बात (y से) होना (*v.i.*) (x) to talk (to y) (W12, p. 65)

(x) की वजह से (*pp*) on account of, because of (x) (T12, p. 103)

कीड़ा (*m*) insect (W7, p. 35)

कीमत (*f*) price (T2, p. 13) (W2, p. 8) (GR 8)

कीर्तन (*m*) devotional song (T17, p. 163)

कुआँ (*m*) a (water) well (W7, p. 35)

कुछ (*pro + adj*) some, something (T7, p. 57) (W6, 8 pp. 28, 41) (GR 15)

कुछ और/और कुछ (*adj*) some (thing) more, else (T15, p. 137) (W8, 12 pp. 41, 65) (GR 15)

कुछ न कुछ (*adj*) something or other (W12, p. 65) (GR 15)

कुछ नहीं (*pro*) nothing (T7, p. 57) (W6, p. 28) (GR 15)

कुछ नहीं रखा है। Nothing is left. (placed) (T21, p. 212)

कुछ भी (*pro*) anything at all (T15, p. 137) (GR 14, 15)

कुतुब मीनार (*f*) Kutub Minar (T13, p. 114)

कुत्ता/कुता (*m*) dog (T6, p. 43)

कुर्ता/कुरता (*m*) shirt (T17, p. 161)

कुर्सी/कुरसी (*f*) chair (T12, p. 100) (W13, p. 71)

कुल (*m*) total (W22, p. 125)

कुल मिलाकर (*adv*) in total, overall (W22, p. 125) (GR 15)

कृपया (*adv*) please (T8, p. 64) (W16, p. 91)

कृपा (*f*) mercy (T4, p. 26)

कृपा लाल (*m*) Kripa Lal (name) (T4, p. 29)

कृष्ण (*m*) Krishna (name of a Hindu deity) (T7, p. 55)

(x) के अलावा (*pp*) in addition to (x) (W10, p. 54)

(x) के आसपास (*pp*) around, nearly (x) (T19, p. 194)

(x) के ऊपर (*pp*) above (x) (T19, p. 187)

(x) के क़रीब (*pp*) close to (x) (T22, p. 215)

(x) के क़ाबिल (*pp*) worthy of (x) (T13, p. 113)

(x) के ख़िलाफ़ (*pp*) against (x) (T22, p. 218)

(x) के द्वारा (*pp*) through the agency of (x) (T21, p. 209)

(x) के नीचे (*pp*) beneath (x) (W10, p. 54)

(x) के/से पहले (*pp*) before (x) (W17, p. 98)

(x) के पास (*pp*) near (x) (T9, p. 72) (W11, p. 60) (GR 9, 13)

(x) के बग़ैर (*pp*) without (x) (T24, p. 137)

(x) के बाद (*pp*) after (x) (T8, p. 66) (W21, p. 120)

(x) के बारे में (*pp*) about (x) (T13, p. 118) (W11, p. 60)

(x) के बिना (*pp*) without (x) (T24, p. 237) (W24, p. 136)

(x) के बीच में (*pp*) amongst (x) (T22, p. 215) (W17, p. 98)

(x) के मारे (*pp*) on account of (x) (T21, p. 212)

(x) के यहाँ (*pp*) at (x)'s place (T20, p. 198) (W17, p. 98)

(x) के लायक़ (*pp*) worthy of (x) (T13, p. 110)

(x) के लिये (*pp*) for (x), in order to (x) (if x is a verb) (T7, p. 53) (W8, p. 41) (GR 13)

(x) के साथ (*pp*) with (x) (T9, p. 70) (W7, 9 pp. 35, 48)

(x) के सामने (*pp*) in front of (x) (T17, p. 167)

(x) के हाथों (*pp*) by the hand(s) of (x) (T21, p. 209)

केवल (*adj*) only, merely (T13, p. 108)

कैंसर (*m*) cancer (T10, p. 78)

कै (*f*) vomiting (T1, p. 5)

कैसा (*adj*) how, what kind of (T5, p. 36) (W3, p. 13) (GR 5)

कैसे (*adv*) how, in what manner (T13, p. 105) (W6, p. 28)

को (*pp*) a postposition denoting accusative and dative case; to; for; on the point of (T7, p. 53) (GR 7, 9, 11, 13, 17, 18, 20)

कोई (*adj + pro*) some, any; someone, anyone (T4, p. 27) (W4, p. 18) (GR 15)

कोई और/और कोई (*adj + pro*) some other/more, any other/more; someone else, anyone else (T15, p. 137) (GR 15)

कोई बात नहीं no matter (W13, p. 71)

कोई भी (*pro*) anyone at all (T15, p. 137) (GR 14, 15)

कोट (*m*) coat (T15, p. 140)

(x की) कोशिश करना (*v.t.*) to endeavor (to x), to try (to x) (used with oblique infinitives) (T15, p. 134)

कोष/कोश (*m*) treasure, dictionary

कौन (*pro*) who (T4, p. 28) (W4, p. 18) (GR 4, 7)

कौन जाने who knows (W23, p. 130)

कौन-सा (*inter adj*) which (T12, p. 103) (W6, p. 28) (W15, 22 pp. 85, 124)

कौशेय (*adj*) silky, silken (T6, p. 48)

क्या (*pro*) what (also marks a question) (T1, p. 6) (W1, p. 3) (GR 1)

क्या-क्या (*adv*) what (the reduplication gives a sense of plurality) (T13, p. 113) (W12, p. 65)

क्या तुम लोगों को याद है? Do you people remember? (T8, p. 66)

क्यों (*inter*) why (T5, p. 38) (W6, p. 28)

क्योंकि (*conj*) because (T7, p. 51)

क्लास (*m/f*) class (T10, p. 76) (W5, p. 23) (GR 7)

क्षण (*m*) moment, an instant (T11, p. 93)

ख

खड़ा (*adj*) standing (T5, p. 108) (W3, p. 13)

खड़ा रहना (*v.i.*) to remain standing (W22, p. 125)

खड़ा होना (*v.i.*) to stand

ख़त (*m*) letter, line, handwriting (T8, p. 65) (W4, p. 18)

ख़त्म करना (*v.t.*) to finish (W16, p. 91)

ख़त्म होना (*v.i.*) to be finished (T22, p. 218) (W16, p. 91)

ख़बर (*f*) news (T18, p. 175) (W8, p. 41)

ख़राब (*adj*) bad (off), broken (T5, p. 37) (W3, p. 13)

ख़राब होना (*v.i.*) to go bad, break, be spoiled (W15, p. 85)

ख़रीदना (*v.t.*) to buy (T3, p. 20) (W12, p. 65)

खाँसी (*f*) cough (W10, 21 pp. 54, 119)

खाता (*m*) an account, ledger (T20, p. 202)

ख़ान मार्केट (*m*) Khan Market (a market in Delhi) (T9, p. 74)

खाना (*m*) food (T3, p. 20) (W8, p. 41)

खाना (*v.t.*) to eat (T3, p. 20) (W8, p. 41)

ख़ाना (*m*) a shelf, column, compartment

खाना खिलाना (*v.t.*) to feed food, to treat (T13, p. 114)

खाना बनवाना (*v.t.*) to have food made (T10, p. 76)

ख़ालिद (*m*) Khalid (name) (T7, p. 52)

ख़ाली (*adj*) empty, free (W3, p. 13)

ख़ास (*adj*) special (W11, p. 60)

ख़ासियत (*f*) quality, special feature (T11, p. 89)

खिड़की (*f*) window (T8, p. 62) (W14, p. 78) (GR 8)

खींचना (*v.t.*) to pull, draw (W22, p. 125)

ख़ुद (*adv*) (by) oneself (T11, p. 85) (W11, p. 60) (GR 11)

ख़ुदा (*m*) God (T7, p. 51) (W15, p. 85) (GR 16)

ख़ुदा हाफ़िज़ May God protect you. (used in Urdu when leaving) (T7, p. 51)

खुलना (*v.i.*) to open (T19, p. 192)

ख़ुश (*adj*) happy (T7, p. 50) (W16, p. 91)

ख़ुशी (*f*) happiness (T5, p. 33)

(x को) ख़ुशी होना (*v.i.*) (x) to be happy, happiness to occur (to x) (T17, p. 165) (GR 18)

ख़ून (*m*) blood (W21, p. 120)

(x का) ख़ून करना (*v.t.*) to murder (x)

ख़ूब (*adj*) a lot, excellent (W11, p. 60)

ख़ूबसूरत (*adj*) beautiful (T5, p. 36) (W3, p. 13)

खेल (*m*) game, match, sport

खेलना (*v.i. + v.t.*) to play (T11, p. 88)

खोना (*v.i. + v.t.*) to lose (W23, p. 130)

खो जाना (*v.i.*) to become lost (W24, p. 137) (GR 19)

खो देना (*v.t.*) to lose, misplace (W22, p. 125) (GR 19)

खोलना (*v.t.*) to open (T8, p. 62) (W17, p. 98)

ख़्याल/ख़याल (*m*) idea, thought, view, opinion (T6, p. 43) (W19, p. 110)

ख़्वाहिश (*m*) desire, wish (T16, p. 147) (GR 16)

ग

गंगा (*f*) Ganges (name of a river in India) (T6, p. 42) (W10, p. 54)

गंदा (*adj*) dirty, filthy, morbid (T8, p. 64)

गँवाना (*v.t.*) to waste, lose (W24, p. 137)

ग़ज़ल (*f*) a genre of Urdu poetry that may also be sung (W11, p. 60)

गपशप मारना (*v.t.*) to gossip (गपशप gossip (*f*) + मारना to beat, strike) (T15, p. 135)

गरम/गर्म (*adj*) hot (T8, p. 62) (W7, p. 35)

गरमी/गर्मी (*f*) heat (T18, p. 174) (W10, p. 54)

ग़रीब (*adj*) poor (T4, p. 26) (W10, p. 54)

गर्म (*adj*) see गरम

गर्मी (*f*) see गरमी

गर्मी के दिन (*m pl*) days of heat, summer (T19, p. 187)

(x को) गर्मी लगना (*v.i.*) (x) to feel hot (T18, p. 174) (GR 18)

ग़लत (*adj*) wrong (W22, p. 125)

गला (*m*) throat (T4, p. 26) (W4, p. 18)

गली (*f*) lane, gully (W24, p. 137)

गाँव (*m*) village (T6, p. 46)

गाड़ी (*f*) car, vehicle, train (T6, p. 48) (W9, p. 48)

गाड़ी चलाना (*v.t.*) to drive a car/vehicle (T11, p. 86) (W15, p. 85)

गाना (*m*) a song

गाना (*v.t.*) to sing (W11, p. 60)

ग़ायब होना (*v.i.*) to disappear (W24, p. 137)

गिरना (*v.i.*) to fall (T24, p. 232)

गिरफ़्तार (*adj*) arrested, seized (W21, p. 120)

गिराना (*v.t.*) to make (something) fall

गुज़रना (*v.i.*) to pass (by) (W20, p. 115)

गुझिया (*f*) gujhiya, a type of Indian sweetmeat (W19, p. 110)

गुड़गाँव (*m*) Gurgaon (name of a suburb of Delhi close to the airport) (T23, p. 222)

गुड़िया (*f*) doll (W8, p. 41)

गुण (*m*) quality (W13, p. 71)

(x से) गुफ़्तगू करना (*v.t.*) to talk, have a conversation (with x) (T16, p. 154) (GR 16)

गुरुद्वारा (*m*) Gurdwara (Sikh temple) (T17, p. 168)

गुरुवार (*m*) Thursday (T10, p. 76) (W9, p. 48) (GR 16)

गुलाब (*m*) rose (T10, p. 77)

गुलाबजामुन (*m*) gulabjamun (fried sweet dumpling)

गुलाम (*m*) slave

गुलाल (*m*) colored powder thrown at the time of Holi (W19, p. 110)

गुसलख़ाना (*m*) bathroom (W7, p. 35)

गुस्सा (*m*) anger, rage, fury (T17, p. 159)

(x को) गुस्सा आना (*v.i.*) (x) to become angry (T18, p. 172) (W18, p. 104) (GR 18)

गुस्सा होना (*v.i.*) to become angry (T17, p. 159)

गूँधना (*v.t.*) to knead (W18, p. 104)

गेहूँ (*m*) wheat (T10, p. 78)

गोभी (*f*) cauliflower (T14, p. 127)

गोली (*f*) tablet, pill, bullet (W13, p. 71)

गोश्त (*m*) meat, flesh (T5, p. 33) (W20, p. 115)

गौरी (*f*) Parvati (wife of lord Shiva)

ग्यारह (*adj*) eleven (T6, p. 43)

ग्यारहवाँ (*adj*) eleventh (T11, p. 85)

ग्राहक/गाहक (*m*) customer, client (T6, p. 45)

घ

घंटा (*m*) hour, bell (T6, p. 44) (W13, 14, 23 pp. 71, 78, 129)

घटिया (*adj, invar*) inferior, of low quality (T3, p. 21) (GR 3)

घड़ी (*f*) watch (T17, p. 166) (W4, 8 pp. 18, 41)

घड़ीसाज़ (*m*) watchmaker (W17, p. 98)

घबराना (*v.i.*) to be nervous, anxious (W24, p. 137)

घर (*m*) home (T3, p. 20)

घर में at home (T7, p. 54) (W5, 6 pp. 23, 28)

घुसना (*v.i.*) to enter, penetrate (W24, p. 137)

घूमना (*v.i.*) to revolve, to wander (T3, p. 20) (W16, p. 91)

च

चंचल (*adj*) fickle, unsteady, transient, quivering, shaking, restless, skittish, playful, coquettish, nimble (T6, p. 43)

चकमा (*m*) trick, trickery, hoodwinking (T6, p. 48)

चक्कर (*m*) circle, revolution, rotation (W22, p. 125)

चक्र (*m*) a wheel, cycle, circle, disc (T6, p. 45)

चटपटा (*adj*) pungent, spicy (W13, p. 71)

चतुर्थ (*adj*) fourth (T16, p. 152)

चप्पल (*f*) sandal, slipper (T6, p. 43)

चमचा (*m*) a large spoon, flunkey, sycophant

चम्मच (*m*) spoon (T6, p. 44)

चलना (*v.i.*) to move (T3, p. 20) (W13, 14 pp. 71, 78)

चला जाना (*v.i.*) to move away (T22, p. 217) (W21, p. 120) (GR 22)

चलाना (*v.t.*) to make move, to drive (T11, p. 86)

चवालीस (*adj*) forty-four (T16, p. 151)

चश्मा (*m*) spectacles; fountain, spring (T6, p. 43)

चाँदनी (*f*) moonlight (T3, p. 20)

चाचा (*m*) paternal uncle (T7, p. 54) (W14, p. 78)

चाची (*f*) paternal uncle's wife, aunt (T14, p. 126)

चाट (*f*) spicy, fast food (T15, p. 132) (W8, p. 41)

चाय (*f*) tea (T7, p. 57) (W7, p. 35)

चार (*adj*) four (T10, p. 76) (W3, p. 13)

चारों (*adj*) all four (T16, p. 153)

चालीस (*adj*) forty (T16, p. 151) (W18, p. 104)

चावल (*m*) rice (T18, p. 169) (W21, p. 120)

चाहना (*v.t.*) to want (T13, p. 112) (W15, 23 pp. 85, 129)

चाहिये/चाहिए (*invar*) wanted/needed (subject takes को) (T7, p. 56) (GR 7)

चिंता (*f*) worry, concern, anxiety (T24, p. 230)

चिकित्सा (*f*) treatment, remedy (W14, p. 78)

चिट्ठी (*f*) letter (T6, p. 44) (W14, 23 pp. 78, 129)

चिड़िया (*f*) bird (T8, p. 59)

चिड़ियाघर (*m*) zoo (T10, p. 78)

चिढ़ाना (*v.t.*) to tease (T4, p. 26)

चित्र (*m*) picture (W8, p. 41)

चिल्लाना (*v.i.*) to scream, to shout (T19, p. 189)

चिह्न/चिह्न (*m*) sign, mark, marking (T6, p. 44)

चीज़ (*f*) thing (T8, p. 60) (W8, 11 pp. 41, 60)

चीन (*m*) China (T18, p. 173)

चीनी (*f*) sugar; Chinese (W4, p. 18)

चुकना (*v.i.*) to be finished, spent, exhausted, completed, paid off (used as a compound verb to give a sense of already having done an activity) (T19, p. 184) (GR 19)

चुप (*adj*) silent

चुप होना (*v.i.*) to be silent

चुप कराना (*v.t.*) to shut up (someone) (W24, p. 137)

चुप रहना (*v.i.*) to remain quiet (T17, p. 161)

चूड़ी (*f*) bangle (W4, p. 18) (GR 8)

चैन (*m*) peace, rest (W23, p. 130)

चोट (*f*) injury, wound, blow, stroke (T18, p. 174)

(x को) चोट लगना (*m*) (x) to become injured (T18, p. 174) (GR 18)

चोर (*m*) thief (T24, p. 232) (W17, p. 98)

(x की) चोरी करना (*v.t.*) to steal (x) (T24, p. 236)

चौंकना (*v.i.*) to become startled, alarmed (T19, p. 192)

चौंकाना (*v.t.*) to startle, alarm (someone)

चौंतीस (*adj*) thirty-four (T16, p. 151)

चौथा (*adj*) fourth (T4, p. 24) (GR 16)

चौदह (*adj*) fourteen (T16, p. 151)

चौदहवाँ (*adj*) fourteenth (T14, p. 120)

चौबीस (*adj*) twenty-four (T13, p. 109)

चौबीसवाँ (*adj*) twenty-fourth (T24, p. 230)

छ

छज्जा (*m*) balcony, terrace (T6, p. 43)

छठा (*adj*) sixth (T6, p. 40) (GR 16)

छत (*f*) roof, ceiling (W8, p. 41)

छत्तीस (*adj*) thirty-six (T16, p. 151)

छपना (*v.i.*) to be printed or stamped, to be published (W17, p. 98)

छपवाना (*v.t.*) to have something printed (by someone) (T20, p. 201)

छपाना (*v.t.*) to print, stamp

छब्बीस (*adj*) twenty-six (T16, p. 151)

छात्र (*m*) student (T9, p. 70)

छियालीस (*adj*) forty-six (T16, p. 151)

छुट्टी (*f*) holiday (T6, p. 44) (W8, p. 41)

छुपना/छिपना (*v.i.*) to hide, to lurk (T20, p. 201)

छूटना (*v.i.*) to depart (W20, p. 115)

छूना (*v.t.*) to touch, to feel (T8, p. 62) (GR 12)

छेद (*m*) hole (W8, p. 41)

छै/छह/छः (*adj*) six (T10, p. 76)

छै बजे (*adv*) at six o'clock (T10, p. 76) (W10, 12, 17 pp. 54, 65, 97)

छोटा (*adj*) small (T19, p. 196) (W6, p. 28)

छोड़ देना (*v.t.*) to leave, abandon, to drop (T20, p. 206)

छोड़ना (*v.t.*) to leave, abandon (T13, p. 110) (W11, p. 60)

ज

जगह (*f*) place, space (T13, p. 119) (W10, 23 pp. 54, 129)

जन (*m*) people, public, folk, person

जनवरी (*f*) January (month) (T16, p. 154) (W10, p. 54) (GR 16)

जनसंख्या (*f*) population (T13, p. 109)

जन्मदिन (*m*) birthday (T7, p. 50) (W9, p. 48)

जब (*rel adv*) when (T23, p. 225) (GR 23)

जब तक (*rel adv*) until when (L 23, p. 228) (GR 23)

जब भी (*adv*) whenever (T23, p. 226) (GR 14, 23)

ज़बरदस्ती करना (*v.t.*) to force (W8, p. 41)

ज़बान (*f*) language (T22, p. 215)

जमात (*f*) class (W12, p. 65)

ज़माना (*m*) age, period (W11, p. 60)

ज़मींदार/ज़मीनदार (*m*) landowner (T13, p. 108)

ज़मीन (*f*) land (W10, p. 54)

ज़रा (*adj, invar*) a little (also softens a request) (T3, p. 21) (W3, 18 pp. 13, 103)

ज़रूर (*adv*) certainly (T3, p. 20) (W7, 16 pp. 35, 91)

ज़रूरत (*f*) necessity (T13, p. 119) (W16, p. 91)

(x की) ज़रूरत होना (*v.i.*) the necessity of (x) to happen (T23, p. 227)

ज़रूरी (*adv*) necessary (T16, p. 148) (W21, p. 120)

जलेबी (*f*) jalebi (a type of Indian sweet) (T8, p. 62) (W9, p. 48)

जल्दी (*adv*) quickly (T6, p. 43) (W16, 20 pp. 91, 114)

जवाब (*m*) answer (T18, p. 172)

जवाब देना (*v.t.*) to answer (W13, p. 71)

जहाँ (*rel adv*) where (T23, p. 225) (GR 23)

जहाँ भी (*rel adv*) wherever (T23, p. 226) (W23, p. 130) (GR 14, 23)

जहाज़ (*m*) ship (T13, p. 105)

(x की) जाँच करना (*v.t.*) to investigate, to test (x)

(x की) जाँच कराना (*v.t.*) to make (someone) investigate (x), to have (x) tested (W21, p. 120)

जाड़ा (*m*) cold, winter (T19, p. 187)

जान (*adj*) dear, beloved (T7, p. 50)

जान (*f*) life, stamina, vitality, energy (T24, p. 238)

जानना (*v.t.*) to know, to perceive (T9, p. 71) (W9, p. 48)

जाना (*v.i.*) to go, to depart, to lose (T8, p. 64) (W9, p. 48) (GR 12, 19, 21, 22)

जानवर (*m*) animal (W15, p. 85)

जापान (*m*) Japan (T18, p. 173)

जामा मस्जिद (*f*) Jama Masjid (the main mosque in Delhi) (T16, p. 143)

ज़िंदा (*adj, invar*) alive (T3, p. 21) (GR 3)

ज़िंदगी (*f*) life (T7, p. 57) (W11, 22 pp. 60, 124)

जितना (*rel adj*) as many, much (T23, p. 225) (GR 23)

जिधर (*rel adv*) where (T23, p. 225) (GR 23)

जिधर भी (*rel adv*) wherever (T23, p. 226) (GR 14, 23)

जिनका (*rel adj pl*) whose (T7, p. 53) (GR 23)

जिन्हें/जिनको (*rel pro*) oblique form of जो + को (T7, p. 53) (GR 7, 23)

जिन्होंने (*rel pro*) जो + ने (T7, p. 53) (GR 12, 23)

जिल्द (*f*) cover, binding (W20, 23 pp. 115, 129)

जिस (*rel pro*) oblique form of जो (T7, p. 53) (GR 7, 23)

जिसका (*rel adj*) whose (rel) (T7, p. 53) (GR 7, 23)

जिसने (*rel pro*) जो + ने (T7, p. 53) (GR 12, 23)

जिसे/जिसको (*rel pro*) oblique form of जो + को (T7, p. 53) (GR 7, 23)

जी (*m*) heart, polite suffix (T2, p. 12) (W2, p. 8)

ज़ी टी॰ वी॰ (*m*) Zee TV (a popular television channel in India) (T12, p. 103)

जी नहीं (*adv*) no (T2, p. 12)

जी हाँ (*adv*) yes (T2, p. 12)

जीवन (*m*) life (T16, p. 148) (W10, 18 pp. 54, 103)

जीवन साथी (*m*) life companion (W20, p. 115)

जीव-विज्ञान (*m*) biology (T11, p. 86)

ज़ुकाम (*m*) a cold (T13, p. 109)

(x को) ज़ुकाम होना (*v.i.*) a cold to occur (to x) (T13, p. 109) (GR 18)

जुमा (*m*) Friday (T16, p. 153) (GR 16)

जुमेरात (*f*) Thursday (T16, p. 153) (GR 16)

जुलाई (*f*) July (month) (T14, p. 123) (GR 16)

जूता (*m*) shoe (T3, p. 20)

जून (*m*) June (month) (T16, p. 154) (GR 16)

जेब (*f*) pocket (W24, p. 137)

जैसा (*rel adj*) like, resembling, similar to (T23, p. 225) (GR 23)

जैसे (*rel adv*) as, like, such as, for instance (T23, p. 225) (GR 23)

जो (*rel pro*) who (T7, p. 53) (GR 23)

जो भी (*rel pro*) whatever, whichever, whoever (T23, p. 226) (W23, p. 130) (GR 14, 23)

जोरू (*f*) wife (T8, p. 60)

ज्ञान (*m*) knowledge, wisdom (T6, p. 45)

ज़्यादा (*adj, invar*) more, much (T10, p. 83) (W13, p. 71) (GR 3)

ज़्यादातर (*adj + adv*) mostly (T13, p. 106)

ज्योति (*f*) light, Jyoti (name) (T24, p. 236)

झ

झट (*adv*) instantly, at once (T11, p. 91) (GR 11)

झटपट (*adv*) quickly, promptly (T11, p. 91) (GR 11)

झपटना (*v.i.*) to make a sudden swoop, to pounce, to snatch (T19, p. 192)

झूठ (*m*) a lie (T6, p. 46)

झूठ बोलना (*v.i.*) to lie (T12, p. 102)

झूमना (*v.i.*) to sway, to swing (T19, p. 192)

ट

टमाटर (*m*) tomato (T6, p. 46)

टहलना (*v.i.*) to stroll (T16, p. 147) (W14, p. 78)

टाइप करना (*v.t.*) to type (T11, p. 85)

टाइम (*m*) time (T18, p. 176)

टिकट (*m/f*) ticket (T6, p. 46)

टिकिया (*f*) a small cake, tablet, patty (W13, p. 71)

टीचर (*m/f*) teacher (T9, p. 70)

टूटना (*v.i.*) to break, to be broken, to be fractured (T21, p. 211)

टेलीविज़न (*m*) television (W11, p. 60)

ट्रेन (*f*) train (T6, p. 45)

ठ

ठंड (*f*) cold (T6, p. 44) (W14, p. 78)

(x को) ठंड लगना (*v.i.*) (x) to feel cold (T18, p. 174) (GR 18)

ठंडा (*adj*) cold (T6, p. 46) (W8, p. 41)

ठाकुर (*m*) lord, master, God (T15, p. 138)

ठीक (*adj*) okay, right, true, proper, appropriate (T5, p. 33) (W5, p. 23)

ठीक करना (*v.t.*) to fix, to correct (W17, p. 98)

ठीक होना (*v.i.*) to be fixed, be okay, appropriate

ठीक से (*adv*) properly (W11, p. 60)

ड

डटकर (*adv*) having taken a stand, resolutely (W19, p. 110)

डटना (*v.i.*) to stand, tarry, to take a position

डर (*m*) fear (T18, p. 174)

(x से) डरना (*v.i.*) to be afraid (of x) (T12, p. 102) (GR 12)

(x को) (y से) डर लगना (*v.i.*) (x) to feel afraid (of y) (T18, p. 174) (W18, p. 104) (GR 18)

डाक (*f*) post, mail (T4, p. 26)

डाकख़ाना (*m*) post office

डाकिया (*m*) postman (T19, p. 192)

डाकू (*m*) bandit, dacoit (T19, p. 193)

डॉक्टर (*m*) doctor (T7, p. 52)

डॉक्टरी (*f*) (the practice of) medicine (W9, p. 48)

डालना (*v.t.*) to put, place (T19, p. 189) (W24, p. 137) (GR 19)

डॉलर (*m*) dollar (T20, p. 202)

डिग्री (*f*) degree (T19, p. 187)

डिफ़ेंस कॉलनी (*f*) Defence Colony (name of a neighborhood in Delhi) (T14, p. 120)

डिलाइट (*m*) Delite (name of a cinema in Old Delhi) (T14, p. 130)

"डी० डी० एल० जे०" *DDLJ (दिलवाले दुल्हनिया ले जाएँगे) (The One with the Heart Gets the Bride — the title of a popular Hindi film)* (T12, p. 103)

डी० यू० (*f*) D.U. (Delhi University) (T14, p. 120)

डी० वी० डी० (*f*) D.V.D. (T15, p. 141)

डूबना (*v.i.*) to sink, drown (T24, p. 238)

डेढ़ (*adj*) one and a half (T16, p. 153) (W7, p. 35) (GR 16, 18)

ढ

ढंग (*m*) manner, method, mode, way

ढाई (*adj*) two and a half (T16, p. 153) (W7, 18 pp. 35, 104) (GR 16, 18)

ढूँढना (*v.t.*) to search, seek (T6, p. 46) (W14, p. 78)

ढेर (*m*) heap, pile (T6, p. 46)

त

तक (*pp*) until, to, till, by, up to (T9, p. 74) (GR 14)

तक़रीबन (*adv*) approximately (T15, p. 138)

तकलीफ़ (*f*) difficulty, bother, distress, trouble (T16, p. 147)

तकलीफ़ उठाना (*v.t.*) to bother, to trouble (T16, p. 147)

तकल्लुफ़ (*m*) formality (W8, p. 41)

तकल्लुफ़ करना (*v.t.*) to stand on formality, ceremony, to be formal (W8, p. 41)

तथ्य (*m*) fact, reality (T6, p. 43)

तनख़्वाह (*f*) salary (T14, p. 129) (W22, p. 125)

तब (*adv*) then, at that time (T11, p. 91) (GR 23)

तब तक (*adv*) until then (T10, p. 84) (W9, p. 48) (GR 23)

तब भी (*adv*) even then (T11, p. 89)

तबीयत (*f*) health, disposition (T12, p. 103)

तभी (*adv*) right then, at that very time (तब + ही) (T14, p. 128) (GR 14)

-तम (*suffix*) -est (superlative) (T19, p. 197) (GR 19)

तय करना (*v.t.*) to decide, settle (T19, p. 194)

-तर (*suffix*) -er (comparative) (T19, p. 197) (GR 19)

तरकारी (*f*) vegetable (W3, p. 13)

तरक़्क़ी (*f*) progress (W22, p. 125)

तरह (*f*) kind, type, sort, manner (T11, p. 89)

तरह-तरह (*adv*) all manner of (W24, p. 137)

-तरीन (*suffix*) -est (superlative) (T19, p. 197) (GR 19)

तलब (*f*) yearning, desire (W20, p. 115)

(x की) तलाश करना (*v.t.*) to search for (x) (W15, p. 85)

तशरीफ़ (*f*) a term signifying honor and respect (T8, p. 63)

तशरीफ़ रखना (*v.t.*) to sit (one's noble self) (T8, p. 63)

तस्वीर (*f*) picture (W8, 10 pp. 41, 54)

तस्वीर खींचना (*v.t.*) to take a picture (W22, p. 125)

तहज़ीब (*f*) culture (W15, p. 85)

ताक़त (*f*) power (T13, p. 109)

ताकि (*conj*) so that (T16, p. 146) (W16, p. 91) (GR 16)

ताज महल (*m*) Taj Mahal (T13, p. 115)

ताज़ा (*adj*) fresh (T3, p. 21) (W3, p. 13) (GR 3)

(x को) ताज्जुब होना (*v.i.*) (x) to be amazed (GR 18)

तापमान (*m*) temperature (T19, p. 187)

तारा (*m*) star (T2, p. 13)

तारीख़ (*f*) date, history (T3, p. 20) (W3, p. 13)

तालिबे इल्म (*m*) student (T22, p. 216)

तीखा (*adj*) spicy, sharp (food) (W21, p. 120)

तीन (*adj*) three (T10, p. 81) (W3, p. 13)

तीन चौथाई (*adj*) three-quarters (T16, p. 153)

तीन बजे (*adv*) at three o'clock (W14, p. 78)

तीन साल पहले (*adv*) three years ago (W10, p. 54)

तीनों (*adj*) all three (T12, p. 99) (GR 16)

तीस (*adj*) thirty (T16, p. 151) (W2, p. 8)

तीसरा (*adj*) third (T3, p. 17) (GR 16)

तुझ (*pro*) oblique form of तू (T7, p. 53) (GR 7)

तुझी (*pro*) तुझ + ही (T14, p. 128) (GR 7, 14)

तुझे/तुझको oblique form of तू + को (T7, p. 53) (GR 7)

तुम (*pro*) you (familiar, *pl*) (T4, p. 27) (GR 4)

तुमने (*pro*) you (तुम + ने) (T7, p. 53) (GR 7, 12)

तुम्हारा (*adj*) your (T4, p. 26) (GR 4)

तुम्हारी मर्ज़ी (*f*) your desire, whatever you want, as you wish (W22, p. 125)

तुम्हारे लिये (*adv*) for you (T7, p. 53) (W4, p. 18)

तुम्हीं (*pro*) you (तुम + ही) (T14, p. 128) (GR 14)

तुम्हें/तुमको (*pro*) oblique form of तुम + को (T7, p. 53) (GR 7)

तुरंत (*conj*) immediately (T11, p. 91)

तू (*pro*) you (intimate, sing) (T4, p. 27) (GR 4)

तूने (*pro*) you (तू + ने) (T7, p. 53) (GR 7, 12)

तृतीय (*adj*) third (T16, p. 152) (GR 16)

तेईस (*adj*) twenty-three (T16, p. 151)

तेईसवाँ (*adj*) twenty-third (T23, p. 222)

तेज़ (*adj*) sharp, strong, harsh (T19, p. 196) (W20, p. 115)

तेज़ी से (*adv*) with speed, quickly (W22, p. 125)

तेरह (*adj*) thirteen (T16, p. 151)

तेरहवाँ (*adj*) thirteenth (T13, p. 105)

तेरा (*adj*) your (T4, p. 28) (GR 4)

तैंतालीस (*adj*) forty-three (T16, p. 151)

तैंतीस (*adj*) thirty-three (T16, p. 151)

तैयार (*adj*) ready, prepared (T13, p. 112) (W8, p. 41)

तैयार करना (*v.t.*) to prepare (W21, p. 120)

तैयार होना (*v.i.*) to be prepared (T13, p. 113) (W8, p. 41)

तैयारी (*f*) preparation (W19, p. 110)

तैरना (*v.i.*) to swim (W24, p. 137)

तो (*conj + part*) so, then (also emphatic particle) (T11, p. 88) (W3, 5, 6 pp. 13, 23, 28) (GR 14)

तोड़ना (*v.t.*) to break, to fracture (T21, p. 211) (W9, p. 48)

त्याग (*m*) abandonment, relinquishment (T6, p. 43)

त्यौहार (*m*) festival (T10, p. 78) (W10, p. 54)

थ

थक जाना (*v.i.*) to become tired (T22, p. 220)

थकना (*v.i.*) to become tired, fatigued

थकान/थकावट (*f*) fatigue, tiredness (T22, p. 220)

(x को) थकान होना (*v.i.*) (x) to be/become tired (T22, p. 220) (GR 18)

था was (*m sing*) (T5, p. 34) (GR 5)

थी was (*f sing*) (T5, p. 34) (GR 5)

थीं were (*f pl*) (T5, p. 34) (GR 5)

थे were (*m pl*) (T5, p. 34) (GR 5)

थैला (*m*) bag

थैली (*f*) bag, small bag, pouch (T14, p. 127)

थोड़ा (*adj*) small, a little, some (T15, p. 141)

थोड़ा बहुत और (*adj*) a little bit more (T23, p. 222)

थोड़ा सा (*adj*) a little-ish (T24, p. 230)

थोड़ी देर बाद (*adv*) after a little while (W19, p. 110)

द

दक्षिण (*m*) south (T14, p. 120)

दफ़्तर (*m*) office (T12, p. 96) (W10, p. 54)

दरबार (*m*) (royal) court (T15, p. 140)

दरवाज़ा (*m*) door (T15, p. 139) (W11, 17 pp. 60, 97)

दरियागंज (*m*) Dariyaganj (name of a neighborhood of Delhi) (T14, p. 130)

दर्द (*m*) pain (T10, p. 78) (W7, p. 35)

दवा (*f*) medicine (T19, p. 185) (W2, 21 pp. 8, 120)

दवाई (*f*) medicine (W21, p. 120)

दवाख़ाना (*m*) pharmacy (W21, p. 119)

दशरथ (*m*) Dasharath (name of Lord Ram's father) (T13, p. 109)

दस (*adj*) ten (T15, p. 138)

दस बजे (*adv*) (at) ten o'clock (W12, p. 65)

दसवाँ (*adj*) tenth (T10, p. 76) (GR 16)

दाँत (*m*) tooth

दादा (*m*) paternal grandfather (T5, p. 34) (GR 7)

दादा-दादी (*m*) paternal grandparents (T5, p. 35)

दादी (*f*) paternal grandmother (T5, p. 34) (GR 8)

दानी (*adj*) generous (W12, p. 65)

दाम (*m*) price (T2, p. 15) (W2, p. 8) (GR 17)

दाल (*f*) pulse (legume), lentil (T16, p. 147)

दिक़ करना (*v.t.*) to harass, trouble (W17, p. 98)

दिक़्क़त (*f*) difficulty (W15, p. 85)

(x को) दिखना (*v.i.*) to be visible (to x) (W10, p. 54)

(x को) दिखाई देना (*v.i.*) to be visible (to x) (W14, p. 78)

दिखाना (*v.t.*) to show (T9, p. 72)

दिन (*m*) day (T10, p. 76) (W5, p. 23)

दिनचर्या (*f*) daily routine (T12, p. 95)

दिन-ब-दिन (*adv*) day after day (W22, p. 125)

दिन-भर (*m + adv*) (for) the entire day (T10, p. 76)

दिमाग़ (*m*) mind, brain, intellect (T13, p. 109)

दिलवाना/दिलाना (*v.t.*) to provide, to cause to be given

दिल्ली (*f*) Delhi (T3, p. 20)

दिवाली/दीपावली (*f*) Diwali (a Hindu festival) (T16, p. 148) (W10, p. 54)

दिसंबर (*m*) December (month) (T16, p. 154)

दीदी (*f*) older sister (T11, p. 88)

दीपक (*m*) lamp, Deepak (name) (T2, p. 13) (W2, p. 8)

दीपावली see दिवाली

दीवार (*f*) wall (T3, p. 20) (W3, p. 13)

दुःख/दुख (*m*) sorrow, sadness (T5, p. 33)

दुखी (*adj*) sad, unhappy (T16, p. 149)

दुआ (*f*) prayer (T2, p. 13)

(ख़ुदा से) दुआ माँगना (*v.t.*) to pray (to God)

दुकान (*f*) shop (T14, p. 142) (W4, p. 18)

दुकानदार (*m*) shopkeeper (T9, p. 126) (W9, p. 48)

दुखिया (*adj invar*) sad, unfortunate (T3, p. 21)

दुनिया (*f*) world (T7, p. 57)

दुनिया में in the world (W5, p. 23)

दुल्हन (*f*) bride (T19, p. 192)

दुश्मन (*m*) enemy

दुष्टात्मा (*adj*) wicked, vicious, vile (W6, p. 25)

दूध (*m*) milk (T3, p. 20) (W4, 14 pp. 18, 78)

दूर (*adv*) far (T14, p. 120) (W11, p. 60)

दूर करना (*v.t.*) to dispel, to get rid of (W13, p. 71)

दूल्हा (*m*) bridegroom

दूसरा (*adj*) second, other, another (T2, p. 9) (GR 16)

दूसरी तरफ़ (*adv*) on the other side

दृढ़ (*adj*) firm, solid (W24, p. 137)

देखना (*v.t.*) to watch, see (T8, p. 65) (W9, p. 48)

देना (*v.t.*) to give (T8, p. 62) (W8, p. 41) (GR 8, 17, 19)

देर (*f*) delay, lateness (T18, p. 173) (W11, 18 pp. 60, 103)

देर तक (*adv*) until late (T9, p. 74)

(x को) देर लगना (*v.i.*) (x) to take time/delay (T18, p. 173) (GR 18)

देर से (*adv*) late (*with lateness*) (W10, p. 54)

(x को) देर होना (*v.i.*) (x) to be late (T21, p. 207) (W23, p. 130) (GR 18)

देवनागरी (*f*) the Hindi script (T18, p. 172)

देवी (*f*) goddess

देश (*m*) country (T5, p. 33) (W6, 11 pp. 28, 60)

देशभक्त (*adj + m*) patriot

दो (*adj*) two (T8, p. 61) (W3, 6 pp. 13, 28)

दो घंटे तक (*adv*) for two hours (W22, p. 125)

दो बजे (*adv*) at two o'clock (T11, p. 93) (W14, p. 78)

दो हफ़्ते बाद (*adv*) after two weeks (W17, p. 98)

दोनों (*adj*) both (T7, p. 50) (W9, p. 48) (GR 16)

दोपहर (*f*) midday, afternoon (T11, p. 93) (W14, 19 pp. 78, 109) (GR 11)

दोबारा (*adv*) twice, a second time (W13, p. 71)

दोशाला (*m*) shawl (T15, p. 140)

दोस्त (*m/f*) friend (T3, p. 22) (W4, p. 18)

दोस्ती (*f*) friendship (T14, p. 130) (W11, p. 60)

दौड़ना (*v.i.*) to run (T11, p. 88) (W22, p. 125)

दौलत (*f*) wealth (W22, p. 125)

द्रव्य (*m*) substance, matter, money (T6, p. 45)

द्वार (*m*) door, doorway (T6, p. 45)

द्वारा (*pp*) by, through, through the medium of (T21, p. 209) (GR 21)

द्वितीय (*adj*) second (T16, p. 152) (GR 16)

ध

धन (*m*) wealth (W7, p. 35)

धनाढ्य (*adj*) wealthy (T6, p. 44)

धनी (*adj*) wealthy

धर्म (*m*) religion, righteous action, duty, justice (T6, p. 44)

धीरे-धीरे (*adv*) slowly (T22, p. 217)

धुआँ (*m*) smoke (W10, p. 54)

धुलना (*v.i.*) to be washed

धूप (*f*) sunshine, incense (T10, p. 78)

धूमधाम (*m*) pomp, fanfare

धूमधाम से (*adv*) with pomp and ceremony (W19, p. 110)

धोना (*v.t.*) to wash (T15, p. 140)

धोबी (*m*) washerman (W7, p. 35)

ध्यान (*m*) attention, meditation, heed, contemplation (T6, p. 43) (W15, p. 85) (x पर) ध्यान देना (*v.t.*) to concentrate (on x) (T24, p. 230)

ध्यान से (*adv*) with attention, carefully (T24, p. 235)

न

न (*adv*) no, not, isn't it? (T7, p. 50) (W6, p. 28) (GR 8)

नक़्शा (*m*) map, shape (W22, p. 125)

नज़दीक (*adv*) close, near (T15, p. 132)

नदी (*f*) river (T17, p. 165) (W10, p. 54)

नन्हाँ (*adj*) small, tiny, wee (said of children) (T6, p. 44)

नब्बे (*adj*) ninety (T16, p. 151)

नमक (*m*) salt (T1, p. 6) (W1, p. 3)

नमकीन (*adj + m*) salty, salted; a salty dish of snacks (T1, p. 6)

नमस्कार (*m*) hello and goodbye (T2, p. 12) (W4, p. 18)

नमस्ते (*m*) hello and goodbye (T2, p. 12) (W2, p. 8)

नमाज़ पढ़ना (*v.t.*) to read the prayer, to pray (W15, p. 85)

नम्बर/नंबर (*m*) grade, mark, number (T7, p. 57)

नया (*adj*) new (T1, p. 7) (W1, p. 3)

नवम्बर (*m*) November (T16, p. 154) (W10, p. 54) (GR 16)

नवाँ (*adj*) ninth (T9, p. 67)

नवाब (*m*) Nawab (a title) (W12, p. 65)

नवाबी (*adj*) Nawabi, aristocratic (W15, p. 85)

नस्तालिक़ (*f*) Nastaliq (name of the Urdu script) (T22, p. 215)

नहलाना (*v.t.*) to bathe (someone) (W10, p. 54)

नहाना (*v.i. + v.t.*) to bathe (T10, p. 76) (W10, p. 54)

नहीं (*adv*) no, not (T2, p. 12)

नहीं तो (*adv*) certainly not, otherwise (T13, p. 18) (W16, p. 91)

ना (*adv*) no (T1, p. 5)

नाई (*m*) barber (T1, p. 5)

नाच (*m*) dance (W10, p. 54)

नाचना (*v.i.*) to dance

नाटक (*m*) drama, play (W10, 17 pp. 54, 97)

नाना (*m*) maternal grandfather (T5, p. 34) (GR 7)

नाना-नानी (*m*) maternal grandparents (T5, p. 35)

नानी (*f*) maternal grandmother (T1, p. 5) (GR 8)

नाम (*m*) name (T2, p. 15) (W2, p. 8)

नामक (*adj*) called (W12, p. 65)

नाव (*f*) boat (T1, p. 6)

नाश्ता (*m*) light refreshment, breakfast (T5, p. 32)

नाश्ता करना (*v.t.*) to eat breakfast (T10, p. 76)

निकलना (*v.i.*) to emerge (T14, p. 130)

निकालना (*v.t.*) to take out (W11, p. 60)

निगाह (*f*) glance, sight (T24, p. 232)

निरंतर (*adv*) continuous, uninterrupted, incessant (T11, p. 91)

निर्बल (*adj*) weak (T6, p. 46)

निश्चय (*m*) decision (T6, p. 45)

(x का) निश्चय करना (*v.t.*) to decide (x) (T23, p. 226)

नींद (*f*) sleep, slumber (T18, p. 172)

(x को) नींद आना (*v.i.*) (x) to fall asleep (T18, p. 172) (GR 18)

(x को) नींद लगना (*v.i.*) (x) to feel sleepy (T22, p. 220) (GR 18)

नीचे (*adv*) beneath, below (T20, p. 204)

नीला (*adj*) blue (T3, p. 22) (W1, p. 3)

ने (*pp*) a postposition denoting the subject case with a transitive verb in the perfective form (T7, p. 53) (GR 7, 12)

नेता (*m*) leader, politician (W10, p. 54) (GR 7)

नौ (*adj*) nine (T10, p. 76)

नौकर (*m*) servant (T9, p. 71)

नौकरी (*f*) employment, work (T3, p. 20) (W17, 20 pp. 98, 114)

नौकरी करना (*v.t.*) to work (for money) (T11, p. 90) (W20, p. 115)

(x की) नौकरी लग जाना (*v.i.*) (x) to start a job, get a job (T22, p. 220)

प

पंखा (*m*) fan, blade (T6, p. 43)

पंद्रह (*adj*) fifteen (T16, p. 151)

पंद्रहवाँ (*adj*) fifteenth (T15, p. 132) (GR 16)

पकड़ना (*v.t.*) to grab, catch (T24, p. 232) (W20, 23 pp. 115, 129)

पकवान (*m*) rich delicacy (food) (W24, p. 137)

पकाना (*v.t.*) to cook (T16, p. 147)

पक्का (*adj*) ripe, strong (T5, p. 38) (W1, p. 3)

पचास (*adj*) fifty (T7, p. 50)

पच्चीस (*adj*) twenty-five (T16, p. 151)

पड़ना (*v.i.*) to fall (T14, p. 125) (W10, p. 54) (GR 19, 20)

पड़ोसी (*m*) neighbor

पड़ोसिन (*f*) neighbor

पढ़ना (*v.t.*) to read, study (T4, p. 26) (W9, p. 48)

पढ़ाई (*f*) study, studies (T4, p. 26) (W16, 19 pp. 91, 109)

पढ़ाई करना (*v.t.*) to do study (T9, p. 70)

पढ़ाना (*v.t.*) to teach, make read (T19, p. 191)

पता (*m*) address, whereabouts (T2, p. 13) (W2, p. 8) (GR 18)

पता करना (*v.t.*) to find out, discover (T18, p. 172) (GR 18)

(x को) पता चलना (*v.i.*) (x) to find out, discover (T18, p. 172) (W18, p. 104) (GR 18)

पता नहीं don't know

(x को) पता लगना (*v.i.*) (x) to find out, discover (T18, p. 172) (GR 18)

पता लगाना (*v.t.*) to find out, discover (T18, p. 172) (GR 18)

(x को) पता होना (*v.i.*) (x) to know, to find out (T18, p. 172) (GR 18)

पति (*m*) husband (T10, p. 81) (W7, p. 35)

पत्ता (*m*) leaf (T6, p. 45)

पत्नी (*f*) wife (W8, p. 41)

पत्र (*m*) letter (T6, p. 46) (W9, p. 48)

पन्ना (*m*) page (W8, p. 41)

परंतु (*conj*) but, however (T15, p. 139)

पर (*pp + conj*) on; but (T8, p. 64) (W3, p. 13) (GR 15)

परचा (*m*) chit, note, prescription (W21, p. 120)

परसों (*adv*) the day before yesterday/after tomorrow (T11, p. 91) (W17, p. 98) (GR 11)

परिवार (*m*) family (T5, p. 35) (W4, p. 18)

परीक्षा (*f*) examination (T6, p. 45) (W15, p. 85)

परीक्षा देना (*v.t.*) to sit for (take) an exam (T17, p. 163) (W20, p. 115)

परीक्षा लेना (*v.t.*) to administer (give) an exam

परेशान (*adj*) troubled, bothered (T18, p. 173) (W18, p. 104)

परेशान लगना (*v.i.*) to seem bothered, troubled (T18, p. 173) (GR 18)

परेशान होना (*v.i.*) to be worried

पर्दा (*m*) curtain, screen, veil (T19, p. 192)

पलंग (*m*) bed (W7, p. 35)

पल (*m*) a moment, a measure of time equal to twenty-four seconds

पवित्र (*adj*) sacred (W10, p. 54) (W6, p. 25)

पश्चाताप (*m*) remorse, compunction, repentance (T18, p. 175)

पश्चिम (*m*) west (T23, p. 222)

पसंद (*adj + f*) approved, liked; liking, choice, taste, preference (T18, p. 170)

(x को) पसंद आना (*v.i.*) (x) to enjoy (one/first time) (T18, p. 170) (GR 18)

(x को) पसंद होना (*v.i.*) (x) to enjoy, to like (T18, p. 170) (W18, p. 104) (GR 18)

पहचानना (*v.t.*) to recognize (W22, p. 125)

पहनना (*v.t.*) to wear, to put on (T1, p. 6) (W9, 23 pp. 48, 129)

पहनाना (*v.t.*) to cause to wear, to dress (someone)

पहला (*adj*) first (T1, p. 1) (W1, p. 3)

पहले (*adv*) ago, before, previously (T8, p. 61) (W10, 16, 17 pp. 54, 91, 97)

पहाड़ (*m*) mountain (W23, p. 130)

पहुँचना (*v.i.*) to arrive (T9, p. 72) (W9, 17 pp. 48, 97)

पाँच (*adj*) five (T10, p. 81) (W3, p. 13)

पाँचवाँ (*adj*) fifth (T5, p. 31) (GR 16)

पागल (*adj*) crazy (T20, p. 201)

पागल होना (*v.i.*) to become crazy (T20, p. 201)

पाठ (*m*) lesson, reading (T1, p. 1) (W18, p. 104)

पाठयपुस्तक (*f*) course book (T6, p. 44)

पात्र (*m*) character (in a play) (W6, p. 28)

पान (*m*) betel leaf (T1, p. 8) (W1, p. 3)

पाना (*v.i. + v.t.*) to find, obtain; to be able to (T17, p. 162) (GR 17, 19)

पानी (*m*) water (T1, p. 7) (W1, p. 3)

पाप (*m*) sin (W15, p. 85)

पार्किंग (*f*) parking (T23, p. 227)

पार्टी (*f*) party (T15, p. 132)

पालक (*m*) spinach (T18, p. 169)

पालकी (*f*) palanquin, sedan chair (T19, p. 192)

पास होना (*v.i.*) to pass (an exam) (W15, p. 85)

(x से) पिंड छूटना (*v.i.*) to be freed (from x) (W21, p. 120)

पिघलना (*v.i.*) to melt (W23, p. 130)

पिचकारी (*f*) water gun, syringe (W19, p. 109)

पिछला (*adj*) previous, prior (T11, p. 92)

पिछले हफ्ते (*adv*) last week (T11, p. 92) (W13, 14 pp. 71, 78)

पिता (*m*) father (T5, p. 34) (W4, p. 18) (GR 7)

पिलाना (*v.t.*) to cause to drink, to serve (T13, p. 110) (W9, p. 48)

पीछे (*adv*) back, behind, after

पीढ़ी (*f*) generation (T22, p. 219)

पीना (*v.t.*) to drink (T1, p. 5) (W9, p. 48)

पीर (*m*) Monday, Muslim saint (T16, p. 153) (GR 16)

पीला (*adj*) yellow (W1, p. 3)

पुकारना (*v.t.*) to call (out) (W24, p. 137)
पुराना (*adj*) old (said of things) (T13, p. 114)
  (W4, 13, 15 pp. 18, 71, 85)
पुरुष (*m*) man (T19, p. 196)
पुलिस (*f*) police (T15, p. 137)
पुस्तक (*f*) book (T6, p. 43)
पुस्तकालय (*m*) library (T10, p. 76) (W14, p. 78)
(x से) पूछना (*v.t.*) to ask (x) (T12, p. 101) (W11, p. 60)
  (GR 16)
पूरा (*adj*) complete (T16, p. 148) (W3, 15 pp. 13, 85)
पूरा करना (*v.t.*) to complete (T16, p. 148) (W13, p. 71)
पूरा होना (*v.i.*) to be completed (W19, p. 110)
पूर्व (*m*) east (T23, p. 222)
पृथ्वी (*f*) the earth, world (T6, p. 43)
पेट (*m*) stomach (T19, p. 185) (W21, p. 120)
पेड़ (*m*) tree (T11, p. 88) (W7, p. 35)
पैंतालीस (*adj*) forty-five (T16, p. 151)
पैंतीस (*adj*) thirty-five (T16, p. 151)
पैदल (*adv*) on foot (T13, p. 105)
पैदल जाना (*v.i.*) to walk (T21, p. 207)
पैदा (*adj, invar*) born (T3, p. 21) (GR 3)
पैदा करना (*v.t.*) to produce, give birth
पैदा होना (*v.i.*) to be produced, to be born (T12, p. 99)
पैना (*adj*) sharp, acute (T1, p. 5)
पैसा (*m*) paisa, money (T7, p. 57) (W2, 7 pp. 8, 35)
पौन (*adj*) three-quarters, quarter to one (T16, p. 153)
  (GR 16, 18)
पौने (*adj*) quarter to (less a quarter) (T16, p. 153)
  (GR 16, 18)
प्यार (*m*) love
प्याला (*m*) cup (W15, p. 85)
प्याली (*f*) cup
प्यास (*f*) thirst (T6, p. 43) (W15, p. 85)
(x को) प्यास लगना (*v.i.*) (x) to be thirsty
  (T18, p. 174) (GR 18)
प्रकार (*m*) type, manner, sort, kind, quality
  (T17, p. 166)
प्रणाम (*m*) reverential salutation; bowing with respect,
  a term used in greeting elders (T7, p. 51)
प्रतिदिन (*adv*) every day (T11, p. 91)
प्रतिशत (*m*) percent
प्रथम (*adj*) first (T16, p. 152) (GR16)
प्रधान मंत्री (*m*) Prime Minister (T20, p. 205)
प्रयाग (*m*) Prayag (Allahabad) (name of a city in U.P.)
  (W14, p. 78)

प्रयोग (*m*) use, experiment, employment, application
(x का) प्रयोग करना (*v.t.*) to use, to experiment,
  to employ, to apply (x)
प्रश्न (*m*) question (T6, p. 46)
प्रसन्नता (*f*) happiness (T, 6, p. 46)
प्राप्त करना (*v.t.*) to obtain (T23, p. 224)
(x को) प्राप्त होना (*v.i.*) (x) to obtain
प्रायः (*adv*) often, approximately (T11, p. 91)
प्रार्थना (*f*) prayer (T6, p. 46)
प्रियतम (*adj*) beloved, dearest (T21, p. 212)
प्रेम (*m*) love (T6, p. 46)
प्रेमचंद (*m*) Premchand (name of a famous Hindi
  author) (T18, p. 173) (W12, p. 65)
प्लैटफ़ार्म (*m*) platform (T23, p. 229) (W14, p. 78)

फ

फटना (*v.i.*) to explode, break, burst, to be torn
  (T22, p. 217)
फ़रमाना (*v.t.*) to request (W8, p. 41)
फ़रवरी (*f*) February (month) (T16, p. 154)
फ़र्क़ (*m*) difference (T22, p. 214)
फ़र्श (*m*) floor (T22, p. 217) (W6, p. 25)
फल (*m*) fruit (W7, 18 pp. 35, 103)
फ़ायदा (*m*) advantage (T17, p. 159)
(x को) फ़ायदा होना (*v.i.*) (x) to be advantaged
फ़िक्र (*f*) worry (T24, p. 230) (W19, p. 110)
(x की) फ़िक्र करना (*v.t.*) to worry (about x)
  (T24, p. 230) (W19, p. 110)
(x को) फ़िक्र होना (*v.i.*) (x) to worry (T24, p. 230)
फिर (*conj*) then; again; afterwards; thereafter;
  in the future; a second time (T8, p. 64)
फिर भी (*conj*) nevertheless (T16, p. 155)
फ़िल्म (*f*) film, movie (T9, p. 72) (W9, p. 48)
फ़ुरसत (*f*) spare time (T4, p. 26)
फूल (*m*) flower (T4, p. 26) (W4, p. 18)
फेरीवाला (*adj*) hawker, street vendor (T24, p. 235)
फैलना (*v.i.*) to spread, to be diffused, to expand
फैलाना (*v.t.*) to spread (T15, p. 139)
फ़ोन (*m*) phone (T8, p. 66) (W16, p. 91)
फ़ोन उठाना (*v.t.*) to pick up the phone (T15, p. 135)
फ़ोन करना (*v.t.*) to phone (T10, p. 84) (W16, p. 91)
फ़ोन रखना (*v.t.*) to place (put down) the phone
  (T17, p. 167)
फ़ौज (*f*) army (T21, p. 210)
फ़ौजी (*m*) soldier; (*adj*) martial

फ़ौरन (*adv*) immediately, instantly, at once (T11, p. 91)

फ़्लैट (*m*) apartment, flat (T20, p. 204)

ब

बंगला (*f*) Bengali language (W15, p. 85)

बंगाली मार्केट (*m*) Bengali Market (T13, p. 114)

बंद (*adj*) closed, off (T15, p. 135)

बंद रहना (*v.i.*) to remain closed (W10, p. 54)

बंद होना (*v.i.*) to be closed, turned off (T15, p. 135)

बँधना (v.i.) to be tied, to be fastened, to be bound (T21, p. 211)

बंबई/बम्बई (*f*) Bombay (T8, p. 61) (W10, 19 pp. 54, 109)

बक़रईद (*f*) name of Eid (W15, p. 85)

बकरा (*m*) goat (T18, p. 169)

बकवास (*f*) nonsense (T18, p. 175) (W9, p. 48)

बग़ल (*f*) flank, armpit, next to (T17, p. 161) (W19, p. 110)

बग़ल में (*adv*) next door (T17, p. 161)

बगीचा (*m*) garden (T14, p. 126) (W14, p. 78)

बग्घी (*f*) buggy (T6, p. 43)

बचना (*v.i.*) to be saved (T24, p. 234)

बचपन (*m*) childhood (T11, p. 88) (W10, p. 54)

बचाना (*v.t.*) to save (T19, p. 193)

बच्चा (*m*) child (T6, p. 43) (W17, p. 98)

बजना (*v.i.*) to be struck, strike (T11, p. 93) (W18, p. 104) (GR 18)

बजे (*adv*) o'clock (T11, p. 93) (GR 18)

बजाना (*v.t.*) to strike

बटुआ (*m*) wallet, purse (T24, p. 236)

बड़ा (*adj*) big (T3, p. 22) (W3, p. 13)

बड़ा इमामबाड़ा (*m*) Bara Imambara (one of the famous historical buildings in Lucknow) (W12, p. 65)

बड़ा होना (*v.i.*) to grow up (T12, p. 99)

बढ़ना (*v.i.*) to be increased, to grow (T23, p. 222) (W22, p. 125)

बढ़ाना (*v.t.*) to increase, to grow

बढ़िया (*adj*) excellent (T3, p. 21) (W7, p. 35)

बताना (*v.t.*) to tell (T9, p. 70) (W8, p. 41) (GR 16)

बत्तीस (*adj*) thirty-two (T16, p. 151)

बद (*adj*) bad, wicked, vile, depraved (T19, p. 197)

बदतर (*adj*) worse (T19, p. 197)

बदतरीन (*adj*) worst (T19, p. 197)

बदलना (*v.i. + v.t.*) to change (T12, p. 102) (W11, 22 pp. 60, 124)

बनना (*v.i.*) to be made (T11, p. 90) (W11, p. 60) (GR 22)

बनवाना (*v.t.*) to cause to be built (T10, p. 76) (W12, p. 65)

बनाना (*v.t.*) to make, produce (T9, p. 73)

बयालीस (*adj*) forty-two (T16, p. 151)

बरगद (*m*) banyan tree (T11, p. 88)

बरस (*m*) year (T11, p. 92) (W24, p. 137)

बरसात (*f*) rainy season (T19, p. 187)

बरिस्ता (*m*) Barista (a chain of coffee shops) (T21, p. 207)

बर्फ़ (*f*) snow (T19, p. 187) (W23, p. 130)

बलवान (*adj*) strong, powerful (T19, p. 196)

बलिदान (*m*) sacrifice (W15, p. 85)

बस (*invar + m*) okay, enough; power (T5, p. 36) (W3, 12 pp. 13, 65)

बसना (*v.i.*) to settle, inhabit (T23, p. 223)

बस्ता (*m*) (school) bag (W10, 23 pp. 54, 129)

बहन (*f*) sister (T4, p. 29) (W2, p. 8)

बहना (*v.i.*) to flow (W10, p. 54)

बहादुर (*adj*) courageous (T21, p. 209)

बहाना (*m*) excuse; (*v.t.*) to make flow (W19, p. 110)

बहाना बनाना (*v.t.*) to make an excuse (W19, p. 110)

बहुत (*adj*) very, a lot, much (T4, p. 29) (W3, p. 13)

बहुत कुछ (*adj*) very much (T7, p. 57)

बहुत देर तक (*adv*) for a long time (W11, p. 60)

बहुत सारा (*adj*) very many (W7, p. 35)

बाँधना (*v.t.*) to tie, to fasten, to bind (T21, p. 211)

बाइओलॉजी (*f*) biology (T11, p. 86)

बाईस (*adj*) twenty-two (T6, p. 49) (W10, p. 54)

बाईसवाँ (*adj*) twenty-second (T22, p. 214)

बाक़ी (*adj*) remaining, rest (T18, p. 177) (W15, 19 pp. 85, 109)

बाग़ (*m*) garden (T16, p. 146)

बाघ (*m*) tiger (W10, p. 54)

बाज़ार (*m*) market (T2, p. 12) (W2, p. 8)

बात (*f*) matter, talk, thing (T5, p. 36) (W4, p. 18)

(x से) बात करना (*v.t.*) to talk, converse (to/with x) (T13, p. 112) (W9, p. 48) (GR 16)

(x की) बात (y से) होना (*v.i.*) (x's) conversation/talk/matter to happen (with y) (T14, p. 123) (W12, p. 65) (GR 16)

(x से) बातचीत करना (*v.t.*) to converse (with x) (T16, p. 154) (W11, p. 60) (GR 16)

बादशाह (*m*) king (T21, p. 209)

बाबा (*m*) grandfather, an old man, ascetic

बार (*f*) time (T11, p. 93) (W11, 15 pp. 60, 85)

बार-बार (*adv*) time and again (T11, p. 91)

बारह (*adj*) twelve (T10, p. 76)

बारहवाँ (*adj*) twelfth (T12, p. 95) (GR 16)

बारिश (*f*) rain (T19, p. 187) (W20, p. 115)

बारी (*f*) turn (W4, p. 18)

बावर्ची (*m*) cook (W21, p. 120)

बासी (*adj*) stale (W3, p. 13)

बाहर (*adv*) outside (T11, p. 94) (W3, p. 13)

बिठाना/बैठाना (*v.t.*) to seat (someone) (T8, p. 65)

बिताना (*v.t.*) to spend, pass (time) (T16, p. 149)

बिलकुल (*adv*) absolutely (T7, p. 50) (W5, p. 23)

बिस्तर (*m*) bedding, bed (W22, p. 125)

बीमार (*adj*) sick, ill (T5, p. 33) (W5, 21 pp. 23, 119)

बीमारी (*f*) illness, sickness (T18, p. 174) (W21, p. 120)

बीस (*adj*) twenty (T16, p. 151) (W10, p. 54)

बीसवाँ (*adj*) twentieth (T20, p. 198) (GR 16)

बीसियों (*adj*) scores (T16, p. 153) (GR 16)

बीसों (*adj*) scores, all twenty (T16, p. 153) (GR 16)

बुख़ार (*m*) fever (T13, p. 110)

(x को) बुख़ार होना (*v.i.*) (x) to have a fever (T13, p. 110) (GR 18)

बुझना (*v.i.*) to be extinguished, quenched (W15, p. 85)

बुधवार (बुध) (*m*) Wednesday (T9, p. 74) (W6, p. 28) (GR 16)

बुरा (*adj*) bad (T18, p. 174) (W11, p. 60)

(x को) बुरा लगना (*v.i.*) (x) to feel bad (T18, p. 174) (GR 18)

बुलाना (*v.t.*) to call, invite (T10, p. 84) (W15, p. 85)

बृहस्पतिवार (*m*) Thursday (T16, p. 153) (W6, p. 28) (GR 16)

बेकार (*adj*) useless, idle, stupid (W5, p. 23)

बेघर (*adj*) homeless

बेचना (*v.t.*) to sell (T8, p. 65)

बेटा (*m*) son (sometimes used affectionately as a mode of address for a girl) (T8, p. 62) (W8, p. 41)

बेवकूफ (*adj*) idiot, foolish (W23, p. 130)

बेवफ़ा (*adj*) unfaithful (W5, p. 23)

बैंक (*m*) bank (T11, p. 85)

बैठक (*f*) sitting room (W17, p. 98)

बैठना (*v.i.*) to sit (T8, p. 62) (W9, p. 48) (GR 19)

बोझ (*m*) burden (W16, p. 91)

बोतल (*f*) bottle (T15, p. 137) (W3, p. 13)

बोर होना (*v.i.*) to become bored (T15, p. 142)

(x से) बोलना (*v.i. + v.t.*) to speak (to x) (T3, p. 20) (W8, 10 pp. 41, 54) (GR 12, 16)

बौद्ध धर्म (*m*) Buddhism (Buddhist religion) (T18, p. 173)

ब्याह (*m*) marriage, wedding (T6, p. 43)

ब्राह्मण (*m*) Brahmin (T6, p. 46)

भ

भई (*m*) brother, friend (W11, p. 60)

भक्त (*m*) devotee (T6, p. 45)

भगवान (*m*) Lord (God) (T16, p. 148) (W11, p. 60)

भगाना (*v.t.*) to chase away

भर (*adj*) entire, all, whole, full

भरना (*v.i. + v.t.*) to be filled, to fill (T19, p. 185)

भरोसा (*m*) faith, trust (T15, p. 139) (W10, p. 54)

(x पर) भरोसा करना (*v.t.*) to trust, to believe (x) (T15, p. 139)

(x पर) भरोसा होना (*v.i.*) to trust, to believe (x) (T24, p. 230)

भविष्य (*m*) future (W17, p. 98)

भाई (*m*) brother (T5, p. 33) (W6, p. 28)

भाई-बहन (*m pl*) brothers and sisters, siblings (T8, p. 61) (W6, p. 28)

भाई-साहब (*m*) Sir! (T7, p. 52)

भागना (*v.i.*) to escape, to flee (T15, p. 140) (W17, p. 98)

भारत (*m*) India (T5, p. 33) (W10, 22 pp. 54, 124)

भारत यात्रा करना (*v.t.*) to travel to India (W22, p. 125)

भारतीय (*adj*) Indian (T9, p. 70)

भालू (*m*) bear (W7, p. 35) (GR 7)

भाव (*m*) cost, price; emotion, sentiment (T17, p. 160)

भावना (*f*) emotion (W24, p. 137)

भाषण (*m*) speech (T23, p. 224) (W22, p. 125)

भाषण देना (*v.t.*) to give a speech (T23, p. 224) (W17, p. 98)

भाषा (*f*) language (T8, p. 60) (W8, p. 41)

भिखारी (*m*) beggar (W22, p. 125)

भी (*part*) also, even, too (T13, p. 114) (W8, p. 41) (GR 14)

भीड़ (*f*) crowd (T20, p. 206)

भुलाना (*v.t.*) to forget

भूख (*f*) hunger (T18, p. 174)

(x को) भूख लगना (*v.i.*) (x) to feel hungry (T18, p. 174) (W18, p. 103) (GR 18)

भूल जाना (*v.i.*) to forget (T21, p. 212)

भूलना (*v.i.*) to forget (T5, p. 33) (GR 12)

भेंट (*f*) gift (W8, p. 41)

भेजना (*v.t.*) to send, to transmit, to remit (T8, p. 63) (W16, 23 pp. 91, 129)

भैया (*m*) brother (affectionate term) (T18, p. 180)

म

मंगलमय (*adj*) auspicious (T16, p. 148)

मंगलवार (*m*) Tuesday (T9, p. 74) (W6, p. 28) (GR 16)

मँगवाना (*v.t.*) to have ordered (T23, p. 227)

मंज़िल (*f*) floor of a building, story (T16, p. 152)

मंत्री (*m*) minister (W7, p. 35)

मंदिर (*m*) temple (T7, p. 55)

मई (*m*) May (month) (T16, p. 154) (W10, p. 54) (GR 16)

मकान (*m*) house (T1, p. 7) (W1, p. 3)

मगर (*conj*) but (T15, p. 139)

मच्छर (*m*) mosquito (T5, p. 33)

मज़दूर (*m*) laborer (T19, p. 185)

मज़ा (*m*) enjoyment, relish (T11, p. 89)

(x को) मज़ा आना (*v.i.*) (x) to enjoy (T11, p. 89) (W19, p. 110) (GR 18)

मज़ाक (*m*) joke (W11, p. 60)

मज़े करना (*v.t.*) to enjoy, have fun (T22, p. 221)

मज़े में (*adv*) at perfect ease (T5, p. 37) (W3, p. 13)

मज़ेदार (*adj*) tasty, enjoyable (W13, p. 71)

मटर (*m*) peas (T18, p. 169)

मत (*adv + m*) don't, not; opinion, view, vote (T8, p. 64) (W8, p. 41) (GR 8)

मतलब (*m*) meaning (T5, p. 35) (W15, p. 85)

मतलबी (*adj*) selfish

मदद (*f*) help (T9, p. 74) (W15, p. 85)

(x की) मदद करना (*v.t.*) to help (x) (T9, p. 74) (W13, p. 71)

मन (*m*) heart, mind (T17, p. 167) (W8, 24 pp. 41, 136)

(x का) मन लगाना (*v.i.*) (x) to feel at home, happy, engaged, to feel easy

मन लगाना (*v.t.*) to apply oneself (W23, p. 130)

मन लगाकर (*adv*) having applied the heart/mind, with industry (GR 15)

मन ही मन (*adv*) in the mind (W24, p. 137)

(x का) मन होना (*v.i.*) to feel like (x); (x) to feel like (T17, p. 167) (W22, p. 125)

मनपसंद (*adj*) favorite (T16, p. 143) (W24, p. 137)

मना (*adj*) forbidden (T13, p. 111)

मनाना (*v.t.*) to appease, to celebrate, to persuade (W15, 19 pp. 85, 109)

मनुष्य (*m*) man, human (T13, p. 108)

मरना (*v.i.*) to die

मर्ज़ी (*f*) desire, will

मशहूर (*adj*) famous (T15, p. 132) (W11, p. 60)

मस्जिद (*f*) mosque (T16, p. 143) (W15, p. 85)

महँगा (*adj*) expensive (T17, p. 161) (W10, p. 54)

महत्त्वपूर्ण (*adj*) important (W15, p. 85)

महल (*m*) palace (T1, p. 6) (W1, p. 3)

महसूस (*adj*) felt, perceived, experienced (T24, p. 236)

महसूस करना (*v.t.*) to feel, perceive

(x को) महसूस होना (*v.i.*) (x) to feel, perceive (T24, p. 236) (GR 18)

महाद्वीप (*m*) continent (T19, p. 196)

महाराज (*m*) king (T14, p. 227)

महाराष्ट्र (*m*) Mahrashtra (a state in India) (T6, p. 46)

महिला (*f*) woman (T13, p. 108) (W13, p. 71)

महीना (*m*) month (T1, p. 6) (W1, p. 3)

माँ (*f*) mother (T2, p. 17) (W2, p. 8)

"माँ, तुझे सलाम" *Salaam to You, Mother* (film title) (T20, p. 198)

माँ-बाप (*m pl*) parents (T4, p. 29) (W2, p. 8)

माँगना (*v.t.*) to demand (T4, p. 26)

माघ (*m*) the name of a month (W10, p. 54)

मानना (*v.t.*) to accept, regard, respect (T1, p. 6) (W11, p. 60)

माफ़ (*adj*) excused, forgiven, pardoned (T12, p. 102)

माफ़ करना (*v.t.*) to forgive, excuse, pardon (T12, p. 102) (W23, p. 130)

माफ़ी (*f*) forgiveness, pardon

मामला (*m*) issue, matter (T13, p. 110) (W13, p. 71)

मामा (*m*) maternal uncle (T1, p. 5) (W2, p. 8) (GR 7)

मामी (*f*) maternal aunty (T9, p. 73) (GR 8)

मारना (*v.t.*) to beat, strike, kill (T19, p. 192)

मार्च (*m*) March (month) (T16, p. 154) (W6, p. 28)

मॉल (*m*) mall (T23, p. 222)

मालकिन (*f*) owner (W7, p. 35)

मालिक (*m*) owner (W7, p. 35)

माली (*m*) gardener (T1, p. 5)

(x को) मालूम होना (*v.i.*) to be known (to x) (T12, p. 104) (W18, p. 104) (GR 18)

माहौल (*m*) atmosphere (T23, p. 229) (W10, p. 54)

मिज़ाज (*m*) mood, temperament

मिटना (*v.i.*) to be effaced, erased (W15, p. 85)

मिट्टी (*f*) soil, earth (T6, p. 46)

मिठाई (*f*) sweetmeat (T13, p. 111) (W8, p. 41)

मित्र (*m*) friend (T6, p. 45)

मिनट (*m*) minute (T8, p. 64) (GR 18)

मिलना (*v.i.*) to meet, to encounter, to be mixed, to be united, to mingle (T2, p. 13) (W10, 18 pp. 54, 103) (GR 17)

मिलाना (*v.t.*) to mix, to unite, to compare, to blend, to cause to meet, to bring together (W22, p. 125)

मिसेस Mrs. (T17, p. 164)

मीठा (*adj*) sweet (T19, p. 193)

मुंबई (*f*) Mumbai (T19, p. 187)

मुँह (*m*) face, mouth, opening (T15, p. 140)

मुझ (*pro*) me (oblique form of मैं) (T7, p. 53) (GR 7)

मुझी (*pro*) me (मुझ + ही) (T14, p. 128) (GR 14)

मुझे/मुझको (*pro*) (to) me (oblique form of मैं + को) (T7, p. 53) (GR 7)

मुझे कुछ काम है। I have work to do. (T20, p. 198)

मुद्रा (*f*) seal, stamp, money, countenance, pose, posture (W6, p. 25)

मुनासिब (*adj*) reasonable, proper, fit, appropriate (T16, p. 148)

मुन्ना (*m*) a term of endearment for a child, dear child (T6, p. 45)

मुन्नी (*f*) a term of endearment for a child, dear child (T6, p. 44)

मुफ़्त (*adj*) free of charge, gratis (T6, p. 42)

मुफ़्त में (*adv*) gratis, for free

मुबारक (*adj*) auspicious, blessed, fortunate (T16, p. 147)

(x) मुबारक हो! may (x) be auspicious! (T16, p. 147) (GR 16)

मुमकिन (*adj*) possible (T16, p. 146) (GR 16)

मुर्ग़ी (*f*) chicken (T18, p. 167)

मुलाक़ात (*f*) meeting (W19, p. 110)

(x से) (य की) मुलाक़ात होना (*v.i.*) (y) to meet (with x), (y's) meeting to take place (with x) (T22, p. 221)

मुश्किल (*adj*) difficult; (*f*) difficulty (T13, p. 115)

मुसलमान (*m*) Muslim (W10, p. 54)

मुस्कराना/मुस्कुराना (*v.i.*) to smile (T19, p. 191) (W19, p. 110) (GR 19)

मुहर्रम (*m*) the month of Imam Hussain's martyrdom which is held sacred and celebrated by Shia Muslims (W10, p. 54)

मूर्ति (*f*) idol, statue (T7, p. 55)

में (*pp*) in (T3, p. 22) (W2, p. 8) (GR 7, 13)

में से (*pp*) from amongst (T15, p. 138) (W7, p. 35)

मेज़ (*f*) table (T8, p. 64) (W3, p. 13)

मेज़ पर on the table (T8, p. 64) (W3, p. 13)

मेट्रो (*f*) Metro (T13, p. 106)

मेधा (*f*) intellect, brilliance, Medha (name) (T10, p. 83)

मेन कैम्पस (मुख्य परिसर) (*m*) main campus (T15 p. 132)

मेरा (*adj*) my (T2, p. 14) (GR 2, 4)

मेरा क्या? What's it to me? (T10, p. 83)

मेरी (बात) कहाँ सुनते हैं? Where do they listen to me (my matter)? (T16, p. 156)

मेरे ख़्याल में (*adv*) in my opinion (T20, p. 202)

मेला (*m*) fair (W10, p. 54)

मेहनत (*f*) hard work (T18, p. 173) (W9, 17, 18 pp. 48, 97, 103)

मेहनत करना (*v.t.*) to work hard (T20, p. 203)

मेहनती (*adj*) hardworking, industrious (T20, p. 202)

मेहरबानी (*f*) kindness, favor (T8, p. 64) (W4, p. 18)

मैं (*pro*) I (T2, p. 14) (GR 2, 4, 7)

मैं चलता हूँ। I'm (*m*) off. (T9, p. 68)

मैंने (*pro*) I (मैं + ने) (T7, p. 53) (GR 7, 12)

मैना (*f*) Indian black bird (T1, p. 5)

मोची (*m*) cobbler (W17, p. 98)

मोटरसाइकिल (*f*) motorcycle (T13, p. 105)

मोटा (*adj*) fat (W19, p. 110)

मोलतोल (*m*) haggling, bargaining (W11, p. 60)

मौक़ा (*m*) opportunity (T18, p. 181)

मौज-मस्ती करना (*v.t.*) to enjoy, have fun (T22, p. 220)

मौसम (*m*) weather, season (T5, p. 37) (W3, p. 13)

य

यदि (*conj*) if (T11, p. 88)

यमुना (*f*) Yamuna (river) (T17, p. 165) (W10, p. 54)

यह (*pro*) he/she/this/it (close to the speaker) (T1, p. 6) (W1, p. 3) (GR 2, 4, 7)

यहाँ (*adv*) here (T5, p. 39) (W2, p. 8) (GR 23)

यहीं (*adv*) right here (यहाँ + ही) (T8, p. 62) (T14, p. 128) (W6, p. 28) (GR 14)

यही (*pro*) this very (person, thing) (यह + ही) (T14, p. 128) (W14, p. 78) (GR 14)

या (*conj*) or (T1, p. 5) (W17, p. 98)

यात्रा करना (*v.t.*) to travel (W10, 22 pp. 54, 124)

याद (*f*) memory (T8, p. 66)

(x को) (य की) याद आना (*v.i.*) (x) to miss (y) (T21, p. 207) (W15, 22 pp. 85, 124) (GR 18)

(x की) याद करना (*v.t.*) to remember (x) (W15, p. 85)

याद होना (*v.i.*) to remember (T18, p. 181)

याद रखना (*v.t.*) to keep in mind (W19, p. 110)

यार (*m*) friend, mate

यूनिवर्सिटी (*f*) university (T18, p. 173)

ये (*pro*) these/he/she/they (pl) (T2, p. 13) (GR 2, 4, 7)

योग्य (*adj*) worthy, qualified, able (T13, p. 113)

र

रंग (*m*) color (W19, 23 pp. 108, 130)

रक्षा (*f*) protection (T16, p. 148)

(x की) रक्षा करना (*v.t.*) to protect (x) (T16, p. 148)

रखना (*v.t.*) to put, place, keep (T8, p. 63) (W17, p. 98) (GR 19)

रजनीश (*m*) the moon, Rajneesh (name) (W11, p. 60)

रफ़्तार (*f*) speed, pace (T6, p. 42) (W22, p. 125)

रविवार (*m*) Sunday (T11, p. 87) (W6, p. 28) (GR 16)

रस (*m*) juice, essence, aesthetic relish, sentiment, pleasure (T15, p. 139)

रस्सी (*f*) rope (W8, p. 41)

रहना (*v.i.*) to live (T9, p. 67) (W9, p. 48) (GR 14, 22)

(x का) रहनेवाला होना (*v.i.*) to be a resident (of x) (T12, p. 99)

राजधानी (*f*) capital (T14, p. 120)

राजा (*m*) king (T7, p. 54) (W7, p. 35)

राज़ी (*adj*) willing, approving

राजीव चौक (*m*) Rajiv Chowk (square) (the new name for Connaught Place in Delhi) (T16, p. 143)

राज्य (*m*) kingdom, state, policy, rule (T6, p. 43)

रात (*f*) night (T9, p. 74) (W6, p. 28)

रात का खाना (*m*) dinner (T9, p. 74)

रात्रि (*f*) night (T8, p. 59)

रानी (*f*) queen (T13, p. 109)

राम राम Ram Ram (an orthodox Hindu greeting) (T7, p. 51)

राष्ट्र (*m*) nation (T6, p. 45) (W6, p. 25)

राह (*f*) way, path (W20, p. 115)

रिक्शा (*m*) rickshaw (T13, p. 105)

रिश्तेदार (*m*) relative (W14, p. 78)

रुई (*f*) cotton

रुकना (*v.i.*) to stop (T19, p. 164) (W24, p. 137)

रुपया (*m*) rupee, money (T2, p. 13)

रुपये (*m pl*) rupees (T13, p. 108) (W2, p. 8)

रुश्दी (*m*) Rushdie (name) (T20, p. 201)

रेडियो (*m*) radio (T23, p. 224)

रेल (*f*) railways, rail (T9, p. 70)

रेलगाड़ी (*f*) train (T13, p. 105) (W14, p. 78)

रोज़ (*adv + m*) daily, day (T3, p. 20) (W7, p. 35)

रोटी (*f*) roti, chapatti, Indian bread (T18, p. 169)

रोना (*v.i.*) to cry (T19, p. 191) (GR 19)

रौनक़ (*f*) color, gaiety, vibrancy (T16, p. 143)

ल

लंबा/लम्बा (*adj*) tall (T6, p. 46) (W19, p. 110)

लक्ष्य (*m*) aim, intention, objective (T23, p. 224)

लखनऊ (*m*) Lucknow (the capital of U.P.) (T16, p. 147) (W11, p. 60)

लगना (*v.i.*) to attach, to seem (T14, 17 pp. 131, 162) (W18, p. 104) (GR 17, 18)

लगभग (*adj*) approximately (T12, p. 103) (W13, p. 71)

लगाना (*v.t.*) to attach (T18, p. 172) (W10, p. 54)

लगातार (*adv + adj*) continuously, incessantly, constantly, continuous, continual (T11, p. 91)

लजाना (*v.i.*) to become shy, to be embarrassed, to blush (T19, p. 192)

लड़का (*m*) boy (T3, p. 20) (W3, p. 13)

लड़की (*f*) girl (T3, p. 20) (W3, p. 13)

लड़ना (*v.i. + v.t.*) to fight (T12, p. 102)

लड्डू (*m*) laddu, an Indian sweet (T6, p. 44)

लाई (*v.i.*) brought (T1, p. 5)

लाख (*m*) one hundred thousand (T16, p. 152) (GR 16)

लाजपत नगर (*m*) Lajpat Nagar (name of a neighborhood in Delhi) (T15, p. 132)

लाठी (*f*) stick (W8, p. 41)

लाना (*v.i.*) to bring (T12, p. 102) (W8, 16, 17, 20 pp. 41, 91, 97, 114)

लॉबी (*f*) lobby (W7, p. 35)

लायक़ (*adj*) worthy, capable, able (T13, p. 110) (W13, p. 71)

लाल (*adj*) red (T3, p. 21) (W1, p. 3)

लाल क़िला (*m*) Red Fort (T13, p. 114)

लाहौर (*m*) Lahore (T20, p. 204)

लिखना (*v.t.*) to write (T8, p. 65) (W9, p. 48)

लिपि (*f*) script (T18, p. 172)

लिफ़ाफ़ा (*m*) envelope (W7, p. 35)

लूटना (*v.t.*) to loot, plunder (T19, p. 193)

ले आना (*v.i.*) to bring (T15, p. 141) (GR 15)

ले जाना (*v.i.*) to take away (T15, p. 141) (W11, p. 60) (GR 15)

लेकिन (*conj*) but (T4, p. 29) (W4, p. 18)

लेख (*m*) article (T22, p. 218) (W17, p. 98)

लेखक (*m*) author (T22, p. 218) (W17, p. 98)

लेना (*v.t.*) to take, to accept, to borrow, to buy (T8, p. 62) (W8, 11 pp. 41, 60) (GR 19)

लोग (*m pl*) people (T4, p. 26) (W4, p. 18)

लोटा (*m*) a small round metal utensil for the household (T14, p. 127)

लोदी गार्डन (*m*) Lodi Garden (name of a popular garden in South Delhi with tombs from the Lodi and Sayyid period, 15th–16th centuries) (T15, p. 132)

लौकी (*f*) gourd (T18, p. 169)

व

व (*conj*) and (T1, p. 5)

वकालत (*f*) advocacy (W10, p. 54)

वक़्त (*m*) time (T11, p. 92) (W13, 18 pp. 71, 103) (GR 24)

वगैरह etcetera (W19, p. 110)

वन (*m*) forest (W1, p. 3)

वर्मा Varma/Verma (name) (T10, p. 81)

वर्ष (*m*) year (T11, p. 92) (W10, p. 54)

वर्षा (*f*) rain (T6, p. 46)

वसंत (*m*) spring (season) (T10, p. 78)

वस्तु (*f*) thing (W8, p. 41)

वह (*pro*) he/she/that/it (far from the speaker) (T1, p. 6) (W1, p. 3) (GR 2, 4, 7)

वह तो है। That's true. (T14, p. 129)

वहाँ (*adv*) (over) there (T5, p. 36) (W3, p. 13) (GR 23)

वहीं (*adv*) right (over) there, only there (वहाँ + ही) (T14, p. 128) (GR 14)

वही (*pro*) only he/she, that very (person/thing) (वह + ही) (T14, p. 128) (GR 14)

वाँ (*adj*) a suffix added to most cardinal numbers to create ordinals (T16, p. 152) (GR 16)

वाक्य (*m*) a sentence (W1, p. 3)

वापस आना (*v.i.*) to return, come back (T17, p. 161)

वापस करना (*v.t.*) to return, to give back

वापस जाना (*v.i.*) to return, to go back (T9, p. 74) (W16, 19 pp. 91, 109)

(x से) वार्तालाप करना (*v.t.*) to converse (with x) (T16, p. 154) (GR 16)

वाला (*adj*) a suffix denoting an agent, doer, owner, possessor, keeper or inhabitant (T1, p. 5) (W12, p. 65) (GR 20)

वालैकुम अस्सलाम And peace be upon you! (a return greeting, see अस्सलाम अलैकुम) (T7, p. 51)

विकल्प (*m*) alternative, option (W20, p. 115)

विकसित होना (*v.i.*) to become developed (T23, p. 222)

विख्यात (*adj*) renowned, well-known, famous (T6, p. 43)

विचार (*m*) thought, idea (T13, p. 109) (W11, 16 pp. 60, 91)

विज्ञान (*m*) science (T11, p. 86) (W6, p. 26)

विदेश (*m*) foreign country (T13, p. 119)

विद्या (*f*) knowledge, learning, education, science (T6, p. 45)

विद्यार्थी (*m*) student (T15, p. 132) (W20, p. 115)

विवश (*adj*) compelled, helpless

विशेष (*adj*) special

विश्वविद्यालय (*m*) university (T9, p. 73) (W9, p. 48)

विश्वास (*m*) belief, confidence, trust, faith, reliance (T13, p. 113)

विश्वास करना (*v.t.*) to believe, to trust (T13, p. 113)

विश्वास होना (*v.i.*) belief to occur, trust to occur

विषय (*m*) subject, topic, matter (T12, p. 104)

वीकेंड (*m*) weekend (T15, p. 132)

वे (*pro*) they/those/he/she (T2, p. 14) (GR 2, 4, 7)

वैवाहिक (*adj*) married, marital (T16, p. 148)

वैसा (*adj*) of that kind/nature, such as that, like that (T23, p. 224) (GR 23)

वैसे (*adv*) that way, in that manner, in the same manner (T7, p. 57) (GR 23)

व्यक्ति (*m*) individual (W6, p. 25)

व्यवहार (*m*) behavior, dealings, treatment, transaction (T6, p. 43)

व्याकरण (*m*) grammar (W15, p. 85)

व्यापार (*m*) business, trade (T6, p. 43)

श

शंकर (*m*) Shankar (name of Shiva) (T6, p. 43)

शक्कर/शकर (*m*) sugar (T6, p. 42)

शक्ल (*f*) countenance, face, shape, form, appearance (T17, p. 165)

शताब्दी (*f*) century (W12, p. 65)

शत्रु (*m*) enemy (T21, p. 210)

शनिवार/शनिश्चर (*m*) Saturday (T5, p. 33) (W6, p. 28) (GR 16)

शब्द (*m*) word (T6, p. 42)

शराब (*f*) alcohol, wine (T5, p. 33) (W9, p. 48)

शराब पीना (*v.t.*) to drink alcohol (T15, p. 133)

शरीफ़ (*adj*) noble, virtuous (T10, p. 81)

शर्बत/शरबत (*m*) sherbert (W15, p. 85)

शर्मिंदा (*adj*) embarrassed (W23, p. 130)

शहर (*m*) city (T10, p. 82) (W13, p. 71)

शांत (*adj*) peaceful, tranquil (T24, p. 236)

शांति (*f*) peace (T7, p. 57) (W7, 18 pp. 35, 103)

शादी (*f*) wedding, marriage (W13, 23 pp. 71, 129)

(x से) शादी करना (*v.t.*) to marry (x) (W20, p. 115)

शानदार (*adj*) grand, glorious (T15, p. 140) (W15, 21 pp. 85, 119)

शाम (*f*) evening (T11, p. 93)

शायद (*conj*) perhaps (T11, p. 90) (W11, p. 60)

शाहजहाँ (*m*) Shah Jahan (name of a 17th century Mughal emperor) (T23, p. 222)

शाह रुख़ ख़ान (*m*) Shah Rukh Khan (name of an actor) (T12, p. 103)

शिक्षक (*m*) teacher (T17, p. 162) (W13, p. 71)

शिक्षिका (*f*) teacher (W15, p. 85)

शिष्य (*m*) disciple (T6, p. 43)

शिष्या (*f*) female disciple (T14, p. 127)

शुक्रवार (*m*) Friday (T10, p. 76) (W6, p. 28) (GR 16)

शुक्रिया (*m*) thank you (W6, p. 28)

शुद्ध (*adj*) pure, unadulterated (T6, p. 45)

शुद्ध शाकाहारी (*adj*) pure vegetarian (T18, p. 169)

शुभ (*adj + m*) auspicious, good; well-being (T16, p. 148)

शुरुआत (*f*) beginning, commencement

शुरू (*m*) beginning, commencement (T5, p. 33)

शुरू करना (*v.t.*) to begin (W19, p. 110)

शुरू होना (*v.i.*) to begin (T18, p. 179)

शून्य (*adj*) empty, void, vacant; (*m*) zero, void (W6, p. 25)

शृंगार (*m*) beautification, adornment, love, the erotic sentiment (T6, p. 45)

शेर (*m*) lion, tiger, a couplet (T10, p. 78)

शौक़ (*m*) interest, hobby (W13, p. 71)

(x को) (y का) शौक़ होना (*v.i.*) (x) to have the interest/ hobby (of y) (T22, p. 215)

श्री (*adj*) an honorific adjective prefixed to male names; Mr.; (*f*) Lakshmi (the goddess of wealth) (T6, p. 46)

स

संकोच (*m*) hesitation (W24, p. 137)

संगम (*m*) confluence (W10, p. 54)

संगीत (*m*) music (T19, p. 192) (W11, p. 60)

संजीव (*m*) Sanjeev (name) (T6, p. 49)

संजय (*m*) Sanjay (name) (T6, p. 43)

संत (*m*) saint (T6, p. 44)

संतरा (*m*) mandarin, orange (T7, p. 57) (W7, p. 35)

संबंध (*m*) relation, association, connection, relationship

संभव (*adj*) possible (T16, p. 146) (W16, p. 91) (GR 16)

संभालना (*v.t.*) to steady, maintain, take care of (W24, p. 137)

संवाददाता (*m*) correspondent (W7, p. 35) (GR 7)

संस्कृत (*f + adj*) Sanskrit language; refined (W6, p. 25) (W21, p. 120)

संस्कृति (*f*) culture (T16, p. 155)

सकना (*v.i.*) to be able (T16, p. 146) (GR 17)

सच (*adj*) true (T16, p. 110) (W19, p. 110)

सचमुच (*adv*) really (T20, p.198) (W23, p. 130)

सच्चाई (*f*) truth (W18, p. 104)

सज़ा (*f*) punishment

सड़क (*f*) street (T17, p. 166)

सड़ना (*v.i.*) to decay, to decompose, to rot (T24, p. 236)

सताना (*v.t.*) to harass, torment, torture, trouble (T16, p. 148)

सत्तर (*adj*) seventy (T16, p. 151)

सत्ता (*f*) being, existence, power, sway, authority (T13, p. 108)

सत्ताईस (*adj*) twenty-seven (T16, p. 151)

सत्रह (*adj*) seventeen (T16, p. 151) (W10, p. 54)

सत्रहवाँ (*adj*) seventeenth (T17, p. 157) (GR 16)

सदा (*adv*) always, ever (T11, p. 91)

सन् (*m*) year (of the Christian calendar)

सफ़र करना (*v.t.*) to travel (T24, p. 234) (W17, p. 98)

सफल (*adj*) successful (W16, p. 91)

सफल होना (*v.i.*) to be successful (W17, p. 98)

सफलता (*f*) success (T23, p. 228)

सब (*adj*) all (T7, p. 50) (W6, p. 28)

सब कुछ (*pro*) everything (T10, p. 78)

सब लोग (*m*) all people (T7, p. 57)

सब्ज़ी (*f*) vegetable (T18, p. 170) (W12, p. 65)

सभी (*adj*) all (सब + ही) (T14, p. 128) (W8, p. 41) (GR 14)

सभ्य (*adj*) civilized (T6, p. 43)

(x की) समझ में आना (*v.i.*) (x) to understand (lit: to come into x's understanding) (W15, p. 85)

समझना (*v.i. + v.t.*) to regard, consider, understand (T6, p. 46) (W11, 23 pp. 60, 129) (T12)

समझाना (*v.t.*) to explain (T19, p. 191)

समय (*m*) time (T10, p. 78) (W15, 23 pp. 85, 129) (GR 24)

समस्या (*f*) problem (W11, p. 60)

समाज (*m*) society (W11, p. 60)

समोसा (*m*) samosa (T3, p. 21) (W8, p. 41)

सरकार (*f*) government (T22, p. 218) (W11, p. 60)

सरदर्द (*m*) headache (T12, p. 103)

सरस्वती (*f*) Sarasvati, name of a deity, river (W10, p. 54)

सर्जरी (*f*) surgery (T9, p. 74)

सर्दी (*f*) cold, a cold, winter (T6, p. 44)

सलवार कमीज़ (*f*) shalwar kameez (a loose fitting trouser and shirt) (T17, p. 160)

सवा (*adj, invar*) one-and-a-quarter (T3, p. 21) (GR 3, 16, 18)

सवाल (*m*) question (T11, p. 90) (W2, 11 pp. 8, 60)

सवेरा (*m*) morning (T11, p. 91) (W11, p. 60)

सस्ता (*adj*) cheap (T2, p. 13) (W2, p. 8)

सहस्र (*adj*) one thousand (T16, p. 152) (GR 16)

सहेली (*f*) female friend of a female (T14, p. 87)

साँस (*f*) breath/breathing (T19, p. 119)

सा (*adj*) "ish", like, similar to, resembling (a suffix) (T24, p. 230)

साइकिल (*f*) bicycle (T13, p. 105)

सागर (*m*) ocean (T22, p. 217)

साठ (*adj*) sixty (T16, p. 151)

साड़ी (*f*) sari (T8, p. 59) (W3, p. 13)

साढ़े (*adj*) plus one half (from three and one half onwards) (T16, p. 153) (GR 16, 18)

सात (*adj*) seven (T10, p. 76)

सातवाँ (*adj*) seventh (T7, p. 50) (GR 16)

साथ साथ (*adv*) together (T18, p. 180)

साधु (*m*) sadhu (T4, p. 26)

साफ़ (*adj*) clear, clean (T11, p. 89) (W10, p. 54)

साफ़-साफ़ कहना (*v.t.*) to say clearly (T24, p. 234)

सामने (*adv*) in front (T17, p. 167) (W2, p. 8)

सामान (*m*) goods, luggage, stuff (W2, p. 8) (W8, p. 41)

सारा (*adj*) entire (T12, p. 96) (W3, 22 pp. 13, 124)

सारे दिन (*adv*) the entire day (T10, p. 76)

साल (*m*) year (T6, p. 48) (W6, 10, 13 pp. 28, 54, 71)

सावधान (*adj*) vigilant, careful, alert, attentive

सावधान रहना (*v.i.*) to remain vigilant, careful (W19, p. 110)

साहब (*m*) sir, sahib (T7, p. 50) (W8, p. 41)

सिखाना (*v.t.*) to teach (T22, p. 214) (W9, p. 48)

सिगरेट (*f*) cigarette (T10, p. 78) (W10, p. 54)

सिगरेट पीना (*v.t.*) to smoke a cigarette (T10, p. 78) (W20, p. 115)

सितंबर (*m*) September (T16, p. 154)

सितार (*m*) sitar (T2, p. 14) (W2, p. 8)

सिनेमाहाल (*m*) movie theatre (T12, p. 95)

सिर (*m*) head (T10, p. 78) (W7, p. 35)

सिर पर होना (*v.i.*) to be on the head (to be imminent) (T24, p. 230) (W19, p. 110)

सी॰ पी॰ (कनॉट प्लेस) (*f*) C.P. (Connaught Place; now known as Rajiv Chowk after Rajiv Gandhi) (T16, p. 143)

सिर्फ़ (*adv*) only, just (W8, p. 41)

सीखना (*v.t.*) to learn (T9, p. 68)

सी॰ डी॰ (*f*) CD (T13, p. 113) (W11, p. 60)

सीधा (*adj*) straight, simple, right, erect

सीधे (*adv*) straight (direction) (W13, p. 71)

सुई (*f*) needle, hand of a watch (W13, p. 71)

सुखमय (*adj*) full of happiness (T16, p. 148)

सुनना (*v.t.*) to hear, listen (T13, p. 113) (W11, 13 pp. 60, 71)

सुनवाही (*f*) (court) hearing (W17, p. 98)

सुनसान (*adj*) desolate, empty (W23, p. 130)

सुनाना (*v.t.*) to tell, relate (T8, p. 63) (W10, 15 pp. 54, 85)

सुनीता (*f*) Sunita (name) (T2, p. 15) (W2, p. 8)

सुन्दर (*adj*) beautiful (T13, p. 118) (W8, p. 41)

सुबह (*f*) morning (T3, p. 20) (W6, 10 pp. 28, 54)

सुहावना (*adj*) charming (T5, p. 37)

सूँड़ (*f*) the trunk of an elephant (T13, p. 109)

सूचना (*f*) information (T15, p. 138)

सूर्य (*m*) sun

सूर्योदय (*m*) sunrise (T22, p. 217)

से (*pp*) from, since, by, with (T4, p. 29) (W6, 12 pp. 28, 65) (GR 16)

(x) से लेकर (y) तक from (x) until (y) (T19, p. 187)

(x) से पहले (*pp*) before (x) (T10, p. 83) (W17, p. 98)

सेना (*f*) army (T9, p. 70)

सेब (*m*) apple (T8, p. 65)

सेल (*m*) cell phone, mobile phone (T10, p. 83)

सेहत (*f*) health (T13, p. 111)

सैंतालीस (*adj*) forty-seven (T16, p. 151)

सैंतीस (*adj*) thirty-seven (T16, p. 151)

सैकड़ों (*adj*) hundreds (T16, p. 152) (GR 16)

सोचना (*v.t.*) to think (T3, p. 20) (W9, p. 48)

सोच में पड़ना (*v.i.*) to be deep in thought (W22, p. 125)

सोना (*v.i.*) to sleep (T10, exercise, p. 79) (W9, p. 48)

सोमवार (*m*) Monday (T9, p. 73) (W5, p. 23) (GR 16)

सोलह (*adj*) sixteen (T16, p. 151)

सोलहवाँ (*adj*) sixteenth (T16, p. 143) (GR 16)

सौ (*adj*) one hundred (T16, p. 151) (W7, p. 35) (GR 16)

स्कूल (*m*) school (T9, p. 70) (W5, p. 23)

स्टेशन (*m*) station (T20, p. 206) (W14, p. 78)

स्ट्यूडेंट (*m*) student (T15, p. 132)

स्त्री (*f*) woman (T19, p. 196)

स्थान (*m*) place, position (W6, p. 28)

स्थिति (*f*) situation, state (T20, p. 202)

स्वयं (*adv*) (by) oneself (T11, p. 85) (GR 11)

स्वर्ग (*m*) heaven (T10, p. 78)

स्वाद (*m*) taste (W24, p. 137)

ह

हँसना (*v.i.*) to laugh (T6, p. 47) (GR 19)

हज़ार (*adj*) one thousand (T16, p. 152) (W7, p. 35) (GR 16)

हज़ारों (*adj*) thousands (T16, p. 153) (GR 16)

हफ़्ता (*m*) week/Saturday (T11, p. 92) (W11, p. 60)

हम (*pro*) we (T2, p. 14) (GR 2, 4, 7)

हमने (*pro*) we हम + ने (T7, p. 53) (GR 7, 12)

हमारा (*adj*) our (T2, p. 14) (GR 2, 4)

हमीं (*pro*) we (emphatic), only we (हम + ही) (GR 14)

हमें/हमको (*pro*) oblique form of हम + को (T7, p. 53) (GR 7)

हमेशा (*adv*) always (T11, p. 86) (W9, p. 48)

हमेशा से (*adv*) (from) always (T18, p. 175)

हर (*adj*) all, every (T9, p. 72) (W9, 22 pp. 48, 124)

हर बार (*adv*) every time (T24, p. 230)

हरेक (*adj*) each (W7, p. 35)

हल्का (*adj*) light (not heavy), weak (W20, p. 115)

हवा (*f*) wind, air (T15, p. 139)

हवाई अड्डा (*m*) airport (T23, p. 222)

हवाई जहाज़ (*m*) airplane (T13, p. 105) (W18, p. 104)

हाँ (*adj*) yes (T2, p. 12) (W3, p. 13)

हाथ (*m*) hand, arm (T13, p. 109) (W14, p. 78)

हाथ-मुँह (*m pl*) hands and face (T15, p. 140)

हाथी (*m*) elephant (T13, p. 109)

हाय (*m*) hi! (a greeting) (W4, p. 18)

हाल (*m*) condition, state (W3, p. 13)

हालत (*f*) state, condition (T21, p. 212)

हिंदी/हिन्दी (*f*) the Hindi language (T6, p. 46)

हिन्दुस्तान/हिंदुस्तान (*m*) India (T3, p. 20) (W8, p. 41)

हिन्दुस्तानी/हिंदुस्तानी (*adj*) Indian (T3, p. 22) (W10, p. 54)

हिफ़ाज़त (*f*) protection, security, safety (T16, p. 148)

(x की) हिफ़ाज़त करना (*v.t.*) to protect (x) (T16, p. 148)

हिम्मत (*f*) courage (T23, p. 224) (W13, p. 71)

हिम्मत जुटाना (*v.t.*) to summon courage (W24, p. 137)

हिलाना (*v.t.*) to shake, wave (W14, p. 78)

हिस्सा (*m*) part, portion (T16, p. 153)

ही (*invar*) only, just; emphatic particle (T1, p. 5) (W5, 6 pp. 23, 28) (GR 14)

हीरालाल (*m*) Hiralal (name) (W9, p. 48)

हूँ (*v.i.*) am (verb *to be*) (T3, p. 20) (W3, p. 13) (GR 4)

हृदय (*m*) heart (T4, p. 26)

हे (*voc*) Hey! (T7, p. 55)

हैं (*v.i.*) is/are (*pl*) (T3, p. 22) (W2, p. 8) (GR 4)

है (*v.i.*) is/are (*s*) (T1, p. 5) (W1, p. 3) (GR 4)

हों (*v.i.*) may be (*pl*) (T16, p. 145) (GR 16)

हो (*v.i.*) are (*pl*); may be (*sing/pl*) (T4, p. 28) (GR 4, 16)

हो सकता है (it) could be, is possible (T16, p. 146) (GR 19)

होटल (*m*) hotel (W7, p. 35)

होना (*v.i.*) to be, become, occur, happen, take place, to exist (T3, p. 20)

होली (*f*) Holi (the Indian festival of colors) (T10, p. 78) (W19, p. 110)

होली खेलना (*v.t.*) to play (celebrate) Holi (W19, p. 110)

होशियार (*adj*) clever, sharp, intelligent, shrewd (T19, p. 195)

ह्रास (*m*) decay, fall, downfall (T6, p. 45)

English-Hindi Glossary

The information in the first set of parentheses provides the first occurrence of the word in the Textbook (T). The information in the second set provides the page number of the glossary or glossaries in which the word occurs in the Workbook (W). The final set of parentheses indicates the lesson in the Textbook in which any relevant grammatical information is located (GR).

(T1, p. 4) = Textbook, Lesson 1, p. 4

(W1, p. 3) = Workbook, Lesson 1 Glossary, p. 3

(GR 8) = Grammar, Textbook Lesson 8

A

आदत छोड़ना (*v.t.*) to abandon a habit

त्याग (*m*) abandonment, relinquishment (T6, p. 43)

क़ाबिल (*adj*) able, worthy, capable (T13, p. 113)

इस बारे में (*adv*) about this (T20, p. 202)

इस मामले में (*adv*) about (in) this matter (T13, p. 110)

(x) के बारे में (*pp*) about (x) (T13, p. 118) (W11, p. 60)

(x) के ऊपर (*pp*) above (x) (T19, p. 187)

बिलकुल (*adv*) absolutely (T7, p. 50) (W5, p. 23)

कर (*invar*) absolutive कर (T15, p. 140) (GR 15)

ए॰ सी॰ (*f*) A.C. (T19, p. 194)

मानना (*v.t.*) to accept, regard, respect (T1, p. 6) (W11, p. 60)

ख़ाता (*m*) an account, ledger (T20, p. 202)

पता (*m*) address, whereabouts (T2, p. 13) (W2, p. 8) (GR 18)

परीक्षा लेना (*v.t.*) to administer (give) an exam

फ़ायदा (*m*) advantage (T17, p. 159)

वकालत (*f*) advocacy (W10, p. 54)

एक घंटे बाद (*adv*) after an hour (T13, p. 110)

थोड़ी देर बाद (*adv*) after a little while (W19, p. 110)

दो हफ़्ते बाद (*adv*) after two weeks (W17, p. 98)

(x) के बाद (*pp*) after (x) (T8, p. 66) (W21, p. 120)

(x) के ख़िलाफ़ (*pp*) against (x) (T22, p. 218)

उम्र (*f*) age (T6, p. 48) (W10, p. 54)

ज़माना (*m*) age, period (W11, p. 60)

पहले (*adv*) ago, before, previously (T8, p. 61) (W10, 16, 17 pp. 54, 89, 97)

आगरा (*m*) Agra (name of a city in U.P.) (T13, p. 115)

आगे (*adv*) ahead, in front, before, in the future (T16, p. 155)

लक्ष्य (*m*) aim, intention, objective (T23, p. 224)

हवाई जहाज़ (*m*) airplane (T13, p. 105) (W18, p. 104)

हवाई अड्डा (*m*) airport (T23, p. 222)

काश (*voc*) Alas!; if only (T15, p. 134) (GR 15)

शराब (*f*) alcohol, wine (T5, p. 33) (W9, p. 48)

अली Ali (name) (T1, p. 5)

ज़िंदा (*adj, invar*) alive (T3, p. 21) (GR 3)

सभी (*adj*) all (सब + ही) (T14, p. 128) (W8, p. 41) (GR 14)

सब (*adj*) all (T7, p. 50) (W6, p. 28)

हर (*adj*) all, every (T9, p. 72) (W9, 22 pp. 48, 124)

चारों (*adj*) all four (T16, p. 153)

तरह-तरह (*adv*) all manner of (W24, p. 137)

सब लोग (*m*) all people (T7, p. 57)

तीनों (*adj*) all three (T12, p. 99) (GR 16)

अल्लाह (*m*) Allah, God (T16, p. 146)

इलाहाबाद (*m*) Allahabad (name of a city in U.P.) (T4, p. 29) (W2, p. 8)

अल्मोड़ा (*m*) Almora (name of a town in the foothills of the Himalayas) (T24, p. 234)

अकेला (*adj*) alone (W22, p. 125)

अकेले (*adv*) alone (W23, p. 130)

भी (*part*) also, even, too (T13, p. 114) (W8, p. 41) (GR 14)

विकल्प (*m*) alternative, option (W20, p. 115)

हमेशा (*adv*) always (T11, p. 86) (W9, p. 48)

सदा (*adv*) always, ever (T11, p. 91)

हमेशा से (*adv*) (from) always (T18, p. 175)

हूँ (*v.i.*) am (verb *to be*) (T3, p. 20) (W3, p. 13) (GR 4)

अमरिका (*m*) America (T4, p. 29)

अमरीकी (*adj*) American (T3, p. 22)

अमिताव घोष (*m*) Amitav Ghosh (name of a famous Indian author) (T12, p. 103)

(x) के बीच में (*pp*) amongst (x) (T22, p. 215) (W17, p. 98)

व (*conj*) and (T1, p. 5)

और (*adj/adv/conj*) and, more (T3, p. 20) (W7, p. 35)

वालैकुम अस्सलाम And peace be upon you! (a return greeting, see अस्सलाम अलैकुम Peace...) (T7, p. 51)

गुस्सा (*m*) anger, rage, fury (T17, p. 159)

जानवर (*m*) animal (W15, p. 85)

अनोखी (*f*) Anokhi (name of a popular clothing store in Khan Market) (अनोखा (*adj*) unique, peculiar) (T17, p. 160)

जवाब (*m*) answer (T18, p. 172)

जवाब देना (*v.t.*) to answer (W13, p. 71)

कोई भी (*pro*) anyone at all (T15, p. 137) (GR 14, 15)

कुछ भी (*pro*) anything at all (T15, p. 137) (GR 14, 15)

कहीं और (*adv*) anywhere/somewhere else (T23, p. 227)

फ़्लैट (*m*) apartment, flat (T20, p. 204)

मनाना (*v.t.*) to appease, to celebrate, to persuade (W15, 19 pp. 85, 109)

सेब (*m*) apple (T8, p. 65)

मन लगाना (*v.t.*) to apply oneself (W23, p. 130)

पसंद (*adj + f*) approved, liked; liking, choice, taste, preference (T18, p. 170)

लगभग (*adj*) approximately (T12, p. 103) (W13, p. 71)

तक़रीबन (*adv*) approximately (T15, p. 138)

अप्पू (*m*) Appu (name) (T11, p. 88)

अप्रैल (*m*) April (month) (T16, p. 154)

हो (*v.i.*) are (*pl*); may be (*sing/pl*) (T4, p. 28) (GR 4, 16)

इलाक़ा (*m*) area, locality, territory (T14, p. 120)

फ़ौज (*f*) army (T21, p. 210)

सेना (*f*) army (T9, p. 70)

(x) के आसपास (*pp*) around, nearly (x) (T19, p. 194)

(x का) इंतज़ाम करना (*v.t.*) to arrange (x) (T13, p. 113)

इंतज़ाम (*m*) arrangement (T13, p. 113)

गिरफ़्तार (*adj*) arrested, seized (W21, p. 120)

पहुँचना (*v.i.*) to arrive (T9, p. 72) (W9, 17 pp. 48, 97)

कला (*f*) art (T1, p. 5)

लेख (*m*) article (T22, p. 218) (W17, p. 98)

जैसे (*rel adv*) as, like, such as, for instance (T23, p. 225) (GR 23)

जितना (*rel adj*) as many, much (T23, p. 225) (GR 23)

आसफ़ुद्दौला (*m*) Asaf-ud-Daula (name) (W12, p. 65)

आश्रम (*m*) ashram (hermitage) (T6, p. 46)

एशिया (*m*) Asia (T19, p. 196)

(x से) पूछना (*v.t.*) to ask (x) (T12, p. 101) (W11, p. 60) (GR 16)

घर में at home (T7, p. 54) (W5, 6 pp. 23, 28)

कम से कम (*adj*) at least (T17, p. 164)

मज़े में (*adv*) at perfect ease (T5, p. 37) (W3, p. 13)

छै बजे (*adv*) at six o'clock (T10, p. 76) (W10, 12, 17 pp. 54, 65, 97)

तीन बजे (*adv*) at three o'clock (W14, p. 78)

दो बजे (*adv*) at two o'clock (T11, p. 93) (W14, p. 78)

किस समय (*inter*) at what time (T20, p. 198)

कितने बजे (*adv*) at what time (T10, p. 76) (W12, p. 65)

(x) के यहाँ (*pp*) at (x)'s place (T20, p. 198) (W17, p. 98)

माहौल (*m*) atmosphere (T23, p. 229) (W10, p. 54)

लगाना (*v.t.*) to attach (T18, p. 172) (W10, p. 54)

लगना (*v.i.*) to attach, to seem (T14, 17 pp. 131, 162) (W18, p. 104) (GR 17, 18)

ध्यान (*m*) attention, meditation, heed, contemplation (T6, p. 43) (W15, p. 85)

अगस्त (*m*) August (T16, p. 154)

मंगलमय (*adj*) auspicious (T16, p. 148)

मुबारक (*adj*) auspicious, blessed, fortunate (T16, p. 147)

शुभ (*adj + m*) auspicious, good; well-being (T16, p. 148)

ऑस्ट्रेलिया (*m*) Australia (T8, p. 61)

ऑस्ट्रेलियन (*adj*) Australian (T10, p. 77)

लेखक (*m*) author (T22, p. 218) (W17, p. 98)

ऑटो(रिक्शा) (*m*) auto(rickshaw) (T13, p. 105)

अय्यर (*m*) Ayyar (name) (T6, p. 43)

B

पीछे (*adv*) back, behind, after

ख़राब (*adj*) bad (off), broken (T5, p. 37) (W3, p. 13)

बुरा (*adj*) bad (T18, p. 174) (W11, p. 60)

बद (*adj*) bad, wicked, vile, depraved (T19, p. 197)

थैला (*m*) bag

बस्ता (*m*) (school) bag (W10, 23 pp. 54, 129)

थैली (*f*) bag, small bag, pouch (T14, p. 127)

छज्जा (*m*) balcony, terrace (T6, p. 43)

डाकू (*m*) bandit, dacoit (T19, p. 193)

चूड़ी (*f*) bangle (W4, p. 18) (GR 8)

बैंक (*m*) bank (T11, p. 85)

बरगद (*m*) banyan tree (T11, p. 88)

बड़ा इमामबाड़ा (*m*) Bara Imambara (one of the famous historical buildings in Lucknow) (W12, p. 65)

नाई (*m*) barber (T1, p. 5)

बरिस्ता (*m*) Barista (a chain of coffee shops) (T21, p. 207)

नहाना (*v.i. + v.t.*) to bathe (T10, p. 76) (W10, p. 54)

नहलाना (*v.t.*) to bathe (someone) (W10, p. 54)

ग़ुसलख़ाना (*m*) bathroom (W7, p. 35)

हों (*v.i.*) may be (*pl*) (T16, p. 145) (GR 16)

होना (*v.i.*) to be, become, occur, happen, take place, to exist (T3, p. 20)

(x का) रहनेवाला होना (*v.i.*) to be a resident (of x) (T12, p. 99)

सकना (*v.i.*) to be able (T16, p. 146) (GR 17)

(x को) फ़ायदा होना (*v.i.*) (x) to be advantaged

(x से) डरना (*v.i.*) to be afraid (of x) (T12, p. 102) (GR 12)

(x को) ताज्जुब होना (*v.i.*) (x) to be amazed (GR 18)

बंद होना (*v.i.*) to be closed, turned off (T15, p. 135)

पूरा होना (*v.i.*) to be completed (W19, p. 110)

कटना (*v.i.*) to be cut (T21, p. 211)

सोच में पड़ना (*v.i.*) to be deep in thought (W22, p. 125)

मिटना (*v.i.*) to be effaced, erased (W15, p. 85)

भरना (*v.i. + v.t.*) to be filled, to fill (T19, p. 185)

ख़त्म होना (*v.i.*) to be finished (T22, p. 218) (W16, p. 91)

चुकना (*v.i.*) to be finished, spent, exhausted, completed, paid off (used as a compound verb to give a sense of already having done an activity) (T19, p. 184) (GR 19)

ठीक होना (*v.i.*) to be fixed, be okay, appropriate

(x से) पिंड छूटना (*v.i.*) to be freed (from x) (W21, p. 120)

(x को) ख़ुशी होना (*v.i.*) (x) to be happy, happiness to occur (to x) (T17, p. 165) (GR 18)

बढ़ना (*v.i.*) to be increased, to grow (T23, p. 222) (W22, p. 125)

(x को) देर होना (*v.i.*) (x) to be late (T21, p. 207) (W23, p. 130) (GR 18)

बनना (*v.i.*) to be made (T11, p. 90) (W11, p. 60) (GR 22)

घबराना (*v.i.*) to be nervous, anxious (W24, p. 137)

सिर पर होना (*v.i.*) to be on the head (to be imminent) (T24, p. 230) (W19, p. 110)

तैयार होना (*v.i.*) to be prepared (T13, p. 113) (W8, p. 41)

छपना (*v.i.*) to be printed or stamped, to be published (W17, p. 98)

पैदा होना (*v.i.*) to be produced, to be born (T12, p. 99)

चुप होना (*v.i.*) to be silent

बजना (*v.i.*) to be struck, strike (T11, p. 93) (W18, p. 104) (GR 18)

सफल होना (*v.i.*) to be successful (W17, p. 98)

बँधना (*v.i.*) to be tied, to be fastened, to be bound (T21, p. 211)

(x को) प्यास लगना (*v.i.*) (x) to be thirsty (T18, p. 174) (GR 18)

(x को) थकान होना (*v.i.*) (x) to be/become tired (T22, p. 220) (GR 18)

(x को) दिखना (*v.i.*) to be visible (to x) (W10, p. 54)

(x को) दिखाई देना (*v.i.*) to be visible (to x) (W14, p. 78)

धुलना (*v.i.*) to be washed

परेशान होना (*v.i.*) to be worried

मारना (*v.t.*) to beat, strike, kill (T19, p. 192)

भालू (*m*) bear (W7, p. 35) (GR 7)

श्रृंगार (*m*) beautification, adornment, love, the erotic sentiment (T6, p. 45)

सुन्दर (*adj*) beautiful (T13, p. 118) (W8, p. 41)

ख़ूबसूरत (*adj*) beautiful (T5, p. 36) (W3, p. 13)

क्योंकि (*conj*) because (T7, p. 50)

ग़ुस्सा होना (*v.i.*) to become angry (T17, p. 159)

(x को) ग़ुस्सा आना (*v.i.*) (x) to become angry (T18, p. 172) (W18, p. 104) (GR 18)

बोर होना (*v.i.*) to become bored (T15, p. 142)

पागल होना (*v.i.*) to become crazy (T20, p. 201)

विकसित होना (*v.i.*) to become developed (T23, p. 222)

(x को) चोट लगना (*m*) (x) to become injured (T18, p. 174) (GR 18)

खो जाना (*v.i.*) to become lost (W24, p. 137) (GR 19)

लजाना (*v.i.*) to become shy, to be embarrassed, to blush (T19, p. 192)

चौंकना (*v.i.*) to become startled, alarmed (T19, p. 192)

थक जाना (*v.i.*) to become tired (T22, p. 220)

थकना (*v.i.*) to become tired, fatigued

पलंग (*m*) bed (W7, p. 35)

बिस्तर (*m*) bedding, bed (W22, p. 125)

(x) से पहले (*pp*) before (x) (T10, p. 83) (W17, pp. 98)

(x) के/से पहले (*pp*) before (x) (W17, p. 98)

भिखारी (*m*) beggar (W22, p. 125)

शुरू होना (*v.i.*) to begin (T18, p. 179)

शुरू करना (*v.t.*) to begin (W19, p. 110)

शुरुआत (*f*) beginning, commencement

शुरू (*m*) beginning, commencement (T5, p. 33)

व्यवहार (*m*) behavior, dealings, treatment, transaction (T6, p. 43)

सत्ता (*f*) being, existence, power, sway, authority (T13, p. 108)

विश्वास (*m*) belief, confidence, trust, faith, reliance (T13, p. 113)

विश्वास होना (*v.i.*) belief to occur, trust to occur

विश्वास करना (*v.t.*) to believe, to trust (T13, p. 113)

प्रियतम (*adj*) beloved, dearest (T21, p. 212)

(x) के नीचे (*pp*) beneath (x) (W10, p. 54)

नीचे (*adv*) beneath, below (T20, p. 204)

बंगला (*f*) Bengali language (W15, p. 85)

बंगाली मार्केट (*m*) Bengali Market (L13, p. 114)

पान (*m*) betel leaf (T1, p. 8) (W1, p. 3)

साइकिल (*f*) bicycle (T13, p. 105)

बड़ा (*adj*) big (T3, p. 22) (W3, p. 13)

अरब (*adj*) a billion; (*m*) Arab (T16, p. 152)

जीव-विज्ञान (*m*) biology (T11, p. 86)

बाइओलॉजी (*f*) biology (T11, p. 86)

चिड़िया (*f*) bird (T8, p. 59)

जन्मदिन (*m*) birthday (T7, p. 50) (W9, p. 48)

करेला (*m*) bitter gourd (T18, p. 169)

कंबल (*m*) blanket (T6, p. 44)

अंधा (*adj*) blind, irrational, unenlightened (T13, p. 108)

खून (*m*) blood (W21, p. 120)

नीला (*adj*) blue (T3, p. 22) (W1, p. 3)

नाव (*f*) boat (T1, p. 6)

बंबई/बम्बई (*f*) Bombay (T8, p. 61) (W10, 19 pp. 54, 109)

किताब (*f*) book (T2, p. 13) (W2, p. 8)

पुस्तक (*f*) book (T6, p. 43)

पैदा (*adj, invar*) born (T3, p. 21) (GR 3)

दोनों (*adj*) both (T7, p. 50) (W9, p. 48) (GR 16)

तकलीफ़ उठाना (*v.t.*) to bother, to trouble (T16, p. 147)

बोतल (*f*) bottle (T15, p. 137) (W3, p. 13)

लड़का (*m*) boy (T3, p. 20) (W3, p. 13)

ब्राह्मण (*m*) Brahmin (T6, p. 46)

टूटना (*v.i.*) to break, to be broken, to be fractured (T21, p. 211)

तोड़ना (*v.t.*) to break, to fracture (T21, p. 211) (W9, p. 48)

साँस (*f*) breath/breathing (T19, p. 119)

दुल्हन (*f*) bride (T19, p. 192)

दूल्हा (*m*) bridegroom

लाना (*v.t.*) to bring (T12, p. 102) (W8, 16, 17, 20 pp. 41, 89, 97, 114)

ले आना (*v.i.*) to bring (T15, p. 141) (GR 15)

भाई (*m*) brother (T5, p. 33) (W6, p. 28)

भैया (*m*) brother (affectionate term) (T18, p. 180)

भई (*m*) brother, friend (W11, p. 60)

भाई-बहन (*m pl*) brothers and sisters, siblings (T8, p. 61) (W6, p. 28)

लाई (*v.i.*) brought (T1, p. 5)

बौद्ध धर्म (*m*) Buddhism (Buddhist religion) (T18, p. 173)

बग्घी (*f*) buggy (T6, p. 43)

इमारत (*f*) building (T2, p. 13) (W12, p. 65)

बोझ (*m*) burden (W16, p. 91)

व्यापार (*m*) business, trade (T6, p. 43)

किंतु (*conj*) but (T15, p. 139)

मगर (*conj*) but (T15, p. 139)

लेकिन (*conj*) but (T4, p. 29) (W4, p. 18)

परंतु (*conj*) but, however (T15, p. 139)

ख़रीदना (*v.t.*) to buy (T3, p. 20) (W12, p. 65)

इत्तफ़ाक़ से (*adv*) by chance (T17, p. 166)

पैदल (*adv*) on foot (T13, p. 105)

(x) के हाथों (*pp*) by the hand(s) of (x) (T21, p. 209)

द्वारा (*pp*) by, through, through the medium of (T21, p. 209) (GR 21)

C

बुलाना (*v.t.*) to call, invite (T10, p. 84) (W15, p. 85)

(x को) (y) कहना (*v.t.*) to call (x) (y) (T14, p. 120)

पुकारना (*v.t.*) to call (out) (W24, p. 137)

नामक (*adj*) called (W12, p. 65)

ऊँट (*m*) camel (T6, p. 47)

कैंसर (*m*) cancer (T10, p. 78)

राजधानी (*f*) capital (T14, p. 120)

गाड़ी (*f*) car, vehicle, train (T6, p. 48) (W9, p. 48)

गोभी (*f*) cauliflower (T14, p. 127)

बनवाना (*v.t.*) to cause to be built (T10, p. 76) (W12, p. 65)

पिलाना (*v.t.*) to cause to drink, to serve (T13, p. 110) (W9, p. 48)

पहनाना (*v.t.*) to cause to wear, to dress (someone)

सी॰ डी॰ (*f*) CD (T13, p. 113) (W11, p. 60)

सेल (*m*) cell phone, mobile phone (T10, p. 83)

शताब्दी (*f*) century (W12, p. 65)

ज़रूर (*adv*) certainly (T3, p. 20) (W7, 16 pp. 35, 89)

नहीं तो (*adv*) certainly not, otherwise (W16, p. 91)

कुर्सी/कुरसी (*f*) chair (T12, p. 100) (W13, p. 71)

बदलना (*v.i. + v.t.*) to change (T12, p. 102) (W11, 22 pp. 60, 124)

पात्र (*m*) character (in a play) (W6, p. 28)

सुहावना (*adj*) charming (T5, p. 37)

भगाना (*v.t.*) to chase away

सस्ता (*adj*) cheap (T2, p. 13) (W2, p. 8)

मुर्गी (*f*) chicken (T18, p. 167)

बच्चा (*m*) child (T6, p. 43) (W17, p. 98)

बचपन (*m*) childhood (T11, p. 88) (W10, p. 54)

चीन (*m*) China (T18, p. 173)

परचा (*m*) chit, note, prescription (W21, p. 120)

सिगरेट (*f*) cigarette (T10, p. 78) (W10, p. 54)

चक्कर (*m*) circle, revolution, rotation (W22, p. 125)

शहर (*m*) city (T10, p. 82) (W13, p. 71)

सभ्य (*adj*) civilized (T6, p. 43)

क्लास (*m/f*) class (T10, p. 76) (W5, p. 23) (GR 7)

कक्षा (*f*) class (T6, p. 46) (W10, p. 54)

जमात (*f*) class (W12, p. 65)

साफ़ (*adj*) clear, clean (T11, p. 89) (W10, p. 54)

होशियार (*adj*) clever, sharp, intelligent, shrewd (T19, p. 195)

नज़दीक (*adv*) close, near (T15, p. 132)

(x) के क़रीब (*pp*) close to (x) (T22, p. 215)

बंद (*adj*) closed, off (L15, p. 135)

कपड़ा (*m*) cloth (T16, p. 144) (W7, p. 35)

कपड़े (*m*) clothes (T15, p. 140)

कोट (*m*) coat (T15, p. 140)

मोची (*m*) cobbler (W17, p. 98)

कॉफ़ी (*f*) coffee (T10, p. 83) (W6, 7 pp. 28, 35)

ठंडा (*adj*) cold (T6, p. 46) (W8, p. 41)

ठंड (*f*) cold (T6, p. 44) (W14, p. 78)

सर्दी (*f*) cold, a cold, winter (T6, p. 44)

जाड़ा (*m*) cold, winter (T19, p. 187)

जुकाम (*m*) cold (T13, p. 109)

(x को) जुकाम होना (*v.i.*) a cold to occur (to x) (T13, p. 109) (GR 18)

इकट्ठा करना (*v.t.*) to collect, gather (T23, p. 226)

इकट्ठा (*adj*) collected, gathered (T23, p. 226)

कॉलेज (*m*) college (T9, p. 70) (W5, p. 23)

रंग (*m*) color (W19, 23 pp. 108, 130)

रौनक़ (*f*) color, gaiety, vibrancy (T16, p. 143)

गुलाल (*m*) colored powder thrown at the time of Holi (W19, p. 110)

कंघी (*f*) comb (T6, p. 43)

आना (*v.i.*) to come (T1, p. 5) (W9, p. 48) (GR 22)

आओ (*v.i.*) come (imperative form with तुम) (W4, p. 18)

आराम से (*adv*) comfortably (T14, p. 126)

आज्ञा (*f*) command, order (W8, p. 41)

विवश (*adj*) compelled, helpless

पूरा (*adj*) complete (L16, p. 148) (W3, 15 pp. 13, 85)

पूरा करना (*v.t.*) to complete (T16, p. 148) (W13, p. 71)

(x पर) ध्यान देना (*v.t.*) to concentrate (on x) (T24, p. 230)

कॉनसर्ट (*m*) concert (W11, p. 60)

इत्तफ़ाक़ (*m*) concurrence, agreement, coincidence, assent, consent (T17, p. 166)

हाल (*m*) condition, state (W3, p. 13)

संगम (*m*) confluence (W10, p. 54)

महाद्वीप (*m*) continent (T19, p. 196)

निरंतर (*adv*) continuous, uninterrupted, incessant (T11, p. 91)

लगातार (*adv + adj*) continuously, incessantly, constantly, continuous, continual (T11, p. 91)

(x की) बात (y से) होना (*v.i.*) (x's) conversation/talk/ matter to happen (with y) (T14, p. 123) (W12, p. 65) (GR 16)

(x से) वार्तालाप करना (*v.t.*) to converse (with x) (T16, p. 154) (GR 16)

(x से) बातचीत करना (*v.t.*) to converse (with x) (T16, p. 154) (W11, p. 60) (GR 16)

बावर्ची (*m*) cook (W21, p. 120)

पकाना (*v.t.*) to cook (T16, p. 147)

संवाददाता (*m*) correspondent (W7, p. 35) (GR 7)

भाव (*m*) cost, price; emotion, sentiment (T17, p. 160)

रुई (*f*) cotton

खाँसी (*f*) cough (W10, 21 pp. 54, 119)

हो सकता है (it) could be, is possible (T16, p. 146) (GR 19)

शक्ल (*f*) countenance, face, shape, form, appearance (T17, p. 165)

देश (*m*) country (T5, p. 33) (W6, 11 pp. 28, 60)

हिम्मत (*f*) courage (T23, p. 224) (W13, p. 71)

बहादुर (*adj*) courageous (T21, p. 209)

पाठ्यपुस्तक (*f*) course book (T6, p. 44)

कचहरी (*f*) court (W17, p. 98)

दरबार (*m*) (royal) court (T15, p. 140)

आँगन (*m*) courtyard (W8, p. 41)

जिल्द (*f*) cover, binding (W20, 23, pp. 115, 129)

ओढ़ना (*v.t.*) to cover, drape, wrap (one's own body) (T15, p. 140)

सी० पी० (कनॉट प्लेस) (*f*) C.P. (Connaught Place; now known as Rajiv Chowk after Rajiv Gandhi) (T16, p. 143)

पागल (*adj*) crazy (T20, p. 201)

भीड़ (*f*) crowd (T20, p. 206)

रोना (*v.i.*) to cry (T19, p. 191) (GR 19)

संस्कृति (*f*) culture (T16, p. 155)

तहज़ीब (*f*) culture (W15, p. 85)

प्याली (*f*) cup

कप (*m*) cup (T24, p. 235)

प्याला (*m*) cup (W15, p. 85)

पर्दा (*m*) curtain, screen, veil (T19, p. 192)

ग्राहक/गाहक (*m*) customer, client (T6, p. 45)

काटना (*v.t.*) to cut, to chop, to bite (T21, p. 211)

D

दिनचर्या (*f*) daily routine (T12, p. 95)

रोज़ (*adv + m*) daily; day (T3, p. 20) (W7, p. 35)

नाच (*m*) dance (W10, p. 54)

नाचना (*v.i.*) to dance

दरियागंज (*m*) Dariyaganj (name of a neighborhood of Delhi) (T14, p. 130)

अंधेरा (*adj*) dark (T24, p. 235) (W22, p. 125)

दशरथ (*m*) Dasharath (name of Lord Ram's father) (T13, p. 109)

तारीख़ (*f*) date, history (T3, p. 20) (W3, p. 13)

दिन (*m*) day (T10, p. 76) (W5, p. 23)

दिन-ब-दिन (*adv*) day after day (W22, p. 125)

परसों (*adv*) the day before yesterday/after tomorrow (T11, p. 91) (W17, p. 98) (GR 11)

गर्मी के दिन (*m pl*) days of heat, summer (T19, p. 187)

"डी० डी० एल० जे०" *DDLJ* (दिलवाले दुल्हनिया ले जाएँगे) (*The One with the Heart Gets the Bride* — the title of a popular Hindi film) (T12, p. 103)

जान (*adj*) dear, beloved (T7, p. 50)

ह्रास (*m*) decay, fall, downfall (T6, p. 45)

सड़ना (*v.i.*) to decay, to decompose, to rot (T24, p. 236)

दिसंबर (*m*) December (month) (T16, p. 154)

तय करना (*v.t.*) to decide, settle (T19, p. 194)

(x का) निश्चय करना (*v.t.*) to decide (x) (T23, p. 226)

निश्चय (*m*) decision (T6, p. 45)

डिफ़ेंस कॉलनी (*f*) Defence Colony (name of a neighborhood in Delhi) (T14, p. 120)

डिग्री (*f*) degree (T19, p. 187)

देर (*f*) delay, lateness (T18, p. 173) (W11, 18 pp. 60, 103)

दिल्ली (*f*) Delhi (T3, p. 20)

डिलाइट (*m*) Delite (name of a cinema in Old Delhi) (T14, p. 130)

माँगना (*v.t.*) to demand (T4, p. 26)

छूटना (*v.i.*) to depart, be released (W20, p. 115)

उतरना (*v.i.*) to descend, come off (T22, p. 217) (W19, p. 110)

इच्छा (*f*) desire (T16, p. 147) (W8, 20 pp. 41, 114)

मर्ज़ी (*f*) desire, will

ख़्वाहिश (*m*) desire, wish (T16, p. 147) (GR 16)

सुनसान (*adj*) desolate, empty (W23, p. 130)

भक्त (*m*) devotee (T6, p. 45)

कीर्तन (*m*) devotional song (T17, p. 163)

मरना (*v.i.*) to die

फ़र्क़ (*m*) difference (T22, p. 214)

अलग (*adj*) different (T11, p. 89)

मुश्किल (*adj*) difficult; (*f*) difficulty (T13, p. 115)

कठिन (*adj*) difficult (T5, p. 33)

दिक़्क़त (*f*) difficulty (W15, p. 85)

तकलीफ़ (*f*) difficulty, bother, distress, trouble (T16, p. 147)

रात का खाना (*m*) dinner (T9, p. 73)

ओर (*f*) direction (T3, p. 20)

गंदा (*adj*) dirty, filthy, morbid (T8, p. 64)

ग़ायब होना (*v.i.*) to disappear (W24, p. 137)

शिष्य (*m*) disciple (T6, p. 43)

आटे दाल का भाव मालूम होना (*v.i.*) to discover a harsh truth (T18, p. 171)

दूर करना (*v.t.*) to dispel, to get rid of (W13, p. 71)

दिवाली/दीपावली (*f*) Diwali (a Hindu festival) (T16, p. 148) (W10, p. 54)

करना (*v.t.*) to do, to perform, to complete, to act, to execute (T8, p. 63) (GR 22)

पढ़ाई करना (*v.t.*) to do study (T9, p. 70)

क्या तुम लोगों को याद है? Do you people remember? (T8, p. 66)

डॉक्टर (*m*) doctor (T7, p. 52)

कुत्ता/कुत्ता (*m*) dog (T6, p. 43)

गुड़िया (*f*) doll (W8, p. 41)

डॉलर (*m*) dollar (T20, p. 202)

मत (*adv + m*) don't, not; opinion, view, vote (T8, p. 64) (W8, p. 41) (GR 8)

पता नहीं don't know

ऐसे मत बनो don't put on an act (T15, p. 141)

दरवाज़ा (*m*) door (T15, p. 139) (W11, 17 pp. 60, 97)

द्वार (*m*) door, doorway (T6, p. 45)

नाटक (*m*) drama, play (W10, 17 pp. 54, 97)

पीना (*v.t.*) to drink (T1, p. 5) (W9, p. 48)

शराब पीना (*v.t.*) to drink alcohol (T15, p. 133)

गाड़ी चलाना (*v.t.*) to drive a car/vehicle (T11, p. 86) (W15, p. 85)

डी० यू० (*f*) D.U. (Delhi University) (T14, p. 120)

डी० वी० डी० (*f*) D.V.D. (T15, p. 141)

E

हरेक (*adj*) each (W7, p. 35)

कान (*m*) ear (W1, p. 3)

पृथ्वी (*f*) the earth, world (T6, p. 43)

पूर्व (*m*) east (T23, p. 222)

आसान (*adj*) easy (W3, p. 13)

खाना (*v.t.*) to eat (T3, p. 20) (W8, p. 41)

नाश्ता करना (*v.t.*) to eat breakfast (T10, p. 76)

अर्थशास्त्र (*m*) economics (T11, p. 86)

ईकनॉमिक्स (*m*) economics (T11, p. 86)

अंडा (*m*) egg (T6, p. 44)

आठ (*adj*) eight (T10, p. 77)

अट्ठारह/अठारह (*adj*) eighteen (T16, p. 151)

अट्ठारहवाँ (*adj*) eighteenth (T18, p. 168) (W12, p. 65)

आठवाँ (*adj*) eighth (T8, p. 59)

अस्सी (*adj*) eighty (T16, p. 151)

हाथी (*m*) elephant (T13, p. 109)

ग्यारह (*adj*) eleven (T6, p. 43)

ग्यारहवाँ (*adj*) eleventh (T11, p. 85)

शर्मिंदा (*adj*) embarrassed (W23, p. 130)

निकलना (*v.i.*) to emerge (T14, p. 130)

भावना (*f*) emotion (W24, p. 137)

नौकरी (*f*) employment, work (T3, p. 20) (W17, 20 pp. 98, 114)

खाली (*adj*) empty, free (W3, p. 13)

शून्य (*adj*) empty, void, vacant; (*m*) zero, void (W6, p. 25)

अंत (*m*) end (W13, p. 70)

आखिर (*m*) the end; (*adv*) finally, in the end (T16, p. 155)

(x की) कोशिश करना (*v.t.*) to endeavor (to x), to try (to x) (used with oblique infinitives) (T15, p. 134)

दुश्मन (*m*) enemy

शत्रु (*m*) enemy (T21, p. 210)

इंग्लैंड (*m*) England (T18, p. 174)

अंग्रेज़ी (*f*) English (T6, p. 46)

मौज-मस्ती करना (*v.t.*) to enjoy, have fun (T22, p. 220)

मज़े करना (*v.t.*) to enjoy, have fun (T22, p. 221)

(x को) मज़ा आना (*v.i.*) (x) to enjoy (T11, p. 89) (W19, p. 110) (GR 18)

(x को) पसंद होना (*v.i.*) (x) to enjoy, to like (T18, p. 170) (W18, p. 104) (GR 18)

(x को) पसंद आना (*v.i.*) (x) to enjoy (one/first time) (T18, p. 170) (GR 18)

मज़ा (*m*) enjoyment, relish (T11, p. 89)

काफ़ी (*adj*) enough, quite (T4, p. 26) (W4, p. 18)

घुसना (*v.i.*) to enter, penetrate (W24, p. 137)

सारा (*adj*) entire (T12, p. 96) (W3, 22 pp. 13, 124)

भर (*adj*) entire, all, whole, full

सारे दिन (*adv*) the entire day (T10, p. 76)

दिन-भर (*m + adv*) (for) the entire day (T10, p. 76)

लिफ़ाफ़ा (*m*) envelope (W7, p. 35)

-तर (*suffix*) -er (comparative) (T19, p. 197) (GR 19)

भागना (*v.i.*) to escape, to flee (T15, p. 140) (W17, p. 98)

-तम (*suffix*) -est (superlative) (T19, p. 197) (GR 19)

-तरीन (*suffix*) -est (superlative) (T19, p. 197) (GR 19)

वगैरह etcetera (W19, p. 110)

अभी भी (*adv*) even now (T10, p. 80)

तब भी (*adv*) even then (T11, p. 89)

शाम (*f*) evening (T11, p. 93)

कभी (*adv*) ever, sometime (कब + ही) (T5, p. 33) (W12, p. 65) (GR 14)

प्रतिदिन (*adv*) every day (T11, p. 91)

हर बार (*adv*) every time (T24, p. 230)

सब कुछ (*pro*) everything (T10, p. 78)

इम्तहान (*m*) examination (T20, p. 202) (W15, 19 pp. 85, 109)

परीक्षा (*f*) examination (T6, p. 45) (W15, p. 85)

इम्तहान (x के) सिर पर होना (*v.i.*) (x's) exams to be imminent (T24, p. 230)

बढ़िया (*adj*) excellent (T3, p. 21) (W7, p. 35)

बहाना (*m*) excuse; (*v.t.*) to make flow (W19, p. 110)

माफ़ (*adj*) excused, forgiven, pardoned (T12, p. 102)

महँगा (*adj*) expensive (T17, p. 161) (W10, p. 54)

अनुभव (*m*) experience (T13, p. 110)

समझाना (*v.t.*) to explain (T19, p. 191)

फटना (*v.i.*) to explode, break, burst, to be torn (T22, p. 217)

एक्सप्रेस (*adj*) express (W14, p. 78)

बुझना (*v.i.*) to be extinguished, quenched (W15, p. 85)

आँख (*f*) eye (T5, p. 20)

F

मुँह (*m*) face, mouth, opening (T15, p. 140)

तथ्य (*m*) fact, reality (T6, p. 43)

मेला (*m*) fair (W10, p. 54)

ईमान (*m*) faith, belief, integrity (T1, p. 7)

भरोसा *(m)* faith, trust (T15, p. 139) (W10, p. 54)

पड़ना *(v.i.)* to fall (T14, p. 125) (W10, p. 54) (GR 19, 20)

गिरना *(v.i.)* to fall (T24, p. 232)

(x को) नींद आना *(v.i.)* (x) to fall asleep (T18, p. 172) (GR 18)

परिवार *(m)* family (T5, p. 35) (W4, p. 18)

मशहूर *(adj)* famous (T15, p. 132) (W11, p. 60)

पंखा *(m)* fan, blade (T6, p. 43)

दूर *(adv)* far (T14, p. 120) (W11, p. 60)

किसान *(m)* farmer, peasant (W10, p. 54)

उपवास *(m)* fast (not eating) (W24, p. 137)

मोटा *(adj)* fat (W19, p. 110)

पिता *(m)* father (T5, p. 34) (W4, p. 18) (GR 7)

थकान/थकावट *(f)* fatigue, tiredness (T22, p. 220)

मनपसंद *(adj)* favorite (T16, p. 143) (W24, p. 137)

डर *(m)* fear (T18, p. 174)

फ़रवरी *(f)* February (month) (T16, p. 154)

खाना खिलाना *(v.t.)* to feed food, to treat (T13, p. 114)

महसूस करना *(v.t.)* to feel, perceive

(x को) महसूस होना *(v.i.)* (x) to feel, perceive (T24, p. 236) (GR 18)

(x को) (y से) डर लगना *(v.i.)* (x) to feel afraid (of y) (T18, p. 174) (W18, p. 104) (GR 18)

(x का) मन लगना *(v.i.)* (x) to feel at home, happy, engaged, to feel easy

(x को) बुरा लगना *(v.i.)* (x) to feel bad (T18, p. 174) (GR 18)

(x को) ठंड लगना *(v.i.)* (x) to feel cold (T18, p. 174) (GR 18)

(x को) गर्मी लगना *(v.i.)* (x) to feel hot (T18, p. 174) (GR 18)

(x को) भूख लगना *(v.i.)* (x) to feel hungry (T18, p. 174) (W18, p. 104) (GR 18)

(x का) मन होना *(v.i.)* to feel like (x); (x) to feel like (T17, p. 167) (W22, p. 125)

(x को) नींद लगना *(v.i.)* (x) to feel sleepy (T22, p. 220) (GR 18)

(x को) अफ़सोस होना *(v.i.)* (x) to feel sorrow (T18, p. 175)

महसूस *(adj)* felt, perceived, experienced (T24, p. 236)

शिष्या *(f)* female disciple (T14, p. 127)

सहेली *(f)* female friend of a female (T14, p. 87)

त्यौहार *(m)* festival (T10, p. 78) (W10, p. 54)

ईद *(f)* the festival of Eid (T16, p. 148) (W12, p. 65)

बुख़ार *(m)* fever (T13, p. 110)

चंचल *(adj)* fickle, unsteady, transient, quivering, shaking, restless, skittish, playful, coquettish, nimble (T6, p. 43)

पंद्रह *(adj)* fifteen (T16, p. 151)

पंद्रहवाँ *(adj)* fifteenth (T15, p. 132) (GR 16)

पाँचवाँ *(adj)* fifth (T5, p. 31) (GR 16)

पचास *(adj)* fifty (T7, p. 50)

लड़ना *(v.i. + v.t.)* to fight (T12, p. 102)

फ़िल्म *(f)* film, movie (T9, p. 72) (W9, p. 48)

पाना *(v.i. + v.t.)* to find, obtain; to be able to (T17, p. 162) (GR 17, 19)

पता करना *(v.t.)* to find out, discover (T18, p. 172) (GR 18)

पता लगाना *(v.t.)* to find out, discover (T18, p. 172) (GR 18)

(x को) पता लगाना *(v.i.)* (x) to find out, discover (T18, p. 172) (GR 18)

(x को) पता चलना *(v.i.)* (x) to find out, discover (T18, p. 172) (W18, p. 104) (GR 18)

ख़त्म करना *(v.t.)* to finish (W16, p. 91)

दृढ़ *(adj)* firm, solid (W24, p. 137)

पहला *(adj)* first (T1, p. 1) (W1, p. 3)

प्रथम *(adj)* first (T16, p. 152) (GR16)

पाँच *(adj)* five (T10, p. 81) (W3, p. 13)

ठीक करना *(v.t.)* to fix, to correct (W17, p. 98)

बग़ल *(f)* flank, armpit, next to (L17, p. 161) (W19, p. 110)

फ़र्श *(m)* floor (T22, p. 217) (W6, p. 25)

मंज़िल *(f)* floor of a building, story (T16, p. 152)

आटा *(m)* flour (T18, p. 171) (W18, p. 104)

बहना *(v.i.)* to flow (W10, p. 54)

फूल *(m)* flower (T4, p. 26) (W4, p. 18)

उड़ना *(v.i.)* to fly (T15, p. 139)

खाना *(m)* food (T3, p. 20) (W8, p. 41)

(x) के लिये *(pp)* for (x), in order to (x) (if x is a verb) (T7, p. 53) (W8, p. 41) (GR 13)

बहुत देर तक *(adv)* for a long time (W11, p. 60)

अपने लिये *(adv)* for oneself (T11, p. 90)

दो घंटे तक *(adv)* for two hours (W22, p. 125)

किसलिये *(inter)* for what reason, why (T15, p. 135)

किसके लिये *(inter adv)* for whom (T7, p. 53) (W4, 7 pp. 18, 35)

तुम्हारे लिये *(adv)* for you (T7, p. 53) (W4, p. 18)

मना *(adj)* forbidden (T13, p. 111)

ज़बरदस्ती करना (*v.t.*) to force (W8, p. 41)

विदेश (*m*) foreign country (T13, p. 119)

वन (*m*) forest (W1, p. 3)

भुलाना (*v.t.*) to forget

भूल जाना (*v.i.*) to forget (T21, p. 212)

भूलना (*v.i.*) to forget (T5, p. 33) (GR 12)

माफ़ करना (*v.t.*) to forgive, excuse, pardon
  (T12, p. 102) (W23, p. 130)

माफ़ी (*f*) forgiveness, pardon

तकल्लुफ़ (*m*) formality (W8, p. 41)

चालीस (*adj*) forty (T16, p. 151) (W18, p. 104)

अड़तालीस (*adj*) forty-eight (T16, p. 151)

पैंतालीस (*adj*) forty-five (T16, p. 151)

चवालीस (*adj*) forty-four (T16, p. 151)

उनचास (*adj*) forty-nine (T16, p. 151)

इकतालीस (*adj*) forty-one (T16, p. 151)

सैंतालीस (*adj*) forty-seven (T16, p. 151)

छियालीस (*adj*) forty-six (T16, p. 151)

तैंतालीस (*adj*) forty-three (T16, p. 151)

बयालीस (*adj*) forty-two (T16, p. 151)

चार (*adj*) four (T10, p. 76) (W3, p. 13)

चौदह (*adj*) fourteen (T16, p. 151)

चौदहवाँ (*adj*) fourteenth (T14, p. 120)

चतुर्थ (*adj*) fourth (T16, p. 152)

चौथा (*adj*) fourth (T4, p. 24) (GR 16)

मुफ़्त (*adj*) free of charge, gratis (T6, p. 42)

ताज़ा (*adj*) fresh (T3, p. 21) (W3, p. 13) (GR 3)

शुक्रवार (*m*) Friday (T10, p. 76) (W6, p. 28) (GR 16)

जुमा (*m*) Friday (T16, p. 153) (GR 16)

दोस्त (*m/f*) friend (T3, p. 22) (W4, p. 18)

मित्र (*m*) friend (T6, p. 45)

यार (*m*) friend, mate

दोस्ती (*f*) friendship (T14, p. 130) (W11, p. 60)

से (*pp*) from, since, by, with (T4, p. 29)
  (W6, 12 pp. 28, 65) (GR 16)

में से (*pp*) from amongst (T15, p. 138) (W7, p. 35)

x से लेकर y तक from x until y (T19, p. 187)

फल (*m*) fruit (W7, 18 pp. 35, 103)

सुखमय (*adj*) full of happiness (T16, p. 148)

भविष्य (*m*) future (W17, p. 98)

G

खेल (*m*) game, match, sport

गंगा (*f*) Ganges (name of a river in India) (T6, p. 42)
  (W10, p. 54)

बग़ीचा (*m*) garden (T14, p. 126) (W14, p. 78)

बाग़ (*m*) garden (T16, p. 146)

माली (*m*) gardener (T1, p. 5)

आम (*adj*) general, ordinary (T1, p. 7)

आम तौर पर (*adv*) generally (W10, p. 54)

पीढ़ी (*f*) generation (T22, p. 219)

उदार (*adj*) generous (W10, p. 54)

दानी (*adj*) generous (W12, p. 65)

ग़ज़ल (*f*) a genre of Urdu poetry that may also be sung
  (W11, p. 60)

उतारना (*v.t.*) to get down, make descend (T15, p. 140)

भेंट (*f*) gift (W8, p. 41)

लड़की (*f*) girl (T3, p. 20) (W3, p. 13)

कन्या (*f*) girl, daughter, virgin (T16, p. 152)

देना (*v.t.*) to give (T8, p. 62) (W8, p. 41) (GR 8, 17, 19)

भाषण देना (*v.t.*) to give a speech (T23, p. 224)
  (W17, p. 98)

निगाह (*f*) glance, sight (T24, p. 232)

काँच (*m*) glass (W4, p. 18)

जाना (*v.i.*) to go, to depart, to lose (T8, p. 64)
  (W9, p. 48) (GR 12, 19, 21, 22)

ख़राब होना (*v.i.*) to go bad, break, be spoiled
  (W15, p. 85)

बकरा (*m*) goat (T18, p. 169)

ईश्वर/ईश्वर (*m*) God (T5, p. 32)

ख़ुदा (*m*) God (T7, p. 51) (W15, p. 85) (GR 16)

इंशाअल्लाह! (*voc*) God willing!

देवी (*f*) goddess

अच्छा (*adj*) good (T5, p. 32) (W4, p. 18)

सामान (*m*) goods, luggage, stuff (W2, p. 8)
  (W8, p. 41)

गपशप मारना (*v.t.*) to gossip (गपशप gossip (*f*) +
  मारना to beat, strike) (T15, p. 135)

लौकी (*f*) gourd (T18, p. 169)

सरकार (*f*) government (T22, p. 218) (W11, p. 60)

पकड़ना (*v.t.*) to grab, catch (T24, p. 232)
  (W20, 23 pp. 115, 129)

नम्बर/नंबर (*m*) grade, mark, number (T7, p. 57)

व्याकरण (*m*) grammar (W15, p. 85)

शानदार (*adj*) grand, glorious (T15, p. 140)
  (W15, 21 pp. 85, 119)

बाबा (*m*) grandfather, an old man, ascetic

मुफ़्त में (*adv*) gratis, for free

बड़ा होना (*v.i.*) to grow up (T12, p. 99)

अमरूद (*m*) guava (T3, p. 21)

गुझिया (*f*) gujhiya, a type of Indian sweetmeat (W19, p. 110)

गुलाबजामुन (*m*) gulabjamun (fried sweet dumpling)

गुरुद्वारा (*m*) Gurdwara (Sikh temple) (T17, p. 168)

गुड़गाँव (*m*) Gurgaon (name of a suburb of Delhi close to the airport) (T23, p. 222)

H

आदत (*f*) habit (T19, p. 191)

आदत पड़ना (*v.i.*) a habit to form

मोलतोल (*m*) haggling, bargaining (W11, p. 60)

हाथ (*m*) hand, arm (T13, p. 109) (W14, p. 78)

हाथ-मुँह (*m pl*) hands and face (T15, p. 140)

प्रसन्नता (*f*) happiness (T, 6, p. 46)

खुशी (*f*) happiness (T5, p. 33)

खुश (*adj*) happy (T7, p. 50) (W16, p. 91)

सताना (*v.t.*) to harass, torment, torture, trouble (T16, p. 148)

दिक़ करना (*v.t.*) to harass, trouble (W17, p. 98)

मेहनत (*f*) hard work (T18, p. 173) (W9, 17, 18 pp. 48, 97, 103)

मेहनती (*adj*) hardworking, industrious (T20, p. 202)

(x को) बुख़ार होना (*v.i.*) (x) to have a fever (T13, p. 110) (GR 18)

खाना बनवाना (*v.t.*) to have food made (T10, p. 76)

(x को) (y का) शौक़ होना (*v.i.*) (x) to have the interest/hobby (of y) (T22, p. 215)

मँगवाना (*v.t.*) to have ordered (T23, p. 227)

छपवाना (*v.t.*) to have something printed (by someone) (T20, p. 201)

मन लगाकर (*adv*) having applied the heart/mind, with industry (GR 15)

डटकर (*adv*) having taken a stand, resolutely (W19, p. 110)

फेरीवाला (*adj*) hawker, street vendor (T24, p. 235)

वह (*pro*) he/she/that/it (far from the speaker) (T1, p. 6) (W1, p. 3) (GR 2, 4, 7)

यह (*pro*) he/she/this/it (close to the speaker) (T1, p. 6) (W1, p. 3) (GR 2, 4, 7)

उसने (*pro*) he/she/it/that (वह + ने) (T7, p. 53) (GR 7, 12)

इसने (*pro*) he/she/it/this (यह + ने) (T7, p. 53) (GR 7, 12)

इन्होंने (*pro*) he/she/they/these (ये + ने) (T7, p. 53) (GR 7, 12)

उन्होंने (*pro*) he/she/they/those (वे + ने) (T7, p. 53) (GR 7, 12)

सिर (*m*) head (T10, p. 78) (W7, p. 35)

सरदर्द (*m*) headache (T12, p. 103)

अक्खड़ (*adj*) headstrong, rude and rough (W6, p. 25)

सेहत (*f*) health (T13, p. 111)

तबीयत (*f*) health, disposition (T12, p. 103)

ढेर (*m*) heap, pile (T6, p. 46)

सुनना (*v.t.*) to hear, listen (T13, p. 113) (W11, 13 pp. 60, 71)

सुनवाही (*f*) (court) hearing (W17, p. 98)

हृदय (*m*) heart (T4, p. 26)

मन (*m*) heart, mind (T17, p. 167) (W8, 24 pp. 41, 136)

जी (*m*) heart, polite suffix (T2, p. 12) (W2, p. 8)

गरमी/गर्मी (*f*) heat (T18, p. 174) (W10, p. 54)

स्वर्ग (*m*) heaven (T10, p. 78)

नमस्ते hello and goodbye (T2, p. 12) (W2, p. 8)

नमस्कार hello and goodbye (T2, p. 12) (W4, p. 18)

मदद (*f*) help (T9, p. 74) (W15, p. 85)

(x की) मदद करना (*v.t.*) to help (x) (T9, p. 74) (W13, p. 71)

अतः hence, therefore, thus (T5, p. 33)

यहाँ (*adv*) here (T5, p. 39) (W2, p. 8) (GR 23)

इधर (*adv*) here, this side, over here (T23, p. 225) (W7, p. 35) (GR 23)

संकोच (*m*) hesitation (W24, p. 137)

अरी (*f voc*) hey! (T7, p. 55)

हे (*voc*) hey! (T7, p. 55)

अरे (*m voc*) hey! (T7, p. 55) (W4, p. 18)

हाय (*m*) hi! (a greeting) (W4, p. 18)

छुपना/छिपना (*v.i.*) to hide, to lurk (T20, p. 201)

ऊँचा (*adj*) high (T3, p. 20) (W5, p. 23)

हिंदी/हिन्दी (*f*) the Hindi language (T6, p. 46)

देवनागरी (*f*) the Hindi script (T18, p. 172)

हीरालाल (*m*) Hiralal (name) (W9, p. 48)

इसका (*adj*) his/her/its (T2, p. 14) (GR 2, 4)

उसका (*adj*) his/her/its (T2, p. 14) (GR 2, 4)

इनका (*adj*) his/her/their (T2, p. 14) (GR 2, 4)

उनका (*adj*) his/her/their (T2, p. 14) (GR 2, 4)

इतिहास (m) history (T11, p. 86)

छेद (*m*) hole (W8, p. 41)

होली (*f*) Holi (the Indian festival of colors) (T10, p. 78) (W19, p. 110)

छुट्टी (*f*) holiday (T6, p. 44) (W8, p. 41)

घर (*m*) home (T3, p. 20)

बेघर (*adj*) homeless

श्री (*adj*) an honorific adjective prefixed to male names; Mr.; (*f*) Lakshmi (the goddess of wealth) (T6, p. 46)

आशा (*f*) hope (T5, p. 33)

उम्मीद (*f*) hope, expectation (W21, p. 120)

(x को) आशा होना (*v.i.*) (x) to hope (W18, p. 104)

अस्पताल (*m*) hospital (W15, 21 pp. 85, 119)

गरम/गर्म (*adj*) hot (T8, p. 62) (W7, p. 35)

होटल (*m*) hotel (W7, p. 35)

घंटा (*m*) hour, bell (T6, p. 44) (W13, 14, 23 pp. 71, 78, 129)

मकान (*m*) house (T1, p. 7) (W1, p. 3)

कैसे (*adv*) how, in what manner (T13, p. 105) (W6, p. 28)

कैसा (*adj*) how, what kind of (T5, p. 36) (W3, p. 13) (GR 5)

कितना (*adj*) how much, many (T5, p. 36) (W3, p. 13) (GR 5)

इंसान (*m*) human being (T24, p. 230)

उमस (*f*) humidity (T19, p. 187)

सैकड़ों (*adj*) hundreds (T16, p. 152) (GR 16)

भूख (*f*) hunger (T18, p. 174)

पति (*m*) husband (T10, p. 81) (W7, p. 35)

I

मैं (*pro*) I (T2, p. 14) (GR 2, 4, 7)

मैंने (*pro*) I (मैं + ने) (T7, p. 53) (GR 7, 12)

मुझे कुछ काम है। I have work to do. (T20, p. 198)

मैं चलता हूँ। I'm (*m*) off. (T9, p. 68)

ख्याल/ख़याल (*m*) idea, thought, view, opinion (T6, p. 43) (W19, p. 110)

बेवकूफ (*adj*) idiot, foolish (W23, p. 130)

मूर्ति (*f*) idol, statue (T7, p. 55)

अगर (*conj*) if (T10, p. 83) (W11, p. 60)

यदि (*conj*) if (T11, p. 88)

बीमारी (*f*) illness, sickness (T18, p. 174) (W21, p. 120)

तुरंत (*conj*) immediately (T11, p. 91)

फ़ौरन (*adv*) immediately, instantly, at once (T11, p. 91)

एकदम (*adv*) immediately, suddenly, in one breath, completely; (*adj*) perfect (T11, p. 91)

महत्त्वपूर्ण (*adj*) important (W15, p. 85)

में (*pp*) in (T3, p. 22) (W2, p. 8) (GR 7, 13)

(x) के अलावा (*pp*) in addition to (x) (W10, p. 54)

सामने (*adv*) in front (T17, p. 167) (W2, p. 8)

(x) के सामने (*pp*) in front of (x) (T17, p. 167)

मेरे ख़्याल में (*adv*) in my opinion (T20, p. 202)

(x) की जगह (*pp*) in place of (x) (W24, p. 137)

असल में (*adv*) in reality (W7, p. 35)

(x) की ओर (*pp*) in the direction of (x) (T24, p. 232) (W17, p. 98)

मन ही मन (*adv*) in the mind (W24, p. 137)

दुनिया में in the world (W5, p. 23)

इस तरह (*adv*) in this way (W11, p. 60)

कुल मिलाकर (*adv*) in total, overall (W22, p. 125) (GR 15)

किस दुकान में (*adv*) in(to) which shop (T17, p. 161)

आय (*f*) income (T1, p. 6)

बढ़ाना (*v.t.*) to increase, to grow

अपने मन का (*adj*) independent, of one's own mind (W10, p. 54)

अपने ढंग से (*adv*) independently

इंडिया (*m*) India (T18, p. 171)

हिन्दुस्तान/हिंदुस्तान (*m*) India (T3, p. 20) (W8, p. 41)

भारत (*m*) India (T5, p. 33) (W10, 22 pp. 54, 124)

इंडिया गेट (*m*) India Gate (T13, p. 114)

हिन्दुस्तानी/हिंदुस्तानी (*adj*) Indian (T3, p. 22) (W10, p. 54)

भारतीय (*adj*) Indian (T9, p. 70)

मैना (*f*) Indian black bird (T1, p. 5)

इंदिरा (*f*) Indira (name) (W10, p. 54)

व्यक्ति (*m*) individual (W6, p. 25)

घटिया (*adj*, *invar*) inferior, of low quality (T3, p. 21) (GR 3)

सूचना (*f*) information (T15, p. 138)

चोट (*f*) injury, wound, blow, stroke (T18, p. 174)

कीड़ा (*m*) insect (W7, p. 35)

अंदर (*adv*) inside (T13, p. 111) (W6, p. 28)

झट (*adv*) instantly, at once (T11, p. 91) (GR 11)

मेधा (*f*) intellect, brilliance, Medha (name) (T10, p. 83)

इरादा (*m*) intention (W9, p. 48)

शौक़ (*m*) interest, hobby (W13, p. 71)

अंतर्मुखी (*adj*) introvertive (W6, p. 25)

(x की) जाँच करना (*v.t.*) to investigate, to test (x)

है (*v.i.*) is/are (*s*) (T1, p. 5) (W1, p. 3) (GR 4)

हैं (*v.i.*) is/are (*pl*) (T3, p. 22) (W2, p. 8) (GR 4)

सा (*adj*) "ish", like, similar to, resembling (a suffix) (T24, p. 230)

मामला (*m*) issue, matter (T21, p. 213) (W13, p. 71)

ऐसी कोई बात नहीं It's not like that (lit: such any matter isn't) (W4, p. 18)

J

जलेबी (*f*) jalebi (a type of Indian sweet) (T8, p. 62) (W9, p. 48)

जामा मस्जिद (*f*) Jama Masjid (the main mosque in Delhi) (T16, p. 143)

जनवरी (*f*) January (month) (T16, p. 154) (W10, p. 54) (GR 16)

जापान (*m*) Japan (T18, p. 173)

जिन्होंने (*rel pro*) जो + ने (T7, p. 53) (GR 12, 23)

जिसने (*rel pro*) जो + ने (T7, p. 53) (GR 12, 23)

मज़ाक (*m*) joke (W11, p. 60)

रस (*m*) juice, essence, aesthetic relish, sentiment, pleasure (T15, p. 139)

जुलाई (*f*) July (month) (T14, p. 123) (GR 16)

जून (*m*) June (month) (T16, p. 154) (GR 16)

K

करीम्स (*m*) Karim's (a famous kabab restaurant in Old Delhi) (T17, p. 168)

याद रखना (*v.t.*) to keep in mind (W19, p. 110)

ख़ालिद (*m*) Khalid (name) (T7, p. 52)

ख़ान मार्केट (*m*) Khan Market (a market in Delhi) (T9, p. 74)

तरह (*f*) kind, type, sort, manner (T11, p. 89)

मेहरबानी (*f*) kindness, favor (T8, p. 64) (W4, p. 18)

राजा (*m*) king (T7, p. 54) (W7, p. 35)

महाराज (*m*) king (T14, p. 227)

बादशाह (*m*) king (T21, p. 209)

राज्य (*m*) kingdom, state, policy, rule (T6, p. 43)

गूँधना (*v.t.*) to knead (W18, p. 104)

जानना (*v.t.*) to know, to perceive (T9, p. 71) (W9, p. 48)

(x को) मालूम होना (*v.i.*) to be known (to x) (T12, p. 104) (W18, p. 104) (GR 18)

(x को) पता होना (*v.i.*) (x) to know, to find out (T18, p. 172) (GR 18)

विद्या (*f*) knowledge, learning, education, science (T6, p. 45)

ज्ञान (*m*) knowledge, wisdom (T6, p. 45)

कृपा लाल (*m*) Kripa Lal (name) (T4, p. 29)

कृष्ण (*m*) Krishna (name of a Hindu deity) (T7, p. 55)

कुतुब मीनार (*f*) Kutub Minar (T13, p. 114)

L

मज़दूर (*m*) laborer (T19, p. 185)

लड्डु (*m*) laddu, an Indian sweet (T6, p. 44)

लाहौर (*m*) Lahore (T20, p. 204)

लाजपत नगर (*m*) Lajpat Nagar (name of a neighborhood in Delhi) (T15, p. 132)

दीपक (*m*) lamp, Deepak (name) (T2, p. 13) (W2, p. 8)

ज़मीन (*f*) land (W10, p. 54)

ज़मींदार/ज़मीनदार (*m*) landowner (T13, p. 108)

गली (*f*) lane, gully (W24, p. 137)

ज़बान (*f*) language (T22, p. 215)

भाषा (*f*) language (T8, p. 60) (W8, p. 41)

चमचा (*m*) a large spoon, flunkey, sycophant

कल रात (*adv*) last night (T11, p. 94) (W12, p. 65) (GR 11)

पिछले हफ़्ते (*adv*) last week (T11, p. 92) (W13, 14 pp. 71, 78)

देर से (*adv*) late (*with lateness*) (W10, p. 54)

हँसना (*v.i.*) to laugh (T6, p. 47) (GR 19)

क़ानून (*m*) law, regulation (W21, p. 120)

नेता (*m*) leader, politician (W10, p. 54) (GR 7)

पत्ता (*m*) leaf (T6, p. 45)

सीखना (*v.t.*) to learn (T9, p. 68)

छोड़ना (*v.t.*) to leave, abandon (T13, p. 110) (W11, p. 60)

छोड़ देना (*v.t.*) to leave, abandon, to drop (T20, p. 206)

कम (*adj*) less, too little (T1, p. 5) (W1, p. 3)

पाठ (*m*) lesson, reading (T1, p. 1) (W18, p. 104)

चिट्ठी (*f*) letter (T6, p. 44) (W14, 23 pp. 78, 129)

पत्र (*m*) letter (T6, p. 46) (W9, p. 48)

ख़त (*m*) letter, line, handwriting (T8, p. 65) (W4, p. 18)

अक्षर (*m*) letter (of the alphabet), character, symbol (W6, p. 26)

पुस्तकालय (*m*) library (T10, p. 76) (W14, p. 78)

झूठ (*m*) a lie (T6, p. 46)

झूठ बोलना (*v.t.*) to lie (T12, p. 102)

जीवन (*m*) life (T16, p. 148) (W10, 18 pp. 54, 103)

ज़िंदगी (*f*) life (T7, p. 57) (W11, 22 pp. 60, 124)

जान (*f*) life, stamina, vitality, energy (T24, p. 238)

जीवन साथी (*m*) life companion (W20, p. 115)

ज्योति (*f*) light, Jyoti (name) (T24, p. 236)

हल्का (*adj*) light (not heavy), weak (W20, p. 115)

नाश्ता (*m*) light refreshment, breakfast (T5, p. 32)

जैसा (*rel adj*) like, resembling, similar to (T23, p. 225) (GR 23)

(x) की तरह (*pp*) like (x) (T16, 155) (W11, p. 60)

(x को) अच्छा लगना (*v.i.*) (x) to like (T18, p. 174) (W18, p. 104) (GR 18)

शेर (*m*) lion, tiger, a couplet (T10, p. 78)

ज़रा (*adj, invar*) a little (also softens a request) (T3, p. 21) (W3, 18 pp. 13, 103)

थोड़ा बहुत और (*adj*) a little bit more (T23, p. 222)

थोड़ा सा (*adj*) a little-ish (T24, p. 230)

रहना (*v.i.*) to live (T9, p. 67) (W9, p. 48) (GR 14, 22)

लॉबी (*f*) lobby (W7, p. 35)

लोदी गार्डन (*m*) Lodi Garden (name of a popular garden in South Delhi with tombs from the Lodi and Sayyid period, 15th–16th centuries) (T15, p. 132)

लूटना (*v.t.*) to loot, plunder (T19, p. 193)

ठाकुर (*m*) lord, master, God (T15, p. 138)

भगवान (*m*) Lord (God) (T16, p. 148) (W11, p. 60)

खोना (*v.i. + v.t.*) to lose (W23, p. 130)

खो देना (*v.t.*) to lose, misplace (W22, p. 125) (GR 19)

खूब (*adj*) a lot, excellent (W11, p. 60)

कमल (*m*) lotus (T1, p. 7) (W1, p. 3)

प्यार (*m*) love

प्रेम (*m*) love (T6, p. 46)

आराम-प्रिय (*adj*) loving relaxation (T10, p. 77)

लखनऊ (*m*) Lucknow (the capital of U.P.) (T16, p. 147) (W11, p. 60)

M

महाराष्ट्र (*m*) Mahrashtra (a state in India) (T6, p. 46)

मेन कैंपस (मुख्य परिसर) (*m*) main campus (T15, p. 132)

बनाना (*v.t.*) to make, produce (T9, p. 73)

बहाना बनाना (*v.t.*) to make an excuse (W19, p. 110)

गिराना (*v.t.*) to make (something) fall

उड़ाना (*v.t.*) to make fly

(x की) जाँच कराना (*v.t.*) to make (someone) investigate (x), to have (x) tested (W21, p. 120)

चलाना (*v.t.*) to make move, to drive (T11, p. 86)

झपटना (*v.i.*) to make a sudden swoop, to pounce, snatch (T19, p. 192)

मॉल (*m*) mall (T23, p. 222)

पुरुष (*m*) man (T19, p. 196)

आदमी (*m*) man (T2, p. 13) (W2, p. 8)

मनुष्य (*m*) man, human (T13, p. 108)

आम (*m*) mango (T1, p. 7) (W1, p. 3)

ढंग (*m*) manner, method, mode, way

आदाब (*m*) manners, salutation ("greetings") (T7, p. 50)

नक्शा (*m*) map, shape (W22, p. 125)

मार्च (*m*) March (month) (T16, p. 154) (W6, p. 28)

बाज़ार (*m*) market (T2, p. 12) (W2, p. 8)

ब्याह (*m*) marriage, wedding (T6, p. 43)

वैवाहिक (*adj*) married, marital (T16, p. 148)

मामी (*f*) maternal aunty (T9, p. 73) (GR 8)

नाना (*m*) maternal grandfather (T5, p. 34) (GR 7)

नानी (*f*) maternal grandmother (T1, p. 5) (GR 8)

नाना-नानी (*m*) maternal grandparents (T5, p. 35)

मामा (*m*) maternal uncle (T1, p. 5) (W2, p. 8) (GR 7)

बात (*f*) matter, talk, thing (T5, p. 36) (W4, p. 18)

मई (*m*) May (month) (T16, p. 154) (W10, p. 54) (GR 16)

ख़ुदा हाफ़िज़ May God protect you. (used in Urdu when leaving) (T7, p. 51)

(x) मुबारक हो! may (x) be auspicious! (T16, p. 147) (GR 16)

मुझी (*pro*) me (मुझ + ही) (T14, p. 128) (GR 14)

मुझ (*pro*) me (oblique form of मैं) (T7, p. 53) (GR 7)

मुझे/मुझको (*pro*) (to) me (oblique form of मैं + को) (T7, p. 53) (GR 7)

मतलब (*m*) meaning (T5, p. 35) (W15, p. 85)

इस बीच (*adv*) meanwhile (W12, p. 65)

गोश्त (*m*) meat, flesh (T5, p. 33) (W20, p. 115)

दवा (*f*) medicine (T19, p. 185) (W2, 21 pp. 8, 119)

दवाई (*f*) medicine (W21, p. 120)

डॉक्टरी (*f*) (the practice of) medicine (W9, p. 48)

मिलना (*v.i.*) to meet, to encounter, to be mixed, to be united, to mingle (T2, p. 13) (W10, 18 pp. 54, 103) (GR 17)

(x से) (y की) मुलाक़ात होना (*v.i.*) (y) to meet (with x), (y's) meeting to take place (with x) (T22, p. 221)

मुलाक़ात (*f*) meeting (W19, p. 110)

पिघलना (*v.i.*) to melt (W23, p. 130)

याद (*f*) memory (T8, p. 66)

कृपा (*f*) mercy (T4, p. 26)

मेट्रो (*f*) Metro (T13, p. 106)

दोपहर (*f*) midday, afternoon (T11, p. 93) (W14, 19 pp. 78, 109) (GR 11)

दूध (*m*) milk (T3, p. 20) (W4, 14 pp. 18, 78)

दिमाग़ (*m*) mind, brain, intellect (T13, p. 109)

मंत्री (*m*) minister (W7, p. 35)

मिनट (*m*) minute (T8, p. 64) (GR 18)

आइना (*m*) mirror (W11, p. 60)

कंजूस (*adj*) miserly, miser (W11, p. 60)

(x को) (y की) याद आना (*v.i.*) (x) to miss (y) (T21, p. 207) (W15, 22 pp. 85, 124) (GR 18)

मिलाना (*v.t.*) to mix, to unite, to compare, to blend, to cause to meet, to bring together (W22, p. 125)

पल (*m*) a moment, a measure of time equal to twenty-four seconds

क्षण (*m*) moment, an instant (T11, p. 93)

सोमवार (*m*) Monday (T9, p. 73) (W5, p. 23) (GR 16)

पीर (*m*) Monday, Muslim saint (T16, p. 153) (GR 16)

महीना (*m*) month (T1, p. 6) (W1, p. 3)

मुहर्रम (*m*) the month of Imam Hussain's martyrdom which is held sacred and celebrated by Shia Muslims (W10, p. 54)

मिज़ाज (*m*) mood, temperament

रजनीश (*m*) the moon, Rajneesh (name) (W11, p. 60)

चाँदनी (*f*) moonlight (T3, p. 20)

ज़्यादा (*adj, invar*) more, much (T10, p. 83) (W13, p. 71) (GR 3)

अधिक (*adj*) more, too much (T19, p. 196) (W10, p. 54)

सवेरा (*m*) morning (T11, p. 91) (W11, p. 60)

सुबह (*f*) morning (T3, p. 20) (W6, 10 pp. 28, 54)

मस्जिद (*f*) mosque (T16, p. 143) (W15, p. 85)

मच्छर (*m*) mosquito (T5, p. 33)

ज़्यादातर (*adj + adv*) mostly (T13, p. 106)

माँ (*f*) mother (T2, p. 17) (W2, p. 8)

अम्मी जान (*f*) mother dear (T7, p. 50)

मोटरसाइकिल (*f*) motorcycle (T13, p. 105)

पहाड़ (*m*) mountain (W23, p. 130)

चलना (*v.i.*) to move (T3, p. 20) (W13, 14 pp. 71, 78)

चला जाना (*v.i.*) to move away (T22, p. 217) (W21, p. 120) (GR 22)

सिनेमाहाल (*m*) movie theatre (T12, p. 95)

मिसेस Mrs. (T17, p. 164)

मुंबई (*f*) Mumbai (T19, p. 187)

(x का) खून करना (*v.t.*) to murder (x)

अजायबघर (*m*) museum (T22, p. 219)

संगीत (*m*) music (T19, p. 192) (W11, p. 60)

मुसलमान (*m*) Muslim (W10, p. 54)

मेरा (*adj*) my (T2, p. 14) (GR 2, 4)

N

नाम (*m*) name (T2, p. 15) (W2, p. 8)

ईद-उज़-जुहा (*f*) name of Eid (W15, p. 85)

ईद-उल-अज़हा (*f*) name of Eid (W15, p. 85)

बक़रईद (*f*) name of Eid (W15, p. 85)

माघ (*m*) the name of a month (W10, p. 54)

नस्तालिक़ (*f*) Nastaliq (name of the Urdu script) (T22, p. 215)

राष्ट्र (*m*) nation (T6, p. 45) (W6, p. 25)

नवाब (*m*) Nawab (a title) (W12, p. 65)

नवाबी (*adj*) Nawabi, aristocratic (W15, p. 85)

क़रीब (*adv*) near (T15, p. 138) (W11, 15 pp. 60, 85)

(x) के पास (*pp*) near (x) (T9, p. 72) (W11, p. 60) (GR 9, 13)

आसपास (*adv*) nearby, around, near about (T19, p. 194) (W7, p. 35)

ज़रूरी (*adv*) necessary (T16, p. 148) (W21, p. 120)

आवश्यक (*adj*) necessary (T5, p. 33)

ज़रूरत (*f*) necessity (T13, p. 119) (W16, p. 91)

(x की) ज़रूरत होना (*v.i.*) the necessity of (x) to happen (T23, p. 227)

सुई (*f*) needle, hand of a watch (W13, p. 71)

पड़ोसी (*m*) neighbor

पड़ोसिन (*f*) neighbor

फिर भी (*conj*) nevertheless (T16, p. 155)

नया (*adj*) new (T1, p. 7) (W1, p. 3)

ख़बर (*f*) news (T18, p. 175) (W8, p. 41)

अख़बार (*m*) newspaper (T5, p. 36) (W4, p. 18)

अगला (*adj*) next, following

बग़ल में (*adv*) next door (T17, p. 161)

अगली बार (*adv*) next time (T11, p. 93) (W15, p. 85)

अगले हफ़्ते (*adv*) next week (T11, p. 92) (W7, p. 35)

रात्रि (*f*) night (T8, p. 59)

रात (*f*) night (T9, p. 73) (W6, p. 28)

नौ (*adj*) nine (T10, p. 76)

उन्नीस (*adj*) nineteen (T12, p. 104)

उन्नीसवाँ (*adj*) nineteenth (T19, p. 183)

नब्बे (*adj*) ninety (T16, p. 151)

नवाँ (*adj*) ninth (T9, p. 67)

ना (*adv*) no (T1, p. 5)

जी नहीं (*adv*) no (T2, p. 12)

नहीं (*adv*) no, not (T2, p. 12)

न (*adv*) no, not, isn't it? (T7, p. 50) (W6, p. 28) (GR 8)

कोई बात नहीं no matter (W13, p. 71)

ऐसे ही (*adv*) no reason, just such (W6, 7 pp. 28, 35) (GR 14)

शरीफ़ (*adj*) noble, virtuous (T10, p. 81)

बकवास (*f*) nonsense (L18, p. 175) (W9, p. 48)

उत्तर (*m*) north (T14, p. 120)

उत्तर भारत (*m*) north India (T19, p. 187)

कापी (*f*) notebook (W1, p. 3)

कुछ नहीं (*pro*) nothing (T7, p. 57) (W6, p. 28) (GR 15)

कुछ नहीं रखा है। Nothing is left. (placed) (T21, p. 212)

उपन्यास (*m*) novel (T12, p. 103)

नवम्बर (*m*) November (T16, p. 154) (W10, p. 54) (GR 16)

अब (*adv*) now (T8, p. 66) (W4, p. 18)

अंक (*m*) number, numeral, figure (T6, p. 46)

O

ओ (*voc*) O! (T7, p. 55) (W3, p. 13)

ऐ (*voc*) O! (T1, p. 5)

बजे (*adv*) o'clock (T11, p. 93) (GR 18)

आपत्ति (*f*) objection (W16, p. 91)

आपको (*pro*) oblique form of आप + को (T7, p. 53) (GR 7)

हमें/हमको (*pro*) oblique form of हम + को (T7, p. 53) (GR 7)

जिस (*rel pro*) oblique form of जो (T7, p. 53) (GR 7, 23)

जिन्हें/जिनको (*rel pro*) oblique form of जो + को (T7, p. 53) (GR 7, 23)

जिसे/जिसको (*rel pro*) oblique form of जो + को (T7, p. 53) (GR 7, 23)

किसे/किसको (*pro*) oblique form of कौन + को (T7, p. 53) (GR 7)

किन्हीं को (*pro pl*) oblique form of कोई + को (T7, p. 53) (GR 7)

तुझ (*pro*) oblique form of तू (T7, p. 53) (GR 7)

तुझे/तुझको oblique form of तू + को (T7, p. 53) (GR 7)

तुम्हें/तुमको (*pro*) oblique form of तुम + को (T7, p. 53) (GR 7)

उन (*pro*) oblique form of वे (T2, p. 14) (GR 7)

उन्हें/उनको (*pro*) oblique form of वे + को (T7, p. 53) (GR 7)

उस (*pro*) oblique form of वह (T2, p. 14) (GR 7)

उसे/उसको (*pro*) oblique form of वह + को (T7, p. 53) (GR 7)

इन (*pro*) oblique form of ये (T2, p. 14) (GR 7)

इन्हें/इनको (*pro*) oblique form of ये + को (T7, p. 53) (GR 7)

इस (*pro*) oblique form of यह (T2, p. 14) (GR 7)

इसे/इसको (*pro*) oblique form of यह + को (T7, p. 53) (GR 7)

उन्हीं (*pro*) उन + ही (T14, p. 128) (GR 14)

उसी (*pro*) उस + ही (T14, p. 126) (GR 14)

इन्हीं (*pro*) इन + ही (T14, p. 128) GR 14

इसी (*pro*) इस + ही (T14, p. 128) (GR 14)

तुझी (*pro*) तुझ + ही (T14, p. 128) (GR 7, 14)

प्राप्त करना (*v.t.*) to obtain (T23, p. 224)

(x को) प्राप्त होना (*v.i.*) (x) to obtain

सागर (*m*) ocean (T22, p. 217)

अक्तूबर (*m*) October (T16, p. 154)

वैसा (*adj*) of that kind/nature, such as that, like that (T23, p. 224) (GR 23)

कहाँ का (*adj*) of where (T4, p. 28) (W7, p. 35)

दफ़्तर (*m*) office (T12, p. 96) (W10, p. 54)

अफ़सर (*m*) officer (T4, p. 26)

अधिकारी (*m*) official, officer (W10, p. 54)

अक्सर (*adv*) often (T11, p. 91) (W9, 22 pp. 48, 124)

प्रायः (*adv*) often, approximately (T11, p. 91)

अरे वाह (*voc*) Oh wow! (T7, p. 50)

ओह (*voc*) oh! (W5, p. 23)

ठीक (*adj*) okay, right, true, proper, appropriate (T5, p. 33) (W5, p. 23)

बस (*invar + m*) okay, enough; power (T5, p. 36) (W3, 12 pp. 13, 65)

पुराना (*adj*) old (said of things) (T13, p. 114) (W4, 13, 15 pp. 18, 71, 85)

दीदी (*f*) older sister (T11, p. 88)

पर (*pp + conj*) on; but (T8, p. 64) (W3, p. 13) (GR 15)

(x) की वजह से (*pp*) on account of, because of (x) (T12, p. 103)

(x) के मारे (*pp*) on account of (x) (T21, p. 212)

दूसरी तरफ़ (*adv*) on the other side

मेज़ पर on the table (T8, p. 64) (W3, p. 13)

एक बार (*adv*) once, one time (T13, p. 118)

एक (*adj*) one (T4, p. 29) (W2, p. 8)

डेढ़ (*adj*) one and a half (T16, p. 153) (W7, p. 35) (GR 16, 18)

एक दिन (*adv*) one day (T11, p. 91)

आधा (*adj*) one half (T16, p. 153) (W14, 23 pp. 78, 129)

सौ (*adj*) one hundred (T16, p. 151) (W7, p. 35) (GR 16)

लाख (*adj*) one hundred thousand (T16, p. 152) (GR 16)

सहस्र (*adj*) one thousand (T16, p. 152) (GR 16)

हज़ार (*adj*) one thousand (T16, p. 152) (W7, p. 35) (GR 16)

सवा (*adj, invar*) one-and-a-quarter (T3, p. 21) (GR 3, 16, 18)

काना (*adj*) one-eyed (T13, p. 108)

एक चौथाई (*adj*) one-quarter (T16, p. 153)

एक तिहाई (*adj*) one-third (T16, p. 153)

अपना (*adj*) one's own (T10, p. 82) (W10, p. 54) (GR 10)

आप ही (*adv*) (by) oneself (T11, p. 85) (GR 11)

स्वयं (*adv*) (by) oneself (T11, p. 85) (GR 11)

अपने-आप (*adv*) (by) oneself (T11, p. 85) (W11, p. 60) (GR 11)

ख़ुद (*adv*) (by) oneself (T11, p. 85) (W11, p. 60) (GR 11)

सिर्फ़ (*adv*) only, just (W8, p. 41)

ही (*invar*) only, just; emphatic particle (T1, p. 5) (W5, 6 pp. 23, 28) (GR 14)

केवल (*adj*) only, merely (T13, p. 108)

वही (*pro*) only he/she, that very (person/thing) (वह + ही) (T14, p. 128) (GR 14)

खुलना (*v.i.*) to open (T19, p. 192)

खोलना (*v.t.*) to open (T8, p. 62) (W17, p. 98)

मौक़ा (*m*) opportunity (T18, p. 181)

ऐश्वर्य (*m*) opulence, prosperity, glory and grandeur (W6, p. 25)

या (*conj*) or (T1, p. 5) (W17, p. 98)

संतरा (*m*) orange, mandarin (T7, p. 57) (W7, p. 35)

ऑर्डर (*m*) order (W8, p. 41)

हमारा (*adj*) our (T2, p. 14) (GR 2, 4)

बाहर (*adv*) outside (T11, p. 94) (W3, p. 13)

अंचल (*m*) the outward fringe of the sari, region, frontier (T6, p. 46)

मालिकिन (*f*) owner (W7, p. 35)

मालिक (*m*) owner (W7, p. 35)

P

पन्ना (*m*) page (W8, p. 41)

दर्द (*m*) pain (T10, p. 78) (W7, p. 35)

पैसा (*m*) paisa, money (T7, p. 57) (W2,7 pp. 8, 35)

महल (*m*) palace (T1, p. 6) (W1, p. 3)

पालकी (*f*) palanquin, sedan chair (T19, p. 192)

कागज़ (*m*) paper (T4, p. 26) (W10, p. 54)

माँ-बाप (*m pl*) parents (T4, p. 29) (W2, p. 8)

पार्किंग (*f*) parking (T23, p. 227)

हिस्सा (*m*) part, portion (T16, p. 153)

पार्टी (*f*) party (T15, p. 132)

गौरी (*f*) Parvati (wife of lord Shiva)

गुज़रना (*v.i.*) to pass (by) (W20, p. 115)

पास होना (*v.i.*) to pass (an exam) (W15, p. 85)

दादा (*m*) paternal grandfather (T5, p. 34) (GR 7)

दादी (*f*) paternal grandmother (T5, p. 34) (GR 8)

दादा-दादी (*m*) paternal grandparents (T5, p. 35)

चाचा (*m*) paternal uncle (T7, p. 54) (W14, p. 78)

चाची (*f*) paternal uncle's wife, aunt (T14, p. 126)

देशभक्त (*adj* + *m*) patriot

शांति (*f*) peace (T7, p. 57) (W7, 18 pp. 35, 103)

चैन (*m*) peace, rest (W23, p. 130)

अस्सलाम अलैकुम Peace be upon you! (a greeting) (T7, p. 51)

शांत (*adj*) peaceful, tranquil (T24, p. 236)

मटर (*m*) peas (T18, p. 169)

कलम (*f*) pen (T1, p. 7) (W1, p. 3)

लोग (*m pl*) people (T4, p. 26) (W4, p. 18)

जन (*m*) people, public, folk, person

प्रतिशत (*m*) percent

शायद (*conj*) perhaps (T11, p. 90) (W11, p. 60)

दवाख़ाना (*m*) pharmacy (W21, p. 120)

फ़ोन (*m*) phone (T8, p. 66) (W16, p. 91)

फ़ोन करना (*v.t.*) to phone (T10, p. 84) (W16, p. 91)

फ़ोन उठाना (*v.t.*) to pick up the phone (T15, p. 135)

तस्वीर (*f*) picture (W8, 10 pp. 41, 54)

चित्र (*m*) picture (W8, p. 41)

स्थान (*m*) place, position (W6, p. 28)

जगह (*f*) place, space (T13, p. 119) (W10, 23 pp. 54, 129)

फ़ोन रखना (*v.t.*) to place (put down) the phone (T17, p. 167)

प्लैटफ़ार्म (*m*) platform (T23, p. 229) (W14, p. 78)

खेलना (*v.i.* + *v.t.*) to play (T11, p. 88)

होली खेलना (*v.t.*) to play (celebrate) Holi (W19, p. 110)

कृपया (*adv*) please (T8, p. 64) (W16, p. 91)

साढ़े (*adj*) plus one half (from three and one half onwards) (T16, p. 153) (GR 16, 18)

जेब (*f*) pocket (W24, p. 137)

कविता (*f*) poem, Kavita (name) (T3, p. 22) (W2, 8 pp. 8, 41)

पुलिस (*f*) police (T15, p. 137)

धूमधाम (*m*) pomp, fanfare

ग़रीब (*adj*) poor (T4, p. 26) (W10, p. 54)

जनसंख्या (*f*) population (T13, p. 109)

आबादी (*f*) population (T19, p. 196) (W11, p. 60)

मुमकिन (*adj*) possible (T16, p. 146) (GR 16)

संभव (*adj*) possible (T16, p. 146) (W16, p. 91) (GR 16)

डाक (*f*) post, mail (T4, p. 26)

डाकख़ाना (*m*) post office

डाकिया (*m*) postman (T19, p. 192)

को (*pp*) a postposition denoting accusative and dative case; to; for; on the point of (T7, p. 53) (GR 7, 9, 11, 13, 17, 18, 20)

ने (*pp*) a postposition denoting the subject case with a transitive verb in the perfective form (T7, p. 53) (GR 7, 12)

आलू (*m*) potato (T7, p. 54) (W3, 13 pp. 13, 71)

ताक़त (*f*) power (T13, p. 109)

अभ्यास (*m*) practice (T6, p. 43) (W23, p. 130)

(x का) अभ्यास करना (*v.t.*) to practice (x) (T11, p. 86)

(ख़ुदा से) दुआ माँगना (*v.t.*) to pray (to God)

प्रयाग (*m*) Prayag (Allahabad) (name of a city in U.P.) (W14, p. 78)

दुआ (*f*) prayer (T2, p. 13)

प्रार्थना (*f*) prayer (T6, p. 46)

प्रेमचंद (*m*) Premchand (name of a famous Hindi author) (T18, p. 173) (W12, p. 65)

तैयारी (*f*) preparation (W19, p. 110)

तैयार करना (*v.t.*) to prepare (W21, p. 120)

पिछला (*adj*) previous, prior (T11, p. 92)

क़ीमत (*f*) price (T2, p. 13) (W2, p. 8) (GR 8)

दाम (*m*) price (T2, p. 15) (W2, p. 8) (GR 17)

प्रधान मंत्री (*m*) Prime Minister (T20, p. 205)

छपाना (*v.t.*) to print, stamp

समस्या (*f*) problem (W11, p. 60)

पैदा करना (*v.t.*) to produce, give birth

तरक्की (*f*) progress (W22, p. 125)

उन्नति (*f*) progress, rise, promotion, improvement, development (W6, p. 25)

उचित (*adj*) proper, appropriate (T16, p. 148)

ठीक से (*adv*) properly (W11, p. 60)

(x की) हिफ़ाज़त करना (*v.t.*) to protect (x) (T16, p. 148)

(x की) रक्षा करना (*v.t.*) to protect (x) (T16, p. 148)

रक्षा (*f*) protection (T16, p. 148)

हिफ़ाज़त (*f*) protection, security, safety (T16, p. 148)

दिलवाना/दिलाना (*v.t.*) to provide, to cause to be given

खींचना (*v.t.*) to pull, draw (W22, p. 125)

दाल (*f*) pulse (legume), lentil (T16, p. 147)

कद्दू/कद्दू (*m*) pumpkin (T6, p. 44)

चटपटा (*adj*) pungent, spicy (W13, p. 71)

सज़ा (*f*) punishment

शुद्ध शाकाहारी (*adj*) pure vegetarian (T18, p. 169)

शुद्ध (*adj*) pure, unadulterated (T6, p. 45)

डालना (*v.t.*) to put, place (T19, p. 189) (W24, p. 137) (GR 19)

रखना (*v.t.*) to put, place, keep (T8, p. 63) (W17, p. 98) (GR 19)

कपड़े पहनना (*v.t.*) to put on clothes (T15 p. 140)

Q

क़व्वाली (*f*) qawwali (a genre of devotional song) (W11, p. 60)

गुण (*m*) quality (W13, p. 71)

ख़ासियत (*f*) quality, special feature (T11, p. 89)

पौने (*adj*) quarter to (less a quarter) (T16, p. 153) (GR 16, 18)

रानी (*f*) queen (T13, p. 109)

सवाल (*m*) question (T11, p. 90) (W2, 11 pp. 8, 60)

प्रश्न (*m*) question (T6, p. 46)

जल्दी (*adv*) quickly (T6, p. 43) (W16, 20 pp. 91, 114)

झटपट (*adv*) quickly, promptly (T11, p. 91) (GR 11)

R

रेडियो (*m*) radio (T23, p. 224)

रेल (*f*) railways, rail (T9, p. 70)

बारिश (*f*) rain (T19, p. 187) (W20, p. 115)

वर्षा (*f*) rain (T6, p. 46)

बरसात (*f*) rainy season (T19, p. 187)

उठाना (*v.t.*) to raise, lift up, wake up (T15, p. 135) (W24, p. 137)

राजीव चौक (*m*) Rajiv Chowk (square) (the new name for Connaught Place in Delhi) (T16, p. 143)

राम राम Ram Ram (an orthodox Hindu greeting) (T7, p. 51)

पढ़ना (*v.t.*) to read, study (T4, p. 26) (W9, p. 48)

नमाज़ पढ़ना (*v.t.*) to read the prayer, to pray (W15, p. 85)

तैयार (*adj*) ready, prepared (T13, p. 112) (W8, p. 41)

असल (*adj*) real, true (W7, p. 35)

असलियत (*f*) reality (W18, p. 104)

सचमुच (*adv*) really (T20, p. 198) (W23, p. 130)

मुनासिब (*adj*) reasonable, proper, fit, appropriate (T16, p. 148)

पहचानना (*v.t.*) to recognize (W22, p. 125)

लाल (*adj*) red (T3, p. 21) (W1, p. 3)

लाल क़िला (*m*) Red Fort (T13, p. 114)

(x से) इनकार करना (*v.t.*) to refuse, to deny (x) (T13, p. 113)

समझना (*v.i. + v.t.*) to regard, consider, understand (T6, p. 46) (W11, 23 pp. 60, 129) (T12)

संबंध (*m*) relation, association, connection, relationship

रिश्तेदार (*m*) relative (W14, p. 78)

आराम करना (*v.t.*) to relax (W12, p. 65)

धर्म (*m*) religion, righteous action, duty, justice (T6, p. 44)

बंद रहना (*v.i.*) to remain closed (W10, p. 54)

चुप रहना (*v.i.*) to remain quiet (T17, p. 161)

खड़ा रहना (*v.i.*) to remain standing (W22, p. 125)

सावधान रहना (*v.i.*) to remain vigilant, careful (W19, p. 110)

बाकी (*adj*) remaining, rest (T18, p. 177) (W15, 19 pp. 85, 109)

इलाज (*m*) remedy, treatment (W13, p. 71)

याद होना (*v.i.*) to remember (T18, p. 181)

(x की) याद करना (*v.t.*) to remember (x) (W15, p. 85)

पश्चाताप (*m*) remorse, compunction, repentance (T18, p. 175)

विख्यात (*adj*) renowned, well-known, famous (T6, p. 43)

किराया (*m*) rent (T20, p. 201) (W7, p. 35)

फ़रमाना (*v.t.*) to request (W8, p. 41)

आदर (*m*) respect, esteem, honor

(x का) आदर करना (*v.t.*) to respect (x)

आराम (*m*) rest, relaxation

वापस आना (*v.i.*) to return, come back (T17, p. 161)

वापस करना (*v.t.*) to return, to give back

वापस जाना (*v.i.*) to return, to go back (T9, p. 74) (W16, 19 pp. 91, 109)

प्रणाम (*m*) reverential salutation; bowing with respect, a term used in greeting elders (T7, p. 51)

घूमना (*v.i.*) to revolve, to wander (T3, p. 20) (W16, p. 91)

चावल (*m*) rice (T18, p. 169) (W21, p. 120)

पकवान (*m*) rich delicacy (food) (W24, p. 137)

रिक्शा (*m*) rickshaw (T13, p. 105)

यहीं (*adv*) right here (यहाँ + ही) (T8, 14 pp. 62, 128) (W6, p. 28) (GR 14)

अभी (*adv*) right now (अब + ही) (T7, 14 pp. 57, 128) (W6, 8 pp. 28, 41) (GR 14)

अभी-अभी (*adv*) right now (W13, p. 71)

तभी (*adv*) right then, at that very time (तब + ही) (T14, p. 128) (GR 14)

वहीं (*adv*) right (over) there, only there (वहाँ + ही) (T14, p. 128) (GR 14)

अंगूठी (*f*) a ring (T6, p. 46)

पक्का (*adj*) ripe, strong (T5, p. 38) (W1, p. 3)

उठना (*v.i.*) to rise, get up (T1, p. 76) (W9, p. 48) (GR 19)

नदी (*f*) river (T17, p. 165) (W10, p. 54)

छत (*f*) roof, ceiling (W8, p. 41)

कमरा (*m*) room (T2, p. 13) (W2, p. 8)

रस्सी (*f*) rope (W8, p. 41)

गुलाब (*m*) rose (T10, p. 77)

रोटी (*f*) roti, chapatti, Indian bread (T18, p. 169)

दौड़ना (*v.i.*) to run (T11, p. 88) (W22, p. 125)

रुपया (*m*) rupee, money (T2, p. 13)

रुपये (*m pl*) rupees (T13, p. 108) (W2, p. 8)

रुशदी (*m*) Rushdie (name) (T20, p. 201)

S

का (*pp*) 's (T1, p. 5) (GR 2)

पवित्र (*adj*) sacred (W10, p. 54) (W6, p. 25)

बलिदान (*m*) sacrifice (W15, p. 85)

उदास (*adj*) sad, dejected, gloomy (T2, p. 13)

दुखिया (*adj invar*) sad, unfortunate (T3, p. 21)

दुखी (*adj*) sad, unhappy (T16, p. 149)

साधु (*m*) sadhu (T4, p. 26)

संत (*m*) saint (T6, p. 44)

"माँ, तुझे सलाम" *Salaam to You, Mother* —film title (T20, p. 198)

तनख़्वाह (*f*) salary (T14, p. 129) (W22, p. 125)

नमक (*m*) salt (T1, p. 6) (W1, p. 3)

नमकीन (*adj + m*) salty, salted; a salty dish of snacks (T1, p. 6)

एक ही (*adj*) same (T15, p. 132)

समोसा (*m*) samosa (T3, p. 21) (W8, p. 41)

चप्पल (*f*) sandal, slipper (T6, p. 43)

संजय (*m*) Sanjay (name) (T6, p. 43)

संजीव (*m*) Sanjeev (name) (T6, p. 49)

संस्कृत (*f + adj*) Sanskrit language; refined (W6, p. 25) (W21, p. 120)

सरस्वती (*f*) Sarasvati, name of a deity, river (W10, p. 54)

साड़ी (*f*) sari (T8, p. 59) (W3, p. 13)

शनिवार/शनिश्चर (*m*) Saturday (T5, p. 33) (W6, p. 28) (GR 16)

बचाना (*v.t.*) to save (T19, p. 193)

बचना (*v.i.*) to be saved (T24, p. 234)

साफ़-साफ़ कहना (*v.t.*) to say clearly (T24, p. 234)

एक बात करना (*v.t.*) to say one thing (T16, p. 149)

(x से) कहना (*v.t.*) to say (to x) (T1, p. 1) (W9, 11 pp. 48, 60) (GR 16)

स्कूल (*m*) school (T9, p. 70) (W5, p. 23)

विज्ञान (*m*) science (T11, p. 86) (W6, p. 26)

बीसियों (*adj*) scores (T16, p. 153) (GR 16)

बीसों (*adj*) scores, all twenty (T16, p. 153) (GR 16)

चिल्लाना (*v.i.*) to scream, to shout (T19, p. 189)

लिपि (*f*) script (T18, p. 172)

मुद्रा (*f*) seal, stamp, money, countenance, pose, posture (W6, p. 25)

ढूँढना (*v.t.*) to search, seek (T6, p. 46) (W14, p. 78)

(x की) तलाश करना (*v.t.*) to search for (x) (W15, p. 85)

ऋतु (*f*) season (T10, p. 78)

बिठाना/बैठाना (*v.t.*) to seat (someone) (T8, p. 65)

द्वितीय (*adj*) second (T16, p. 152) (GR 16)

दूसरा (*adj*) second, other, another (T2, p. 9) (GR 16)

परेशान लगना (*v.i.*) to seem bothered, troubled (T18, p. 173) (GR 18)

मतलबी (*adj*) selfish

बेचना (*v.t.*) to sell (T8, p. 65)

भेजना (*v.t.*) to send, to transmit, to remit (T8, p. 63) (W16, 23 pp. 91, 129)

ऐंद्रिय (*adj*) sensual (W6, p. 25)

वाक्य (*m*) a sentence (W1, p. 3)

अलग-अलग (*adj*) separate, different (T11, p. 89)

सितंबर (*m*) September (T16, p. 154)

नौकर (*m*) servant (T9, p. 71)

बसना (*v.i.*) to settle, inhabit (T23, p. 223)

सात (*adj*) seven (T10, p. 76)

सत्रह (*adj*) seventeen (T16, p. 151) (W10, p. 54)

सत्रहवाँ (*adj*) seventeenth (T17, p. 157) (GR 16)

सातवाँ (*adj*) seventh (T7, p. 50) (GR 16)

सत्तर (*adj*) seventy (T16, p. 151)

कई (*adj*) several (T13, p. 108) (W5, 15 pp. 23, 85)

कई बार (*adv*) several times (T15, p. 135)

शाहजहाँ (*m*) Shah Jahan (name of a 17th century Mughal emperor) (T23, p. 222)

शाह रुख़ ख़ान (*m*) Shah Rukh Khan (name of an actor) (T12, p. 103)

हिलाना (*v.t.*) to shake, wave (W14, p. 78)

सलवार कमीज़ (*f*) shalwar kameez (a loose fitting trouser and shirt) (T17, p. 160)

शंकर (*m*) Shankar (name of Shiva) (T6, p. 43)

पैना (*adj*) sharp, acute (T1, p. 5)

तेज़ (*adj*) sharp, strong, harsh (T19, p. 196) (W20, p. 115)

दोशाला (*m*) shawl (T15, p. 140)

ख़ाना (*m*) a shelf, column, compartment

शर्बत/शरबत (*m*) sherbert (W15, p. 85)

जहाज़ (*m*) ship (T13, p. 105)

कुर्ता/कुता (*m*) shirt (T17, p. 161)

कमीज़ (*f*) shirt (T2, p. 13)

जूता (*m*) shoe (T3, p. 20)

दुकान (*f*) shop (T14, p. 142) (W4, p. 18)

दुकानदार (*m*) shopkeeper (T9, p. 126) (W9, p. 48)

दिखाना (*v.t.*) to show (T9, p. 72)

चुप कराना (*v.t.*) to shut up (someone) (W24, p. 137)

बीमार (*adj*) sick, ill (T5, p. 33) (W5, 21 pp. 23, 119)

चिह्न/चिह्न (*m*) sign, mark, marking (T6, p. 44)

चुप (*adj*) silent

कौशेय (*adj*) silky, silken (T6, p. 48)

पाप (*m*) sin (W15, p. 85)

कब से since when, for how long (W6, p. 28)

गाना (*v.t.*) to sing (W11, p. 60)

डूबना (*v.i.*) to sink, drown (T24, p. 238)

साहब (*m*) sir, sahib (T.7, p. 50) (W8, p. 41)

भाई-साहब! (*m*) Sir! (T7, p. 52)

बहन (*f*) sister (T4, p. 29) (W2, p. 8)

बैठना (*v.i.*) to sit (T8, p. 62) (W9, p. 48) (GR 19)

तशरीफ़ रखना (*v.t.*) to sit (one's noble self) (T8, p. 63)

परीक्षा देना (*v.t.*) to sit for (take) an exam (T17, p. 163) (W20, p. 115)

सितार (*m*) sitar (T2, p. 14) (W2, p. 8)

बैठक (*f*) sitting room (W17, p. 98)

स्थिति (*f*) situation, state (T20, p. 202)

छै/छह/छः (*adj*) six (T10, p. 76)

सोलह (*adj*) sixteen (T16, p. 151)

सोलहवाँ (*adj*) sixteenth (T16, p. 143) (GR 16)

छठा (*adj*) sixth (T6, p. 40) (GR 16)

साठ (*adj*) sixty (T16, p. 151)

ग़ुलाम (*m*) slave

नींद (*f*) sleep, slumber (T18, p. 172)

सोना (*v.i.*) to sleep (T10, exercise, p. 79) (W9, p. 48)

धीरे-धीरे (*adv*) slowly (T22, p. 217)

छोटा (*adj*) small (T19, p. 196) (W6, p. 28)

थोड़ा (*adj*) small, a little, some (T15, p. 141)

नन्हाँ (*adj*) small, tiny, wee (said of children) (T6, p. 44)

टिकिया (*f*) a small cake, tablet, patty (W13, p. 71)

लोटा (*m*) a small round metal utensil for the household (T14, p. 127)

मुस्कराना/मुस्कुराना (*v.i.*) to smile (T19, p. 191) (W19, p. 110) (GR 19)

धुआँ (*m*) smoke (W10, p. 54)

सिगरेट पीना (*v.t.*) to smoke a cigarette (T10, p. 78) (W20, p. 115)

बर्फ़ (*f*) snow (T19, p. 187) (W23, p. 130)

तो (*conj + part*) so, then (also emphatic particle) (T11, p. 88) (W3, 5, 6 pp. 13, 23, 28) (GR 14)

ताकि (*conj*) so that (T16, p. 146) (W16, p. 91) (GR 16)

समाज (*m*) society (W11, p. 60)

मिट्टी (*f*) soil, earth (T6, p. 46)

फ़ौजी (*m*) soldier; (*adj*) martial

किन्हींने (*pro pl*) some (oblique form of कोई + ने) (T7, p. 53) (GR 7, 12)

कोई (*adj + pro*) some, any; someone, anyone (T4, p. 27) (W4, p. 18) (GR 15)

कुछ (*pro + adj*) some, something (T7, p. 57) (W6, 8 pp. 28, 41) (GR 15)

कोई और/और कोई (*adj + pro*) some other/more, any other/more; someone else, anyone else (T15, p. 137) (GR 15)

किन्हीं का (*adj*) some (people)'s (oblique form of कोई [*pl*]) (T7, p. 53) (GR 7)

कुछ और/और कुछ (*adj*) some (thing) more, else (T15, p. 137) (W8, 12 pp. 41, 65) (GR 15)

किसीने (*pro sing*) someone/anyone/some/any (oblique form of कोई + ने) (T7, p. 53) (GR 7, 12)

किसी को (*pro*) (to) someone, anyone, oblique form of कोई + को (T7, p. 53) (GR 7)

किसी का (*adj*) someone's, anyone's (T4, p. 28) (GR 4)

कुछ न कुछ (*adj*) something or other (W12, p. 65) (GR 15)

कभी-कभी (*adv*) sometimes (T9, p. 70) (W9, p. 48)

कहीं (*adv*) somewhere (कहाँ + ही) (T14, p. 128)

बेटा (*m*) son (sometimes used affectionately as a mode of address for a girl) (T8, p. 62) (W8, p. 41)

गाना (*m*) a song

अफ़सोस (*m*) sorrow, grief (T18, p. 175)

दुःख/दुख (*m*) sorrow, sadness (T5, p. 33)

दक्षिण (*m*) south (T14, p. 120)

फ़ुरसत (*f*) spare time (T4, p. 26)

(x से) बोलना (*v.i. + v.t.*) to speak (to x) (T3, p. 20) (W8, 10 pp. 41, 54) (GR 12, 16)

विशेष (*adj*) special

ख़ास (*adj*) special (W11, p. 60)

ऐनक (*f*) spectacles (T1, p. 7)

चश्मा (*m*) spectacles; fountain, spring (T6, p. 43)

भाषण (*m*) speech (T23, p. 224) (W22, p. 125)

रफ़्तार (*f*) speed, pace (T6, p. 42) (W22, p. 125)

बिताना (*v.t.*) to spend, pass (time) (T16, p. 149)

चाट (*f*) spicy, fast food (T15, p. 132) (W8, p. 41)

तीखा (*adj*) spicy, sharp (food) (W21, p. 120)

पालक (*m*) spinach (T18, p. 169)

चम्मच (*m*) spoon (T6, p. 44)

फैलाना (*v.t.*) to spread (T15, p. 139)

फैलना (*v.i.*) to spread, to be diffused, to expand

वसंत (*m*) spring (season) (T10, p. 78)

बासी (*adj*) stale (W3, p. 13)

खड़ा होना (*v.i.*) to stand

डटना (*v.i.*) to stand, tarry, to take a position

तकल्लुफ़ करना (*v.t.*) to stand on formality, ceremony, to be formal (W8, p. 41)

खड़ा (*adj*) standing (T5, p. 108) (W3, p. 13)

तारा (*m*) star (T2, p. 13)

(x की) नौकरी लग जाना (*v.i.*) (x) to start a job, get a job (T22, p. 220)

चौंकाना (*v.t.*) to startle, alarm (someone)

हालत (*f*) state, condition (T21, p. 212)

स्टेशन (*m*) station (T20, p. 206) (W14, p. 78)

संभालना (*v.t.*) to steady, maintain, take care of (W24, p. 137)

(x की) चोरी करना (*v.t.*) to steal (x) (T24, p. 236)

लाठी (*f*) stick (W8, p. 41)

पेट (*m*) stomach (T19, p. 185) (W21, p. 120)

रुकना (*v.i.*) to stop (T19, p. 164) (W24, p. 137)

आँधी (*f*) storm, dust-storm (T6, p. 47)

कहानी (*f*) story (T2, p. 13) (W1, p. 3)

कथा (*f*) story (W10, p. 54)

सीधे (*adv*) straight (direction) (W13, p. 71)

सीधा (*adj*) straight, simple, right, erect

अजीब (*adj*) strange, peculiar (T19, p. 192)

सड़क (*f*) street (T17, p. 166)

बजाना (*v.t.*) to strike

टहलना (*v.i.*) to stroll (T16, p. 147) (W14, p. 78)

बलवान (*adj*) strong, powerful (T19, p. 196)

स्ट्यूडेंट (*m*) student (T15, p. 132)

विद्यार्थी *(m)* student (T15, p. 132) (W20, p. 115)

तालिबे इल्म *(m)* student (T22, p. 216)

छात्र *(m)* student (T9, p. 70)

पढ़ाई *(f)* study, studies (T4, p. 26) (W16, 19 pp. 91, 109)

विषय *(m)* subject, topic, matter (T12, p. 104)

द्रव्य *(m)* substance, matter, money (T6, p. 45)

सफलता *(f)* success (T23, p. 228)

सफल *(adj)* successful (W16, p. 91)

इतनी कम दूर *(adv)* such a little distance (T21, p. 207)

ऐसा *(adj)* such, of this type (T11, p. 89) (W4, p. 18) (GR 23)

अचानक *(adv)* suddenly (T18, p. 174) (W19, p. 110)

कष्ट *(m)* suffering, pain, hardship, distress (T6, p. 43)

वाँ *(adj)* a suffix added to most cardinal numbers to create ordinals (T16, p. 152) (GR 16)

वाला *(adj)* a suffix denoting an agent, doer, owner, possessor, keeper or inhabitant (T1, p. 5) (W12, p. 65) (GR 20)

शक्कर/शकर *(m)* sugar (T6, p. 42)

चीनी *(f)* sugar; Chinese (W4, p. 18)

हिम्मत जुटाना *(v.t.)* to summon courage (W24, p. 137)

सूर्य *(m)* sun

आफ़ताब *(m)* the sun; Aftab (name) (T7, p. 57)

रविवार *(m)* Sunday (T11, p. 87) (W6, p. 28) (GR 16)

इतवार *(m)* Sunday (T11, p. 94) (W9, p. 48) (GR 16)

सुनीता *(f)* Sunita (name) (T2, p. 15) (W2, p. 8)

सूर्योदय *(m)* sunrise (T22, p. 217)

धूप *(f)* sunshine, incense (T10, p. 78)

उमड़ना *(v.i.)* to surge, swell, to flood, to gust (T22, p. 217)

झूमना *(v.i.)* to sway, to swing (T19, p. 192)

मीठा *(adj)* sweet (T19, p. 193)

कलकल *(m)* sweet and soft sound (of a flowing stream) (T1, p. 6)

मिठाई *(f)* sweetmeat (T13, p. 111) (W8, p. 41)

तैरना *(v.i.)* to swim (W24, p. 137)

T

मेज़ *(f)* table (T8, p. 64) (W3, p. 13)

गोली *(f)* tablet, pill, bullet (W13, p. 71)

ताज महल *(m)* Taj Mahal (T13, p. 115)

लेना *(v.t.)* to take, to accept, to borrow, to buy (T8, p. 62) (W8, 11 pp. 41, 60) (GR 19)

ले जाना *(v.i.)* to take away (T15, p. 141) (W11, p. 60) (GR 15)

निकालना *(v.t.)* to take out (W11, p. 60)

तस्वीर खींचना *(v.t.)* to take a picture (W22, p. 125)

(x को) देर लगना *(v.i.)* (x) to take time/delay (T18, p. 173) (GR 18)

(x से) बात करना *(v.t.)* to talk, converse (to/with x) (T13, p. 112) (W9, p. 48) (GR 16)

(x से) गुफ़्तगू करना *(v.t.)* to talk, have a conversation (with x) (T16, p. 154) (GR 16)

(x) की बात (y से) होना *(v.i.)* (x) to talk (to y) (W12, p. 65)

लंबा/लम्बा *(adj)* tall (T6, p. 46) (W19, p. 110)

स्वाद *(m)* taste (W24, p. 137)

मज़ेदार *(adj)* tasty, enjoyable (W13, p. 71)

चाय *(f)* tea (T7, p. 57) (W7, p. 35)

सिखाना *(v.t.)* to teach (T22, p. 214) (W9, p. 48)

पढ़ाना *(v.t.)* to teach, make read (T19, p. 191)

शिक्षक *(m)* teacher (T17, p. 162) (W13, p. 71)

टीचर *(m/f)* teacher (T9, p. 70)

शिक्षिका *(f)* teacher (W15, p. 85)

अध्यापक *(m)* teacher, educator, lecturer (T6, p. 43) (W17, p. 98)

चिढ़ाना *(v.t.)* to tease (T4, p. 26)

टेलीविज़न *(m)* television (W11, p. 60)

बताना *(v.t.)* to tell (T9, p. 70) (W8, p. 41) (GR 16)

सुनाना *(v.t.)* to tell, relate (T8, p. 63) (W10, 15 pp. 54, 85)

तापमान *(m)* temperature (T19, p. 187)

मंदिर *(m)* temple (T7, p. 55)

दस *(adj)* ten (T15, p. 138)

करोड़ *(adj)* ten million (T16, p. 152)

दस बजे *(adv)* (at) ten o'clock (W12, p. 65)

दसवाँ *(adj)* tenth (T10, p. 76) (GR 16)

मुन्नी *(f)* a term of endearment for a child, dear child (T6, p. 44)

मुन्ना *(m)* a term of endearment for a child, dear child (T6, p. 45)

तशरीफ़ *(f)* a term signifying honor and respect (T8, p. 63)

शुक्रिया *(m)* thank you (W6, p. 28)

कि *(conj)* that, for (T10, p. 83) (GR 12)

वैसे *(adv)* that way, in that manner, in the same manner (T7, p. 57) (GR 23)

वह तो है। That's true. (T14, p. 129)

तब *(adv)* then, at that time (T11, p. 91) (GR 23)

फिर *(conj)* then; again; afterwards; thereafter; in the future; a second time (T8, p. 64)

उधर (*adv*) there, over there (T23, p. 225)

वहाँ (*adv*) (over) there (T5, p. 36) (W3, p. 13) (GR 23)

इसमें कोई शक नहीं है । There is no doubt about (in) this. (T20, p. 202)

इसलिये (*conj*) therefore (W10, p. 54)

आजकल (*adv*) these days (T4, p. 29) (W2, p. 8)

ये (*pro*) these/he/she/they (*pl*) (T2, p. 13) (GR 2, 4, 7)

वे (*pro*) they/those/he/she (T2, p. 14) (GR 2, 4, 7)

चोर (*m*) thief (T24, p. 232) (W17, p. 98)

चीज़ (*f*) thing (T8, p. 60) (W8, 11 pp. 41, 60)

वस्तु (*f*) thing (W8, p. 41)

सोचना (*v.t.*) to think (T3, p. 20) (W9, p. 48)

तृतीय (*adj*) third (T16, p. 152) (GR 16)

तीसरा (*adj*) third (T3, p. 17) (GR 16)

प्यास (*f*) thirst (T6, p. 43) (W15, p. 85)

तेरह (*adj*) thirteen (T16, p. 151)

तेरहवाँ (*adj*) thirteenth (T13, p. 105)

तीस (*adj*) thirty (T16, p. 151) (W2, p. 8)

अड़तीस (*adj*) thirty-eight (T16, p. 151)

पैंतीस (*adj*) thirty-five (T16, p. 151)

चौंतीस (*adj*) thirty-four (T16, p. 151)

उनतालीस (*adj*) thirty-nine (T16, p. 151)

इक्तीस (*adj*) thirty-one (T16, p. 151)

सैंतीस (*adj*) thirty-seven (T16, p. 151)

छत्तीस (*adj*) thirty-six (T16, p. 151)

तैंतीस (*adj*) thirty-three (T16, p. 151)

बत्तीस (*adj*) thirty-two (T16, p. 151)

इतना (*adj*) this much, so much, so (T8, p. 66) (W3, 21 pp. 13, 119) (GR 23)

यही (*pro*) this very (person, thing) (यह + ही) (T14, p. 128) (W14, p. 78) (GR 14)

विचार (*m*) thought, idea (T13, p. 109) (W11, 16 pp. 60, 89)

हज़ारों (*adj*) thousands (T16, p. 153) (GR 16)

तीन (*adj*) three (T10, p. 81) (W3, p. 13)

तीन साल पहले (*adv*) three years ago (W10, p. 54)

तीन चौथाई (*adj*) three-quarters (T16, p. 153)

पौन (*adj*) three-quarters, quarter to one (T16, p. 153) (GR 16, 18)

गला (*m*) throat (T4, p. 26) (W4, p. 18)

(x) के द्वारा (*pp*) through the agency of (x) (T21, p. 209)

गुरुवार (*m*) Thursday (T10, p. 76) (W9, p. 48) (GR 16)

जुमेरात (*f*) Thursday (T16, p. 153) (GR 16)

बृहस्पतिवार (*m*) Thursday (T16, p. 153) (W6, p. 28) (GR 16)

टिकट (*m/f*) ticket (T6, p. 46)

बाँधना (*v.t.*) to tie, to fasten, to bind (T21, p. 211)

बाघ (*m*) tiger (W10, p. 54)

समय (*m*) time (T10, p. 78) (W15, 23 pp. 85, 129) (GR 24)

वक़्त (*m*) time (T11, p. 92) (W13, 18 pp. 71, 103) (GR 24)

बार (*f*) time (T11, p. 93) (W11, 15 pp. 60, 85)

टाइम (*m*) time (T18, p. 176)

बार-बार (*adv*) time and again (T11, p. 91)

आज (*m + adv*) today (T2, p. 13) (W3, p. 13)

साथ साथ (*adv*) together (T18, p. 180)

एक साथ (*adv*) together (W10, p. 54)

टमाटर (*m*) tomato (T6, p. 46)

दाँत (*m*) tooth

कुल (*m*) total (W22, p. 125)

छूना (*v.t.*) to touch, to feel (T8, p. 62) (GR 12)

ऐतिह्य (*m*) tradition (W6, p. 25)

रेलगाड़ी (*f*) train (T13, p. 105) (W14, p. 78)

ट्रेन (*f*) train (T6, p. 45)

सफ़र करना (*v.t.*) to travel (T24, p. 234) (W17, p. 98)

यात्रा करना (*v.t.*) to travel (W10, 22 pp. 54, 124)

भारत यात्रा करना (*v.t.*) to travel to India (W22, p. 125)

कोष/कोश (*m*) treasure, dictionary

चिकित्सा (*f*) treatment, remedy (W14, p. 78)

पेड़ (*m*) tree (T11, p. 88) (W7, p. 35)

चकमा (*m*) trick, trickery, hoodwinking (T6, p. 48)

परेशान (*adj*) troubled, bothered (T18, p. 173) (W18, p. 104)

सच (*adj*) true (T16, p. 110) (W19, p. 110)

सूँड़ (*f*) the trunk of an elephant (T13, p. 109)

(x पर) भरोसा होना (*v.i.*) to trust, to believe (x) (T24, p. 230)

(x पर) भरोसा करना (*v.t.*) to trust, to believe (x) (T15, p. 139)

सच्चाई (*f*) truth (W18, p. 104)

मंगलवार (*m*) Tuesday (T9, p. 74) (W6, p. 28) (GR 16)

बारी (*f*) turn (W4, p. 18)

बारहवाँ (*adj*) twelfth (T11, p. 95) (GR 16)

बारह (*adj*) twelve (T10, p. 76)

बीसवाँ (*adj*) twentieth (T20, p. 198) (GR 16)

बीस (*adj*) twenty (T16, p. 151) (W10, p. 54)

अट्ठाईस (*adj*) twenty-eight (T16, p. 151)

इक्कीसवाँ (*adj*) twenty-first (T21, p. 206)

पच्चीस (*adj*) twenty-five (T16, p. 151)

चौबीस (*adj*) twenty-four (T13, p. 109)

चौबीसवाँ (*adj*) twenty-fourth (T24, p. 230)

उनतीस (*adj*) twenty-nine (T16, p. 151)

इक्कीस (*adj*) twenty-one (T16, p. 151) (W10, p. 54)

बाईसवाँ (*adj*) twenty-second (T22, p. 214)

सत्ताईस (*adj*) twenty-seven (T16, p. 151)

छब्बीस (*adj*) twenty-six (T16, p. 151)

तेईसवाँ (*adj*) twenty-third (T23, p. 222)

तेईस (*adj*) twenty-three (T16, p. 151)

बाईस (*adj*) twenty-two (T6, p. 49) (W10, p. 54)

दोबारा (*adv*) twice, a second time (W13, p. 71)

दो (*adj*) two (T8, p. 61) (W3, 6 pp. 13, 28)

ढाई (*adj*) two and a half (T16, p. 153) (W7, 18 pp. 35, 104) (GR 16, 18)

प्रकार (*m*) type, manner, sort, kind, quality (T17, p. 166)

टाइप करना (*v.t.*) to type (T11, p. 85)

U

(x की) समझ में आना (*v.i.*) (x) to understand (lit: to come into x's understanding) (W15, p. 85)

बेवफ़ा (*adj*) unfaithful (W5, p. 23)

यूनिवर्सिटी (*f*) university (T18, p. 173)

विश्वविद्यालय (*m*) university (T9, p. 73) (W9, p. 48)

तक (*pp*) until, to, till, by, up to (T9, p. 74) (GR 14)

देर तक (*adv*) until late (T9, p. 74)

तब तक (*adv*) until then (T10, p. 84) (W9, p. 48) (GR 23)

जब तक (*rel adv*) until when (L 23, p. 228) (GR 23)

उर्दू (*f*) Urdu (language) (T17, p. 167) (W21, p. 120)

प्रयोग (*m*) use, experiment, employment, application

(x का) प्रयोग करना (*v.t.*) to use, to experiment, to employ, to apply (x)

बेकार (*adj*) useless, idle, stupid (W5, p. 23)

उत्तर प्रदेश (*m*) Uttar Pradesh (North Province) (a state in north India) (W21, p. 120)

उत्तराखंड (*m*) Uttarakhand (a state to the northwest of Uttar Pradesh) (T12, p. 99)

V

वर्मा Varma/Verma (name) (T10, p. 81)

सब्ज़ी (*f*) vegetable (T18, p. 170) (W12, p. 65)

तरकारी (*f*) vegetable (W3, p. 13)

बहुत (*adj*) very, a lot, much (T4, p. 29) (W3, p. 13)

बहुत सारा (*adj*) very many (W7, p. 35)

बहुत कुछ (*adj*) very much (T7, p. 57)

सावधान (*adj*) vigilant, careful, alert, attentive

गाँव (*m*) village (T6, p. 46)

आवाज़ (*f*) voice, noise (W2, p. 8)

कै (*f*) vomiting (T1, p. 5)

W

(x का) इंतज़ार करना (*v.t.*) to wait (for x) (T15, p. 134) (W22, p. 125)

इंतज़ार (*m*) waiting (T15, p. 134)

पैदल जाना (*v.i.*) to walk (T21, p. 207)

दीवार (*f*) wall (T3, p. 20) (W3, p. 13)

बटुआ (*m*) wallet, purse (T24, p. 236)

चाहना (*v.t.*) to want (T13, p. 112) (W15, 23 pp. 85, 129)

चाहिये/चाहिए (*invar*) wanted/needed (subject takes को) (T7, p. 56) (GR 7)

था (*m sing*) was (T5, p. 34) (GR 5)

थी (*f sing*) was (T5, p. 34) (GR 5)

धोना (*v.t.*) to wash (T15, p. 140)

धोबी (*m*) washerman (W7, p. 35)

गँवाना (*v.t.*) to waste, lose (W24, p. 137)

घड़ी (*f*) watch (T17, p. 166) (W4, 8 pp. 18, 41)

देखना (*v.t.*) to watch, see (T8, p. 65) (W9, p. 48)

घड़ीसाज़ (*m*) watchmaker (W17, p. 98)

पानी (*m*) water (T1, p. 7) (W1, p. 3)

पिचकारी (*f*) water gun, syringe (W19, p. 110)

राह (*f*) way, path (W20, p. 115)

हम (*pro*) we (T2, p. 14) (GR 2, 4, 7)

हमने (*pro*) we (हम + ने) (T7, p. 53) (GR 7, 12)

हमीं (*pro*) we (emphatic), only we (हम + ही) (GR 14)

निर्बल (*adj*) weak (T6, p. 46)

दौलत (*f*) wealth (W22, p. 125)

धन (*m*) wealth (W7, p. 35)

धनी (*adj*) wealthy

अमीर (*adj*) wealthy (T11, p. 85)

धनाढ्य (*adj*) wealthy (T6, p. 44)

पहनना (*v.t.*) to wear, to put on (T1, p. 6) (W9, 23 pp. 48, 129)

मौसम (*m*) weather, season (T5, p. 37) (W3, p. 13)

शादी (*f*) wedding, marriage (W13, 23 pp. 71, 129)

बुधवार (बुध) (*m*) Wednesday (T9, p. 74) (W6, p. 28) (GR 16)

हफ़्ता (*m*) week/Saturday (T11, p. 92) (W11, p. 60)

वीकेंड (*m*) weekend (T15, p. 132)

अच्छी तरह (*adv*) well, in a good manner (T22, p. 215) (W23, p. 130)

कुआँ (*m*) a (water) well (W7, p. 35)

थीं (*f pl*) were (T5, p. 34) (GR 5)

थे (*m pl*) were (T5, p. 34) (GR 5)

पश्चिम (*m*) west (T23, p. 222)

क्या (*pro*) what (also marks a question) (T1, p. 6) (W1, p. 3) (GR 1)

क्या-क्या (*adv*) what (the reduplication gives a sense of plurality) (T13, p. 113) (W12, p. 65)

और क्या what else, of course! (T9, p. 70)

मेरा क्या? What's it to me? (T10, p. 83)

जो भी (*rel pro*) whatever, whichever, whoever (T23, p. 226) (W23, p. 130) (GR 14, 23)

गेहूँ (*m*) wheat (T10, p. 78)

चक्र (*m*) a wheel, cycle, circle, disc (T6, p. 45)

कब (*adv*) when (T11, p. 91) (W9, p. 48) (GR 23)

जब (*rel adv*) when (T23, p. 225) (GR 23)

कब की बात when's matter (when did it happen) (W6, p. 28)

जब भी (*adv*) whenever (T23, p. 226) (GR 14, 23)

जहाँ (*rel adv*) where (T23, p. 225) (GR 23)

जिधर (*rel adv*) where (T23, p. 225) (GR 23)

कहाँ (*inter*) where (T4, p. 28) (W2, p. 8)

मेरी (बात) कहाँ सुनते हैं? Where do they listen to me (my matter)? (T16, p. 156)

जिधर भी (*rel adv*) wherever (T23, p. 226) (GR 14, 23)

जहाँ भी (*rel adv*) wherever (T23, p. 226) (W23, p. 130) (GR 14, 23)

कौन-सा (*inter adj*) which (T12, p. 103) (W6, p. 28) (W15, 22 pp. 85, 124)

कौन (*pro*) who (T4, p. 28) (W4, p. 18) (GR 4, 7)

जो (*rel pro*) who (T7, p. 53) (GR 23)

किन्होंने (*pro pl*) who/that/which (कौन + ने) (T7, p. 53) (GR 7, 12)

किसने (*pro*) who/that/which (कौन + ने) (T7, p. 53) (GR 7, 12)

कौन जाने who knows (W23, p. 130)

किसको/किसे (*inter pro*) (to) whom (oblique form of कौन + को) (T7, p. 53) (GR 7, 11)

किनका (*inter adj*) whose (oblique form of कौन [*pl*]) (T4, p. 28) (GR 4, 7)

किसका (*inter adj*) whose (oblique form of कौन) (T4, p. 28) (W4, p. 18) (GR 4)

जिनका (*rel adj pl*) whose (T7, p. 53) (GR 23)

जिसका (*rel adj*) whose (rel) (T7, p. 53) (GR 7, 23)

क्यों (*inter*) why (T5, p. 38) (W6, p. 28)

दुष्टात्मा (*adj*) wicked, vicious, vile (W6, p. 25)

जोरू (*f*) wife (T8, p. 60)

पत्नी (*f*) wife (W8, p. 41)

राज़ी (*adj*) willing, approving

हवा (*f*) wind, air (T15, p. 139)

खिड़की (*f*) window (T8, p. 62) (W14, p. 78) (GR 8)

ध्यान से (*adv*) with attention, carefully (T24, p. 235)

धूमधाम से (*adv*) with pomp and ceremony (W19, p. 110)

तेज़ी से (*adv*) with speed, quickly (W22, p. 125)

(x) के साथ (*pp*) with (x) (T9, p. 70) (W7, 9 pp. 35, 48)

(x) के बिना (*pp*) without (x) (T24, p. 237) (W24, 137)

(x) के बगैर (*pp*) without (x) (T24, p. 237)

महिला (*f*) woman (T13, p. 108) (W13, p. 71)

स्त्री (*f*) woman (T19, p. 196)

औरत (*f*) woman (T3, p. 21)

शब्द (*m*) word (T6, p. 42)

कार्य (*m*) work, business

काम (*m*) work, business (T8, p. 63) (W1, p. 3)

काम करना (*v.t.*) to work (T9, p. 70) (W9, p. 48)

नौकरी करना (*v.t.*) to work (for money) (T11, p. 90) (W20, p. 115)

मेहनत करना (*v.t.*) to work hard (T20, p. 203)

दुनिया (*f*) world (T7, p. 57)

फ़िक्र (*f*) worry (T24, p. 230) (W19, p. 110)

चिंता (*f*) worry, concern, anxiety (T24, p. 230)

(x की) फ़िक्र करना (*v.t.*) to worry (about x) (T24, p. 230) (W19, p. 110)

(x को) फ़िक्र होना (*v.i.*) (x) to worry (T24, p. 230)

बदतर (*adj*) worse (T19, p. 197)

बदतरीन (*adj*) worst (T19, p. 197)

(x) के लायक़ (*pp*) worthy of (x) (T13, p. 110)

(x) के क़ाबिल (*pp*) worthy of (x) (T13, p. 113)

लायक़ (*adj*) worthy, capable, able (T13, p. 110) (W13, p. 71)

योग्य (*adj*) worthy, qualified, able (T13, p. 113)

लिखना (*v.t.*) to write (T8, p. 65) (W9, p. 48)

ग़लत (*adj*) wrong (W22, p. 125)

Y

यमुना (*f*) Yamuna (river) (T17, p. 165) (W10, p. 54)

वर्ष (*m*) year (T11, p. 92) (W10, p. 54)

बरस (*m*) year (T11, p. 92) (W24, p. 137)

साल (*m*) year (T6, p. 48) (W6, 10, 13 pp. 28, 54, 71)

सन् (*m*) year (of the Christian calendar)

तलब (*f*) yearning, desire (W20, p. 115)

पीला (*adj*) yellow (W1, p. 3)

जी हाँ (*adv*) yes (T2, p. 12)

हाँ (*adj*) yes (T2, p. 12) (W3, p. 13)

कल (*m*) yesterday, tomorrow (T1, p. 5) (W5, p. 23)

तुम (*pro*) you (familiar, pl) (T4, p. 27) (GR 4)

तू (*pro*) you (intimate, sing) (T4, p. 27) (GR 4)

आप (*pro*) you (plural polite) (T2, p. 14) (GR 4)

तूने (*pro*) you (तू + ने) (T7, p. 53) (GR 7, 12)

तुम्हीं (*pro*) you (तुम + ही) (T14, p. 128) (GR 14)

तुमने (*pro*) you (तुम + ने) (T7, p. 53) (GR 7, 12)

आपने (*pro*) you (आप + ने) (T7, p. 53) (GR 7, 12)

आपका (*adj*) your (T2, p. 14) (GR 4)

तुम्हारा (*adj*) your (T4, p. 26) (GR 4)

तेरा (*adj*) your (T4, p. 28) (GR 4)

तुम्हारी मर्ज़ी (*f*) your desire, whatever you want, as you wish (W22, p. 125)

Z

ज़ी टी० वी० (*m*) Zee TV (a popular television channel in India) (T12, p. 103)

चिड़ियाघर (*m*) zoo (T10, p. 78)

💿 Audio CD Track List

Together with the *Elementary Hindi* Textbook and Workbook, the Audio CD (which is packaged with the Textbook) offers Hindi examples, conversations and activities to help you learn.

"Practice" sections are found in the **Textbook**.
"Activities" are found in the **Workbook**.

LESSON 1

Track		
	1	Activity 1.1
	2	Activity 1.2
	3	Activity 1.4

LESSON 2

Track		
	4	Activity 2.1
	5	Activity 2.3
	6	Activity 2.4
	7	Activity 2.5

LESSON 3

Track		
	8	Activity 3.1
	9	Lesson 3 Practice: Meeting Kavita
	10	Activity 3.2
	11	Activity 3.4

LESSON 4

Track		
	12	Activity 4.1
	13	Lesson 4 Practice: More About Deepak
	14	Activity 4.3
	15	Activity 4.4

LESSON 5

Track		
	16	Activity 5.1
	17	Lesson 5 Practice: Meeting Kavita's Family
	18	Lesson 5 Practice: How Are You? How's the Weather?
	19	Activity 5.3
	20	Activity 5.4

LESSON 6

Track		
	21	Activity 6.1
	22	Lesson 6 Practice: Meeting Deepak's Family
	23	Activity 6.3
	24	Activity 6.4
	25	Activity 6.5

LESSON 7

Track		
	26	Lesson 7 Practice: Outside the Library
	27	Activity 7.2
	28	Activity 7.3
	29	Lesson 7 Practice: What Does Kavita Want?
	30	Activity 7.4
	31	Activity 7.5

LESSON 8

Track *32* Lesson 8 Practice:
How Many Brothers and Sisters
Do You Have?

33 Activity 8.2

34 Activity 8.3

35 Lesson 8 Practice:
What Does Deepak Want?

36 Activity 8.5 Conversation

LESSON 9

Track *37* Activity 9.1

38 Lesson 9 Practice:
What Do You Do?

39 Activity 9.2

40 Activity 9.3

41 Lesson 9 Practice:
What Do You Do on Monday?

42 Activity 9.5

LESSON 10

Track *43* Lesson 10 Practice:
What Time Do You…

44 Activity 10.1

45 Lesson 10 Practice:
Where Did Kavita and Deepak
Use to Live?

46 Activity 10.2

47 Lesson 10 Practice:
Whose Cell Phone?
Whose Friends?

48 Activity 10.3

49 Activity 10.4

LESSON 11

Track *50* Activity 11.1

51 Lesson 11 Practice:
What Do You Study?

52 Activity 11.2

53 Activity 11.3

54 Lesson 11 Practice:
If I Were a Rich Man…

55 Activity 11.4

56 Activity 11.5

LESSON 12

Track *57* Lesson 12 Practice:
What's Your Daily Routine?

58 Lesson 12 Practice:
Where Were You Born?
Where Did You Grow Up?

59 Activity 12.2

60 Lesson 12 Practice:
Did You Watch the Film Last
Night?

61 Activity 12.3

LESSON 13

Track *62* Lesson 13 Practice:
How Do You Go to College?

63 Activity 13.1

64 Lesson 13 Practice:
Do You Have Money, Kavita?

65 Activity 13.2

66 Lesson 13 Practice:
What Is Worth Seeing in Delhi?

67 Activity 13.3

68 Activity 13.4

69 Lesson 13 Practice:
Have You Ever Been to America?
How Many Times?

LESSON 14

Track *70* Lesson 14 Practice: My City Delhi
71 Activity 14.1
72 Lesson 14 Practice:
How Long Have You Been
Learning Hindi?
73 Activity 14.2
74 Activity 14.3
75 Activity 14.4
76 Activity 14.5
77 Lesson 14 Practice:
I Too Want to Go See the Film

LESSON 15

Track *78* Lesson 15 Practice:
Student Life in Delhi
79 Lesson 15 Practice:
I Tried to Call You
80 Activity 15.2
81 Activity 15.3
82 Activity 15.4
83 Lesson 15 Practice:
What Did You Do When You Got
Home Yesterday Evening?

LESSON 16

Track *84* Lesson 16 Practice:
My Favorite Place in Delhi
85 Activity 16.1
86 Lesson 16 Practice:
I Want You to Talk to Vrinda
87 Activity 16.2
88 Activity 16.3
89 Lesson 16 Practice:
May I Ask You a Question?

LESSON 17

Track *90* Activity 17.1
91 Lesson 17 Practice:
How Much Is That?
92 Activity 17.2
93 Activity 17.3
94 Lesson 17 Practice:
I Have Just Had Tea, Thanks
95 Activity 17.4
96 Activity 17.5
97 Lesson 17 Practice:
Where Shall We Meet?

LESSON 18

Track *98* Lesson 18 Practice:
You Must Have Eaten Indian
Food
99 Activity 18.1
100 Activity 18.2
101 Lesson 18 Practice:
What Do You Like?
102 Activity 18.3
103 Activity 18.4
104 Lesson 18 Practice:
Pleased to Meet You

LESSON 19

Track *105* Lesson 19 Practice:
I Want to Leave at Five-Thirty
106 Activity 19.1
107 Lesson 19 Practice:
The Weather in North India
108 Activity 19.2, slow speed
109 Activity 19.2, normal speed
110 Lesson 19 Practice:
It's So Hot! I'm So Thirsty!

Practice your Hindi with the included MP3 audio files!

This CD contains <u>MP3 audio files</u>.

You can play MP3 files on your computer (most computers include a default MP3 player); in your portable MP3 player; on many mobile phones and PDAs; and on some newer CD and DVD players.

You can also convert the MP3 files and create a regular audio CD, using software and a CD writing drive.

To play your MP3 files:

1. Open the CD on your computer.
2. Click on the MP3 file that you wish to play, to open it. The file should start playing automatically. *(If it doesn't, then perhaps your computer does not have an MP3 player; you will need to download one. There are dozens of players available online, and most of them are free or shareware. You can type "mp3 player" or "music downloads" into your search engine to find some.)*